The Complete Guide to Market Breadth Indicators

The Complete Guide to Market Breadth Indicators

How to Analyze and Evaluate
Market Direction and Strength

Gregory L. Morris

McGraw-Hill
New York   Chicago   San Francisco
Lisbon   London   Madrid   Mexico City   Milan
New Delhi   San Juan   Seoul   Singapore
Sydney   Toronto

The McGraw·Hill Companies

Copyright © 2006 by The McGraw-Hill Companies. All rights reserved. Printed in the United States of America. Except as permitted under the United States Copyright Act of 1976, no part of this publication may be reproduced or distributed in any form or by any means, or stored in a data base or retrieval system, without the prior written permission of the publisher.

4 5 6 7 8 9 0   EPAC/EPAC   0 1 0 9

ISBN-13: 978-0-07-144443-9

ISBN-10: 0-07-144443-2

McGraw-Hill books are available at special quantity discounts to use as premiums and sales promotions, or for use in corporate training programs. For more information, please write to the Director of Special Sales, Professional Publishing, McGraw-Hill, Two Penn Plaza, New York, NY 10121-2298. Or contact your local bookstore.

This publication is designed to provide accurate and authoritative information in regard to the subject matter covered. It is sold with the understanding that neither the author nor the publisher is engaged in rendering legal, accounting, or other professional service. If legal advice or other expert assistance is required, the services of a competent professional person should be sought.
—*From a Declaration of principles jointly adopted by a Committee of the American Bar Association and a Committee of Publishers.*

Printed in Mexico

Library of Congress Cataloging-in-Publication Data

Morris, Gregory L., 1948-
    The complete guide to market breadth indicators / by Gregory L. Morris.
       p.   cm.
Includes bibliographical references and index.
    ISBN 0-07-144443-2 (hardcover : alk. paper)
    1. Investment analysis. 2. Stock price forecasting. 3. Stocks—Prices—Mathematical models. I. Title.

HG4529.M675 2005
332.63'2042—dc22
                                                      2005005850

To Laura

Contents

List of Charts, Tables, and Figures   ix
Foreword by John Murphy   xv
Preface   xvii
Acknowledgments   xix

Chapter 1	Introduction	1
Chapter 2	Necessary Breadth Information	11
Chapter 3	Breadth Indicators	19
Chapter 4	Advance Decline Difference Indicators	31
Chapter 5	Advance Decline Ratio Indicators	91
Chapter 6	Advance Decline Miscellaneous Indicators	109
Chapter 7	New High, New Low Indicators	131
Chapter 8	Up Volume, Down Volume Indicators	163
Chapter 9	Composite Indicators	195
Chapter 10	The McClellan Indicators	243
Chapter 11	Putting Breadth to Work	255
Chapter 12	Conclusions	263

Appendix A Indicators and Trading Systems—What's the Difference?	**271**
Appendix B Time Frames for Analysis	**277**
Appendix C Miscellaneous Information	**281**
Bibliography	**285**
Index	**287**

List of Charts, Tables, and Figures

Chart 1–1	Advances, Declines, and Unchanged, all as a Percentage of Total Issues.
Chart 1–2	New Highs and New Lows as a Percentage of Total Issues.
Chart 1–3	Up Volume and Down Volume as a Percentage of Total Issues.
Chart 3–1	Advances and Declines.
Chart 3–2	Advances and Declines Adjusted for Total Issues.
Chart 3–3	New Highs and New Lows.
Chart 3–4	New Highs and New Lows Adjusted for Total Issues.
Chart 3–5	Up Volume and Down Volume.
Chart 3–5b	Up Volume and Down Volume Plotted Using Semilog Scaling.
Chart 3–6	Up Volume and Down Volume Adjusted for Total Volume.
Chart 4–1	Advances Minus Declines Smoothed by 21 days.
Chart 4–2	Advances Minus Declines Exponentially Smoothed by 3 days.
Chart 4–2b	Advances Minus Declines Exponentially Smoothed by 3 days with +1000 and −1000 zones.
Chart 4–3	Advances Decline 10 and 30 Smoothed Difference—Mamis.
Chart 4–4	Advance Decline Overbought Oversold.
Chart 4–5	Advance Decline Overbought Oversold with Levels at +400, +150, −150, and −400.
Chart 4–6	Advance Decline Technique—Lindsay.
Chart 4–7	Advance Decline—Kinsman.
Chart 4–8	Plurality Index.
Chart 4–9	Plurality Index with New Zones.
Chart 4–10	Fugler Three-Day Advance Decline Technique.
Chart 4–11	Advance Decline Line.
Chart 4–12	Advance Decline Line Nonconfirmation—1987.
Chart 4–13	Advance Decline Line Nonconfirmation—1998.
Chart 4–14	Advance Decline Line Divergences.
Chart 4–15	Advance Decline Line—Weekly.

Chart 4–16	Momentum Index—Weinstein.
Chart 4–17	1% Advance Decline—Swenlin.
Chart 4–18	Eakle Advance Decline Index.
Chart 4–19	Eakle Advance Decline Index—Weekly.
Chart 4–20	Advance Decline Line Normalized—5 days.
Chart 4–21	Advance Decline Line Normalized—21 days.
Chart 4–22	Bolton Advance Decline Line.
Chart 4–23	Bolton Advance Decline Ratio—21-day Smooth.
Chart 4–24	Advance Decline Line Adjusted for Total Issues.
Chart 4–25	Big Movers Only—35 Percent.
Chart 4–26	Big Movers Only—50 Percent.
Chart 4–27	Advance Decline Line Oscillator.
Chart 4–28	Advance Decline Line Oscillator—Appel.
Chart 4–29	Absolute Breadth Index—50-day Smooth.
Chart 4–30	Absolute Breadth Index—21-Day Smooth with 300 and 1100 Levels.
Chart 4–31	Absolute Breadth Index—21 day with 250 and 600 Levels.
Chart 4–32	Absolute Breadth Index Adjusted by Total Issues—21-day Smooth with 10 and 30 Levels.
Chart 4–33	McGinley Advance Decline (AD) Power.
Chart 4–33b	Weekly McGinley AD Power.
Chart 4–34	Coppock Breadth Indicator.
Chart 4–35	Haurlan Index—Short-Term.
Chart 4–36	Haurlan Index—Intermediate-Term.
Chart 4–37	Haurlan Index—Long-Term.
Chart 4–38	McClellan Oscillator.
Chart 4–39	McClellan Summation Index—Traditional.
Chart 4–40	McClellan Summation Index—Miekka.
Chart 4–41	McClellan Summation Index—Swenlin.
Chart 4–42	McClellan Summation Index—Pring.
Chart 4–43	Merriman NYSE Breadth Model.
Chart 4–44	Swenlin IT Breadth Momentum Oscillator.
Chart 4–45	Swenlin Trading Oscillator—Breadth.
Chart 4–46	Zahorchak Method—Daily.
Chart 4–47	Zahorchak Method—Weekly.
Chart 5–1	Advance Decline Ratio—1965–2004.
Chart 5–2	Advance Decline Ratio—1996–2004.
Chart 5–3	Breadth Thrust.
Chart 5–4	Breadth Thrust with Simple 10-day Smooth.
Chart 5–5	Breadth Thrust with Exponential 8-day Smooth.
Chart 5–6	Breadth Thrust Continuation
Chart 5–7	Duarte Market Thrust—Weekly.
Chart 5–8	Eliades Sign of the Bear.

List of Charts, Tables, and Figures

Chart 5–9	Hughes Breadth Momentum Oscillator.
Chart 5–10	Hughes Breadth Momentum % Oscillator.
Chart 5–11	Panic Thrust.
Chart 5–12	STIX—Short-Term Trading Index.
Chart 5–13	STIX—with 10-Day Smooth.
Chart 6–1	Schultz Advances/Issues Traded Ratio.
Chart 6–2	Schultz Advance/Total Issues—Smoothed.
Chart 6–3	Advance Decline Divergence Oscillator.
Chart 6–4	Advance Decline Diffusion Index.
Chart 6–5	Breadth Climax.
Chart 6–6	Declining Issues TRIX.
Chart 6–7	Advancing Issues TRIX.
Chart 6–8	Disparity between NYSE Index and Advance Decline Line.
Chart 6–9	Disparity Index.
Chart 6–10	Walter Heiby Dynamic Synthesis.
Chart 6–11	Walter Heiby Dynamic Synthesis as a Percentage of Total Issues.
Chart 6–12	Walter Heiby Dynamic Synthesis Indicator.
Chart 6–13	Unchanged Issues.
Chart 6–14	Unchanged Issues—21-Day Smooth.
Chart 6–15	Unchanged Issues as a Percentage of Total Issues.
Chart 6–15b	Unchanged Issues/Total Issues—1987.
Chart 6–16	Velocity Index.
Chart 7–1	New Highs–New Lows—21-Day Smooth.
Chart 7–2	New Highs, New Lows Percent Total Issues—Hayes.
Chart 7–3	New Highs, New Lows Line.
Chart 7–4	New Highs, New Lows Line—21-Day Smooth.
Chart 7–5	New Highs and New Lows Oscillator.
Chart 7–6	New Highs and New Lows Oscillator—Appel.
Chart 7–7	New Highs, New Lows—Morris.
Chart 7–8	High Low RSI.
Chart 7–9	High Low Stochastic.
Chart 7–10	New Highs, New Lows Ratio—21-Day Smooth.
Chart 7–11	New Highs, New Lows Ratio—10-day Smooth.
Chart 7–12	New High, New Low—Cohen.
Chart 7–13	New Highs, New Lows Ratio—Merrill.
Chart 7–14	Weekly New Highs—Hayes.
Chart 7–15	New Highs—Hayes.
Chart 7–16	New Highs and New Lows Cross.
Chart 7–17	New High, New Low Cross—10-Day Smooth.
Chart 7–18	New Highs, New Lows—Burk.
Chart 7–19	New Highs Percent Total Issues.
Chart 7–20	New Highs Percent Total Issues Rate of Change.
Chart 7–21	Weekly New Highs, New Lows—Hayes.

Chart 7–22   New Lows Percent Total Issues.
Chart 7–23   New Lows Percent Total Issues Rate of Change.
Chart 7–24   High Low Logic Index.
Chart 7–25   High Low Logic Index—Weekly.
Chart 7–26   High Low Logic—Appel.
Chart 7–27   Low High Logic Index.
Chart 7–28   High Low Validation Index.
Chart 8–1   Up Volume—21-Day Smooth.
Chart 8–2   Up Volume—10-Day Smooth.
Chart 8–3   Up Volume—21-Day Detrended.
Chart 8–4   Down Volume—21-Day Smooth.
Chart 8–5   Down Volume—21-Day Detrended.
Chart 8–6   Changed Volume—21-Day Smooth.
Chart 8–7   Up Volume and Down Volume.
Chart 8–8   McClellan Oscillator—Volume.
Chart 8–9   McClellan Summation—Volume.
Chart 8–10   Merriman NYSE Volume.
Chart 8–11   Swenlin IT Volume Momentum Oscillator.
Chart 8–12   Swenlin Trading Oscillator—Volume.
Chart 8–13   Up Volume, Down Volume Line.
Chart 8–14   Cumulative Volume Ratio.
Chart 8–15   Cumulative Volume Ratio—10-Day Smooth.
Chart 8–16   ADOBV with OBV Similarity.
Chart 8–17   ADOBV with Trendline Divergence.
Chart 8–18   ADOBV Oscillator.
Chart 8–19   Volume Percent Ratio.
Chart 8–20   Up Volume−Down Volume.
Chart 8–21   Upside Downside Volume Ratio.
Chart 8–22   Upside Downside Volume—McMillan.
Chart 8–23   Peterson Up Down.
Chart 8–24   Zweig Up Volume.
Chart 8–25   Zweig Double 9 Up Volume.
Chart 8–26   Zweig Double 9 Down Volume.
Chart 9–1   Arms Index.
Chart 9–2   Arms Index Oscillator 21–55.
Chart 9–3   Arms Index —4 Day with Bands.
Chart 9–4   Arms Index —21-Day Smooth with Divergence.
Chart 9–5   Arms Index —10-Day Smooth Inverted.
Chart 9–6   Arms Index —2.65 Days Shown.
Chart 9–7   Arms Index —40 Average.
Chart 9–8   Arms Open Index —10-Day Smooth.
Chart 9–9   Arms Open and with Bollinger Bands.

List of Charts, Tables, and Figures xiii

Chart 9–10	WTRIN10.
Chart 9–11	Bretz TRIN-5.
Chart 9–12	Bretz TRIN-5 Inverted.
Chart 9–13	Cash Flow Index.
Chart 9–14	Composite Tape Index—Medium.
Chart 9–15	Composite Tape Index—Short.
Chart 9–16	Composite Tape Index—Long.
Chart 9–17	Dysart Positive and Negative.
Chart 9–18	Eliades New TRIN.
Chart 9–19	Haller Theory.
Chart 9–20	Hindenburg Omen.
Chart 9–21	Market Thrust.
Chart 9–22	Market Thrust Oscillator.
Chart 9–23	Market Thrust Summation.
Chart 9–24	Market Thrust Oscillator 21 and 55.
Chart 9–25	McClellan Oscillator—Morris.
Chart 9–26	McClellan Oscillator—Morris with Smoothing.
Chart 9–27	McClellan Summation—Morris.
Chart 9–28	Moving Balance Indicator Using Lloyd Signals.
Chart 9–29	Moving Balance Indicator with Stewart Smoothing.
Chart 9–30	Moving Balance Indicator Buy at 40.
Chart 9–31	Technical Index.
Chart 9–32	Technical Index Rate of Change.
Chart 9–33	Titanic Syndrome—1988.
Chart 9–34	Titanic Syndrome—1991.
Chart 9–35	Titanic, 1995—Flying Titanic.
Chart 9–36	Trend Exhaustion Index.
Chart 9–37	Trend Explosion Index.
Chart 10–1	McClellan NYSE Ratio Adjusted Volume Minus Ratio Adjusted Advance Decline Summation Index.
Chart 10–2	T-bonds and McClellan Uncommon Advance Decline Ratio Adjusted Summation Index.
Chart 10–3	Russell 2000 Index and McClellan Up Down Volume Line.
Chart 10–4	After-Tax Profits as Percent of GDP and McClellan NYSE Ratio Adjusted AD Line.
Table 10–1	Desired Sequence.
Figure 10–1	McClellan Oscillator with Neutral Point.
Figure 10–2	McClellan Oscillator with Neutral Point Multiplied by 30.
Table 10–2	Market Changes versus MCOSI.
Chart 11–1	Dominant Index.
Chart 11–2	Nasdaq Advance Decline Model.
Chart 11–3	Nasdaq High Low Model.
Table 11–1	Dominant Market Research.

Table 11–2	Trend Capturing Research.
Table 11–3	McClellan Summation Research.
Table 12–1	Primary Indicators.
Chart 12–1	McClellan Summation Study.
Chart A–1	Advance Decline Line with 30-Day Smooth.
Chart A–2	Advance Decline Line Smoothed 7 Days and 30-Day Smooth.
Table B–1	Time Frames for Analysis.
Chart B–1	Market Cycles—20 Percent.
Chart B–2	90-Day T-bills Rate of Change.

Foreword

I was pretty surprised when I received an advance copy of Greg Morris' new book, *Market Breadth Indicators*. Not only because of its size, but because of the amount of information included on the subject. It reminded me of the same surprise I got when I received a copy of my first book, *Technical Analysis of the Futures Markets*, nearly 20 years ago. I had started off writing a book that included most of the technical theories and indicators that I used in my work. At first, I didn't think there was enough material to actually fill a book. I expected a relatively small volume. What I got in the mail from my publisher was a 600-page monster. And I left some things out. One of the subjects that I left out was market breadth. That was mainly because my first book dealt with futures markets, where market breadth isn't that important. In the 1999 rewrite of the book (which was broadened to include all financial markets), I devoted a chapter to market breadth. I thought that was adequate. Until I read Greg Morris' work.

Morris starts off with a brief introduction to technical analysis and a primer on breadth information. For those new to the subject, he explains the difference between breadth and price, between daily and weekly data, and some of the terminology used in this area. He introduces the three main areas of breadth analysis, which are advancing and declining issues, new highs and new lows, and up and down volume. He even covers some of the advantages and disadvantages of breadth analysis. For one thing, Morris points out that more than half the issues traded on the New York Stock Exchange are interest rate sensitive, which even includes preferred stocks and closed-end bond funds. Because their inclusion can sometimes distort the NYSE breadth data, Morris suggests some ways that market analysts deal with that potential problem.

Chapters 4 through 10 really get into the meat of market breadth. I knew something about most of the indicators included, but I saw a few that were new to me. I was amazed at the amount of variation in the construction and plotting of the breadth data. Morris has done a lot of his own original work over the years, which he relies on in his writing. But he also incorporates the valuable work of other well-known technical authors and analysts like Richard Arms, Ned Davis, Sherman and Tom McClellan, Arthur Merrill, Carl Swenlin, and Martin Zweig to name just a few. It's an eye-opener to see how many ways there are to manipulate only six pieces of information that can be found in your morning newspaper—the number of advancing and declining issues, the number of new 52-week highs and new lows, and the amount of advancing and declining volume. He devotes an entire chapter to the McClellan indicators (the oscillator and summation index), which are extremely popular in technical circles. To add a practical note to the book, he interviews a technically oriented money manager to find out how he uses breadth data in his work.

With today's computers, traders are limited only by their own creativity and imagination in finding ways to incorporate market breadth into their trading and investment decisions. Because most of the available technical literature has dealt mainly with price and volume analysis, Morris gets into an area of market analysis that hasn't been given the attention it deserves. His new book should go a long way towards rectifying that oversight. The book has something for everyone. It provides more than enough information to keep professional number-crunchers busy. It provides a lot of information that's new even to old-timers like myself. It should also be of interest to the individual investor. It's not necessary to be a professional technical analyst to benefit from the study of market breadth. As is often the case in market analysis, simpler approaches often work the best.

The simplest breadth indicator of all is the daily NYSE advance-decline line, which plots the difference between the number of big board advancing and declining issues. If the AD line is rising, that means there are more issues rising than falling. That's good. A falling AD line is bad. The reason it's bad is that the AD line has a tendency to peak ahead of the rest of the market. The last time that happened was in the 2 years from 1998 to 2000. During those 2 years, the NYSE Advance-Decline fell while the NASDAQ advance continued. Seasoned analysts like myself warned that there were a lot more stocks falling than rising during those two years, which was traditionally a sign of a major market top. Other analysts countered that the advance-decline was no longer relevant in the new dot.com era. The worst bear market in 70 years started in the spring of 2000—exactly 2 years after the NYSE advance-decline peaked.

John Murphy
Author of *Technical Analysis of the Financial Markets*
and *Intermarket Analysis*

Preface

Look beneath the surface of the market. Breadth indicators hold a wealth of information about the market's condition, a condition that is not always obvious.

Market breadth is generally misunderstood, misused, and more often than not, it is totally ignored by most. I began writing this book in the mid–1990s because I felt that it was the one subject that had not been adequately addressed in the multitude of books on technical analysis and charting. Many good books by such popular names as John Murphy and Martin Pring only devote a single chapter to the subject.

For many years I have wondered why there was not a single reference devoted to market breadth indicators and analysis. Maybe the subject isn't as popular or useful as I think it is. It might be a difficult subject to sell, because it deals with many unfamiliar data items and components of the stock market. Well, I'm going to find out. This book is devoted to market breadth indicators and covers the topic as thoroughly and as accurately as possible. I have been collecting breadth-related material for more than 20 years, and I firmly believe that the understanding and use of breadth indicators will give you an edge when it comes to your analysis.

Breadth analysis also seems to be the one subject that does not garner a great deal of interest from the financial media. I truly believe that is probably a good thing because they might do it an injustice. If you don't understand something, you probably shouldn't talk about it. Gleaning information from market breadth data and breadth indicators is truly one of the most consistent methods for market analysis, if not the best. Breadth data is simply the best measure of market liquidity there is. This book will attempt to prove that.

Solid analysis with a defined plan of action is crucial for investment success. You should always understand that the analysis might be flawed and that the investment decisions might need to be reversed, and that is just part of a good, solid plan. During a bull market, anyone can buy just about any stock and appear to have an insight into the markets. This reminds me of the old Wall Street axiom: Don't confuse brains with a bull market. However, the table turns when the market turns. The market bubble that ended in early 2000 is a classic example. How many folks held onto their positions, firmly believing that the market would correct itself and then continue its insane climb to lofty heights? The markets have a unique cleansing effect at times, and in the case of the last bull market, it was long overdue. Using market breadth as an analysis tool is essential to a solid and successful investing style. You must utilize some means of controlling your emotions. Breadth analysis is the answer. I have expanded views on this and personal opinions on lots of things in Chapter 1.

This book is laid out in a textbook manner, with each breadth subject adhering to a fairly rigid format. It can be read from cover to cover, or used as a reference guide when desiring information about a particular breadth indicator or topic. For those not too familiar with breadth, I would recommend that you read everything up to the chapters on Breadth Indicators (Chapters 4–10) prior to tackling those chapters. The chapters that delve into the actual breadth indicators (Chapters 4–10) can be studied after the other material is understood. They can be read in sequence or used like an encyclopedia to look up the details on a particular breadth indicator. Chapter 2 is important, as it explains all the variances and terminology that is needed to assist in understanding the chapters on the breadth indicators. If you were to pick only one chapter to read in preparation for reading the breadth indicator chapters, Chapter 2 would be the one.

I used the clean chart concept for the more than 190 charts in this book. On occasion, I highlighted something in particular on a chart, but much more often than not, the description was made in the text that is associated with the chart. The intention is that you can take a straightedge and align the data to see signals much better if the charts are not cluttered. I also insisted that they be displayed in portrait mode so that you could view them without having to turn the book 90 degrees.

You will thoroughly enjoy Chapter 11, on "Putting Breadth to Work." This is a real-life situation and how a successful company uses breadth analysis for managing clients' accounts and a number of large mutual funds. It is kind of a breadth validation chapter, if you will.

In Chapter 1 I take the liberty of pointing out a number of misconceptions that I believe are prevalent in the financial marketplace. Some others are sprinkled throughout the book, hopefully in an appropriate place. It is not my intent to offend anyone who adapts or adheres to a technique that I believe is not correct, just my concern that they might not fully understand it. In a few places I rant excessively and am quite possibly controversial.

In Chapter 12, "Conclusions," I provide a table of all indicators arranged in the order they were presented in the book. I show what breadth components are used in the indicator, whether the indicator works better at market tops, bottoms, or for trend analysis, and whether or not the indicator is short or long term in nature. I also take the liberty of offering a list of my favorite breadth indicators, and I present a short discussion on the importance of the McClellan Summation Index to show its value in your investment approach.

Every attempt has been made to identify the creator or author of these indicators. One major source of information has been *Stocks and Commodities* magazine. If you are a student of the market, and in particular the technical side, this is the one periodical you must have. Subscription information and a special offer are in the back of the book. There is also a special offer in the back of the book to acquire all of the indicators used in this book, plus many more, for use with MetaStock software.

Acknowledgments

I was blessed with loving and caring parents, Dwight and Mary Morris. They are almost single-handedly responsible for any good that I have ever done. As I said in my 1992 book *Candlestick Charting Explained*, and it is still true today, anything bad surely must have come from being a Navy fighter pilot. I owe a lifetime debt of thanks to Keith and Irene Eppler. They guided me in my younger years and Keith sparked the flying bug—which led to more than 21,000 flying hours starting in 1967 and flying every type of aircraft imaginable. When you read my biography at the end of this book, it reads like someone who can't hold a job. That is, until you get to the part that all along, during all the other endeavors, I was a captain for a major airline.

Early in my investment life, my good friend Tom Zellner introduced me to a book by Michael Zahorchak called *The Art of Low Risk Investing*. Being an engineer, I had previously moved toward the technical side of market analysis, but this was the book that solidified my belief in that approach. Before that I was stumbling along with earnings reports, product analysis, management styles, and generally a wide array of fundamental ratios and information that never seemed to have anything to do with the stock price movements. It sure made me feel good, though, to buy a stock because the financial ratios were good. Fortunately, I quickly learned that feeling good has very little to do with making money in the markets.

In the early 1980s I had the privilege of working with Norman North, of N-Squared Computing. We pumped out a lot of DOS-based charting and analysis software back then, including the first program to automatically identify Japanese candle patterns. Another product we developed was one that analyzed breadth data, usually what was available from the Barrons Market Laboratory pages. One customer for that product became and remains a good friend, Ron Salter of Salter Asset Management.

Tim Chapman and Don Beasley, of PMFM, Inc., have been good friends and business associates for a number of years. A friendship with these two first-class individuals is as valuable as it can get.

A special thanks to Tom McClellan, of The McClellan Market Report, who tirelessly responded to questions I had about the McClellan indicators and, with his dad Sherman, provided some good material for this book. Sherman also assisted in proofreading the initial manuscript with his usual engineerlike attention to detail.

Thanks also to Jim Miekka, of the Sudbury Bull and Bear Report, for his thorough analysis of the McClellan Summation index and details on his Hindenburg Omen indicator. Jim added significantly to the value of this book.

The following individuals also deserve recognition for their unselfish assistance with the creation of this book:

Lynn Dufrenne of Equis International assisted me with some coding issues for some of the indicators.
Carl Swenlin of Decision Point (www.decisionpoint.com) was a great source for indicator details and historical information.

John McGinley of Technical Trends helped with some of the old breadth indicators that seem to have disappeared. John was Arthur Merrill's sidekick and produced the Technical Trends service.

Dennis Meyers of Meyers Analytics unconditionally gave me the code for some of his advanced composite indicators.

Ed Pavia, of Pinnacle Data, for providing quality and reliable breadth data.

Jon DeBry, of www.debry.com, for providing breadth manipulation tools in a software package.

Nick Laird, of www.sharelynx.com, for offering the use of his giant market-related database.

Mark Lundeen for providing his huge database of market information and statistics.

A special thanks to the folks at Equis International for their MetaStock software. The charts in this book were almost exclusively created by MetaStock.

Stephen Isaacs of McGraw-Hill was a delight to work with.

And saving the best and most important for last is my loving and wonderful wife and partner, Laura. She is always there for me.

As is the accepted standard, and certainly in this case the fact, whatever factual errors and omissions are sadly, but most certainly, my own.

Breadth Hall of Fame

I would like to honor the following individuals who have made sizable contributions to breadth market analysis. This really is not a wise thing to do for fear of leaving out someone who belongs in this list. After more than 20 years of collecting material and researching the subject of breadth, the following names surfaced often and usually with lasting and important contributions. If anyone was not included that should be, it is totally my oversight. If you are convinced that someone was not included that should be on this list, please let me know.

Gerald Appel
Richard Arms
Leonard Ayres
Tushar Chande
Ned Davis
Norman Fosback
Joseph Granville
Tim Hayes
P.N. Haurlan

James Hughes
Marian McClellan
Sherman McClellan
Tom McClellan
John McGinley
Arthur Merrill
Richard Russell
Martin Zweig

The Complete Guide to Market Breadth Indicators

1
Introduction

The noblest pleasure is the joy of understanding. Leonardo da Vinci

How can you even begin to predict or forecast the market if you are not using the correct tools to determine its present state? If you do not fully grasp the present state of the market, your prediction, whether real or anticipated, will be off by an amount equivalent to at least the error of your current analysis. And your error will be compounded based upon the time frame of your prediction or forecast. Breadth analysis is like quantum mechanics; it does not predict a single definite result. Instead it predicts a number of different possible outcomes and tells us how likely each one will be. Breadth directly represents the market, no matter what the indices are doing. It is the footprint of the market and the best measure of the market's liquidity.

Market breadth indicators are sometimes referred to as broad market indicators. Probably the simplest way to think of them is to realize that they generally do not refer to, or use information relating to, an individual issue. Breadth will treat all stocks in an index equally. The stock with the largest capitalization and the smallest are both equal in breadth analysis. Most breadth analysis is total-market related in that it deals with the complete market. A rising tide raises all ships is the more picturesque way to grasp its meaning.

Market breadth uses market data such as advancing and declining issues, new highs and new lows, up and down volume, etc. This is an area of market analysis that deals only with the stock market and does so in a generic way. It cannot be used on individual stocks, mutual funds, or futures. It is a broad approach to overall market analysis that helps investors and traders realize the underlying strength or weakness associated with a market move. The analysis normally is done on the New York market, the American Stock Exchange market, and the Nasdaq market, but can be applied to any exchange or index of securities for which breadth data is available.

Actually, breadth calculations can be accomplished on any sector of the market or industry group as long as you have a method of determining the components mentioned above. I'm quite certain that with the explosive use of computers for analysis, this is just around the corner, if not already being done in some places.

Technical Analysis

I know of no way of judging the future but by the past. Patrick Henry

The subject of market breadth indicators falls squarely into the field of technical analysis. What is technical analysis? Books are filled with definitions and interpretations on technical analysis. A significant part of technical analysis is the art of studying the past, attempting to identify a pattern or event that seems to represent or reflect the market being studied, and then believing that it will work with some certainty in the foreseeable future.

My definition for technical analysis and my adherence to using it comes from a belief that everyone needs something to believe in or rely upon. I believe in technical analysis because of its close relationship to the supply and demand of the market. Fundamental analysis, which is by far a more popular method of analysis, is generally flawed in that it does not address the issue of "when." When should I buy or when should I sell? Researching the hundreds of different fundamental ratios is the full-time job of thousands of securities analysts. However, think about this simple fact. Almost all fundamental ratios involve price. So why not analyze price? Most forms of technical analysis do just that.

Is technical analysis the same as market timing? Sometimes it is; sometimes it isn't. Market timing has received a bad rap, especially by those who believe it is a process by some who blindly follow some overoptimized mechanical system without utilizing money management or an asset commitment plan. In that regard, its bad rap is appropriate. The analysis of risk and reward is not market timing in the sense that many think of when using that often-misused term. Determining when the market has too much risk is not market timing, but prudent and discretionary investing. Next time you hear a brokerage firm analyst mention that no one can time the market, or that technical analysis does not work, ask to see his record during the bear market of 2000–2002.

Another challenge to technical analysis is that of whether it is an art or a science. I cannot believe anyone would seriously ask this, and I suspect the question comes almost totally from the nonscientific or the innumerate among us. I do believe that scientists, engineers, and mathematically inclined investors migrate toward technical analysis over time because of its ability to look back in history and see how supply and demand played out. It is certainly a more analytical approach to market analysis.

Those who get excited and experience a warm feeling about the overused adjectives of quality, strong, healthy, etc. when Wall Street talks about investing in specific companies are surely the ones who think technical analysis is witchcraft. Years ago I used to be entertained by watching *Wall Street Week* and was humored by the fundamental analysts who would talk endlessly about how they liked to pick good quality companies and hold onto them. They then quickly point out the Ibbotson study that shows that equities have performed at about a 9 percent annual rate for the last 100 years. Hogwash! While the study is true, it is totally irrelevant, as one does not have a 100-year investment horizon, and it is therefore not applicable to humans. Most investors have a good 15-to 20-year period in which to make their serious investments. There were many, many 15-to 20-year periods in the last 100 years that resulted in negative returns. The most egregious example is if you had bought in 1929, you did not break even until 1954, 25 years later. And guess what. Getting even is not what investing is all about.

A good detective will tell you that some of the least reliable information comes from eye witnesses. When people observe an event, it seems their backgrounds, educations, and other influences unrelated to the observed event, color their perception of what occurred. Most will also be influenced by what they hear from others. This is also amplified by a number of individual studies done by behavioral psychologists. In a nutshell, they all agree that groups of people will tend to amplify the consensus view rather than challenge it. A group's ability to focus on common knowledge and not uncover anything new is commonplace. Plus, if someone in the group is acknowledged as an expert, that opinion can totally dominate the thinking for the group and can lead to what is known as the "herd" mentality. Talk radio is a perfect example of this.

One should remember that things are quite often not what they seem. It is absolutely amazing to me how much people believe what is not true. Some believe water runs out of a bathtub faster as it gets toward the end. Assuming that the tub's sides are straight, the pressure is constant, it only appears to drain faster because you observe it starting to swirl toward the end, something you could not observe when the tub was full. How many think that George Washington cut down a cherry tree? George Washington did not cut down a cherry tree. That was a story told so that adults could teach their children that it was bad to tell lies. Even our founding father didn't tell lies. Parson Mason Locke Weems, the author who wrote about it, was trying to humanize Washington. Question: Did Washington throw a silver dollar across the Potomac River? Hint: The Potomac River is almost a mile wide at Mount Vernon, and silver dollars did not exist at that time. What about the Battle of Bunker Hill? It was fought at Breed's Hill in Charleston, Massachusetts. Here's one of the best: Dogs sweat through their tongues. Guess what? Dogs don't sweat. Their tongues have large salivary glands that keep them wet. Okay, one more! He drinks like a fish, but fish don't drink. Hopefully, you are getting my point. In the last few years the Internet has been the source and exploitation of much hype and false information. How many times have you received an e-mail from a friend (who probably did not originate it), and believed it to be true but did not bother to check it out, but forwarded it anyhow? You should start verifying them because many of them are a hoax. Believable misinformation flourishes.

I don't want to turn this into a science book, but I am adamant about correcting the proliferation of bad or incorrect information that exists in the financial markets, and showing you similar misconceptions that you may have believed before is the best way to get your attention. If you believed one or more of the above misconceptions, then how many market-related ones do you also believe?

Technical analysis will let you deal with reality and keep you from falling victim every time the evening news offers its expert opinion on why the markets did what they did today. As I write this, the Indonesian earthquake tidal waves have killed thousands of people, but you cannot begin to know how many. Most news sources are stating guesses anywhere from 15,000 to well over 150,000. Many news sources cannot even keep the number consistent within their own articles. Do you think they can also tell you why the markets did what they did on a daily basis? Stick to technical analysis; it will increase your understanding of the markets, if only by the fact that you are uncovering information about market behavior.

Here are some comments on technical analysis that I read over 30 years ago in *The Commodities Futures Game* by Richard Teweles, and believe to be just as valid today. Almost all methods of technical analysis generate useful information, which if used for nothing more than uncovering and organizing facts about market behavior will increase the investor's understanding of the markets. The investor is made painfully aware that technical competence does not ensure competent investing. Speculators who lose money do so not always because of bad analysis, but because of the inability to transform their analysis into sound practice. Bridging the gap between analysis and action requires overcoming the threat of greed, hope, and fear.

Technical analysis will keep your emotions from being a part of your investment decision making. While not infallible, it certainly gives you the tools to help control your emotions. It will also assist you in overcoming the human traits of ignorance and bliss. Ignorance is an intellectual state and appears to be chronic in many people with regards to the stock market. Bliss is an emotional state, and it characterizes many investors as long as the market is going up. Deluded by emotions, one cannot begin to be successful in the investing arena without some means of controlling greed, fear, and hope. This is what technical analysis does.

Technical Indicators

Those who cannot remember the past are condemned to repeat it. George Santayanna

An indicator is defined by Webster as a pointer or directing device, an instrument for measuring or recording. What, then, is a technical indicator? Technical indicators are mathematical manipulations of data so that specific values or levels can reflect the market or security being indicated upon (analyzed). There are other types of market indicators that are commonly used, such as economic time series, interest rates, etc. Stock market indicators use open, high, low, close, volume, and open interest, which are the basic components of stock and futures data. Here, we will use market breadth indicators.

He who does not know the supreme certainty of mathematics is wallowing in confusion. Leonardo da Vinci

I hope that the mention of mathematics doesn't scare anyone. You don't always have to understand mathematics to know that it will work. Most people believe that Leonardo da Vinci was a mathematician, when he was actually far from it. He had a close friendship with Luca Pacioli, who inspired Leonardo. Leonardo did, however, create a number of mathematical instruments and measuring devices, but his knowledge of mathematics was not exceptional; his friendship with one, whose mathematical knowledge was exceptional, was where the confusion may lie. One word of caution here; do not confuse mathematics with numerology.

A simple series of numbers can sometimes get misinterpreted (promoted) to be something magical. Personally, I see no value in the actual numbers that make up the Fibonacci series (a series developed by an Italian mathematician (Fibonacci) in the thirteenth century to help understand the propagation of rabbits). First I must say that I do value the ratio of the numbers that are expanded in a Fibonacci-like series (1,1,2,3,5,8,13,21,34,55,89,...). That ratio is 0.618 (and its reciprocal 1.618), often called the golden ratio because of its wide occurrence in nature. Here is a fact: the actual numbers in the Fibonacci series have little to do with the ratio. Any two numbers expanded in the same manner will produce the same "golden" ratio. Here is a test: Try it with 2 and 19. Add them together, and then add the total to the previous number just like in the Fibonacci series (2+19=21, 19+21=40, 21+40=61, etc.). Expand this until you get to some four-digit numbers so that the accuracy will be acceptable (2, 19, 21, 40, 61, 101, 162, 263, 425, 688, 1113, 1801, 2914, 4716,. . .). The last two numbers in this sequence are the two numbers that I will use for this example: 2914 and 4716. Now divide the first number by the second number, and you will get 0.618. This is exactly the same as with the one obtained using the Fibonacci series of numbers. So why did I pick 2 and 19 for this example? Hint: the second letter in the alphabet is B. Think about it. What is the nineteenth letter? And that is what numerology is all about. One last thing, the Fibonacci series also failed at understanding or predicting the propagation of rabbits. It is the ratio that is important, not the actual numbers in the series. So, when you hear someone say they are going to use a 34-day moving average because 34 is a Fibonacci number, you can immediately begin to have reservations about the rest of his analysis.

Most breadth indicators are at best coincident indicators, and usually somewhat lagging. Any of the indicators that are smoothed with moving averages are certainly lagging. Lagging means that the indicator is only telling you what is happening after it has happened. Lagging is not a problem, once you realize that picking exact tops and bottoms in the market is better left to gamblers. The confirmation of lagging indicators, however, is very important. Some breadth indicators, especially some of the ratios, can offer leading indications based upon the identification and use of previous levels or thresholds that are consistent with similar market action. An oscillator that reached a threshold level, either positive or negative, with consistency relative to market tops and bottoms is such an indicator. Many breadth indicators work in this manner.

No indicator is right all of the time; fortunately you don't have to be right all of the time. You just need to ensure that you do not hold onto losers, and keep your emotions out of the game. Choose some good, reliable indicators and stick with them. Learn how they respond during different market environments and master the interpretation of them. And remember, when your favorite indicator fails you, avoid thinking that this time is different; it probably is not.

Drawing Trendlines on Charts

Almost all references on supply and demand are directly tied to price. This involves the pricing of goods and services, as well as securities. It seems that some analysts have not understood this concept and draw trendlines all over a chart without any real understanding as to what it is they are trying to accomplish, unless, of course, it is to support (sic) their hypotheses.

Can you use support and resistance for oscillators, ratios, and accumulated values like you do with price-based issues? I believe this is carrying the supply and demand analysis a little too far, yet many analysts are doing it. Can an oscillator made up of internal breadth components have a support line or a resistance line? No, but it can reach certain levels on a consistent basis, and if that is what is being represented, then so be it, but it is not support or resistance. Similarly, I see some who will draw trendlines across moving average peaks or troughs. This is irrelevant analysis and does not represent any type of support or resistance. Like most things, there are exceptions to all this. An analyst may point out that the 200-day moving average offers support for the issue being analyzed. This may well hold out to be true, only because of that particular moving average's popularity. It probably would not hold true if an average that is less familiar or a totally random average were picked, say 163 periods.

Also, and in fairness to these analysts, drawing trendlines on some indicators such as the advance decline line is not done to identify support and resistance, but to assist the analyst in identifying divergence with price. This example should put it into perspective. You cannot relate rates of change linearly. Sun City is 20 miles from Keith's home in Pratt. He drives 60 mph going to a meeting in Sun City, but coming home he drives 30 mph. What is his average speed for the time he is on the road? Going to Sun City took 1/3 of an hour. Coming home took 2/3 of an hour. So the total 40 miles took one hour. Therefore the average speed is 40 mph. Many will believe it was 45 mph ((60 + 30) / 2). You cannot average rates of change like you can constants and linear relationships. Distance is rate multiplied by time ($d = rt$). We are dealing with the harmonic mean here and not average rates. This is one reason drawing trendlines on rates of change oscillators is not support and resistance identification.

A Familiar Breadth Indicator

Most investors are familiar with the long-running Friday night show, *Wall Street Week*, on Public Broadcasting hosted by Louis Rukeyser, who, every week would comment on his elves (his term for technical analysts) and the Wall Street Week Index. What you may not have known is that this index was a composite of 10 indicators, 3 of which were breadth-based. Robert Nurock, long-time panelist and Chief Elf, created it. Robert Nurock was the editor of the Astute Investor, a technical newsletter for many years.

The Arms Index was one of the indicators in the Wall Street Week Index. A 10-day moving average was used with bullish signals given when it was about 1.2 and bearish when it was below 0.8. The advances minus the declines were used over a 10-day period, and bullish signals were from the point where the index exceeds 1000 to a peak and down to a point 1000 below the peak. Bearish signals were just the opposite. The third breadth indicator used was the new highs compared to the new lows. Bullish signals were an expansion of the 10-day average of new highs from less than 10 up to the 10-day average of new lows. Similarly, bearish signals were an expansion of the 10-day average of new lows from less than 10 until it exceeds the 10-day average of new highs.

Breadth Relationships

In the chapters on Breadth Indicators (4–10), you will see these market components used in almost every conceivable method and mathematical combination, by themselves, or in combination with other breadth components. After they are mathematically arranged, they are then again smoothed, averaged, summed, and normalized.

There are some basic tenants that have been created over the years; each one has its place in analysis history, and here we will not attempt to say which is better or worse. Here is a list of various advance decline relationships and the analyst(s) that is(are) credited with initially using them. Many times they were the first to write about them. A student of the market will recognize many of these names.

The primary breadth components for this example are: Advances = A, Declines = D, Unchanged = U. A component between | | means absolute value. For example, the absolute value of 3 is 3 and the absolute value of –3 is also 3.

Relationship	Analyst
$A - D$	McClellan, Miekka, Haurlan, Eakle, Fugler, Arms
$|A - D|$	Fosback, McGinley
A / D	Nicoski, Zweig, Arms
$(A - D) / (A + D)$	Swenlin, Miekka, McClellan, Tabell
$(A - D) / (A + D + U)$	Hughes
$|A - D| / (A + D + U)$	Fosback
$A / (A + D)$	Appel, Zweig
$A / (A + D + U)$	Schultz
$(A - D) / U$	Merrill
$|A - D| / U$	Bolton

Similar types of relationships can be made using new highs, new lows, up volume, and down volume, but the advance decline relationship is used the most.

In the Beginning...

Who was the first to use breadth for market analysis? And when?

Colonel Leonard P. Ayres, of Cleveland Trust Company, is generally credited with being the first to count the advancing issues and declining issues. In 1926, he produced his first work, which he called "making the count of the market." However, 25 years earlier, Charles H. Dow, of Dow Theory fame, commented in his June 23, 1900 editorial in the *Wall Street Journal* about the number of advances and declines thusly, "Of these 174 stocks, 107 advanced, 47 declined, and 20 stood still." However, it is widely accepted that Colonel Ayres and his associate, James F. Hughes popularized the concept that is widely used today.

The Breadth Dance

Here is an attempt (possibly lame) to help you understand the longer term bullish and bearish moves in the market and how the various breadth components play their part. And no, I do not dance well.

The big dance is about to begin (bullish up move). Some of those that showed up are the advances, the declines, the unchanged, the new highs, new lows, and the ever-present volume twins (up and down). The dance partners are always the volume pair. As the music begins to play, there are only a few dancers on the floor—mainly the advances and primarily with the up volume. The number of dancers is good, but more show up as the evening continues. As the evening gets under-

Chart 1-1 Advances, Declines, and Unchanged, all as a Percentage of Total Issues.

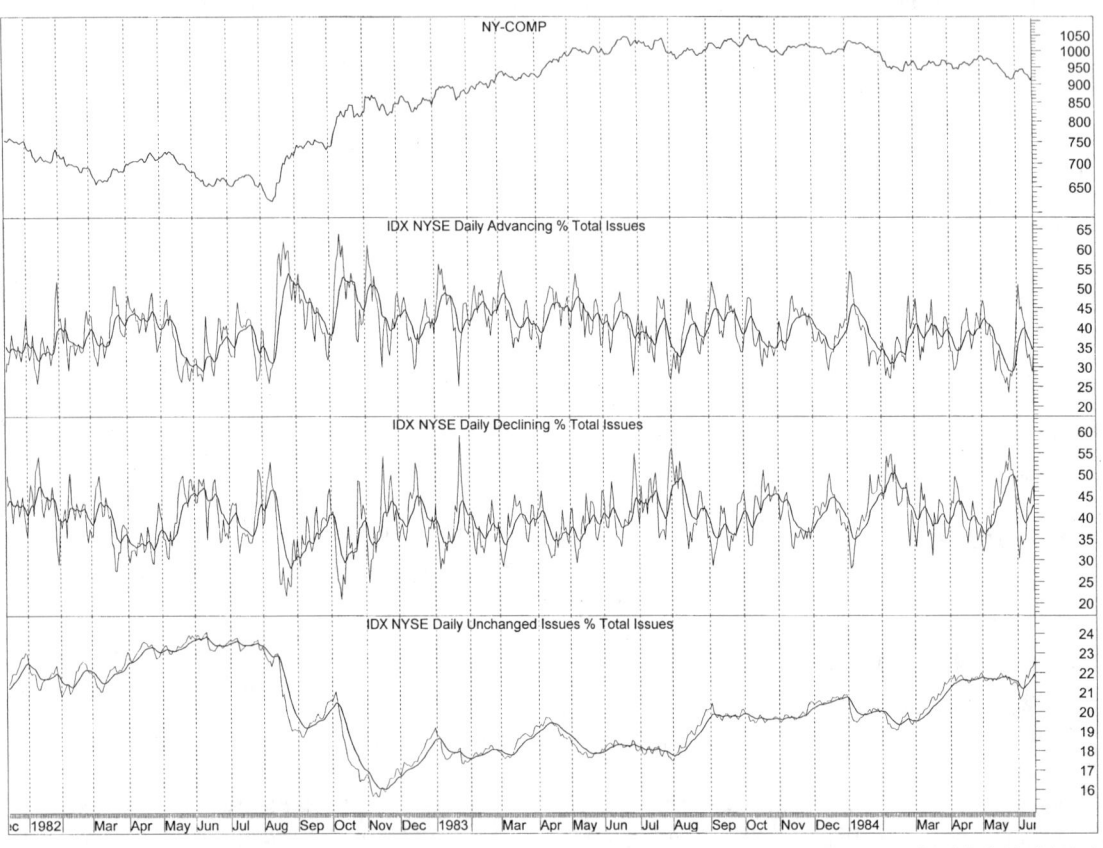

way, more and more advances start to dance, and always with the up volume. The declines, kind of a nerdy group, only dance at certain times, usually only when it is an unpopular song (short corrections).

As the evening moves on, a few of the new highs start to dance. They did not dance earlier because there have not been too many dances of late. The usual small group of the unchanged are dancing, but most are without dates and just watch from the side. As the night continues, the advances, who have been dancing most of the night, begin to sit out a dance here and there. They are worn out. Because of that, the unchanged are starting to dance more while the declines still are not doing much dancing.

With the beginning of the last music set (topping action in the market), the sound is high; everyone is at the dance. The advances have been totally worn out and only dance now and then when a really popular song is played (short up moves). The unchanged are doing a lot of dancing, even though there just aren't that many of them, and the declines, realizing the night is coming to an

Introduction 9

end, begin to dance more. As the last few songs are played, the declines get a second wind and are doing most of the dancing. Most of the advances have gone home with the new highs. The new lows are still on the sidelines, but some of the declines are taking a second look at them. As the last couple of songs are played, the only ones dancing are the declines and the new lows, both of whom are dancing with the down volume; some of the unchanged are also dancing with the new lows. The music stops and the dance is over. On the way home (established down move) the declines do most of the driving, initially by themselves, then more and more with the down volumes, and as they get closer to home (market bottom), the declines are accompanied by the new lows. As they all approach home, the declines and the down volume are almost the only ones who are not there yet. They talk about the next dance.

Charts 1–1, 1–2, and 1–3 show the period from early 1982 to the summer of 1984. This was a period where a bearish market was followed by the beginning of a big bull market (August, 1982), and then by a slow rolling-top formation into mid–1984. You can follow along with the breadth

Chart 1-2 New Highs and New Lows as a Percentage of Total Issues.

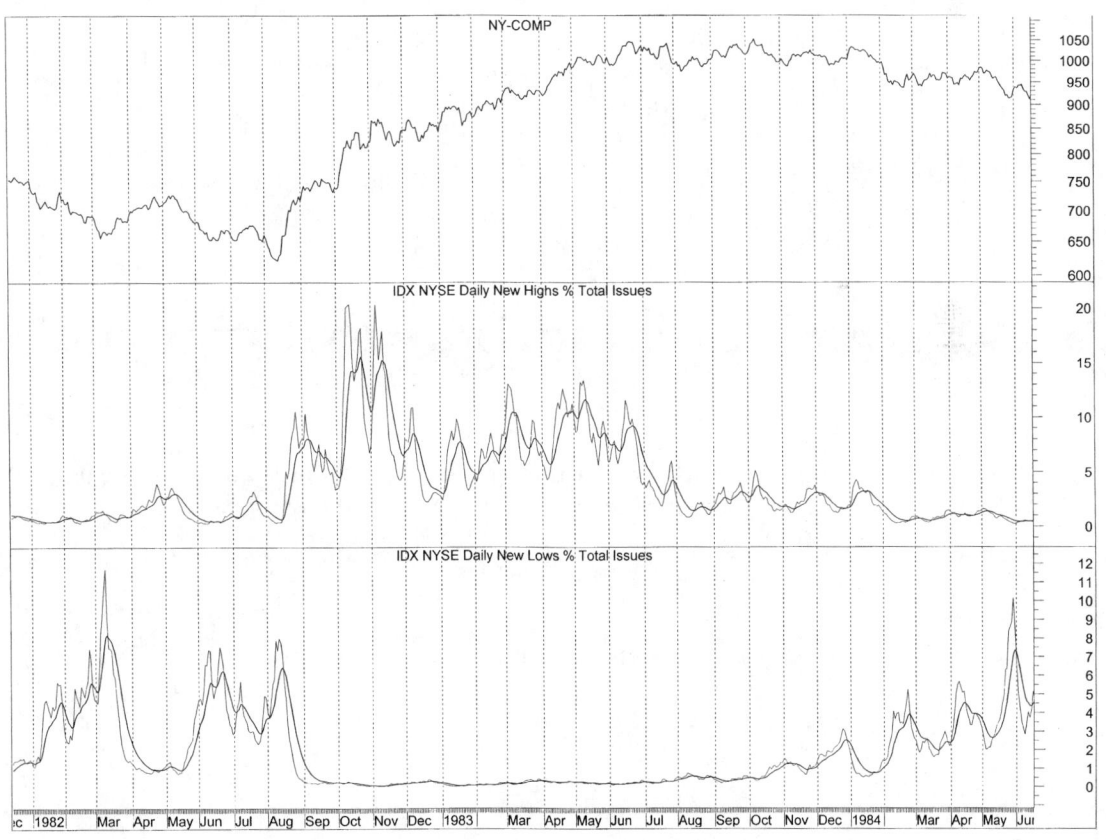

Chart 1-3 Up Volume and Down Volume as a Percentage of Total Issues.

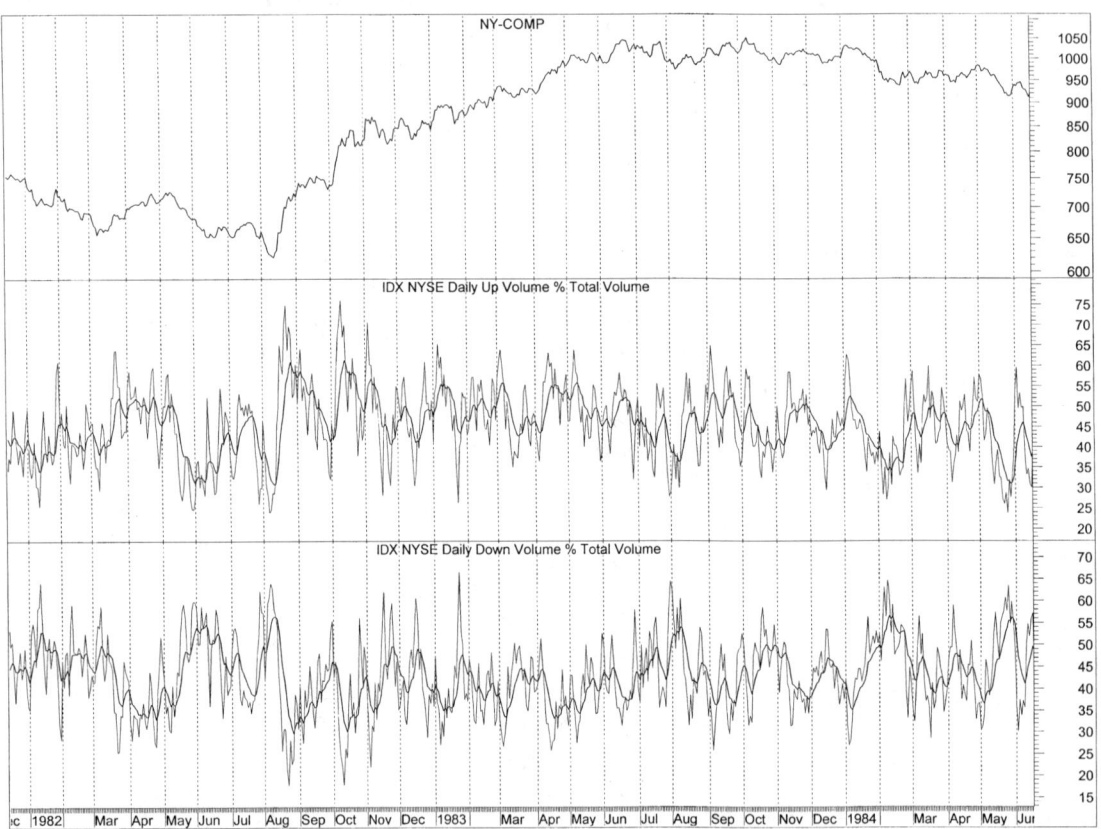

dance and verify the information on Charts 1–1 through 1–3. The raw breadth data is the lighter of the two lines. The darker line is a 10-day exponential average of the raw data.

References

Bramly, Serge. *Leonardo, the Artist and the Man.* New York: Penguin Books, 1994.

2
Necessary Breadth Information

This chapter provides a lot of basic information to assist you in understanding the remainder of this book. There are definitions, mathematical formulae, explanations of anomalies, indicator formulae, historical events that affect the data, differing methods of calculation, and a host of other important information normally found in an appendix. It is of such importance to understand this material that it belongs prior to the discussion of breadth indicators.

Breadth Components

Breadth components are readily available from newspapers, online sources, etc. and consist of daily and weekly statistics. They are: Advances, Declines, Unchanged, Total Issues, Up Volume, Down Volume, Total Volume, New Highs, and New Lows.

From one day to the next, any issue can advance in price, decline in price, or remain unchanged. Also, any issue can make a new high or a new low. Here are more specific definitions:

Advancing Issues or Advances (A)—Stocks that have increased in price from one day to the next, even if only by 1 cent, are considered as advancing issues or advances.

Declining Issues or Declines (D)—Stocks that have decreased in price from one day to the next are considered declining issues or declines.

Unchanged Issues or Unchanged (U)—Stocks that do not change in price from one day to the next are considered unchanged issues or unchanged.

Note: Prior to July, 1997, stock prices were measured in eighths of a point, or about 12.5 cents as the minimum trading unit. In July, 1997 the NYSE went from using eighths to sixteenths. This made the minimum trading unit about 6.25 cents. On January 2, 2002 they went to a decimalization pricing that made the minimum trading price equal to 1 cent (a penny). This is dealt with in more detail in the unchanged issues section.

Total Issues (TI)—This is the total of all issues available for trading on a particular exchange. If you added the advances, declines, and unchanged issues together, it would equal the total issues.

Advancing Volume or Up Volume (UV)—This is the volume traded on a day for each of the stocks that are advancing issues. It is the total volume of all the advances.

Declining Volume or Down Volume (DV)—This is the total volume for all the declines for a particular day.

Total Volume (V)—This is the total volume of all trading for a particular day. Total volume is the sum of Up Volume, Down Volume, and Unchanged Volume. To find Unchanged Volume, subtract the sum of Up Volume and Down Volume from the Total Volume. Total volume is not generally considered a breadth component, but is many times used in a ratio with the up or down volume to alleviate the increase in trading activity over long periods of time.

New High (H)—Whenever a stock's price reaches a new high price for the last 52 weeks, it is termed a new high.

New Low (L)—Whenever a stock's price reaches a new low price for the last 52 weeks, it is termed a new low.

Note: The NYSE new highs and new lows are now computed on a fixed, 52-week moving time window starting on January 1, 1978. Before that, the new highs and new lows were computed on a variable time window of anywhere from $2\frac{1}{2}$ months to $14\frac{1}{2}$ months. This rendered the new-high-new-low data prior to 1978 almost useless, if not certainly confusing to use.

Breadth versus Price

Breadth does not consider the amount or magnitude of price change. It also does not consider the number of shares traded (volume). And it does not consider the shares outstanding for individual stocks. Most stock market indices, such as the New York Stock Exchange Composite Index, the Nasdaq Composite Index, S&P 500 Index, the Nasdaq 100, etc. weigh each stock based upon its price and number of outstanding shares. This makes their contributions to the index based upon their values and are sometimes called market-value weighted indices or capitalization weighted indices. Because of this (at this writing), Microsoft, Qualcomm, Intel, Cisco, eBay, Nextel, Dell, Amgen, Comcast, and Oracle account for over 40 percent of the Nasdaq 100 Index and its ETF, QQQQ. Ten percent of the components account for 40 percent of the price movement of the index. This can lead to an incorrect analysis of the markets, especially if some of these large-cap stocks experience price moving events. Many times the reference to the large-cap issues is that of the generals, while the small caps are referred to as the soldiers. As you will find out, the generals are not always the leaders.

Breadth treats each stock the same. An advance of 1 cent in Microsoft is equally represented in breadth analysis as the advance of 30 cents of the smallest, least capitalized stock. Breadth is truly the best way to accurately measure the liquidity of the market.

The Difference between Daily and Weekly Breadth Data

You just cannot add up daily breadth data for the week to get the weekly data. Here is a scenario that will explain why.

Necessary Breadth Information

Stock: XYZ Corp.	Day	Price	Daily A − D	Weekly A − D
	Friday	12.00		
	Monday	13.00	+1	
	Tuesday	14.00	+1	
	Wednesday	15.00	+1	
	Thursday	16.00	+1	
	Friday	11.00	−1	−1
Total			+3	−1

Here's the narrative: An advance or decline for the week should be based upon its price change from the previous Friday close to the close of the current week. It has absolutely nothing to do with the daily data. Take a single stock; its previous Friday close price was $12.00. On Monday it was up $1.00 to $13.00. It went up a dollar each day for the first four days of the week and closed on Thursday at $16.00. However, on Friday it dropped $5.00 to $11.00. For the week it was down $1.00, which would be one decline for the week. However, on a daily basis, it accounted for four advances and one decline, or a net three advances.

John McGinley, past editor of Technical Trends, and sidekick of Arthur Merrill's, sent this note: "I strongly believe that in creating weekly figures for the advances and declines, one does not use the published weekly data for they disguise and hide what really went on during the week. For instance, imagine a week with 1500 net advances one day and the other four days even. The weekly data would hide the devastation which occurred that dramatic day."

Advantages and Disadvantages of Using Breadth

Breadth data seems to not be consistent among the data providers. If you think about it, if a stock is up, it is an advance for the day, so why is there a disparity? Some data services will not include all stocks on the exchange. They will eliminate preferred issues, warrants, rights, etc. This is fine as long as they tell you that is what they are doing.

In the last few years, the number of interest-sensitive issues on the New York Stock Exchange has increased so that they account for more than half of all the issues. These issues are preferred stocks, closed-end bond funds, electric utility stocks, to mention a few.

Many analysts such as Sherman and Tom McClellan, Carl Swenlin, and Larry McMillan use common-stocks-only breadth indicators. Richard Russell and Paul Desmond refer to it as an operating company only index. Using stocks that have listed options available is another good way to avoid the interest-sensitive issues, because most stocks that have listed options are common stocks.

Indicators and Terminology You Should Know

There are basically four different indicator types: differences, ratios, percentage, and cumulative. Differences are most common and should be adjusted for time-independent scaling. As the number of issues increases over time, the scaling will get expanded and thresholds that worked in the past will need to be adjusted. One way to do this is to normalize the indicator so the scaling is always between 0 and one 100.

Absolute Value—In mathematical script this is denoted with || around the value that you want to have as its absolute value. Absolute value calculations ignore the sign (positive or negative) of the number. In regard to breadth data, absolute value ignores market direction and only deals with market activity. The absolute value of +3 is 3, and the absolute value of −3 is also 3.

Accumulated / Summed ( ) (also see cumulative below)—This is the term used to add up a series of numbers. For example, the advance decline line is an accumulation of the difference between the advances and the declines. That difference is summed with each new day's difference added to the previous value. Also used with the term cumulate. In many formulae in this book, it is shown either as Previous Value + Today's Value or .

Arithmetic / Simple Moving Averages—To take an average of just about anything numerical, you add up the numbers and divide by the number of items. For example, if you have 4 + 6 + 2, the sum is 12, and the average is 12 / 3 = 4. A moving average does exactly this, but as a new number is added, the oldest number is removed. In the example above, let's say that 8 was the new number, so the sequence would be 6 + 2 + 8. The first 4 was removed because we are averaging only 3 numbers (3-period moving average). In this case the new average would be 16 / 3 = 5.33. So by adding an 8 and removing a 4, we increased the average by 1.33 in this example. For those so inclined: 8 − 4 = 4, and 4 / 3 = 1.33.

In technical analysis the simple or arithmetic average is used extensively. One thing that you should keep in mind is that with the simple average, each component is weighted exactly the same. This tends to make the simple average stale if using it for large amounts of data. For example, the popular 200-day average means that the price 200 days ago is carrying the same weight, or having the same effect on the average as the most recent price. It, therefore, is also much slower to change direction.

Cumulative—Cumulative indicators can be differences, ratios, or percentage. You are adding the daily results to the previous total. The advance decline line is a good example of a cumulative indicator. It is sometimes referred to as accumulate or summed.

Detrend—Denotes when you subtract the price from a moving average of the price. This will amplify the price relative to its smoothed value (moving average). To visualize this, pretend you had the ability to take both ends of the moving average line and pull it taut so that the price line falls into its same relative position to the now straight moving average line. Doing this allows you to more easily see cycles of a length greater than that of the number of periods used in the moving average.

Divergence—When an indicator and price do not confirm each other. At market tops, many times the price will continue to make new highs, while an indicator will reverse and not make a new high. This is a negative divergence.

Exponential Moving Averages—This method of averaging was developed by scientists, such as Pete Haurlan, in an attempt to assist and improve the tracking of missile guidance systems. More weight is given to the most recent data, and it is therefore much faster to change direction. It is sometimes represented as a percentage (trend %) instead of by the more familiar periods. Here is a formula that will help you convert between the two:

$K = 2 / (N + 1)$ where K = the smoothing constant (trend %) and N = periods. Algebraically solving for N: $N = (2 / K) - 1$.

For example, if you wanted to know the smoothing constant of a 19-period exponential average, you could do the math, $K = 2 / (19 + 1) = 2 / 20 = 0.10$ (smoothing constant) or 10% (trend), as it is many times expressed.

Here is something very important in regard to exponential moving averages; by the nature of their formula, they will always change direction when they move through the price that is used to calculate them. This means that during an uptrend in prices and their exponential average, when the prices drop below the average, the average will immediately begin to decline. A simple or arithmetic average will not do this.

Momentum—See Rate of Change.

Normalize—This is a mathematical procedure to reduce the scaling of unlike data so it can be more easily compared. To normalize a series of data, one usually wants the resultant data to fall in a range from 0 to 100. The easiest way to do this is by the following formula:

$$\frac{(\text{Current Value} - \text{Lowest Value in the Series})}{(\text{Highest Value in the Series} - \text{Lowest Value in the Series})} * 100$$

Some of you might notice that this is similar to the formula for George Lane's %K Stochastic indicator, with the exception that for stochastics, the highest and lowest values are set by the number of periods you want to use. Many indicators are served well by looking at their normalized values for a predetermined number of periods. For example, if there was a good identifiable cycle in the market being analyzed, the number of periods of that cycle length might be a good number to use for normalization. A number of the breadth indicators in this book are normalized in that manner.

Oscillator—A term used to explain a number of technical indicators such as rate of change, momentum, stochastics, RSI, etc. These are all indicators that oscillate above and below a common value, which is often 0. Other times they oscillate between zero and one hundred.

Overbought / Oversold—These terms have to be the most overused terms when talking about the markets. Overbought refers to the time in which the prices have risen to a level that seems as if they cannot go any higher. Oversold is the opposite; prices have dropped to a point where it seems as they cannot go any lower. While this sounds simple enough, the term is usually based upon someone's personal observation of price levels and not on sound analysis.

Overlay—Refers to the act of putting an indicator on top of another one. A simple example would be displaying a moving average of an indicator on the same plot. In this case the indicator and its moving average would utilize the same scaling. Many times an unrelated indicator can be overlayed on another using totally independent price scaling.

Percentage—Percentage is generally better than a ratio because you are making the item relative to its related base. For example, the number of new highs by itself can be meaningful in the short term, but over long periods of time and with more and more issues traded, the relationship cannot remain consistent. If you took the number of new highs as a percentage of the total issues traded, then the scaling will always be from 0 to 100, and large amounts of data can be viewed with some consistency.

Rate of Change—Used interchangeably with momentum, rate of change is looking at a piece of data relative to a like piece of data at an earlier time. For example, with stock data, a 10-day rate of change would take today's price and subtract or divide by the stock's price 10 days ago. If one takes the difference in price and then divides by the older price, you will see percentage changes. Generally, it is not the value of the rate of change that is important, but the direction and pattern associated with it. However, some oscillators have consistent levels that can be used as overbought and oversold. Rate of Change seems to more often than not be in reference to the difference in values, whereas momentum is more often the ratio of values. The line shape will be the same; only the numbers that make up the line will be different.

Ratio—A ratio is when you divide one data component by another. This keeps them in perspective and will alleviate many of the problems associated with using just the difference. Sometimes the numerator and denominator are not balanced and you get a nonsymmetrical problem similar to what you get with the Arms Index. This is really not a problem as long as you are aware that it exists. Finally, a ratio of positive numbers (or similar signs) is always going to be greater than zero.

Smoothing—this is in reference to averaging data either by a simple or exponential moving average. It is a better adverb to use than always trying to explain that you take the moving average of it or take the exponential moving average of it; just say you are "smoothing" it. It is also used as a verb in as if you can "smooth" it.

Support and Resistance—First the definitions of support and resistance, then an explanation as to what they are. More elaborate definitions are available in almost any text on technical analysis. One of the best discussions of it is in Steven Achelis' book, *Technical Analysis from A to Z*, where he ties it to supply and demand. Support is the price at which an issue has trouble dropping below. Resistance is the price level that it has trouble rising above.

Note: Behavioral psychologists often use a term called anchoring. Using a stock-market-related example, anchoring is when an investor gets focused on a particular price and measures everything relative to that price. Usually it is the price the investor paid for the stock and sometimes it is a recent new high made by the stock. When the price nears one of those prices, the investor is more likely to make a decision about selling the stock. This is one explanation as to why support and resistance works, especially if the support and resistance levels are based on price.

About the Charts in this Book

Most breadth indicators are mathematical equations that use breadth data such as advances, declines, up volume, down, volume, new highs, new lows, etc. Usually the indicator can be displayed as a line plot, and in this book will almost always be displayed below the New York Composite Index. The New York Composite Index is a capitalization-weighted index of all stocks listed on the New York Stock Exchange. This plot of the index is also scaled logarithmically on the price axis. Semi-log scaling (logarithmically on only one axis) is best for long-term charts where the distance between each price point depends on its value. The distance between 10 and 20 is the same as the distance between 30 and 60; both are 100 percent increases.

Each plot on a chart will have a title. The title for the New York Stock Exchange Composite Index will be: NY-COMP. A few times, the indicator was developed to work with the Dow Jones Industrial

Average whose plot title is DJI-CLSE. The titles above the indicator plots will be similar to this example: IDX NYSE Daily Advance Decline Line. IDX refers to the data source used, NYSE refers to the exchange whose data is being analyzed, and Daily refers to the use of daily data (versus weekly). The remainder of the title is the indicator name as it was created in MetaStock's formula language. Sometimes there was further manipulation of the formula to get the desired indicator, and that is not readily apparent by the chart title.

The time frame for the chart was chosen to best reflect the value of the indicator. Some indicators are shown over the full 40-year period, while others are shown only over a few years. Many times the shorter time frames were chosen because of the frequent fluctuations (noise) of the indicator. Chart annotations were intentionally avoided to allow the chart to remain clean and uncluttered. This way you can take a straightedge and align the data to see the details of the indicators.

Some breadth indicators are combinations of various conditions that must be met in order for a buy or a sell signal to be generated. These are displayed as plots that have upward and downward spikes and sometimes steps. The upward spikes are generally for buy signals, and the downward spikes are for sell signals. Some of the plots have spikes of different lengths. This is an indication that the process of reaching a signal is a multistep process and all of the steps are displayed. In most cases, the longest spike is the final or best signal to act upon. A few indicators step higher and higher to their maximum then reverse and step downward in a similar manner. These are usually the ones that have multiple buy and sell parameters that must be met. Each upward step means one more buy parameter has been met over a sell parameter, and the opposite on the downside. Always read the associated discussion near the chart to ensure that you are interpreting the information correctly.

Multicollinearity

If you find a group of indicators that are essentially telling you the same thing and with consistency, you need to pick one of them to use and then drop the others. If they are all saying the same thing, they are not assisting you in your analysis. This is known as multicollinearity and is a trap you need to avoid. Ensure that you are using indicators that measure the markets differently and are diversified. While breadth indicators are different than most price-based indicators, there are many breadth indicators that are essentially revealing the same thing.

Many times, investors think that they are more correct in their analysis if many indicators are telling them the same thing. They are supportive of your analysis only if the indicators are not collinear. If they are collinear, then the support the investor feels from having a lot of indications agree is misleading and dangerous. The support for their analysis gives them a false confidence.

3
Breadth Indicators

This is the first chapter that will highlight the process of presenting details on all known indicators of market breadth. It will attempt to identify the creator of the indicator or methodology, the source of the information, and as much research on the indicator as possible. The formula will be disclosed in most cases, along with a number of different charts to assist you in understanding and interpreting these indicators. Finally, the author gives an opinion on the indicator and its interpretation.

Individual Breadth Indicator Format

All indicators in this book are presented using the format below. If you see that an item below is not included with the coverage of an indicator, it is because there was no information available for that particular item.

Also Known As: Many times an indicator is known by multiple names. A good example of this is the Arms Index, which is also known as TRIN and MKDS. This will also be where you can get information about very similar indicators located elsewhere in this book.

Author/Creator: Most indicators were created by someone. I have attempted to give credit when the information is available.

Data Components Required: These are the components of breadth data that are required to calculate the indicator.

Description: This is a brief description of the indicator, which will also try to clear up any problems with any interpretation of the math.

Interpretation: Here is the generally accepted industry interpretation of the indicator, using value levels, zones, smoothing values, etc. A number of different analysts' various techniques are also mentioned here.

Chart: Here is a chart that best displays the indicator. Enough data is used in the chart so that only "hand-picked" areas are avoided. There are some indicators or breadth-based systems that were beyond the capabilities for creating a chart, and they will be so noted. Many times there will be a number of charts showing different interpretations or uses of the indicator from various analysts.

Author Comments: Here the author tries to offer a personal interpretation, opinion, and use of the indicator. Because the author does not use all of them, he still offers this interpretation, including some modifications and ideas for further analysis. In some instances, he will also offer a modification that he believes will enhance the indicator. A few indicators were designed for buy signals or sell signals, but not both. On these he attempted to create the complementary indicator.

Formula: This is intended as an algebraic formula for the indicator. There are some math symbols that will assist you:

means the formula after it is accumulated or summed.

means the square root of the formula.

There are a number of formulae that are just too complex for this section. If I felt that was the case, I attempted to write a descriptive narrative on the formula. And in a few instances, the indicator was purely designed to be a visual display, and no formulae would assist your understanding.

References: This is a bibliography where you can find additional information on the indicator and/or its creator. This method was preferred over a formal bibliography and at times, there are notes about a particular book or magazine article included here. Displaying them here is a much more useful location for references, in my opinion.

Chapter Format

Because of the large number of breadth indicators, the chapters on the breadth indicators are divided into different categories based upon the mathematical relationship between the breadth pairs. An indicator pair relates to the advances and declines, the new highs and new lows, and the up volume and down volume. Pairs can be mathematically related in a number of ways. The difference between the two and the division of the two are the two primary ways these pairs have been used to create breadth indicators.

Indicator Categories

A − D	AD Difference
A / D	AD Ratio
AD	AD Miscellaneous
H − L	HL Difference
H / L	HL Ratio
HL	HL Miscellaneous
UV DV	Volume
A D H L UV DV	Composite

When necessary, the numerator controls in which category the indicator will be. If A − D is in the numerator, it is in the AD Difference category. A number of indicators could be in either the difference or the ratio category. For example, the ratio used by Sherman McClellan, Tom McClellan and Carl Swenlin has $(A - D)$ in the numerator and $(A + D)$ in the denominator $(A - D) / (A + D)$. The numerator will usually control the direction of an indicator, so that is what was used to determine the category the indicator will be in.

General Advance and Decline Information

Advancing issues (advances) are those whose price increased from the previous closing price. Declining issues (declines) are those whose price decreased from the previous closing price. A bullish market will take many, if not most, issues with it. As the market rises, the number of advances will remain fairly high with the usual oscillations as traders move in and out of the market. Most often the advancing issues will start to decline in number well before the price action reflects a market starting to peak. This is because fewer and fewer issues are continuing to rise. The prices continue to rise because most market averages are capitalization weighted, and the generals continue to lead the charge. It is when the declines begin to rise that the topping formation is reaching its final stages.

If you are analyzing data over a long term (greater than 1 year), it is highly recommended to adjust any raw forms of the data by using a ratio of it to a more universal component. For example, viewing the advancing issues as a percentage of total issues is better than just looking at advancing issues. The same goes for the declining issues and the unchanged issues. Chart 3–1 shows the raw advance and decline data. Chart 3–2 shows the advance and decline data as a percentage of the total issues. On Chart 3–2 is also a nearly horizontal line representing the least squares fit for all the data. For the advancing issues as a percentage of total issues, its value changed by less than 13 percent over the 40 years shown in the chart. For the declines, it changed less than 1.3 percent. The greater increase in the advances is probably because of the overall upward move of the market in the last 40 years.

General New High and New Low Information

The new highs and the new lows are not related like the advances and declines. An advance or decline is based on a single day's price change. A new high or new low is based on the previous year's price changes.

As previously stated, a bullish market will take many issues with it. As the market continues to rise, the number of new highs should continue to increase. Many times the new highs will surge at the beginning of a bull market, then drop off, only to return toward the end of a long bullish advance. This is because stocks that have broken out of congestion areas and are rising above their resistance levels have unlimited upward potential on a technical basis. As the market's upward move starts to falter, the first thing that happens is the number of new highs stops increasing. Then the number of new highs will begin to decline. As the topping process matures, the number of new lows will slowly begin to increase, but will not do so dramatically until the market really begins to fall.

If the number of new highs begins to drop during a market advance, this is quite bearish. In a strong upward market move, even if the new highs do not continue to increase, it is a bearish

Chart 3-1 Advances and Declines.

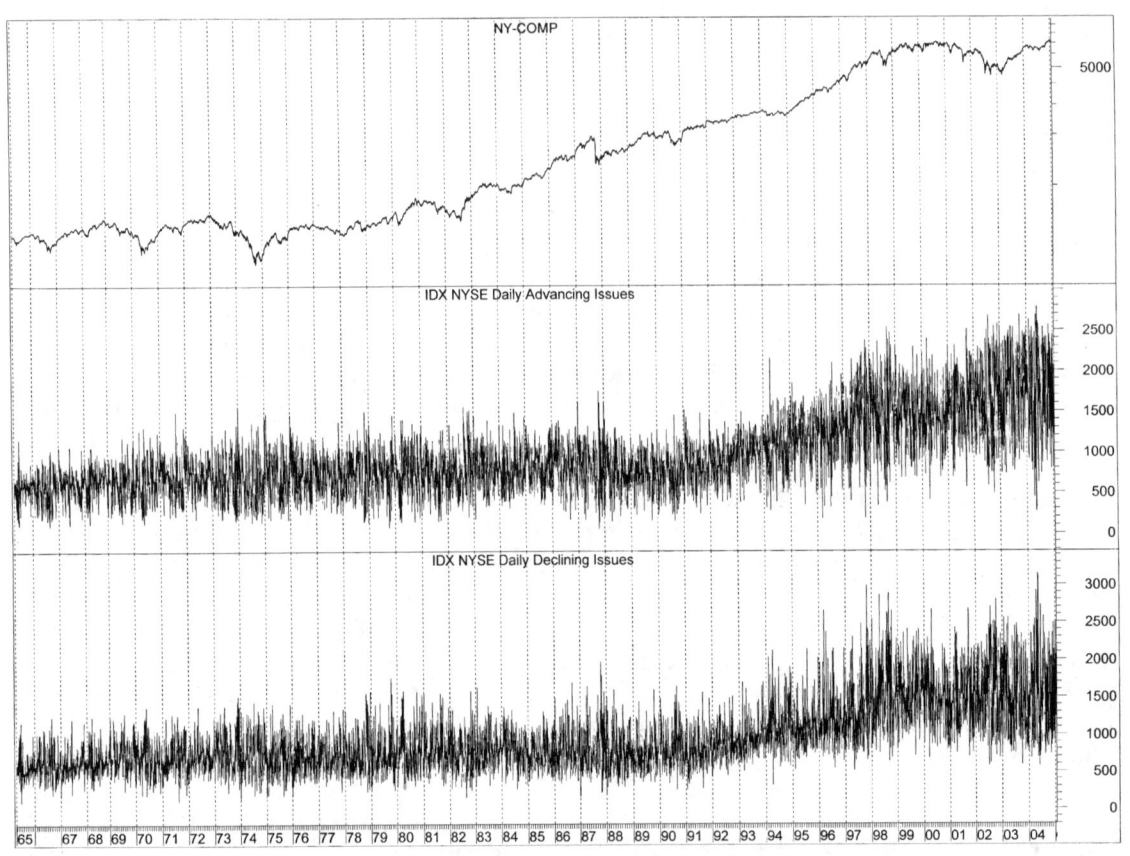

warning. They do not have to drop in number; just the fact that they are no longer increasing is not good for the upward movement.

Charts 3-3 and 3-4 use the new highs and new lows. Chart 3-3 is the raw numbers and Chart 3-4 is the new highs and new lows as a percentage of total issues. The dark line through the plots on Chart 3-4 is the linear least squares fit of the data. The increase in the regression fit for the new highs was a little over 13 percent, similar to the advances. The regression fit through the new lows actually declined over the 40-year period.

General Up Volume and Down Volume Information

Up Volume refers to the volume for the day of the advancing issues. Down volume is that volume for the declining issues. Stocks can still advance, and the amount of volume will be the first

Breadth Indicators

Chart 3-2 Advances and Declines Adjusted for Total Issues.

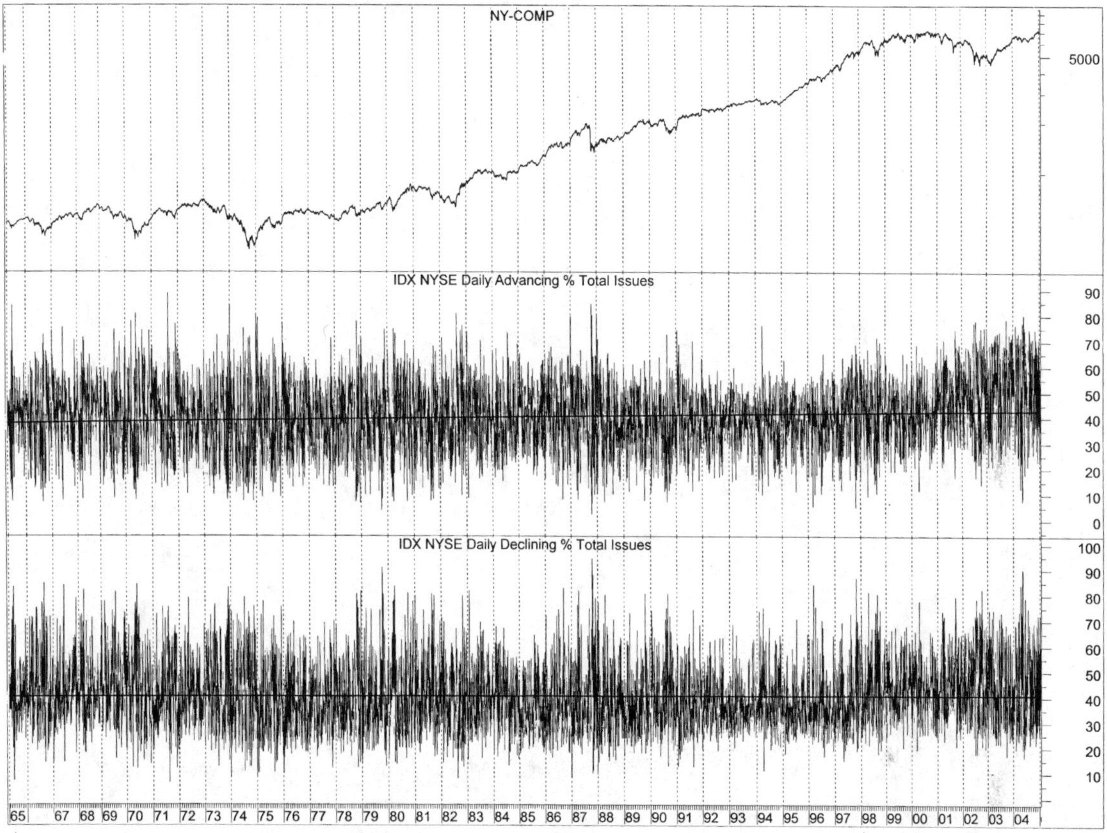

indication of a weakening advance. As an up move begins to falter, the up volume will be one of the first hints that all is not well. It is generally not the case that the declining volume will lead the declining issues when the market is in a maturing top formation. Markets can drop merely from a lack of up volume; they do not need a large increase in down volume. As a market declines, the down volume will come back into play and can be used to help identify the beginning of a bottom. The down volume will quickly dry up and the up volume will rise quickly at a market bottom.

Charts 3–5, 3–5b, and 3–6 use the up volume and down volume. Chart 3–5 is the raw numbers, and you can see that over the last 40 years, the giant increase in volume has rendered this almost useless. Chart 3–5b shows the exact same data, but the scaling for the up and down volume has been changed to semi-log scaling, which greatly enhances the chart. Chart 3–6 is the up and down volume as a percentage of total volume. In Chart 3–6 the regression line is white in hopes that it will be more easily seen. As expected, the up volume as a percentage of total volume increased

Chart 3-3 New Highs and New Lows.

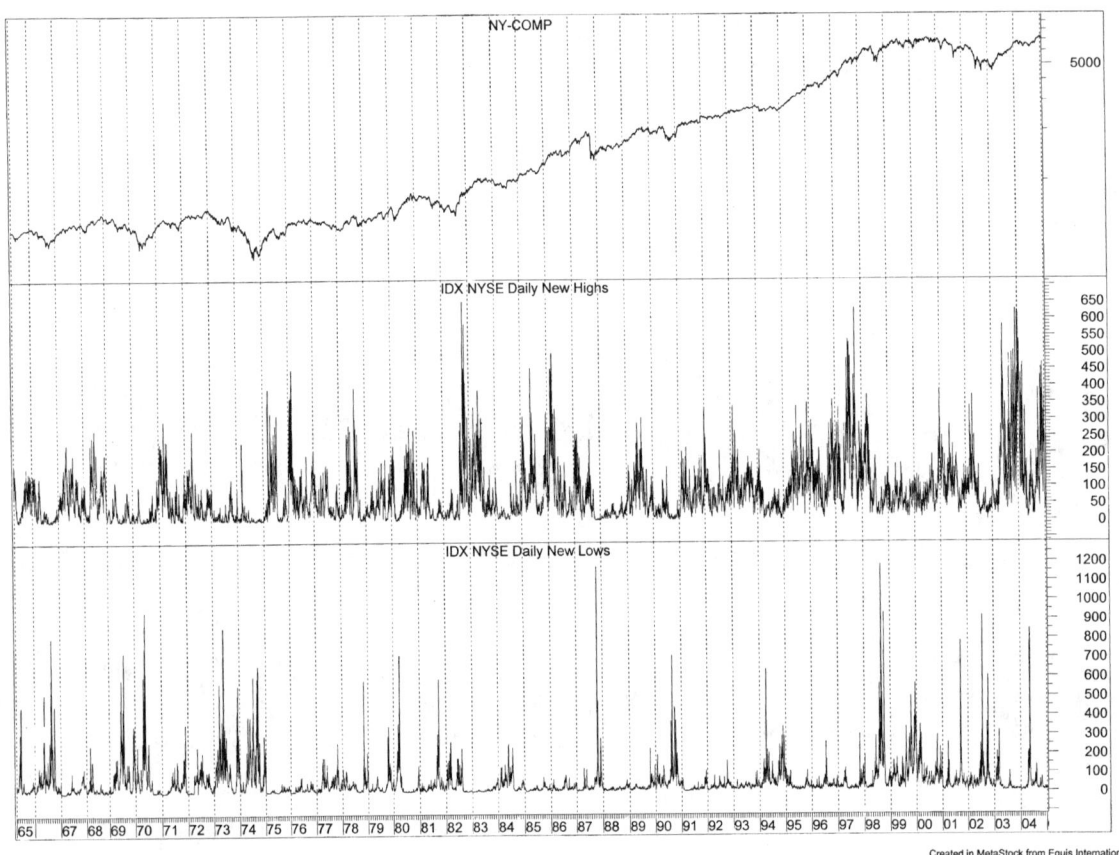

(based on the least squares fit) by about 1.5 percent. Interestingly, but not surprisingly, the down volume also increased over this 40-year period.

Complete List of Breadth Indicators
Chapter 4—Advance Decline Difference

Advances—Declines
Advance Decline Overbought Oversold
Plurality Index
Advance Decline—Fugler
Advance Decline Line
Advance Decline Line—1%

Advance Decline Line—Eakle
Advance Decline Line—Normalized
Advance Decline Line—Bolton
Advance Decline Line—Adjusted Total Issues
Big Movers Only
Advance Decline Line Oscillator

Breadth Indicators

Chart 3-4 New Highs and New Lows Adjusted for Total Issues.

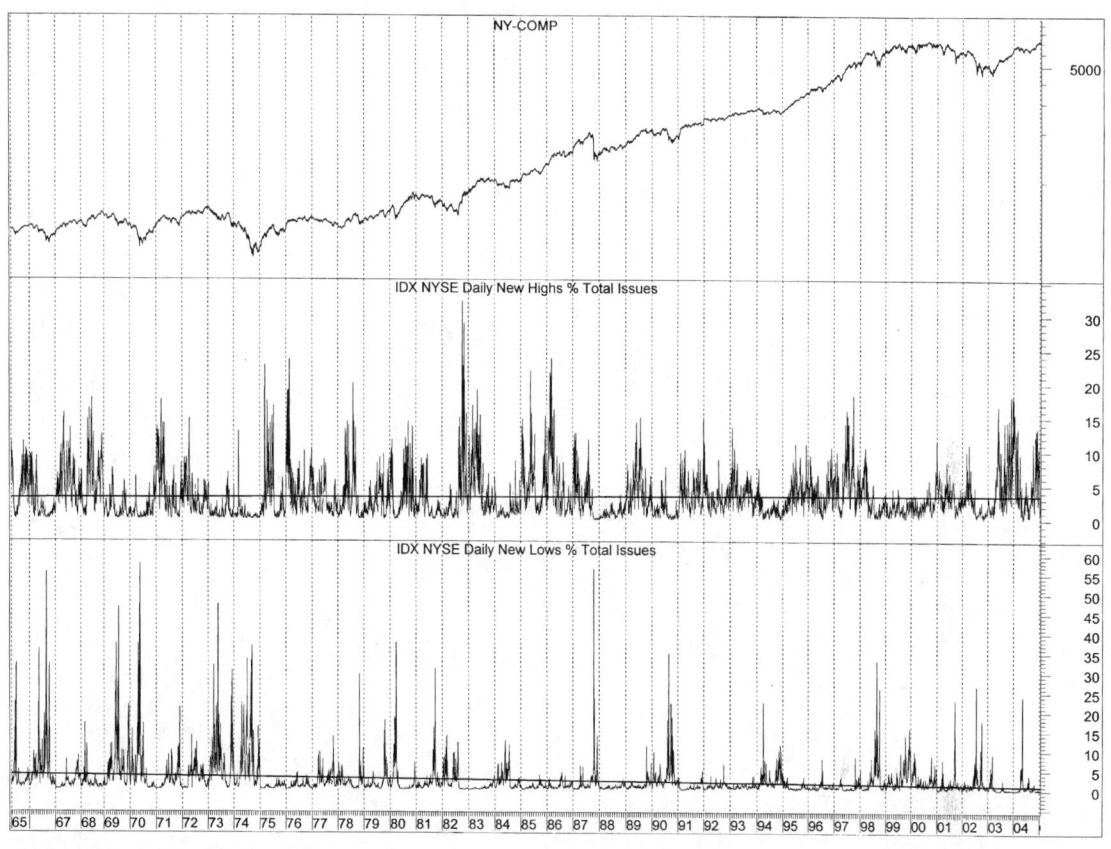

Absolute Breadth Index
Absolute Breadth Index—Adjusted
Advance Decline Power
Coppock Breadth Indicator
Haurlan Index
McClellan Oscillator

McClellan Summation Index
Merriman Breadth Model
Swenlin IT Breadth Momentum Oscillator
Swenlin Trading Oscillator—Breadth
Zahorchak Method

Chapter 5—Advance Decline Ratio

Advance / Decline Ratio
Breadth Thrust
Breadth Thrust Continuation
Duarte Market Thrust Indicator

Eliades Sign of the Bear
Hughes Breadth Momentum Oscillator
Panic Thrust
STIX—Short-Term Trading Index

Chart 3-5 Up Volume and Down Volume.

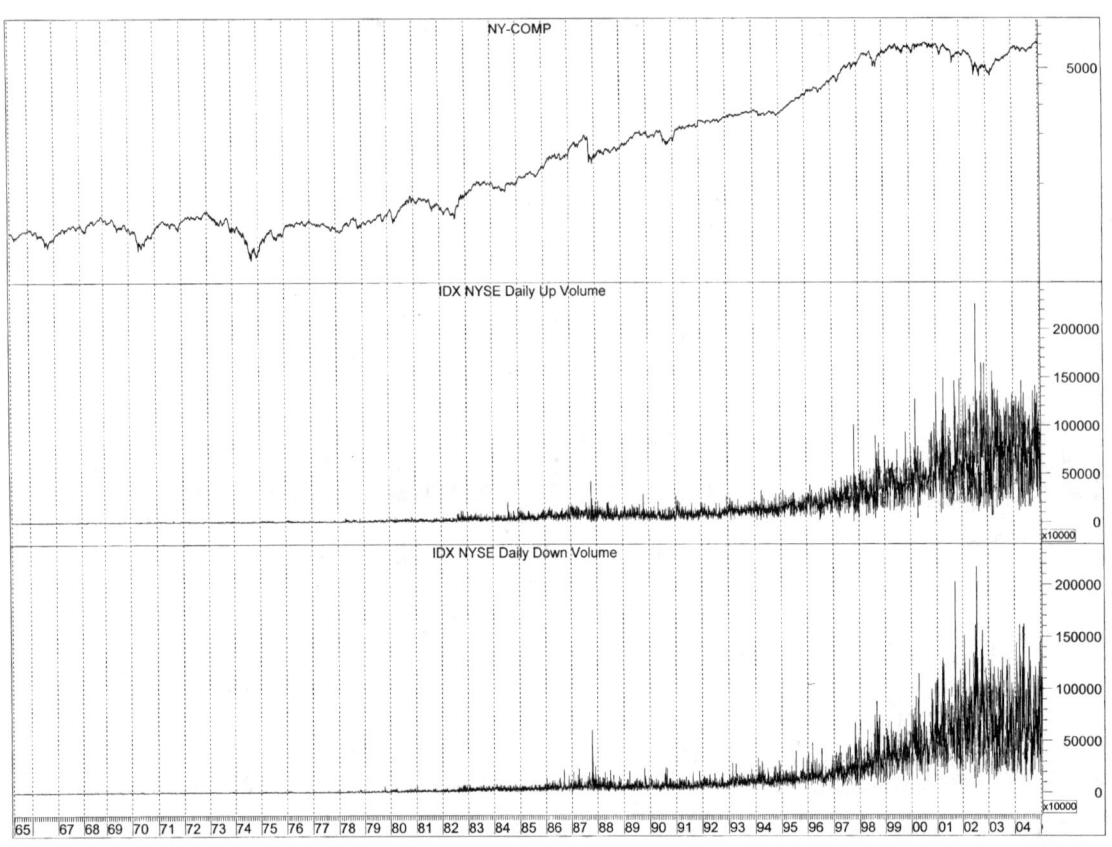

Chapter 6—Advance Decline Miscellaneous

Advances / Issues Traded
Advance Decline Divergence Oscillator
Advance Decline Diffusion Index
Breadth Climax
Declining Issues TRIX

Disparity Index
Dynamic Synthesis
Unchanged Issues
Velocity Index

Chapter 7—New Highs, New Lows Indicators

High Low Difference

New Highs−New Lows
New High New Low Line

New Highs and New Lows Oscillator
New Highs and New Lows Derivations

Breadth Indicators

Chart 3-5b Up Volume and Down Volume Plotted Using Semilog Scaling.

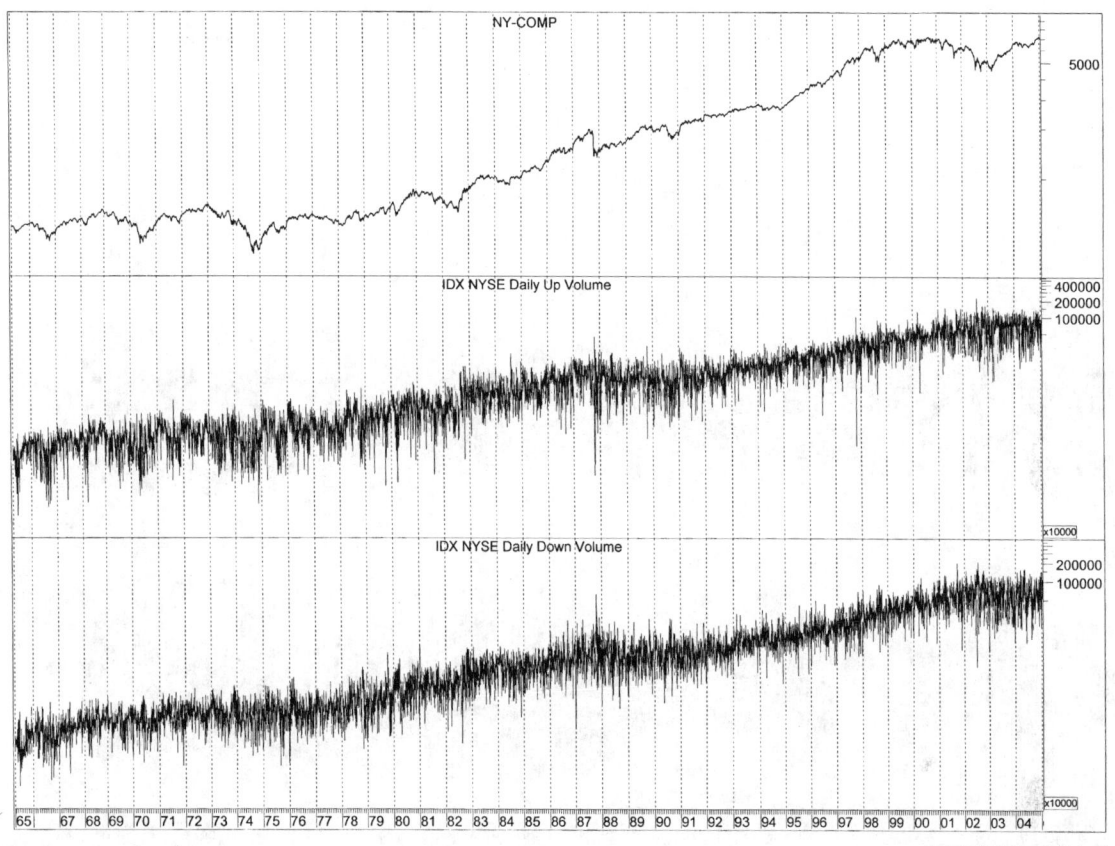

High Low Ratio
New Highs / New Lows Ratio

High Low Miscellaneous
New Highs and New Lows
New Highs % Total Issues
New Lows % Total Issues

High Low Logic Index
High Low Validation

Chapter 8—Up Volume, Down Volume Indicators
Up Volume
Down Volume

Changed Volume
Up and Down Volume

Chart 3-6 Up Volume and Down Volume Adjusted for Total Volume.

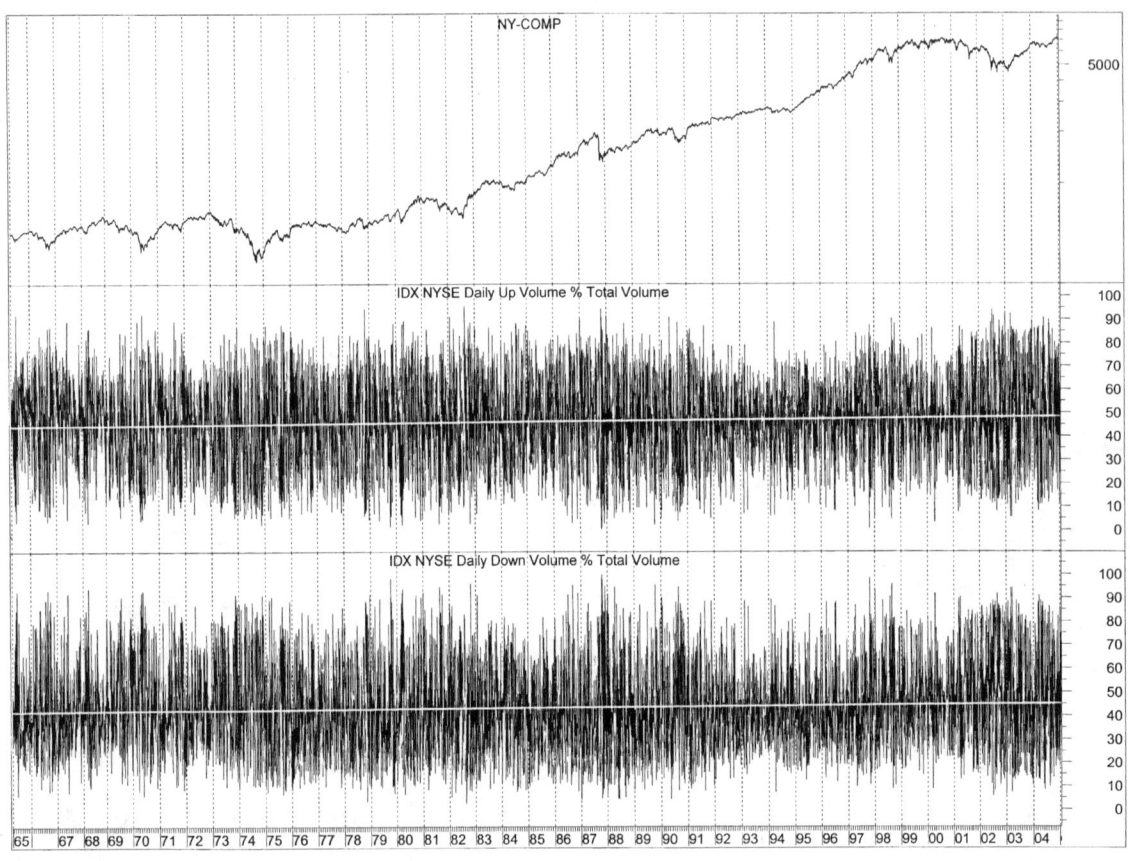

McClellan Oscillator—Volume
McClellan Summation Index—Volume
Merriman's Volume Model
Swenlin IT Volume Momentum Oscillator
Swenlin Trading Oscillator—Volume
Up Volume Down Volume Line

Cumulative Volume Ratio
Up Down On Balance Volume (OBV)
Volume Percentage Ratio
Upside−Downside Volume
Upside / Downside Volume Ratio
Zweig Up Volume Indicator

Chapter 9—Composite Indicators

Arms Index
Arms Open Index
Advance Decline New High New Low
Bretz TRIN-5

Cash Flow Index
Composite Tape Index
Dysart Positive Negative Volume
Eliades New TRIN

Breadth Indicators

Haller Theory
Hindenburg Omen
Market Thrust
McClellan Oscillator with Volume
McClellan Summation Index with Volume

Meyers Systems
Moving Balance Indicator
Technical Index
Titanic Syndrome
Trend Exhaustion Index

4

Advance Decline Difference Indicators

Advances − Declines

The breadth indicators in this chapter all utilize the difference between the advances and the declines as their primary relationship.

Advance Decline Difference Indicators

Advances − Declines
Advance Decline Overbought Oversold
Plurality Index
Advance Decline—Fugler
Advance Decline Line
Advance Decline Line—1%
Advance Decline Line—Eakle
Advance Decline Line—Normalized
Advance Decline Line—Bolton
Advance Decline Line—Adjusted Total Issues
Big Movers Only
Advance Decline Line Oscillator

Absolute Breadth Index
Absolute Breadth Index—Adjusted
Advance Decline Power
Coppock Breadth Indicator
Haurlan Index
McClellan Oscillator
McClellan Summation Index
Merriman Breadth Model
Swenlin IT Breadth Momentum Oscillator
Swenlin Trading Oscillator—Breadth
Zahorchak Method

Advances − Declines

Also Known As: Overbought Oversold
Data components required: Advances (A), Declines (D)

Description

This is the difference between the advancing issues and the declining issues (Advances minus Declines).

Interpretation

Anytime you deal with the difference or the ratio of two items, it is always best to smooth the data because the raw information will be too erratic to be useful. Here is the 21-day moving average of the advance decline difference. You can see that it is generally above the zero line during up moves and below it during down moves. The arithmetic smoothing has a couple of anomalies with it; it unfortunately delays the crossings of the zero line, but then avoids a large number of whipsaws (short-term crossing that reverses direction quickly). Using shorter term periods would help the timing of the crossings but increase the whipsaws. A few vertical lines have been displayed on Chart 4-1 to assist in aligning some of the signals.

Chart 4-1 Advances Minus Declines Smoothed by 21 Days.

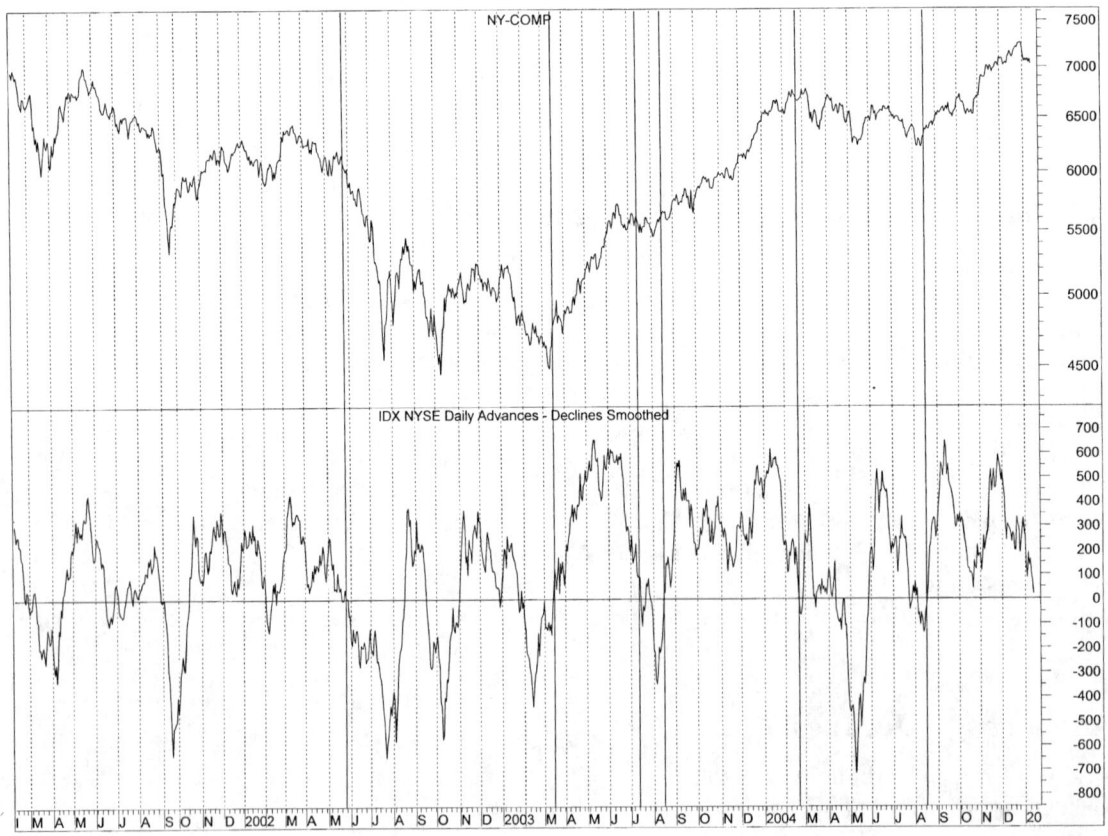

Advance Decline Difference Indicators

Chart 4-2   Advances Minus Declines Exponentially Smoothed by 3 Days.

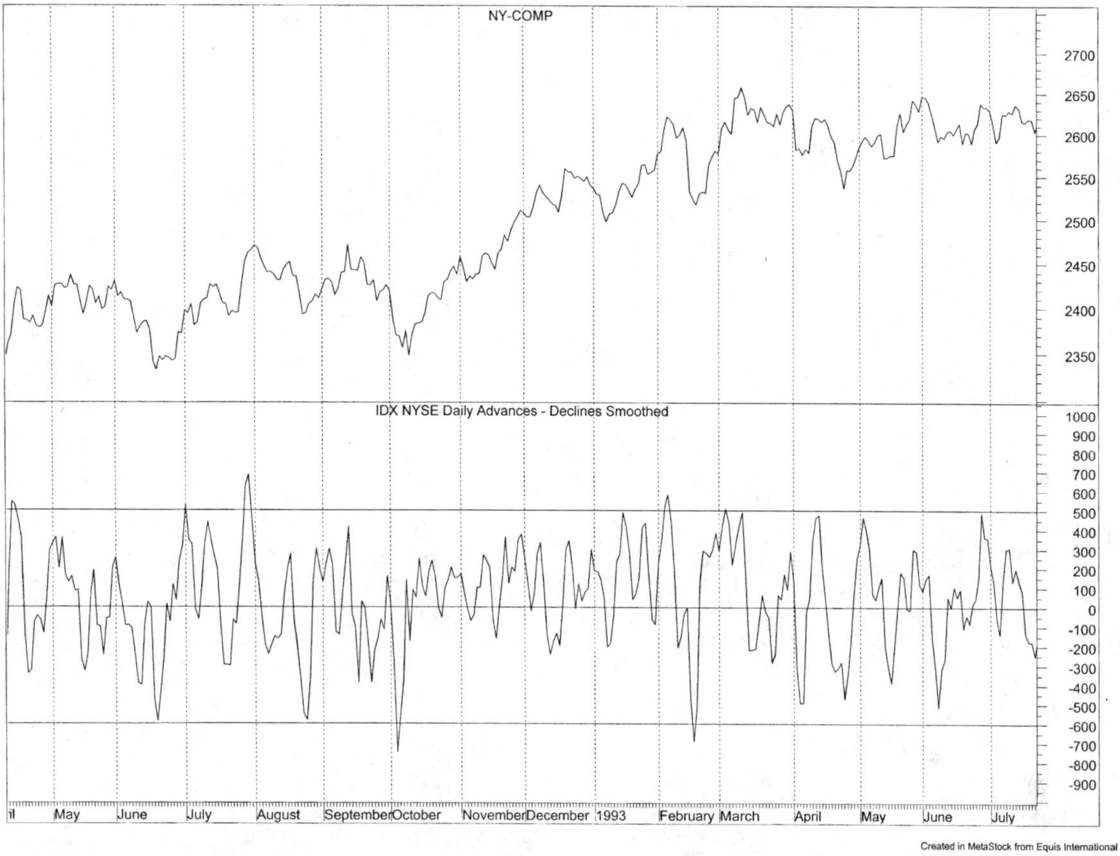

Author Comments

Gerald Appel has stated that he looks at this difference in Advances and Declines by smoothing it with a 3-day exponential average. He said in a 1994 interview that when this indicator went above 500, it could be the start of a good rally. Also, if it goes below −600, stand by for a good down move. Chart 4–2 shows this indicator up to late 1993, just prior to his interview. You can see that his zones worked well for short-term action.

Soon after the interview with Gerald Appel, the volume and number of issues on the New York Stock Exchanges began to increase significantly. Chart 4–2b shows this advance decline indicator with the zones changed to +1000 and −1000. These seem to keep his concept alive and up-to-date. Justin Mamis, who, with Stan Weinstein started the Professional Tape Reader newsletter, likes to look at the 10-day average of the Advance Decline difference (dotted line) plotted with the 30-day average of the difference (solid line). The rectified (squared corners) line (darkest line) in Chart 4–3 is showing the times when the 10-day average is above the 30-day average. Whenever it is above the zero line, the 10 day is above the 30 day and it is bullish. If you are familiar with a moving aver-

Chart 4-2b Advances Minus Declines Exponentially Smoothed by 3 Days with +1000 and −1000 Zones.

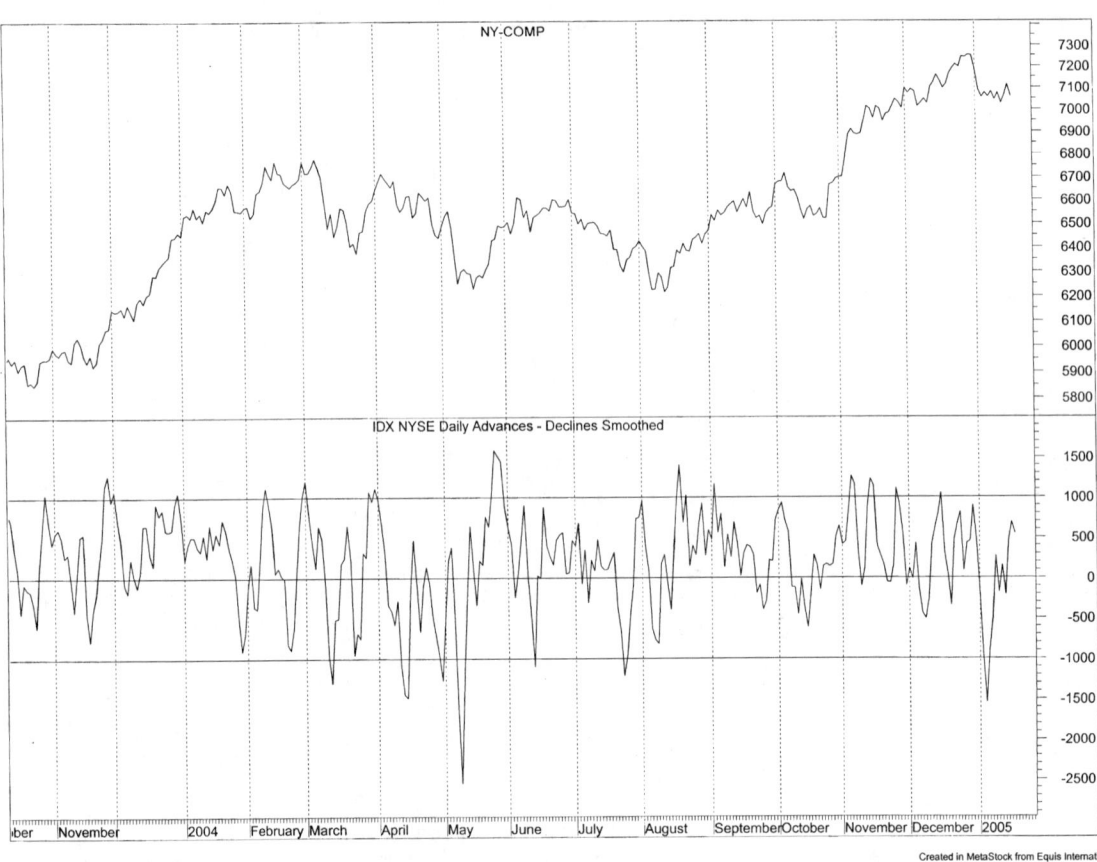

age crossover system, this is very similar; instead of using price, this indicator uses the difference between advances and declines.

$$\text{Formula: } A - D$$

References

Appel, Gerald, "Gerald Appel, with Systems and Forecasts." *Stocks and Commodities*, Volume 12, March 1994, pp 98–105.

Mamis, Justin, "Justin Mamis and the Meaning of Life." *Stocks and Commodities*, Volume 13, August 1995 pp 359–365.

Advance Decline Overbought Oversold

Also See: Advances − Declines
Data components required: Advances (*A*), Declines (*D*)

Advance Decline Difference Indicators 35

Chart 4-3 Advances Decline 10 and 30 Smoothed Difference—Mamis.

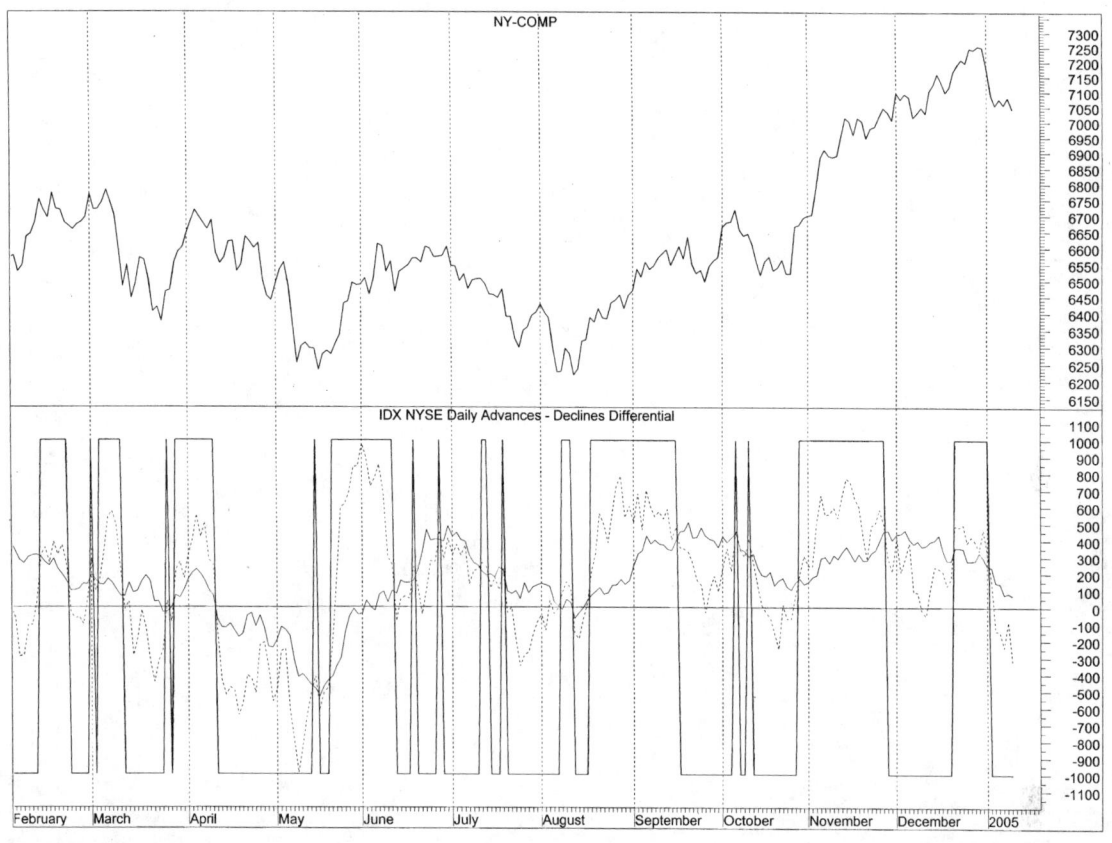

Description

There are many derivatives on the relationship of the Advances and Declines, and this is just one of them. This is a smoothed version of the advances minus the declines. This is actually a continuation of the previous section because there are some analysts who refer to this as the overbought oversold indicator.

Interpretation

Taking the difference between the Advances and the Declines produces an oscillator that moves above and below a zero line. Smoothing that line will reduce the daily fluctuations and provide a better tool for determining overbought and oversold. While it seems to show overbought and oversold areas well, it does not do so with the consistency one would desire for this indicator. Steve Achelis claims that a range between +200 and −200 will yield good overbought and oversold signals. Chart 4–4 shows the overbought oversold indicator using a 10-day exponential smoothing.

Chart 4-4 Advance Decline Overbought Oversold.

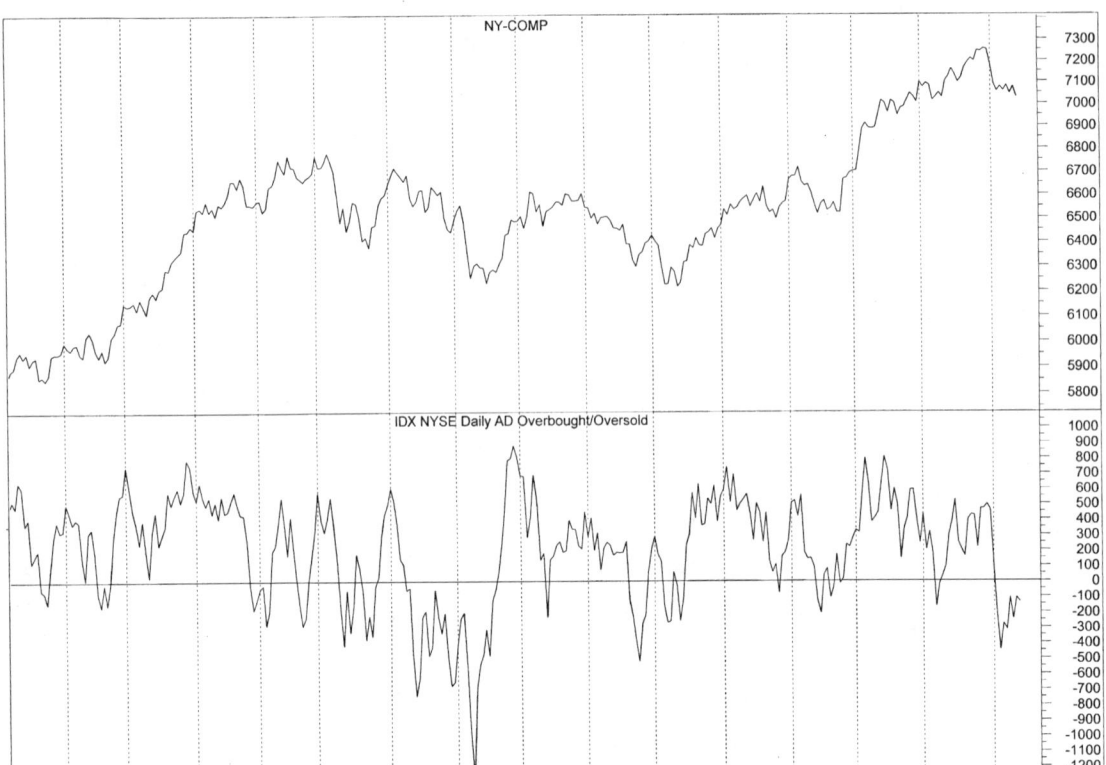

Author Comments

This is a good example of an indicator that has two definitions from two respected market technicians. Norman Fosback uses the ratio of Advances to Declines for the overbought/oversold indicator. Steven Achelis uses the difference of Advances and Declines for the overbought/oversold indicator. Either case can be easily justified; it just becomes confusing to newcomers. They both accomplish essentially the same goal, and that is a relationship between the advances and the declines.

I have generally gotten away from the somewhat standard 10-period smoothing and prefer to use a 21-day smoothing for most work. In an oscillator such as this, it greatly reduces the noise and sharpens the interpretation of the indicator. You can see from Chart 4–5 that the area between the zero line and +400 is when the market is bullish. Similarly, the area between the zero line and −400 points out down markets well. One way to further improve this is to broaden the area around the zero line to define the neutral areas. For example, the area between +150 and +400 is

Advance Decline Difference Indicators

Chart 4-5 Advance Decline Overbought Oversold with Levels at +400, +150, −150, and −400.

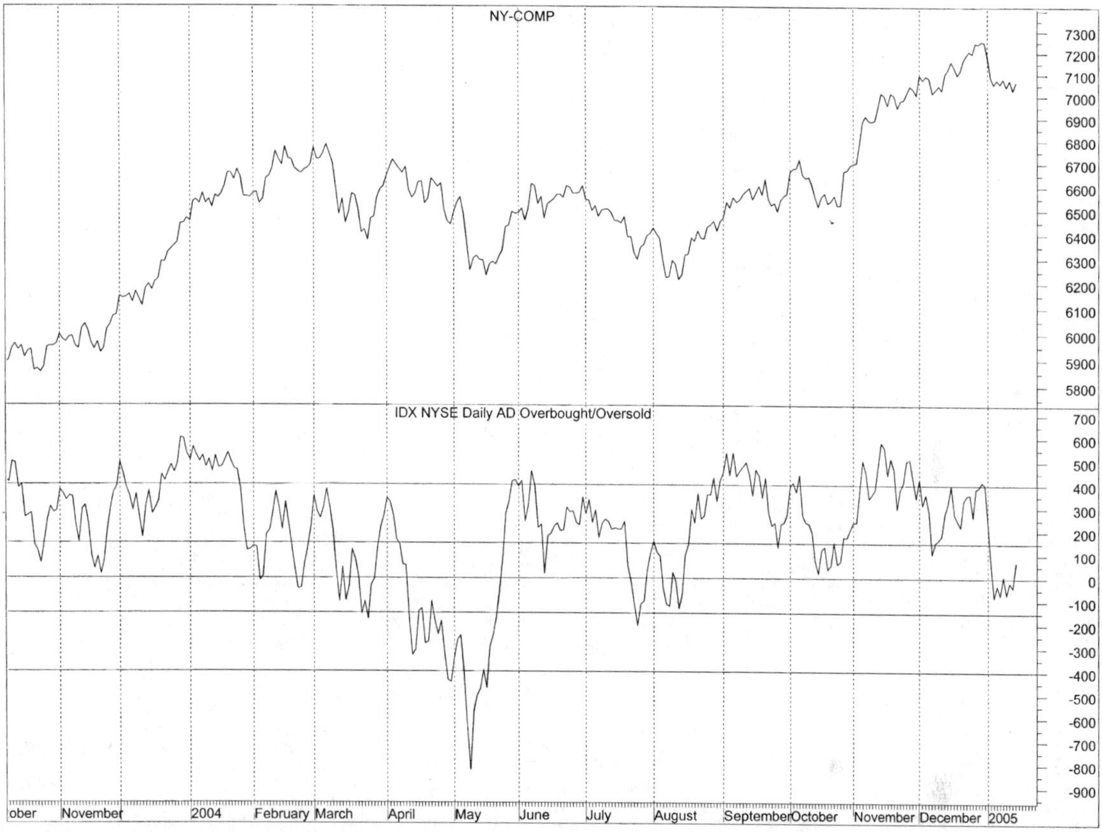

bullish, and the area between −150 and −400 is bearish. Above +400 continues to represent overbought and below −400 oversold.

George Lindsay used an unsmoothed version of the difference between Advances and Declines. He looked for a triple zigzag pattern in the plot of raw advances minus declines. Three successively higher peaks in the Dow Jones Industrial Average, along with three successively lower peaks in the advance decline difference, would be his sell signal. This is typical negative divergence; it is used by many today and is also difficult to quantify and totally subjective. Chart 4–6 shows a couple of examples of Lindsay's technique.

Robert Nurock, who created the Wall Street Week Index, also used an advance decline component. He used a 10-day sum of the difference. A bullish signal was generated when from a point where the index exceeds 1000 to a peak and then down to a point 1000 below the peak. A bearish signal was from the point where the index drops below −1000 to a trough and then up to a point 1000 above the trough. The concept here was to give the indicator an opportunity to reverse and not try to pick the actual top or bottom.

Chart 4-6 Advance Decline Technique—Lindsay.

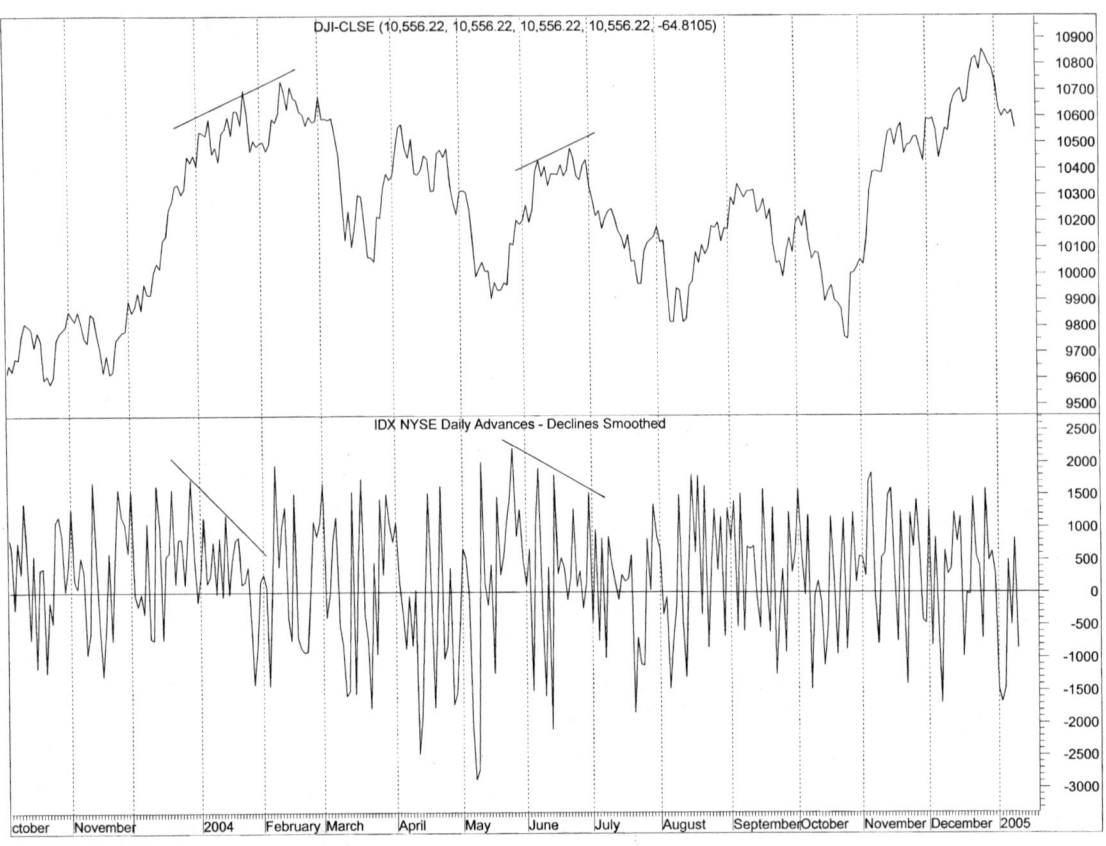

Robert Kinsman used a 7-period exponential average and called it the Kinsman smoothed $A - D$. His concept was to identify the general high-low range for this oscillator and then look for spikes outside that range. He further states that large spikes outside the range are more revealing than just trading opportunities, but are a precursor to significant trend changes in the market. Chart 4–7 shows lines at +600 and −600. You can see that the spikes outside those bands generally identified turning points in the market.

Formula: 21-day Moving Average $(A - D)$

References

Achelis, Steven, "Forecasting the market with the overbought/oversold indicator." *Stocks and Commodities*, July, 1987, pp 231–232.

Favors, Jerry, "The Lindsay A − D Indicator." *Stocks and Commodities*, Volume 10, February 1992, pp 75–76.

Chart 4-7 Advance Decline—Kinsman.

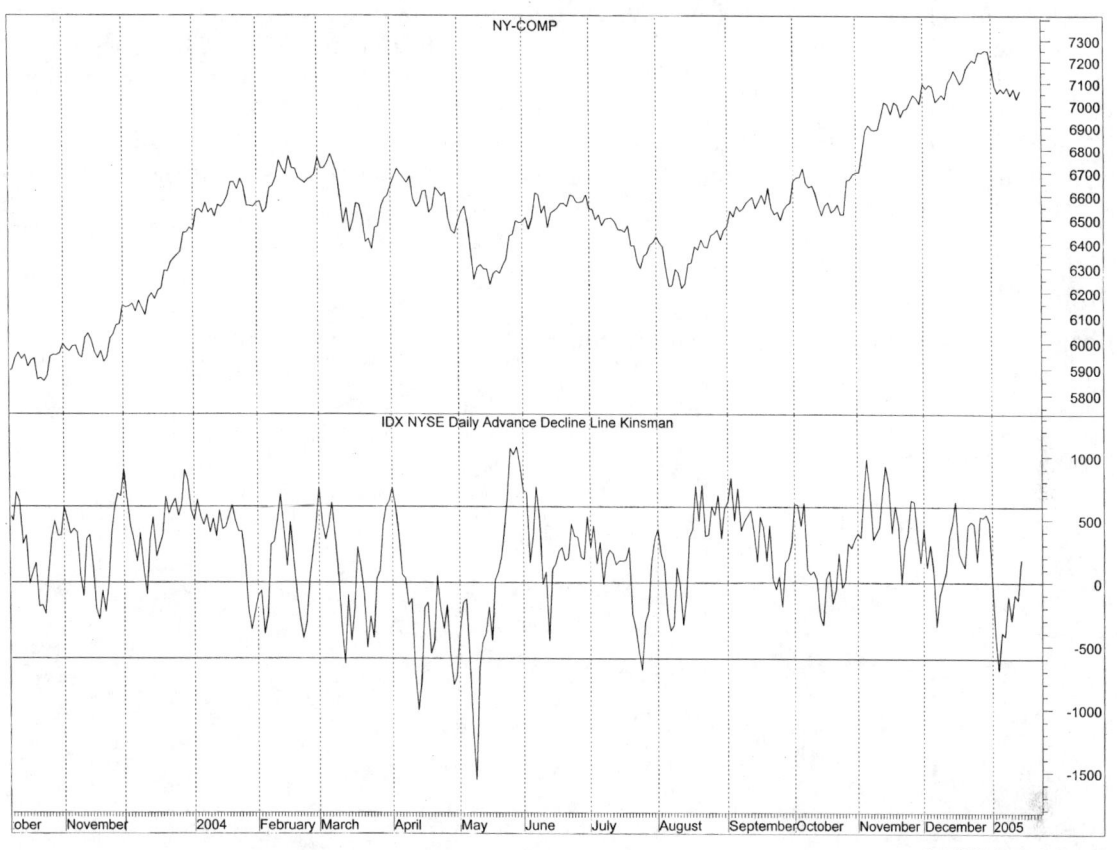

Kinsman, Robert, "Advance – Decline Line Redux." *Stocks and Commodities*," Volume 14, January 1996, 29–33.

Plurality Index

Author/Creator: Paul Dysart wrote about it in 1937, Ralph Rotnem used it, and Alan Shaw named it.
Data components required: Advances (A), Declines (D).

Description

This is a moving total of the absolute difference between advances and declines over a 25-day period. According to James Alphier, this was part of Paul Dysart's broader "Theory of Equalization."

Interpretation

Alan Shaw used benchmarks of 6000 and 12,000. If the indicator drops below 6000, a sell warning is signaled. He then waits until the index turns back up, at which point the signal becomes a definite sell. If the indicator rises above 12,000, it gives a buy alert, at which point he waits until it starts to drop, when it gives a definite buy signal. Chart 4–8 shows this technique.

The reasoning behind this indicator is that there is usually complacency at the top and panic at the bottom. John McGinley, of Technical Trends, says that a bull market dies of exhaustion. While at market bottoms, everyone is rushing in to buy.

Author Comments

I have seen the Plurality Index calculated using a moving average, instead of a sum. They look similar, but the zones need to be reset.

Chart 4-8 Plurality Index.

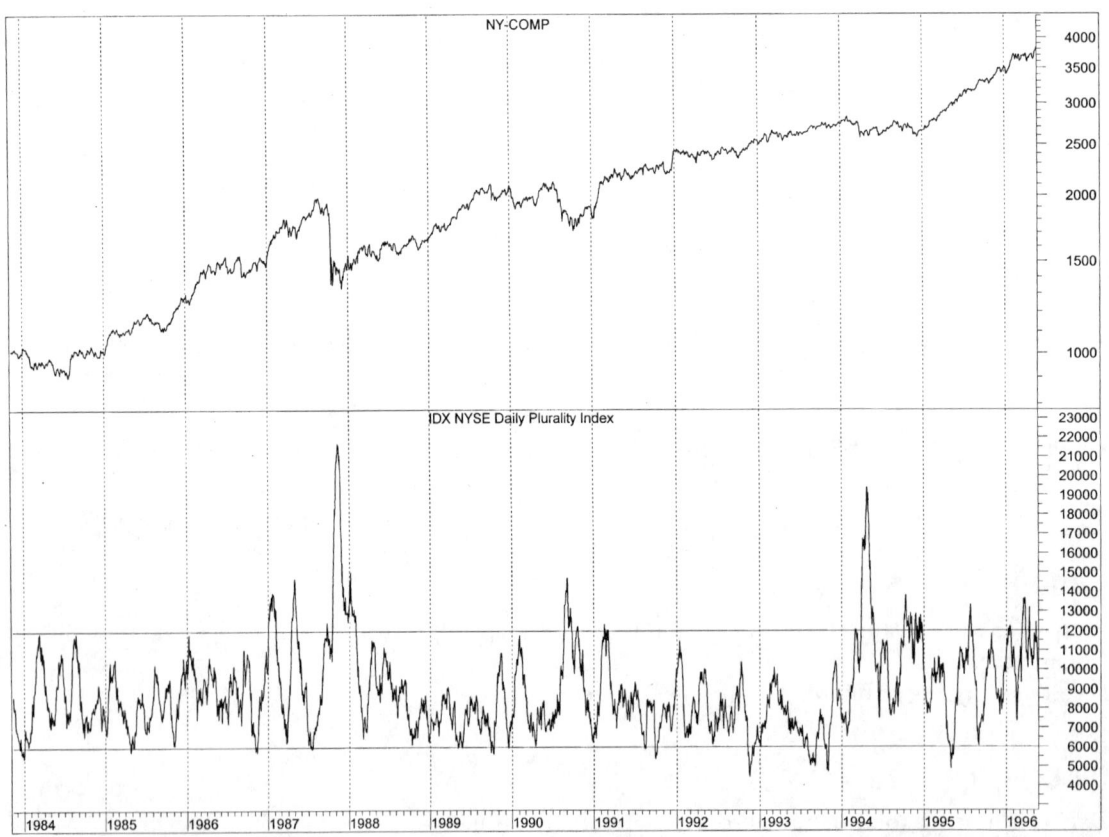

Since 1994 this indicator has had an upward bias that makes Alan Shaw's zones in need of adjustment. It would appear that 23,000 can replace Shaw's 12,000 zone, and that 14,000 can replace the 6000 zone. Incidentally, I'm quite sure Alan Shaw knows this or at least uses different zones than when Art Merrill wrote about it in 1990. Art Merrill claims that this must be a daily indicator and not one that uses weekly data. Alan Shaw says that this indicator doesn't always give a signal, but when it does, it should be noted. Chart 4–9 shows zones at 23,000, 14000, and 12,000.

Formula: $|A - D|$ over 25 days.

References

Merrill, Arthur A., "Plurality." *Stocks and Commodities*, Volume 8, April 1990, pp 137–138.

Chart 4-9 Plurality Index with New Zones.

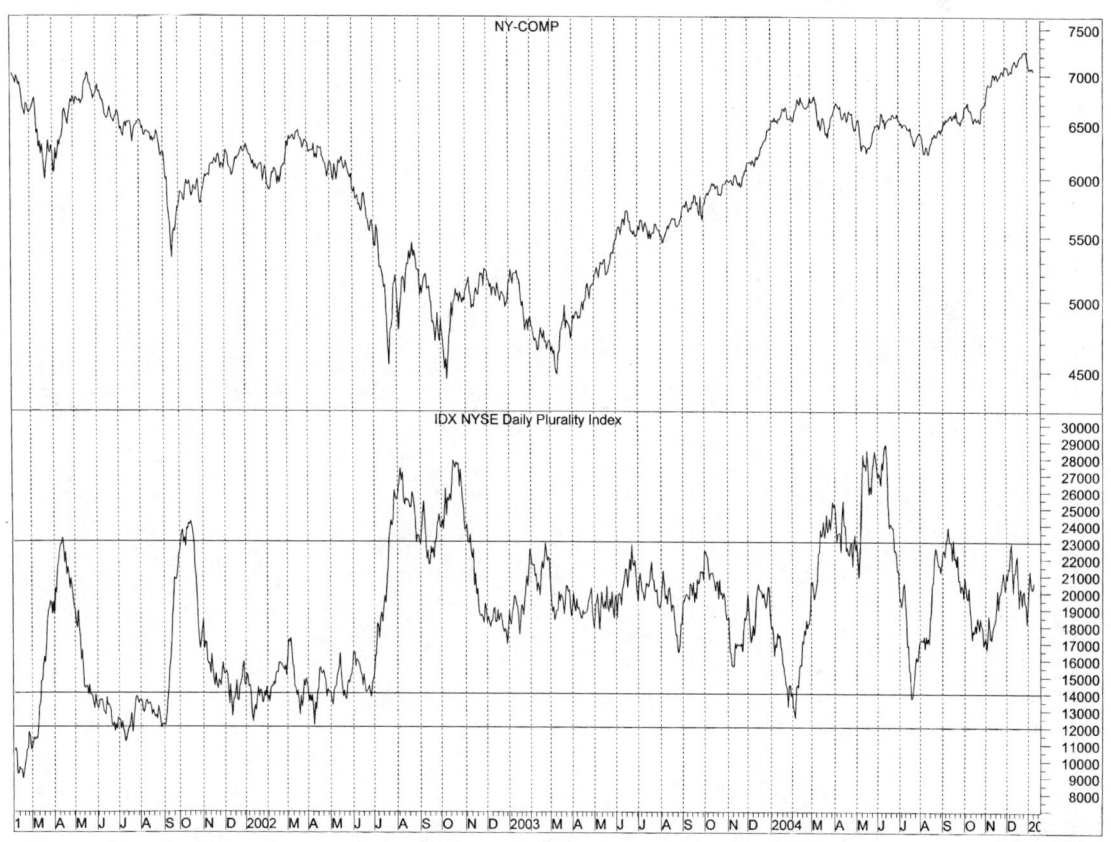

Advance Decline—Fugler

Author/Creator: George Fugler
Data components required: Advances (*A*), Declines (*D*)

Description

George Fugler called this his "quick and dirty" indicator. If the value of Advances minus Declines is positive on three successive trading days, an up (buy) signal in generated. If they are negative on three successive days, a down (sell) signal is generated.

Interpretation

Arthur Merrill said that his indicator is afflicted with whipsaws, but it stays in gear during a trend. Chart 4–10 shows each signal for up and down. The up spikes represent the buy signals, and the

Chart 4–10 Fugler Three-Day Advance Decline Technique.

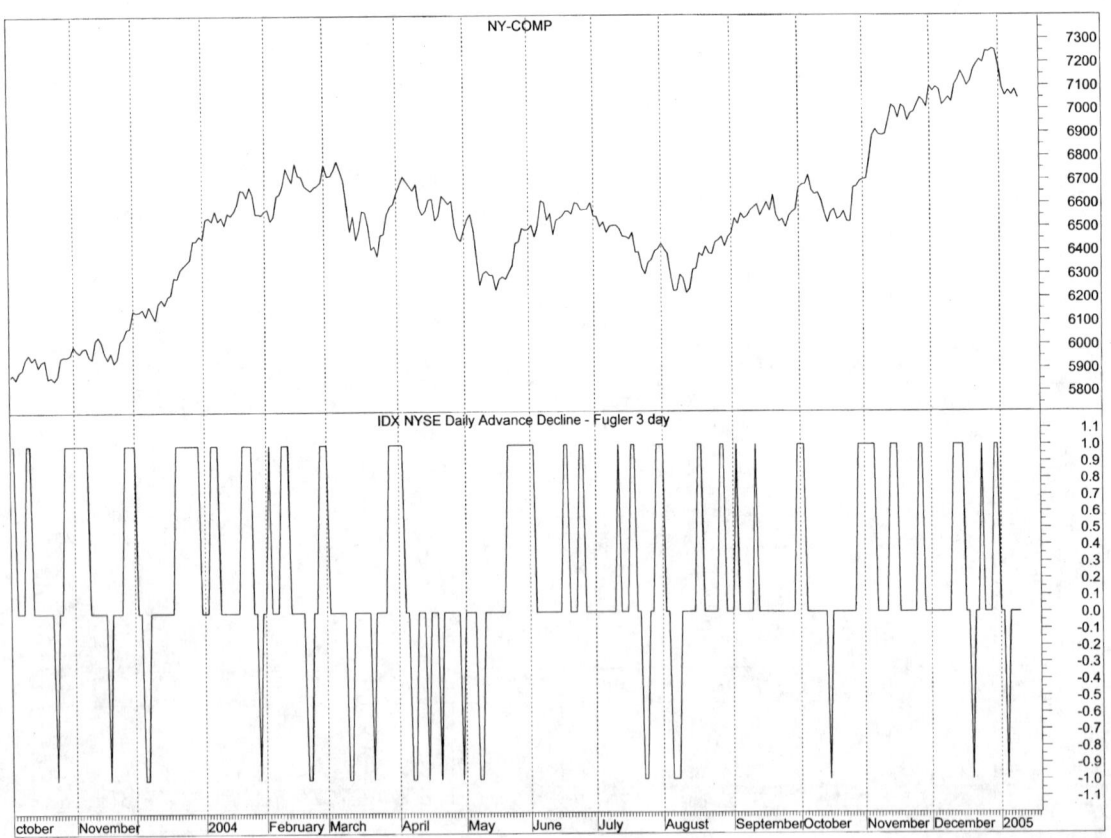

downward spikes represent the sell signals. There are usually a few similar signals in a row before a reversal, so one should ignore multiple signals.

Author Comments
Arthur Merrill is correct when he said this has lots of whipsaws. He was never one to mince words.

$$\text{Formula: } (A - D)$$

References
Merrill, Arthur, "More Trend Detection." *Stocks & Commodities*, Volume 6, Sept, 1988, pp. 219.

Advance Decline Line

Author/Creator: Colonel Leonard P. Ayres
Data components required: Advances (A), Declines (D)

Description
The Advance Decline Line is one of the most popular ways to measure the breadth of the market. The number of declining stocks is subtracted from the number of advancing stocks each day. If the advances outnumber the declines, the net difference is added to the previous total. If the declines outnumber advances, the net difference is subtracted from the previous total. In a nutshell, when there are more advances than declines, the line goes up. When there are more declines than advances, the line goes down. The Advance Decline Line can be used with either daily or weekly data.

For example, if 800 stocks advance for the day, and 450 fall, the advance decline difference for the day would be +350. This value is then added to the previous day's advance decline line value. If the number of declines was greater than the number of advances and the difference between the two was −200, then that amount would be subtracted from the Advance Decline Line's previous value. Note: You do not subtract −200 because that, mathematically, would be adding it. Here is another example:

Day	Advances (A)	Declintes (D)	$A - D$	Cumulative $A - D$
Monday	800	1200	−400	−400
Tuesday	1000	950	50	−350
Wednesday	800	1150	−350	−700
Thursday	950	1300	−350	−1050
Friday	1600	700	900	−150

Interpretation
The Advance Decline Line is usually compared to one of the popular market price indices, preferably the index that is also related to the advances and declines that are being used. For example, the New York Composite Index should be used with the New York Stock Exchange advances and

declines. They should trend in the same direction. When the Advance Decline Line begins to diverge from the index, an early indication is given of a possible trend reversal.

During a strong advance, the Advance Decline Line normally will move more than the NYSE Composite Index. If the market averages reach a new high and the Advance Decline Line fails to follow suit that can be an early indication of nonconfirmation. Chart 4–11 shows the advance decline line for the last 40 years. The numbers on the scale to the right of the chart are essentially meaningless because they reflect the summed difference from the first date on the chart. The numbers will change based on when you start the calculation.

Author Comments

The material in this section (Advance Decline Line) was reviewed by Tom McClellan, along with some added material from him with my sincere appreciation. You'll learn more about Tom and his family in later sections.

Chart 4–11 Advance Decline Line.

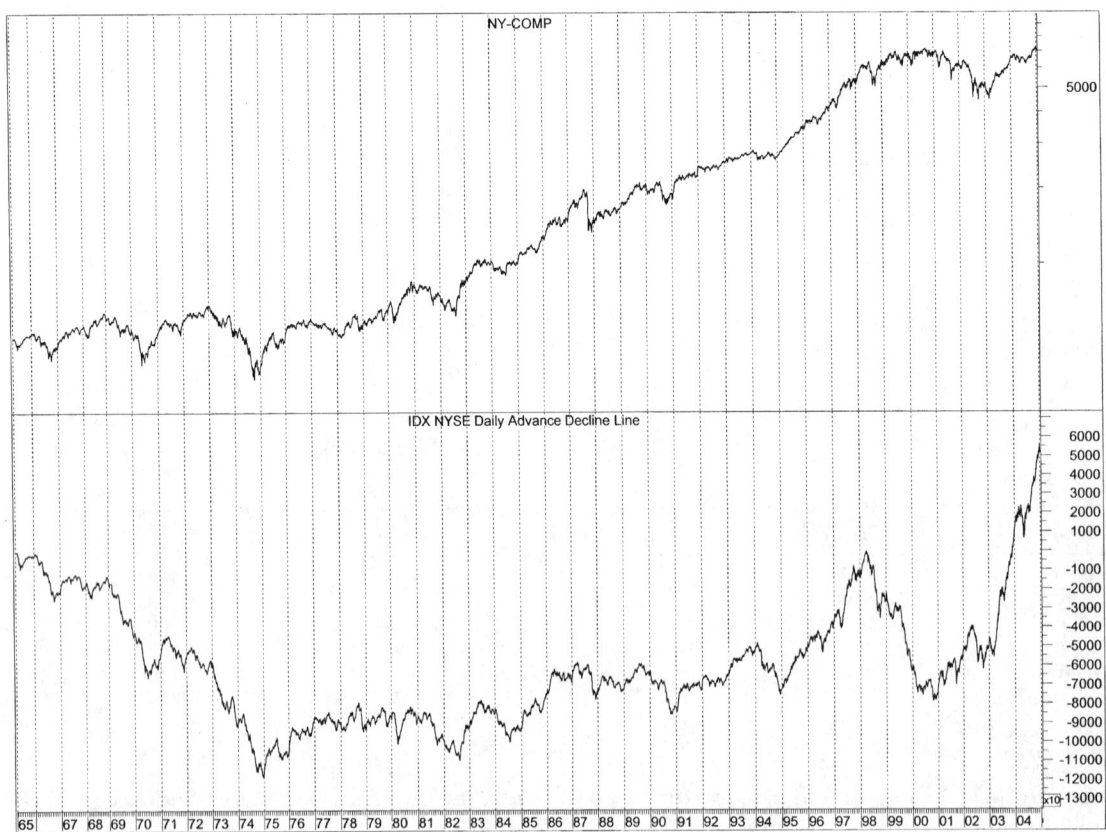

Advance Decline Difference Indicators

If there is one breadth indicator that has been analyzed, modified, adjusted, and discussed more than any other, the Advance Decline Line is probably the winner. Like many of the other versions of this popular breadth indicator, it seems best at determining the ends of longer term up moves in the market. It seems that the Advance Decline Line gives a lot of false signals at tops, but is much better at market bottoms. It is not the absolute numerical value of the advance decline line that matters, but its acceleration (up and down) or lack thereof that is important.

A common misconception of analysts is to compare the rate of change of the Advance Decline Line with a market index. One is based on movement and the other is based on price. Because the units are different, such comparisons are difficult to make in a consistent way. The one analogy that seems to fit this best is that the smart money always leaves the market first, usually quite a bit of time ahead of the masses. The smart money is also the first to get into the market after a decline. Chart 4–12 shows the divergence that occurred in 1987 that helped identify the drop in the markets that started in August of that year, but is usually only remembered by the October 19th plunge. A close examination of the Advance Decline Line shows it was dropping significantly before that day.

Chart 4–12 Advance Decline Line Nonconfirmation—1987.

Chart 4-13 Advance Decline Line Nonconfirmation—1998.

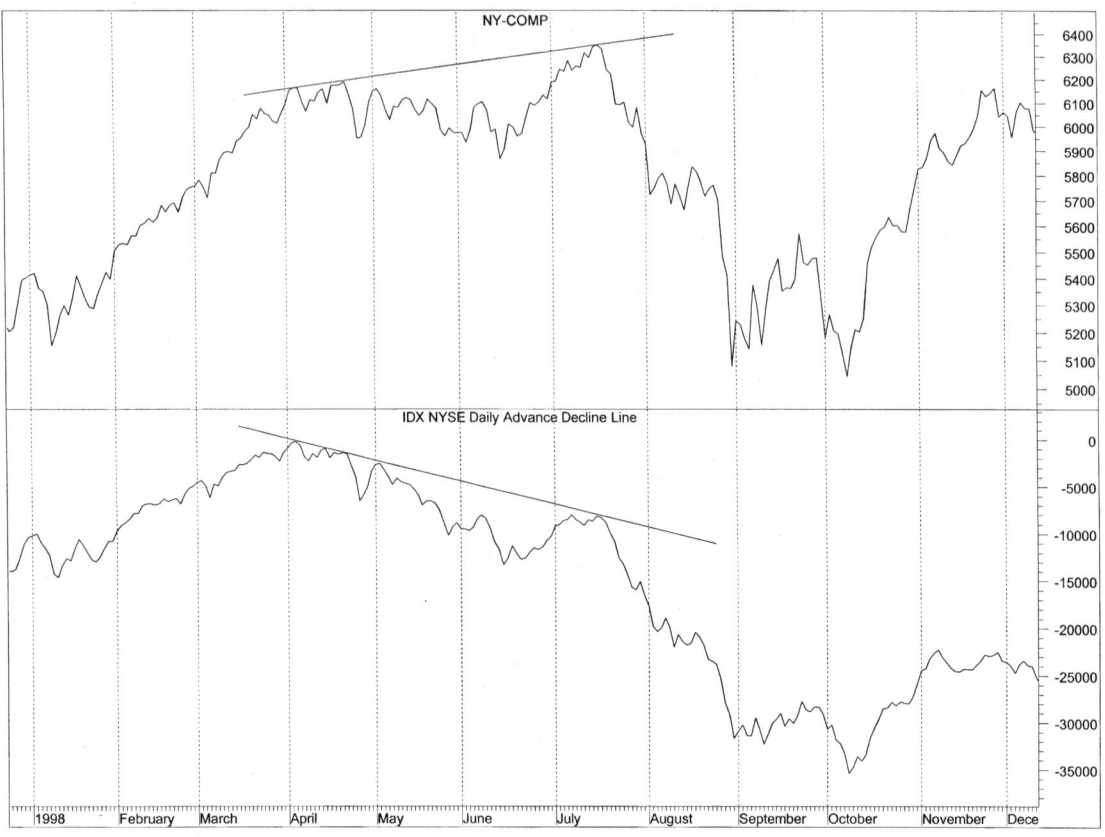

Chart 4–13 shows the topping divergence in the advance decline line in 1998 a time when everyone believed the markets were never going to stop rising. This very early warning panned out as the markets rallied again in late 1998 through much of 1999, then began one of the biggest bear markets most will see in their lifetime.

Chart 4–14 shows five divergent patterns over the last 20 years. Three of them are identifying market tops in 1987, 1990, and 1999, while the other two are identifying market bottoms in early 2003 and mid-2004.

The chief value of looking at the Advance Decline Line comes from its relationship to liquidity. When there is a lot of money coming into the market, it tends to spread itself out into a majority of issues, which shows up in the breadth statistics with more advances than declines.It is impossible to get a majority of stocks to go up unless there is sufficient liquidity to spread around. Conversely, when liquidity is tight, then the dwindling supply of money tends to go into only the highest quality issues, resulting in more declines than advances. It is possible for the major price indices to remain aloft while the Advance Decline Line starts declining, provided that the limited amount of liquidity is channeled into the right stocks to keep the price indices up. But this is a

Advance Decline Difference Indicators

Chart 4-14 Advance Decline Line Divergences.

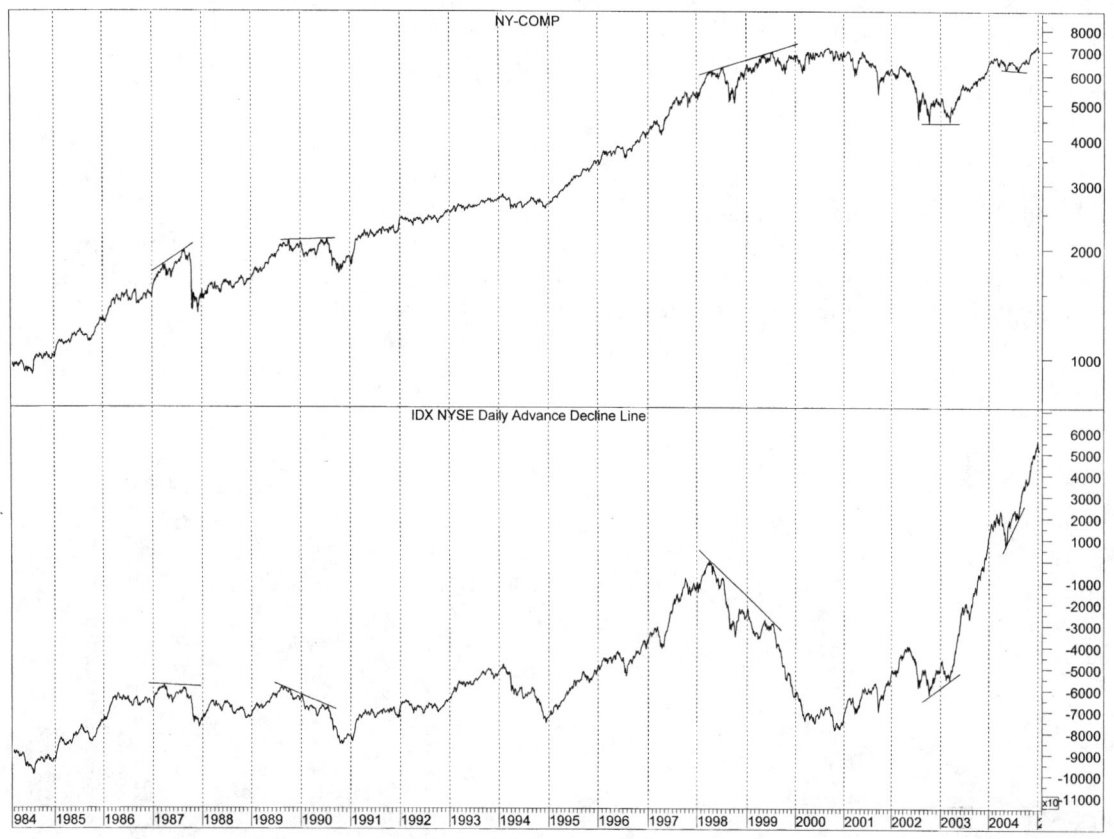

very weak condition for the market, and it usually resolves itself with an eventual negative outcome for the price indices. The 1998–2001 period was a great example of this.

The Advance Decline Line has an inherent downward bias, especially compared to price indices. This is because of the of the survivorship bias in the price indices. Only the big, established, and successful large-cap companies get to see their stock performance have much of an impact on the price indices. But the Advance Decline Line is a much more egalitarian indicator, where every single listed stock gets an equal vote, both the great ones and the lousy ones. Companies that go public and then end up going bankrupt will see a lot of days of counting toward the declines as the price goes from the IPO (initial public offering) price to zero. This is especially true for the Nasdaq Advance Decline Line because the Nasdaq market has lower standards for listing of companies than the NYSE.

It is because of this inherent downward bias that analysts are better served by focusing on the upward or downward acceleration taking place in the Advance Decline Line rather than on the raw position of it.

One problem with the standard Advance Decline Line is that the changing number of issues traded on the exchange affects the amplitudes of the Advance Decline Line's movements. Also, the change of quoting prices from eighths to sixteenths, followed a few years later by going to decimalization (see details in Chapter 2) affected the Advance Decline Line. Many analysts adjust for these by dividing the advance decline difference by the total number of issues traded, or more simply by the total of advances plus declines:

$$\frac{(A - D)}{(A + D)}$$

The daily values are then summed as with the original version.

In addition to using daily advance decline data to construct an Advance Decline Line, one can also use weekly data. Chart 4–15 shows the weekly advance decline line. Remember that this uses weekly data for the advances and declines and is not a derivation of the daily data.

Formula: $(A - D)$

Chart 4–15   Advance Decline Line—Weekly.

References
McClellan, Sherman and Tom, "The McClellan Market Report."
Just about any technical analysis book that covers technical market indicators will have information on the advance decline line.

Advance Decline Line—1%
Also known as: Momentum Index by Stan Weinstein
Author/Creator: Carl Swenlin and Stan Weinstein
Data components required: Advances (A), Declines (D)

Description
This is the Advance Decline difference with a long-term smoothing of 200 days. Carl Swenlin prefers using an exponential moving average, and Stan Weinstein prefers a simple / arithmetic moving average.

Interpretation
Stan Weinstein suggests that it gives buy and sell signals when it crosses the zero line. From below to above the zero line was bullish and from above to below was bearish. He further refines it to say that the longer it remained on one side of the zero line before crossing it, the better the signal. Also, the further into positive (above zero) or negative (below zero) territory that it had been would add to the value when it did cross the zero line. His most meaningful bearish signal is when the indicator has been in positive territory for quite a while and moved to an extreme. Chart 4–16 shows Weinstein's Momentum Index.

Author Comments
I found Weinstein's comment that this was more helpful at spotting tops than bottoms to be interesting. This is not usually the case when it comes to technical indicators. I believe the fact that he used a simple moving average might be the reason. Remember, with a simple average, the data from 200 days ago is carrying the same weight as the most recent data. To really make this point, the data from 6 to 8 months ago (60+ days) is carrying the same weight as the data in the last 3 months. Most market tops are long spread out affairs of distribution and take a while to be put in place. This would somewhat explain that, and also why Weinstein thought it was not that good at bottoms, as most bottoms are sharp and decisive.

I have always preferred to use exponential smoothing when using large time periods. In this case the Swenlin version seems better at keeping you in most of the move, either up or down. Additionally, Carl uses the ratio of the difference between advances and declines divided by the sum of advances and declines. Here is what Carl Swenlin says about it: "I find it much more useful to watch where this indicator forms tops and bottoms. For example, in 1990, when the Dow

Chart 4-16 Momentum Index—Weinstein.

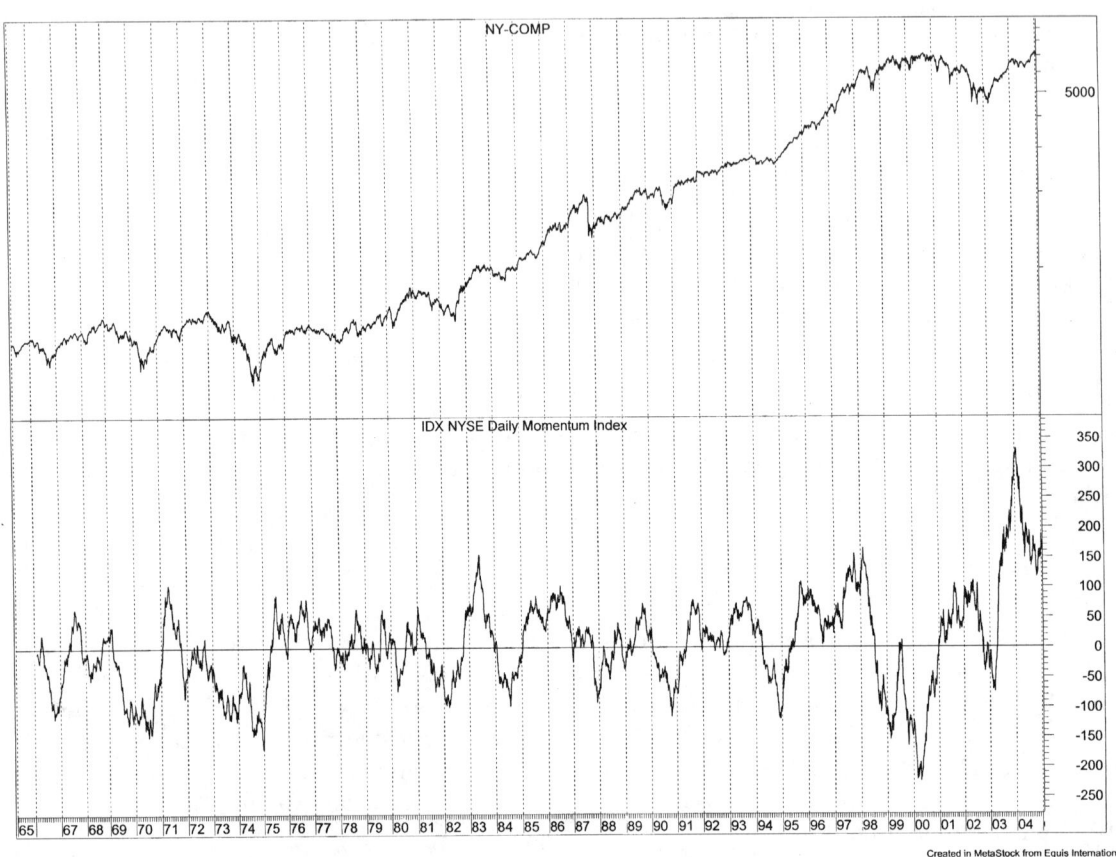

made two successive new highs, the 1% Advance Decline Line was topping below the zero line. The 1990 bear market followed immediately after the second top. Again in late 1994, as the Dow was putting in a double top, this indicator was topping below the zero line. The market subsequently went to its final low prior to the monster rally of 1995, which leads to the significance of bottoms on this indicator. When you see it bottoming in the area of −100 to −150, chances are that the market is putting in a major low. This happened in late 1994, late 1990, late 1987, and mid-1984. The bottom in 1981 did not lead to a major rally, but it was followed in 1982 by two higher indicator bottoms corresponding with two lower market lows, the final low being in August, 1982." Chart 4–17 shows Carl Swenlin's exponential version of the momentum index, which he calls 1% EMA (exponential moving average) of Advance Declines. While it offers more whipsaws, it is also considerably more timely than the Weinstein version.

Formula: Previous Value + (A − D) smoothed by 200 days.

Advance Decline Difference Indicators

Chart 4-17 1% Advance Decline—Swenlin.

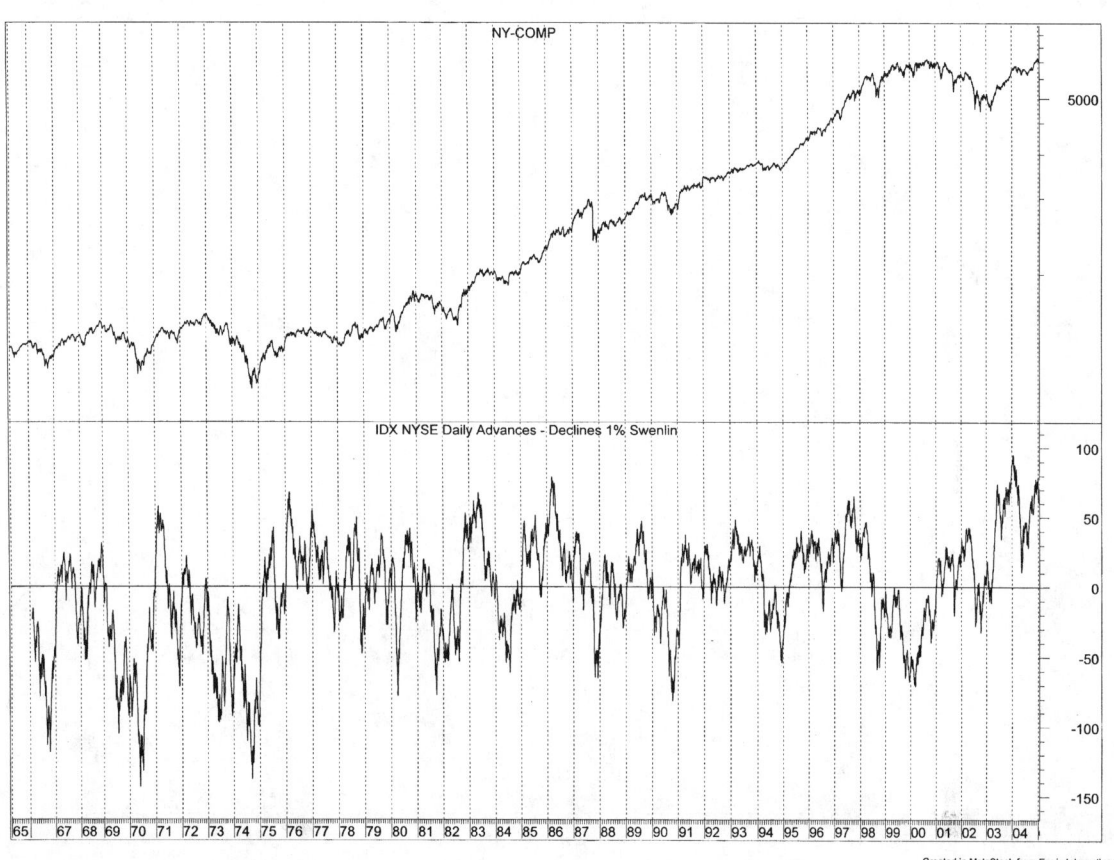

References
Weinstein, Stan. *Secrets for Profiting in Bull and Bear Markets.* Dow Jones-Irwin, Homewood, IL., 1988
Swenlin, Carl, www.decisionpoint.com

Advance Decline Index—Eakle

Author/Creator: Eakle
Data components required: Advances (A), Declines (D)

Description

This is a smoothed rate of change of the Advance Decline Line. It was originally used as a weekly indicator with a smoothing of 35 weeks and then a 2-week rate of change.

Chart 4-18 Eakle Advance Decline Index.

Interpretation

Because of the simplicity of this indicator, using the concept on daily data seemed reasonable. Chart 4-18 shows the Eakle advance decline index using a 10-day (2-week) rate of change and a 175-day (35 week) smoothing.

Author Comments

The only source for this was John McGinley's Technical Trends service. Because the daily version in Chart 4-18 did not seem to work very well, here, in Chart 4-19 is the weekly version as it was originally designed to be used. Market bottoms seem to be well identified by the downward spikes in the indicator and whenever the indicator is above the zero line, the market is generally bullish. However it does tend to stay bullish too long and does not seem be work well for tops.

$$\text{Formula:} \quad (A - D)$$

Advance Decline Difference Indicators 53

Chart 4-19 Eakle Advance Decline Index—Weekly.

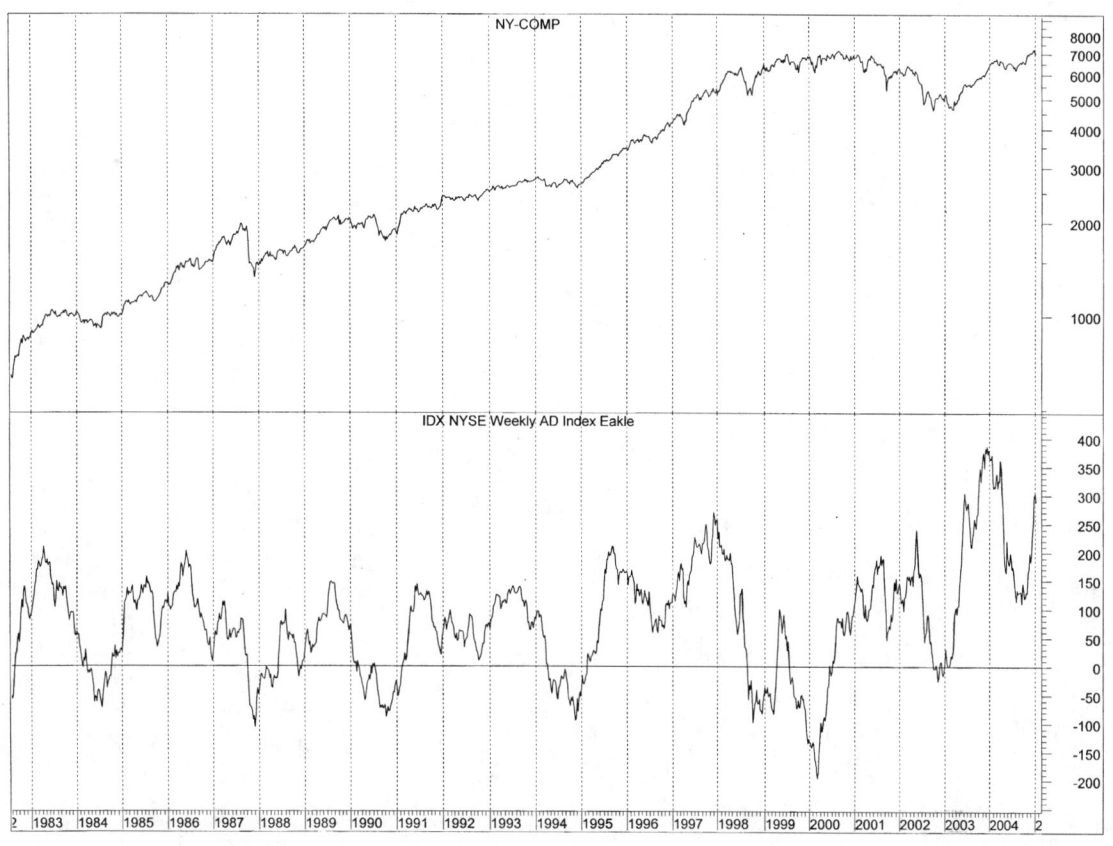

References
McGinley, John. *Technical Trends.* Wilton, CT.

Advance Decline Line—Normalized

Author/Creator: Tushar Chande
Data components required: Advances (*A*), Declines (*D*)

Description
This is the adjusted Advance Decline Line normalized with a moving 5-day formula similar to that used in George Lane's stochastics. This process shows extremes in the Advance Decline Line. Also like stochastics, the use of 20 for oversold and 80 for overbought works well.

Chart 4-20 Advance Decline Line Normalized—5 Days.

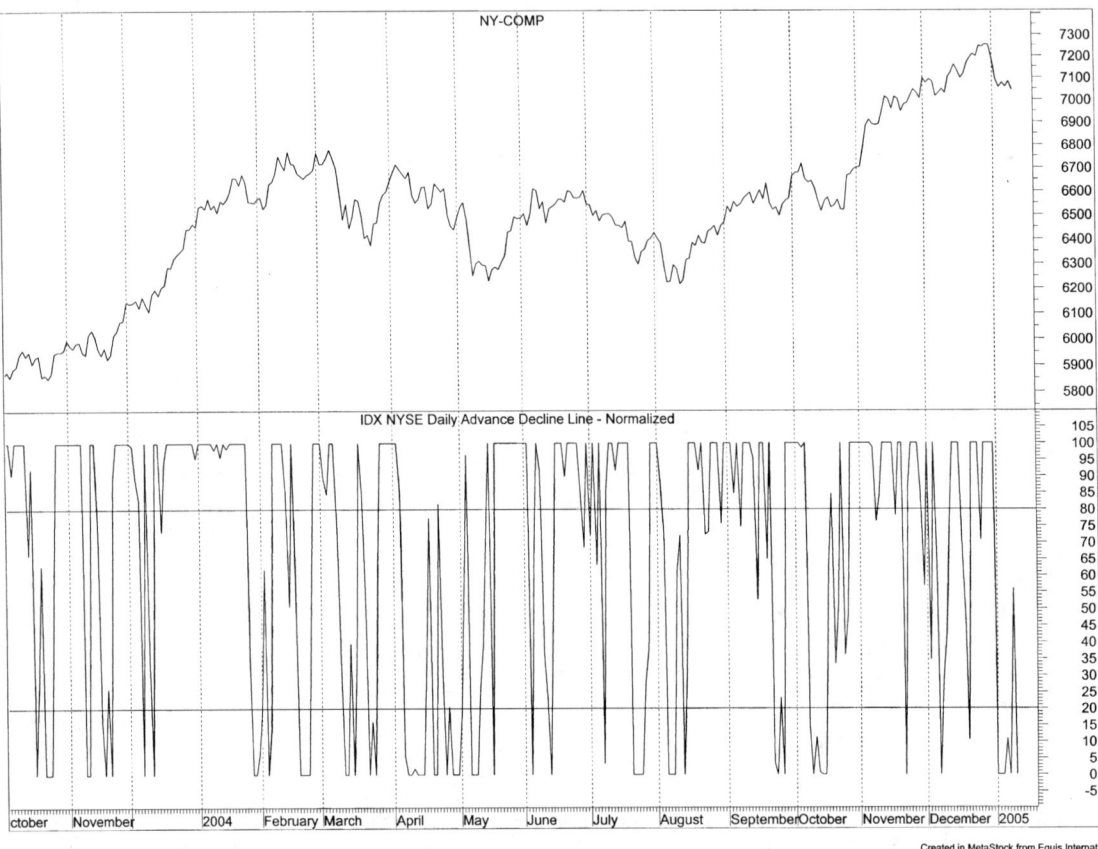

Interpretation

Using a short period such as 5 days makes this more of a trading oscillator. Chande says that oversold values of zero and overbought values of 100 would be good for trading. Chart 4–20 shows the normalized advance decline line for trading as Chande suggests.

Author Comments

Tushar Chande has been a big contributor to the field of technical analysis, so I pay particularly close attention, not only to his work, but also to try to understand the concept he is revealing. To take this normalizing concept and reduce the signals, I used a 21-day period for the normalization and then smoothed the results with a 7-day exponential average. This makes the indicator slower and better for intermediate analysis. You can see in Chart 4–21 that when the indicator is rising and goes above 50, it is the early part of a market rise. After the indicator goes above 80, and then drops back below 80, you can leg out of your long position. Sell all of it when it goes below 50.

Advance Decline Difference Indicators

Chart 4-21 Advance Decline Line Normalized—21 Days.

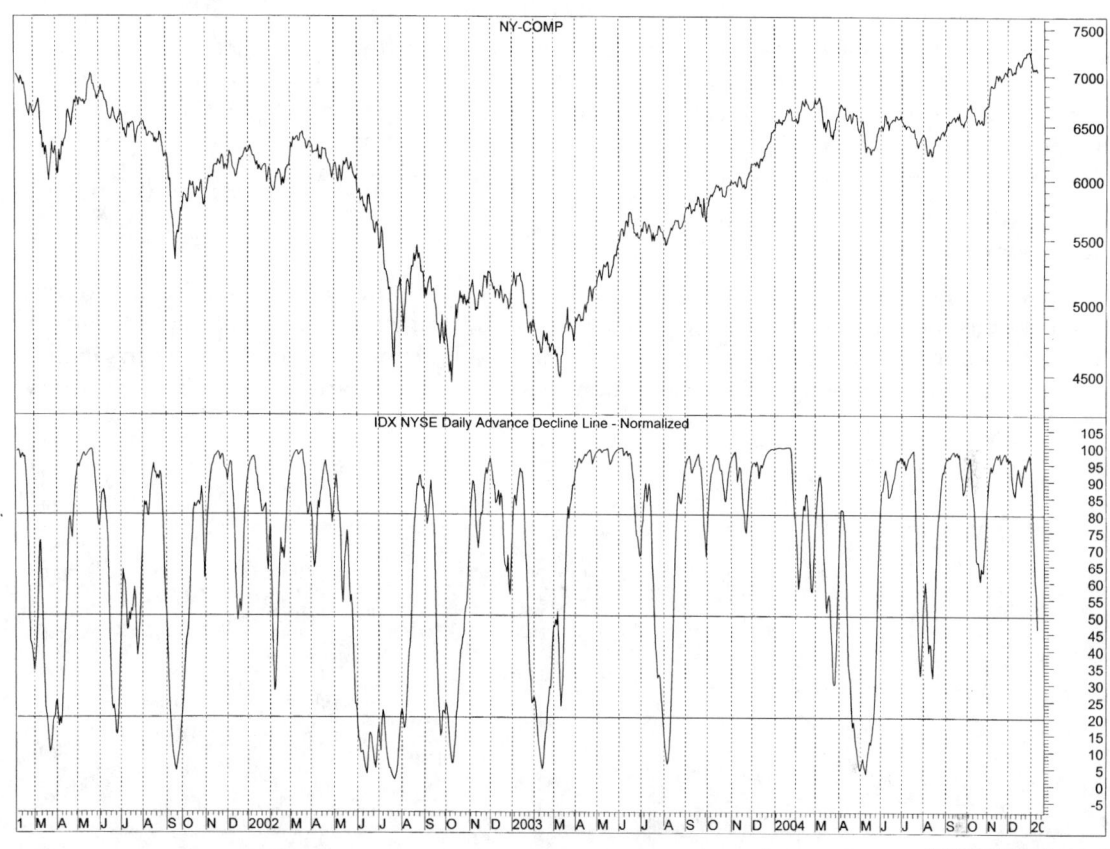

Formula: Previous Value + Today's $(A - D) = AD$, $(((AD - \text{lowest value } (AD)) / (\text{highest value } (AD) - \text{lowest value } (A))) * 100$

References

Chande, Tushar, "Breadth Stix and Other Tricks." *Stocks and Commodities*, Volume 12, May 1994, pp. 211–214.

Advance Decline Line—Bolton

Also Known As: Bolton Tremblay
Author/Creator: Hamilton Bolton
Data components required: Advances (A), Declines (D), Unchanged (U)

Description

This was an attempt by Bolton to remove downward bias in the Advance Decline Line. It was the square root of the difference of advances and declines, with that difference divided by the unchanged issues. This is an enhanced Advance Decline Line, in that, when the market is strong, it gives a slight push to either the advancing side or the declining side, depending on which is stronger.

Interpretation

This is yet another version of the Advance Decline Line. Considering its attempt to remove downward bias, this version should definitely be considered. By giving the unchanged issues weight, it can allow for this version to start to slow down its ascent a little sooner than the more traditional version. This follows the logic of the discussion that as a market starts to peak, the number of

Chart 4-22 Bolton Advance Decline Line.

unchanged issues will expand. Chart 4–22 shows the Bolton version of the Advance Decline Line.

Author Comments

Martin Pring uses this version, and that is good enough for me. Pring says that Bolton developed this because it was better at reflecting the unweighted indices such as the Value Line composite. Because the Value Line data was not available prior to the 1960s, this gave him a way to evaluate unweighted data for many years prior to that.

There isn't much written about this; I remember it from the old CompuTrac days and found references to it in Pring's and Colby's books. I believe the square root of a negative number is the reason you do not find this in charting software. I made a few assumptions to overcome it, and I believe have displayed it correctly in Chart 4–22. Also, I found the 21-day smoothed version of the ratio to be interesting as shown in Chart 4–23.

Formula: Previous Value + Square Root of $((A - D) / U)$

Chart 4-23 Bolton Advance Decline Ratio—21-Day Smooth.

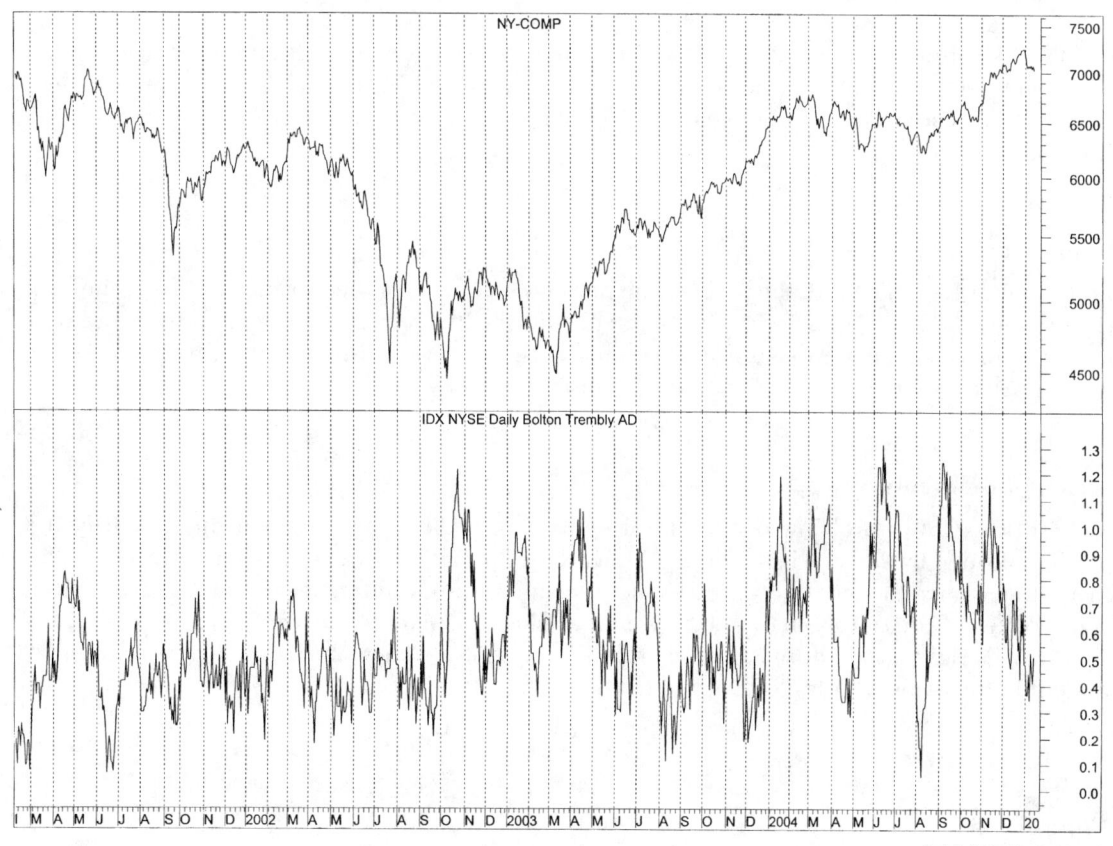

References

Dworkin, Fay, "Defining Advance / Decline Indicators." *Stocks and Commodities*, Volume 8, July 1990, pp. 274–278.

Pring, Martin, "Internal Market Momentum." *Stocks and Commodities*, Volume 11, July 1993, pp. 298–305.

Pring, Martin J. *Technical Analysis Explained.* McGraw-Hill, 1985.

Colby, Robert W. *The Encyclopedia of Technical Market Indicators.* New York : McGraw-Hill, 2003.

Advance Decline Line—Adjusted Total Issues

Also Known As: The Advance Decline Ratio
Author/Creator: Richard Russell
Data components required: Advances (A), Declines (D), Total Issues (TI)

Description

Richard Russell says that this was conceived by Colonel Leonard P. Ayres and James Hughes in 1926, and that it remained relatively obscure until he started his newsletter, Dow Theory Letters, in 1957. This indicator is an attempt to reduce the large increase in issues and normalize the difference between the advances and declines by dividing that difference by the total issues traded. Then it is calculated like the Advance Decline Line by adding each successive difference to the previous one.

Interpretation

Looking for divergence with the index is the most common use of the Advance Decline Line, and this version is no different. It is a normal tendency, during bull moves, for there to be more advancing days than declining days, and in down markets, the reverse is true. Chart 4–24 shows the Advance Decline Line adjusted for the total number of issues.

Author Comments

Richard Russell was probably one of the first to use the difference between the advances and declines divided by the total issues in his "A − D Ratio" published as a book of charts in 1962. This seems to enhance the more popular Advance Decline Line and offers very good long-term divergence patterns. You can see in the Chart 4–24 that when the market is in a good uptrend, this indicator trends right along with it. However, the first sign of weakness in the price action is readily evident in the adjusted Advance Decline Line.

$$\text{Formula:} \quad ((A - D) / TI)$$

References

Russell, Richard, 1975, *Dow Theory Letters*, San Diego, CA.

Chart 4-24 Advance Decline Line Adjusted for Total Issues.

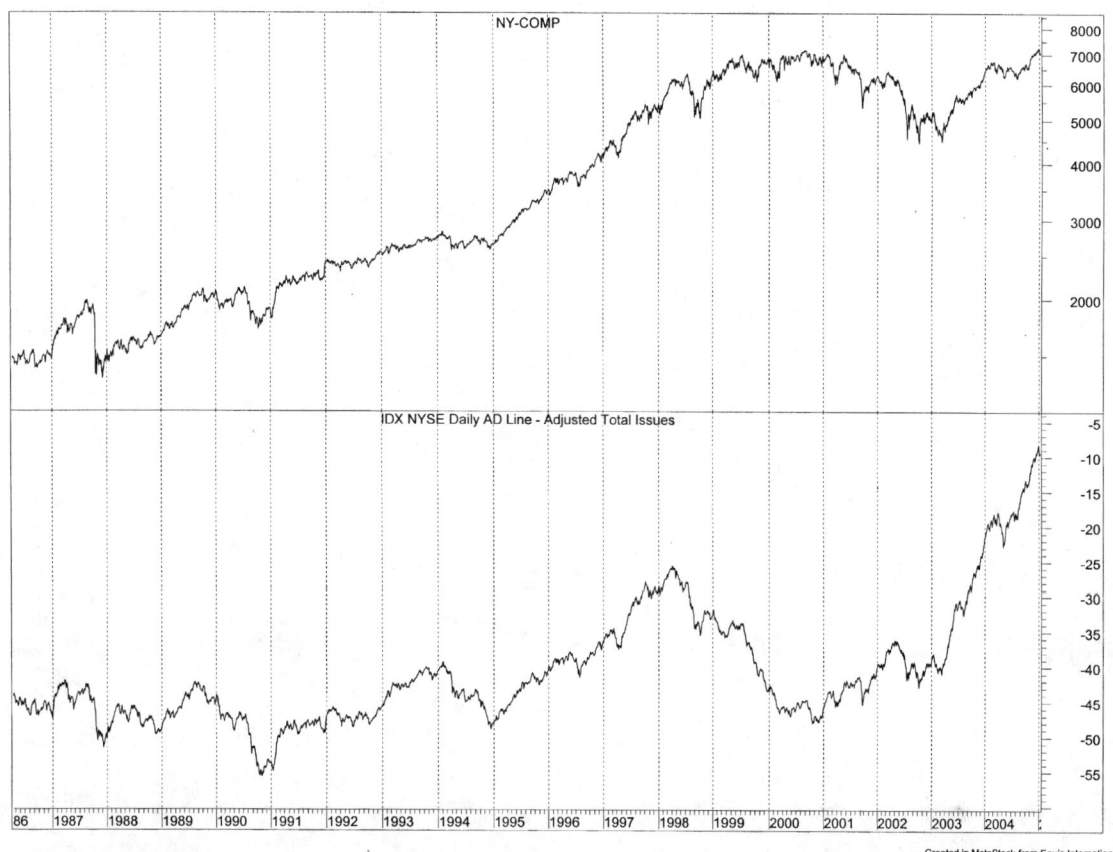

Big Movers Only

Author/Creator: Greg Morris
Data components required: Advances (A), Declines (D), Total Issues (TI)

Description

This is the Advance Decline Line using only days when either the advances, declines, or both were above a predetermined percentage of total issues traded. Initially, this was developed in an attempt to remove days of very inactive trading, such as the Friday after Thanksgiving, days in which the exchanges were not open all day, etc.

Interpretation

The intent was to filter out the boring days in the standard Advance Decline Line and use only data when either the number of advances or declines are significant. Long periods of inactivity in

Chart 4-25 Big Movers Only—35 Percent.

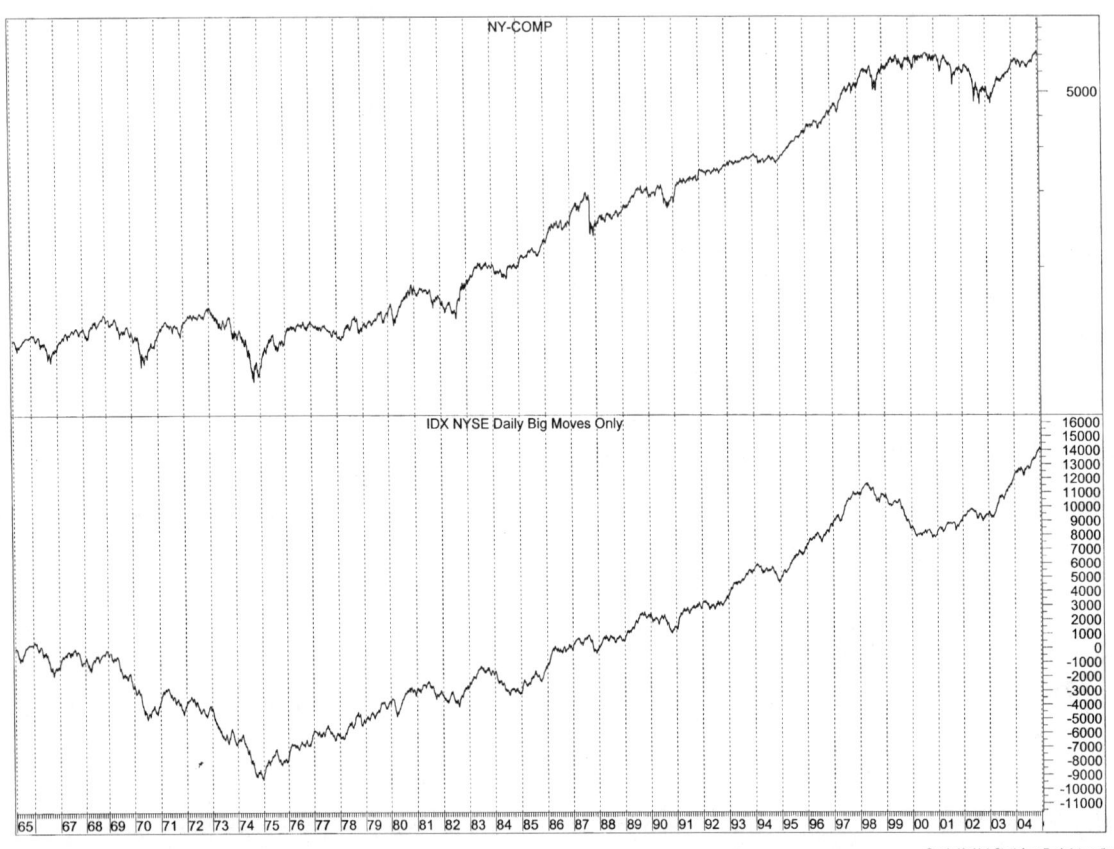

the market can still have a bias either upward or downward. It was felt that those trading days did not adequately reflect the underlying trends of the market. By removing a certain percentage of inactive days, this modification to the advance decline line reflects only the more powerful moves in the market. Chart 4-25 shows the Advance Decline Line where days with less than 35 percent of total issues (either advances or declines) removed. It seems to reflect the market quite well.

Author Comments

When I first developed this back in the 1980s, I used a fixed number of 1200 for the limit on whether the advances or declines for that day would be part of this indicator. Like most breadth indicators, adjusting for the big increase in issues traded was necessary. If you look at a long-term chart of this indicator, you will see that it will better reveal longer term trends than most Advance Decline Line indicators used in the standard or more generally accepted manner. This is good for keeping the "big picture" in mind during your analysis. Chart 4-26 removes all advance decline data less than 50 percent of total issues. It is interesting how, during one of the big bull markets in history, from

Advance Decline Difference Indicators

Chart 4-26 Big Movers Only—50 Percent.

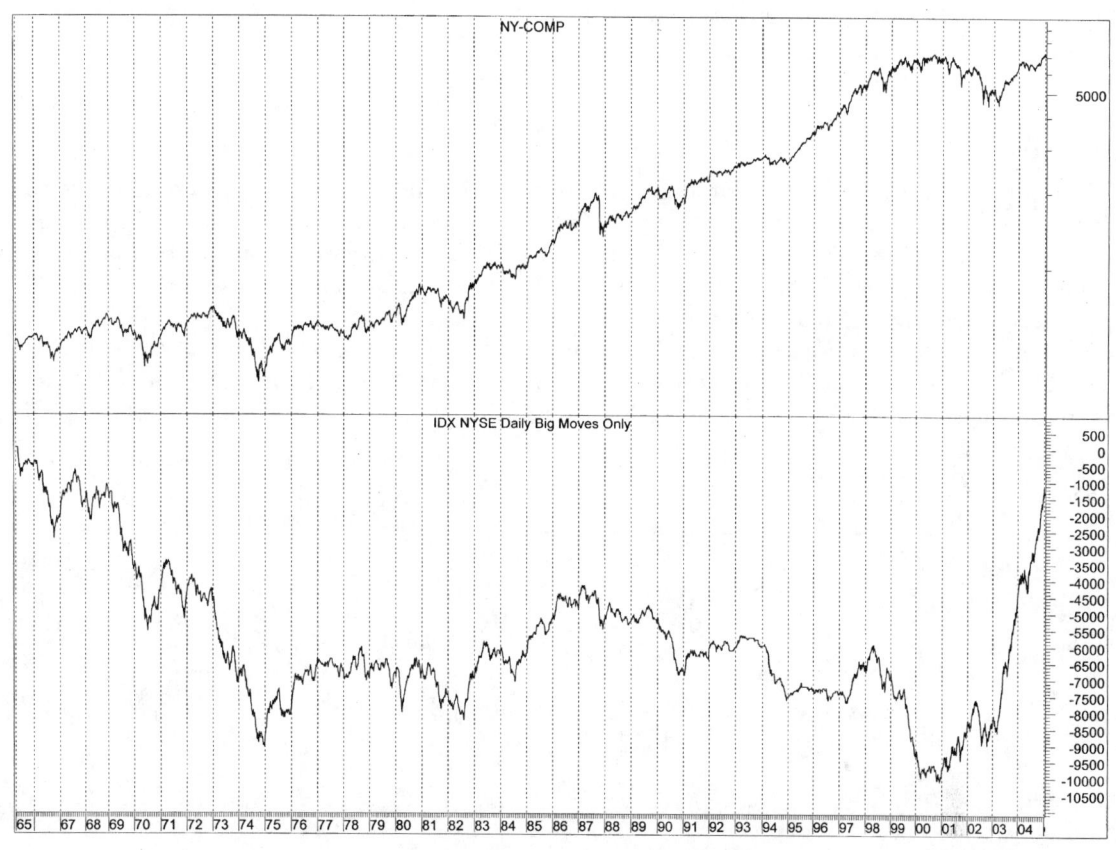

1988 to 2000, this went down. What does that mean? Somewhere between 35 percent and 50 percent of the large breadth moves of the market were not present in those years. This is also proven true by looking at Zweig's Breadth Thrust (Chapter 5) where, beginning in 1984, there were no breadth thrust signals until 2004. This Big Movers line limited to the top 50 percent breadth days also reflects that.

Formula: $(A > \%TI - D > \%TI)$.

References
Morris, Greg, 1995, "Indicators and Trading Systems Software," G. Morris Corporation, Dallas, TX.

Advance Decline Line Oscillator

Data components required: Advances (A), Declines (D)

Description

This is a 21-day rate of change of the advance decline line. Rate of change is where you take today's indicator value and subtract the value from 21 days ago.

Interpretation

Like most oscillators, this is good for identifying overbought and oversold areas. Putting levels on this indicator, like most oscillators, requires a visual technique because most advance decline line numbers are meaningless by themselves. It all depends on where you start the calculation that determines the numbers (values) that make up the advance decline line. Chart 4–27 uses zones at +1000 and −1000, and they seem to work very well.

Gerald Appel likes to use a 10-day rate of change of the advance decline line and +3000 and −3000 as the zones. He states that if it gets to +5000 or +6000, it is good indicator of market strength. Chart 4–28 shows the Appel version with lines at −3000, 0, +3000, and +6000. Appel

Chart 4–27 Advance Decline Line Oscillator.

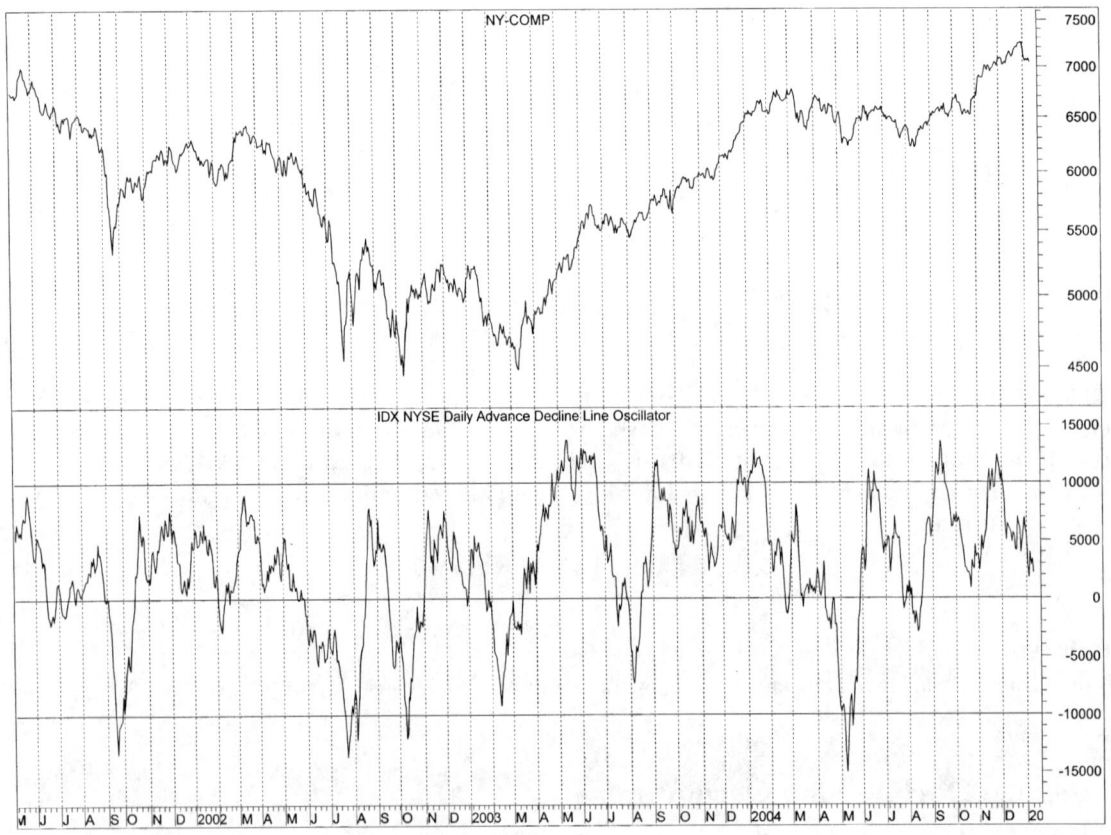

also likes to use a 21-day oscillator, which is described at the beginning of this section. He mentions that he also uses this as a divergence indicator with the market.

Author Comments

Most oscillators, especially those with short-term parameters will yield short-term signals. The Advance Decline Line Oscillator does not disappoint in that regard. I prefer the 21-day rate of change as the signals are more defined.

$$\text{Formula: } \{\text{Cumulated } (A - D) - (A - D) \text{ input periods ago } (ROC)\}$$

References

Appel, Gerald, "Gerald Appel, with Systems and Forecasts." *Stocks and Commodities*, Volume 12, March 1994, pp. 98–105.

Chart 4-28 Advance Decline Line Oscillator—Appel.

Absolute Breadth Index

Author/Creator: Norman G. Fosback
Data components required: Advances (A), Declines (D)

Description

This indicator was termed by Norman Fosback as a "going nowhere" indicator because you take the absolute value of the difference between advancing issues and declining issues. It does not matter whether there are more or fewer advances or declines; it is the absolute difference between them that the Absolute Breadth Index measures. It totally disregards market direction. It shows market activity or lack thereof.

Interpretation

The thinking behind the creation of the Absolute Breadth Index is that when the difference between the advances and declines is high, the price changes are also big, which, in turn, can mean the market is more prone to being at a bottom than at a top. This is an indication of good market activity. Similarly, if the difference between the advances and declines is small (low Absolute Breadth Index values), the market is not going anywhere and probably more near a top. This indicates a lack of activity in the market. In Chart 4–29 you can easily see that when the Absolute Breadth Index is smoothed by 50 days, it clearly is pointing out market bottoms and tops.

Author Comments

This indicator was one of the early ones, as is most of Fosback's work. It is also one of the good ones, and because it seems so simplistic, many times I forget to look at it. I prefer to smooth it with 21 days and watch it as it goes over 1100 for bottoms and below 300 for market tops. These are the current settings. Because the number of issues has increased so much in recent years, these levels needed to be spread further apart. You can see this in Chart 4–30.

During the 1970s and 1980s, the levels that seemed to work best were 250 and 600. This is merely because of fewer issues being traded. See Chart 4–31. A more current method of using the Absolute Breadth Index would be the Absolute Breadth Index adjusted for the total issues the way so many indicators from the past can and should be used this way. See Absolute Breadth Index Adjusted in this chapter.

$$\text{Formula: } |A - D|$$

References

Fosback, Norman G. *Stock Market Logic*, Fort Lauderdale, FL: The Institute for Economic Research, Inc., 1976.

Chart 4-29 Absolute Breadth Index—50-Day Smooth.

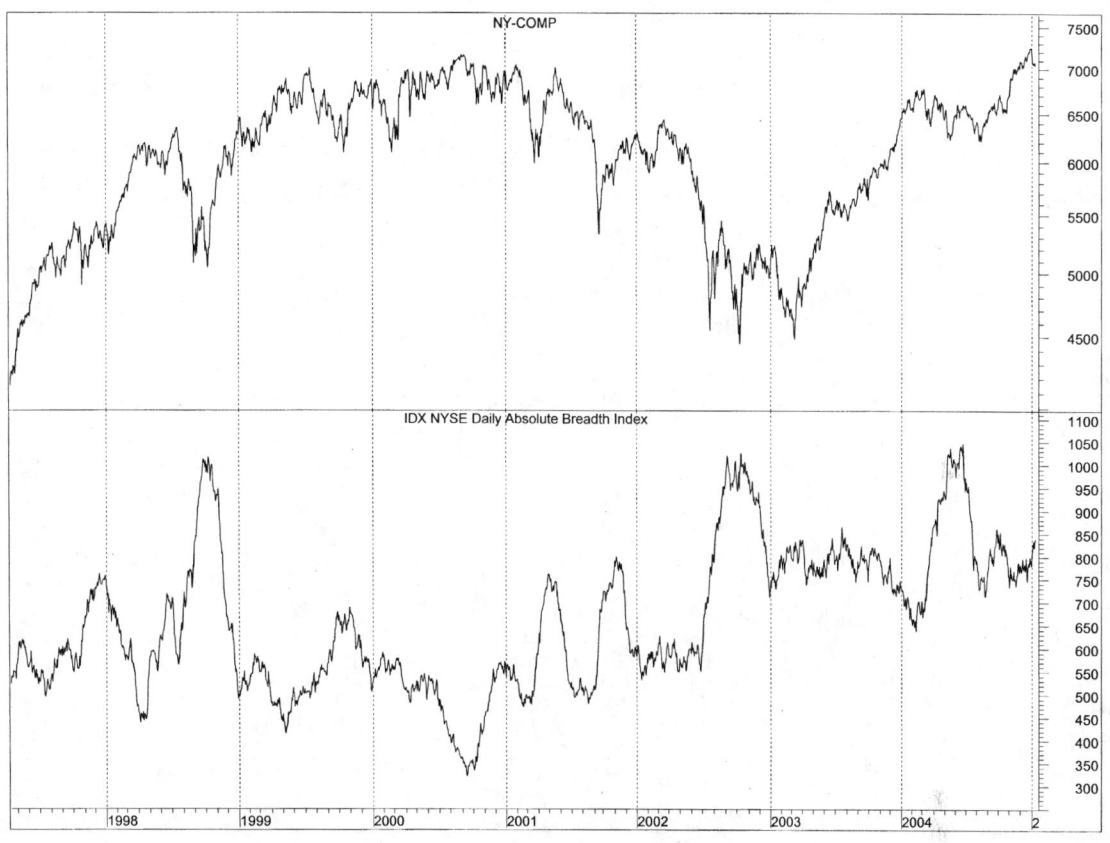

Absolute Breadth Index—Adjusted

Author/Creator: Norman G. Fosback was the creator of the original ABI.
Data components required: Advances (A), Declines (D), Total Issues (TI)

Description

The original version of this indicator was termed by Fosback as a "going nowhere" indicator because you take the absolute value of the difference between advancing issues and declining issues. It does not matter whether there are more advances or declines; it is the absolute difference between them that this indicator measures.

Chart 4-30 Absolute Breadth Index—21-Day Smooth with 300 and 1100 Levels.

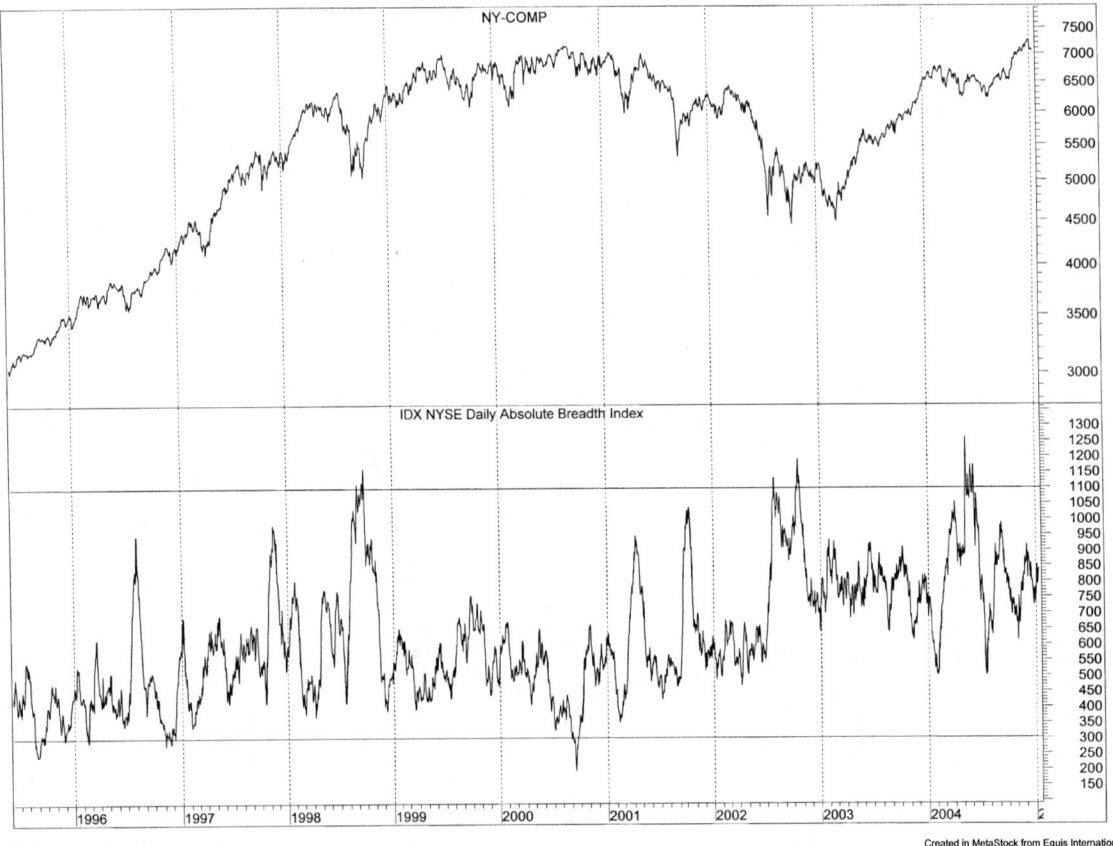

Interpretation

The thinking behind the creation of the Adjusted Absolute Breadth Index is that when the difference between the advances and declines is high, the price changes are also big, which, in turn, can mean the market is more prone to being at a bottom than at a top. Similarly, if the difference between the advances and declines is small (low Absolute Breadth Index values), the market is not going anywhere and is probably more near a top.

Author Comments

This is one of those indicators that needed to be adjusted because of the large increase in the number of issued being traded. As with most adjusted indicators, all you need to do is create a ratio.

Advance Decline Difference Indicators

Chart 4-31 Absolute Breadth Index—21-Day with 250 and 600 Levels.

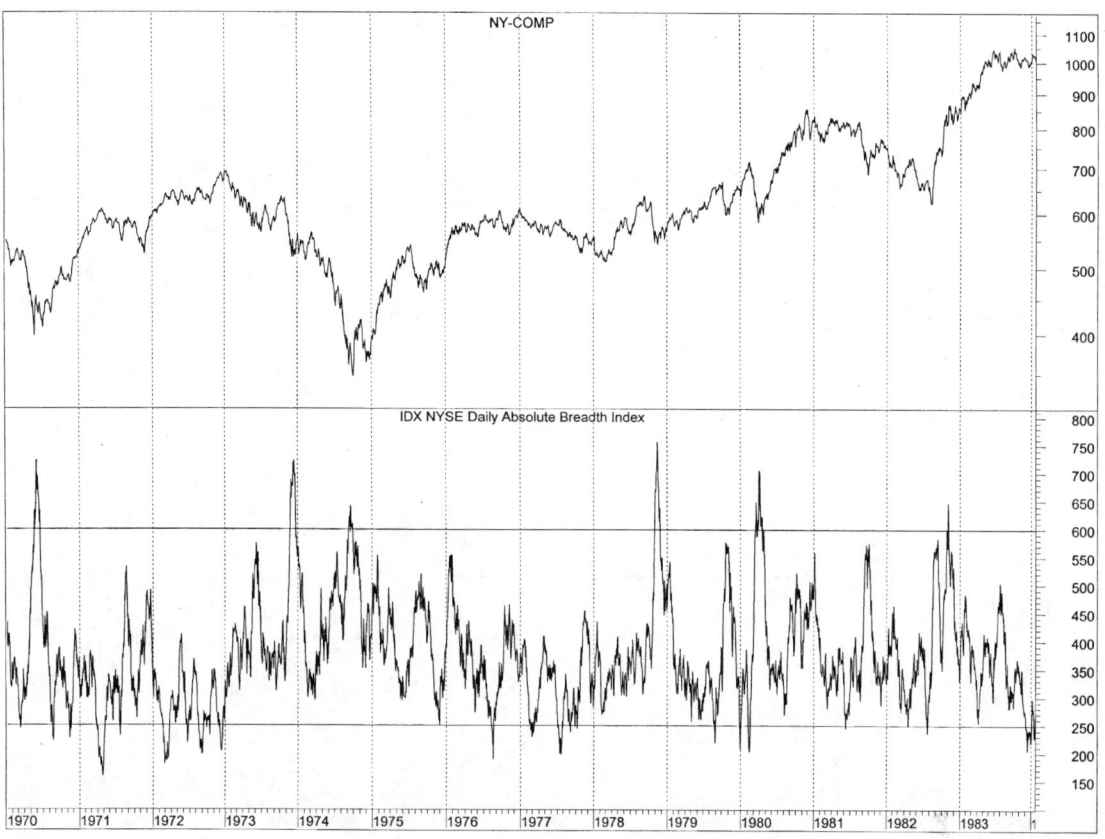

In this case, just divide by the total issues traded. Just like the Absolute Breadth Index, I prefer to smooth it with 21 days and watch it as it goes over 30 for bottoms and below 10 for market tops. Robert Colby, in his book *The Encyclopedia of Technical Market Indicators* further adjusted the formula to multiply by 100 to remove the decimal values of the adjusted absolute breadth index. Chart 4-32 shows the Adjusted Absolute Breadth Index.

$$\text{Formula: } |A - D| / TI * 100$$

References

Fosback, Norman G. *Stock Market Logic*, Fort Lauderdale, FL: The Institute for Economic Research, Inc., 1976.

Colby, Robert W. *The Encyclopedia of Technical Market Indicators*. New York : McGraw-Hill, 2003.

Chart 4-32 Absolute Breadth Index Adjusted by Total Issues—21-Day Smooth with 10 and 30 Levels.

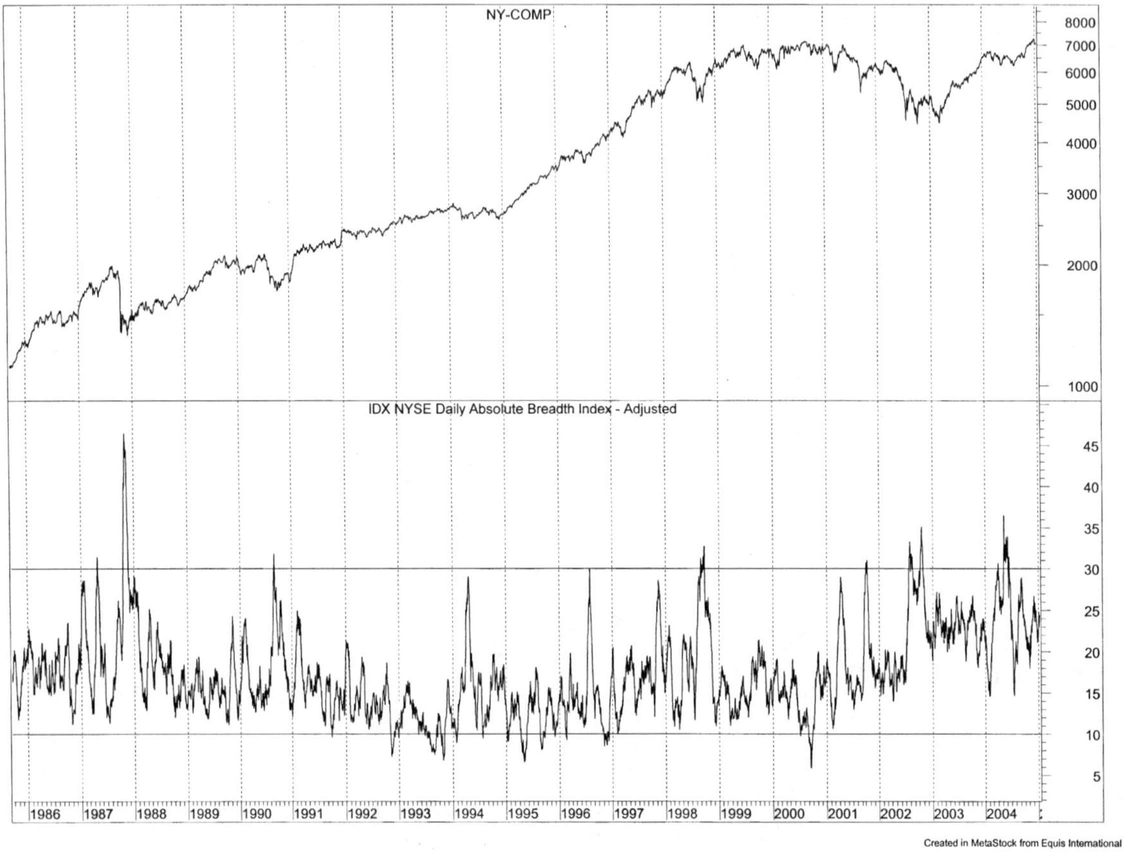

Advance Decline Power

Also Known As: AD Power
Author/Creator: John McGinley / Joe Granville
Data components required: Advances (A), Declines (D), Market Index (MKT).

Description

Originally based on weekly data, this is the difference between advances and declines divided by the absolute change in the Dow Jones Industrial average.

Interpretation

Originally, the concept was to identify relative strength between the broad market (advances and declines) and the Dow Industrial average (the market). Chart 4–33 is the daily AD Power with a 21-day smoothing.

Chart 4-33 McGinley Advance Decline (AD) Power.

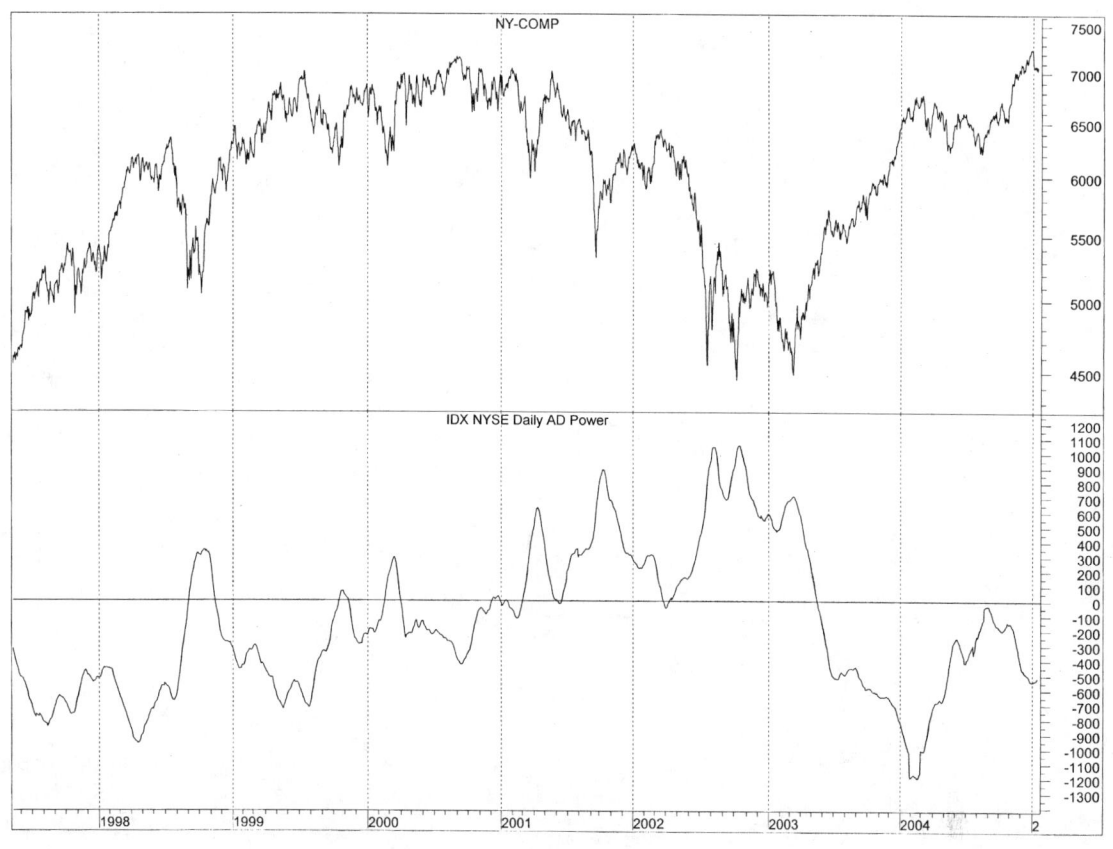

Author Comments

By taking a ratio of the advance decline difference and the absolute change in the Dow Industrials, this indicator is relating to momentum or acceleration values. It certainly appears that this indicator is good for identifying significant market bottoms. While it seems to reflect many market tops by its downward spikes, it is somewhat like many of the economic indicators that are in use today where they identify 12 of the last 8 recessions. In keeping with the original formula, Chart 4–33b shows the AD Power index using weekly data. You can see that there isn't that much difference with the daily version.

$$\text{Formula: } (A - D) \, / \, |MKT - MKT(52 \text{ weeks ago})|$$

References

McGinley, John, *Technical Trends*, Wilton, CT.

Chart 4-33b Weekly McGinley AD Power.

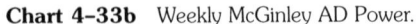

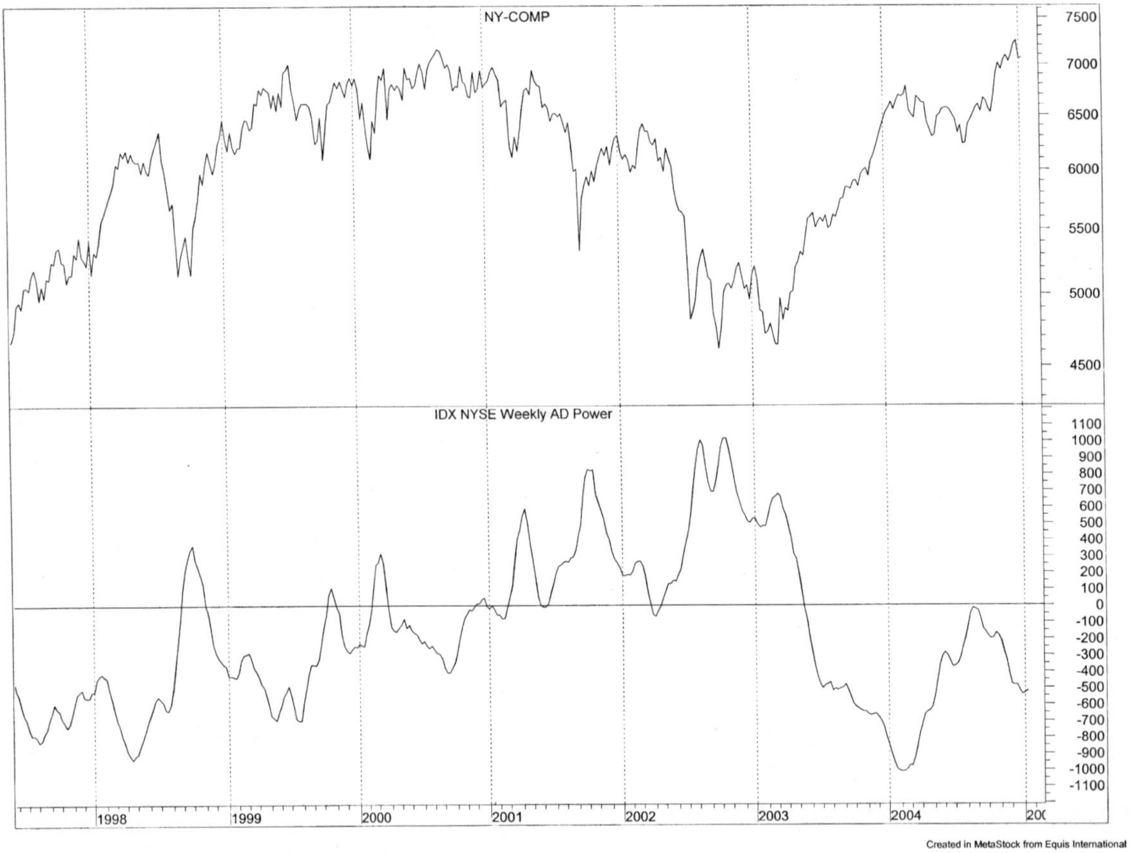

Coppock Breadth Indicator

Author/Creator: Edwin Sedgwick Chittenden Coppock
Data components required: Advances (*A*), Declines (*D*), Total Issues (*TI*)

Description

This indicator, created in the early 1960s, uses an adjusted advance decline line as its basis. Subtract the declines from the advances and divide that difference by the total issues traded. Then calculate a cumulative total as you would with the advance decline line. A second line is calculated as a weighted moving average of the raw cumulated line. Originally developed as a weekly indicator, the Coppock Breadth Indicator can also be adapted to daily breadth data.

Advance Decline Difference Indicators

Interpretation

Coppock's interpretation was simple; when the cumulative line crossed its own 15-week weighted moving average, a signal was generated. Most times, it is the simple concepts that seem to work the best. Chart 4–34 uses daily data adjusted to a 75-day weighted smooth instead of the 15-week version. When the middle plot is equal to 10, the advance decline line is above its weighted moving average. When it is at −10, it is below the average.

Author Comments

Sedge Coppock was as interesting in person as his early stock market innovations. Most are familiar with his Coppock Curve, not the name he gave it, but one that is generally accepted in the trade. He called it the Trendex Very Long Term Risk Index for Listed Stocks. It was an 11- and 14-month

Chart 4–34 Coppock Breadth Indicator.

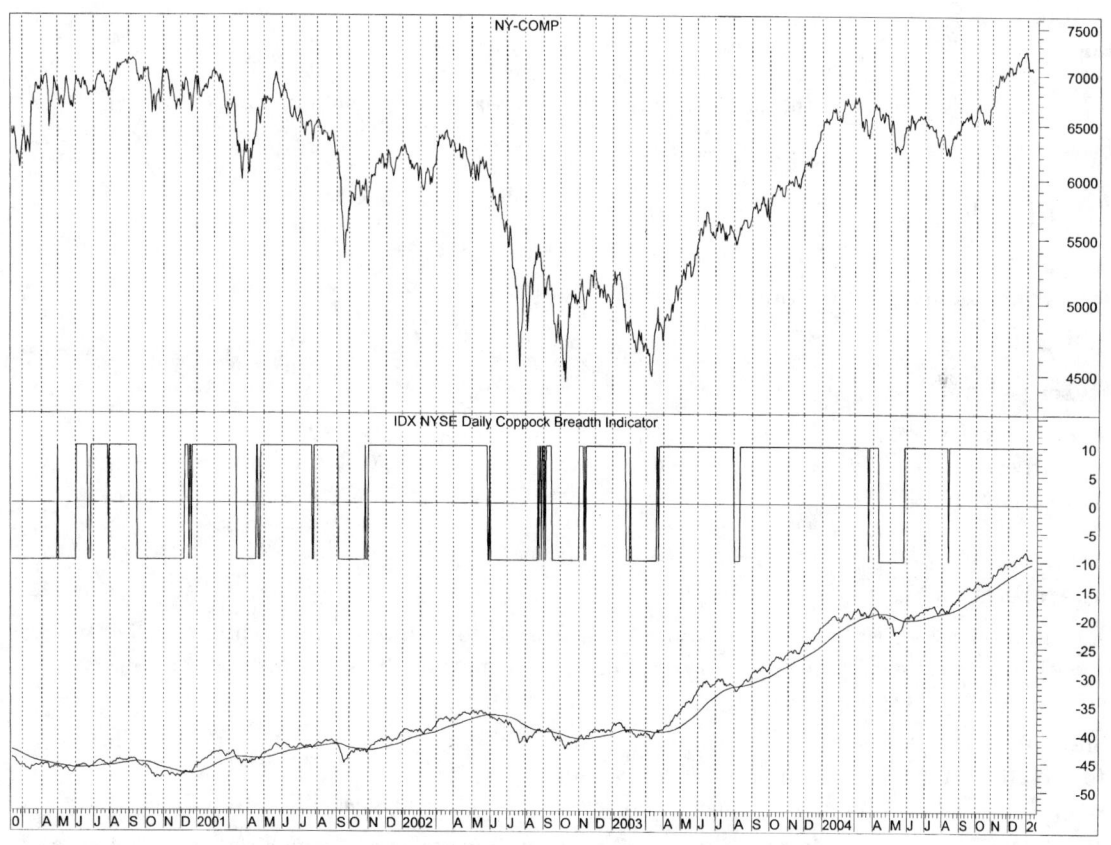

percentage change of the Dow Jones Industrial Average added together, and then a 10-month weighted moving average of that. He was once asked why he picked 11 and 14 months for this indicator. He said an undertaker friend told him that the period of time for a grieving family after the death of a close family member was usually between 11 and 14 months.

I had the pleasure of meeting Sedge Coppock in 1988 at the Market Technician's Association (MTA) conference where he was awarded the MTA's annual award for contribution to the field of technical analysis. Prior to that, I had a few communications with him in regard to a local group of analysts in Dallas, Texas, that I was working with. He sent us a tape about his beliefs and observations of almost 40+ years in the stock market. He did not hold back any punches in regard to uninformed investors, those who are always looking for the quick way to profits, and how most will not do the work required to make it in the markets. That tape, and three monographs that he wrote, are some of the best investment advice one could ever get.

$$\text{Formula: Previous Value} + (A - D) / TI$$

References
Coppock, E. S. C., 1977, "Low-Risk Investing," Trendex Research Corp, San Antonio.
—E. S. C., "Emotions Make Prices," Trendex Research Corp, San Antonio.
—E. S. C., "Realistic Stock Market Speculation," Trendex Research Corp, San Antonio.

Haurlan Index

Author/Creator: P.N. (Pete) Haurlan
Data components required: Advances (A), Declines (D)

Description
The Haurlan Index is an exponential moving average of the advances minus the declines. There are three variations for short-, intermediate-, and long-term analysis, using three different exponential averages.

Interpretation
All three versions give buy signals as they cross from below the zero line to above it. Sell signals are when it goes from above to below the zero line. Paul Carroll assigned the following buy and sell zones, which seem to work well:

Short-Term Haurlan Index (3-day smooth):	−550 for buy and +550 for sell.
Intermediate-Term Haurlan Index (20-day smooth):	−200 for buy and +200 for sell.
Long-Term Haurlan Index (200-day smooth):	He suggests using trendlines.

Gerald Appel also claims that these are ideal for trendline analysis, particularly with the short and intermediate versions. Appel also agrees with Carroll that −550 and +550 for the short version

Advance Decline Difference Indicators

Chart 4–35 Haurlan Index—Short-Term.

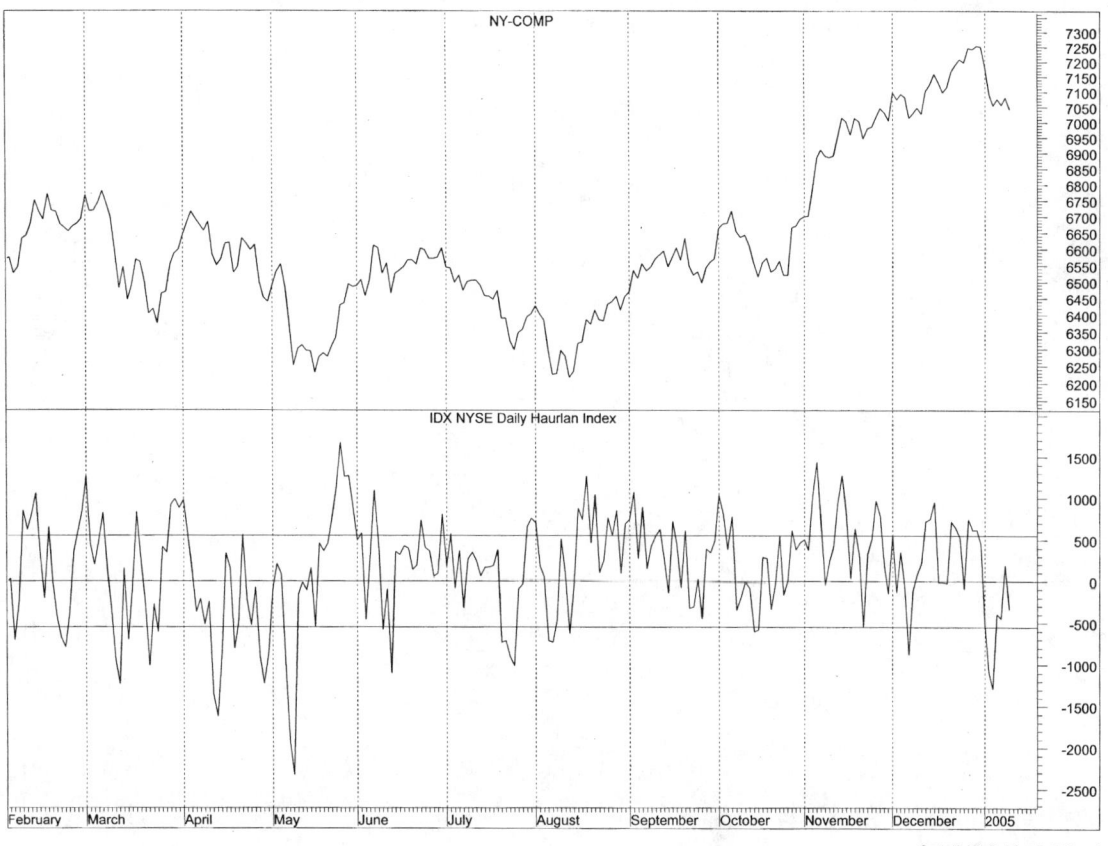

indicate the immediacy of a short-term market reversal or consolidation. Chart 4–35 shows the short-term version of the Haurlan Index with the thresholds used by Carroll and Appel.

Chart 4–36 is the intermediate term Haurlan Index showing the +200 and −200 thresholds.

Chart 4–37 is the long-term Haurlan Index with a couple of trendline breaks identifying market turns.

Author Comments

This is another twist on the advance decline difference. Some of the best indicators are also the simplest ones. Pete Haurlan was a true rocket scientist who worked for the Jet Propulsion Laboratory. His market interest and contributions to the field were under his advisory firm, Trade Levels.

$$\text{Formula: Exp. Avg. } (A - D)$$

Chart 4-36 Haurlan Index—Intermediate-Term.

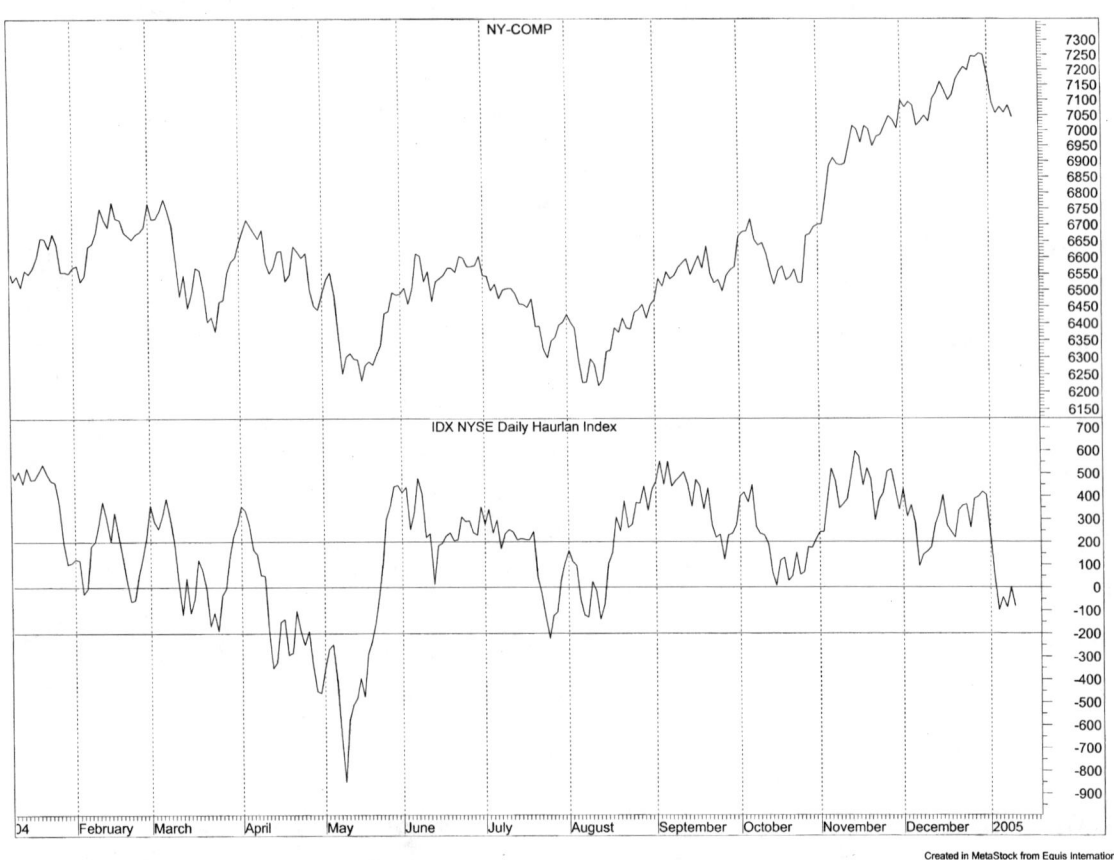

References
Haurlan, P.N., *Trade Levels, Inc.* Pasadena, CA.
Carroll, Paul E., "The Haurlan Index." *Stocks and Commodities*, Volume 12, January, 1994, pp. 23–25.
Appel, Gerald. *Winning Market Systems*. Greenville: Traders Press, 1973.

McClellan Oscillator

Author/Creator: Sherman and Marian McClellan
Data components required: Advances (A), Declines (D)

Description

The McClellan Oscillator is the difference between the 19-day (10 percent trend) and the 39-day (5 percent trend) exponential moving averages of the daily net advances minus declines figure.

Advance Decline Difference Indicators

Chart 4-37 Haurlan Index—Long-Term.

These two smoothing values were used because they reflect the two most dominant short-to-intermediate cycles in the market. These two exponential averages also were chosen in order to optimize speed in generating a directional signal, while minimizing whipsaws. They were also chosen for their ease of hand calculation at a time when calculators and computers were not available. The oscillator tends to lead the market because it will indicate overbought and oversold situations prior to the market. It will pass through zero at or very soon after an important market turning point.

Interpretation

The McClellan Oscillator is an intermediate-term indicator, but it can be used for shorter-term timing when it bottoms in oversold areas such as −100 and below. Usually, McClellan Oscillator crossings above the zero line are positive/bullish and below the zero line are negative/bearish. Readings above +100 are overbought readings, while below −100 are oversold. The +130 and −130 levels are also important. When the oscillator drops to −130 and then rallies, quite often the rally will fail and give a good sell signal. The opposite occurs when the oscillator rises to +130. Very negative readings in the −150 area are considered as selling climax levels. Another component of the McClellan Oscillator is divergent pattern formations compared to the market, in particular, a triple-top formation of the oscillator. In *Patterns for Profit*, there is also mention of using standard trendline analysis with the oscillator. That book further mentions a strong 22–24 week cycle appears in the oscillator, and that was true at the time the book was written. This cycle no longer appears in the patterns of the Oscillator, and it likely disappeared due to changes in U.S. tax laws related to holding periods for determination of capital gains taxes. Chart 4–38 shows the McClellan Oscillator and the +150 and −150 thresholds mentioned above.

Author Comments

Exponential moving averages and percentage of trend smoothing are confusing to most. They really are equal other than small rounding differences. A 19-period exponential average is the same

Chart 4-38 McClellan Oscillator.

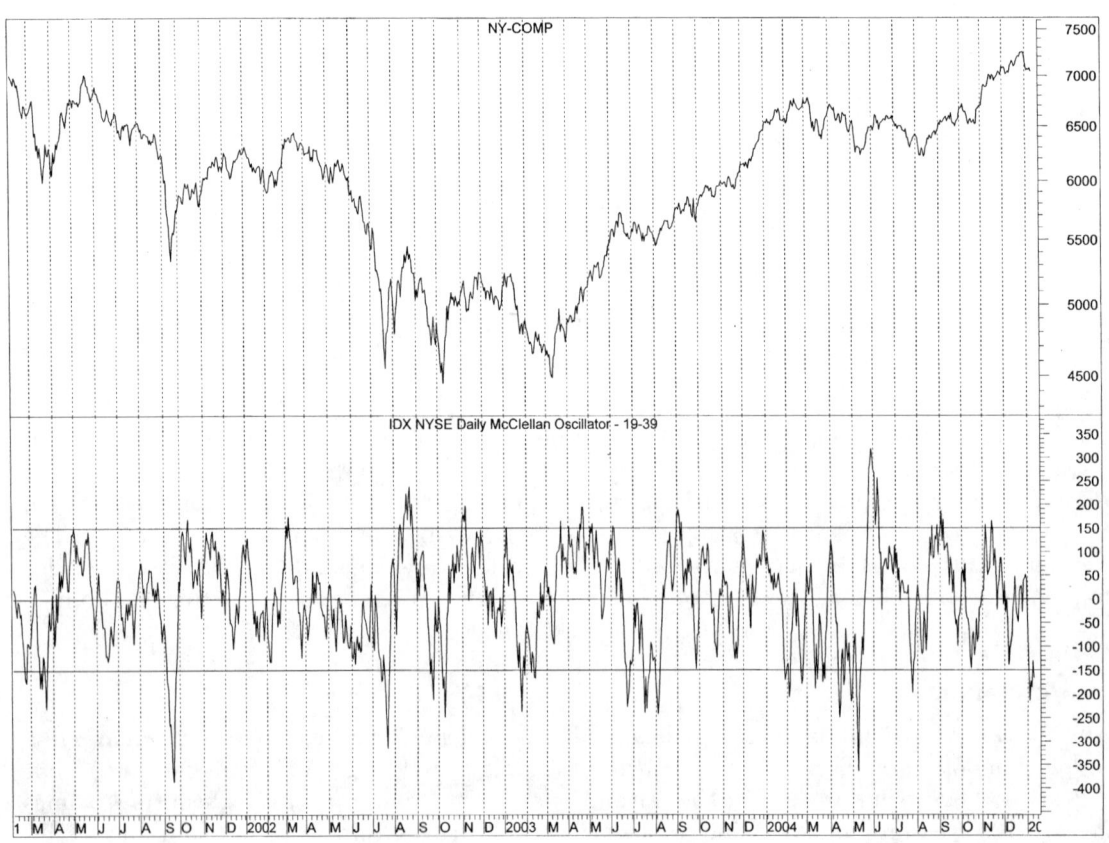

Advance Decline Difference Indicators

as a 10 percent trend smoothing. One needs to be cautious to avoid relying on data and results at the beginning of the data file in order to let the indicators adjust to reflect recent data value. See the additional information in Chapter 10 (The McClellan Indicators) for the mathematical details.

The McClellan indicators use the advance decline line concept. A point often not understood about the advance decline line is that its numerical value has no meaning, because different start points in the $A - D$ data will result in different numerical values for the sum of all previous $A - D$ readings. The $A - D$ Line's relative position to past structures can have importance, such as making a higher high or a divergence relative to prices. Of even greater importance is the $A - D$ Line's acceleration, both up and down. This is why the McClellan indicators are such a significant contribution to breadth analysis.

Sherman McClellan, in an interview in *Stocks and Commodities* magazine in 1994, said that McClellan Oscillator readings in the neighborhood of -125 to -130 represented a bearish indication. A reading that low or lower that arises after a prolonged period without deeply negative readings means the market is becoming illiquid. In effect, it can be a warning shot of larger problems to come. A subsequent deeply negative reading does not have the same "warning shot" implications; it is instead the fulfillment of what the warning shot was predicting.

We make mention here of numerical values for the Oscillator, but readers are urged not to focus so closely on the number. Varying amounts of market volatility can affect amplitudes, and so analysis is better done by examining a chart of the Oscillator's path rather than by looking at a single numerical value and drawing conclusions from that. A chart will reveal what levels have marked recent extremes, and will also allow the analyst to spot Oscillator structures that have interpretive significance, such as complex or simple structures and divergences relative to price action.

When the Oscillator crosses through the zero line in one direction, and then makes a direct turn around to head back across zero in the other direction, that is a sign of weakness for that side of the zero line. If, however, the Oscillator builds a "complex" structure on one side of the zero line, doing a lot of chopping up and down without crossing zero, then that implies strength for that side. A complex structure above zero implies that the bulls have control, and although the bears might summon enough energy for a momentary downward correction, further gains should be expected. Occasionally, periods will occur in which neither side of zero will see a complex structure; the Oscillator may just go from a simple structure above zero to a simple structure below zero and back again, meaning that neither side has the willingness or ability to take control of the market.

The history of how Sherman and Marian McClellan developed the Oscillator and Summation Index is rich in technical analysis history and development. It begins with contact from Gene Morgan, who hosted *Charting the Market* on KWHY television in the 1960s and who gave the indicators their names. Kennedy Gammage comes into the picture, as does Pete Haurlan. The single best accounting on this was done by Sherman McClellan at the Market Technician's Association meeting on May 14, 2004, when he was awarded the Lifetime Achievement Award. His son, Tom, provides this presentation and Sherman's acceptance speech on their site. Go to: http://www.mcoscillator.com/user/MTAspeech.pdf. Tom also was kind enough to add comments on this section and the section on the McClellan Summation Index.

More details on the McClellan Indicators can be found in Chapter 10.

Formula: (Today's 19 exp average of $(A - D)$ − (Today's 39 exp average of $(A - D)$

References

McClellan, Sherman and Marian. *Patterns for Profit*. Lakewood, WA: McClellan Financial Publications, Inc., 1989. This book was originally published by Trade Levels in 1970.

McClellan Family Interview, "It's All In the Family: Sherman, Marian, and Tom McClellan." *Stocks and Commodities*, Volume 12, June 1994, pp. 264–273.

McClellan Summation Index

Author/Creator: Sherman and Marian McClellan
Data components required: Advances (A), Declines (D)

Description

The McClellan Summation Index is the cumulative sum of all daily McClellan Oscillator readings, and provides a long-range view of market breadth. The Summation Index therefore changes each day by the value of the Oscillator, rising when the Oscillator is positive and declining when the Oscillator is negative. The Summation Index has developed a life of its own as time has added additional information to its interpretation. Originally (in the 1960–1970s) the summation index moved in the range of +2000 and −1500. Because the Oscillator and Summation Index debuted before the days when computers or even hand-held calculators were available, all calculations were done manually. So that folks would not have to work with negative numbers except under very unusual (and important) circumstances, the McClellans arbitrarily set a neutral level at +1000. This was done by adding 1000 to the calculation. Since the advent of personal computers, this is no longer necessary, but is also not easily changed because so much is written about it and so many folks follow it. Tom McClellan (Sherman and Marian's son) told me it was not worth the possible confusion to change it.

Interpretation

A basic mathematical fact is that when the McClellan Oscillator is positive (above the zero line), the McClellan Summation Index will be rising. The levels of the Summation index are as important as the direction. Chart 4–39 shows the McClellan Summation Index back to 1997.

Author Comments

This is probably one of the best breadth indicators available. It has a multitude of uses. Not only its direction, but the level it is at is important. It is discussed here in keeping with the conventions used in this book and is further elaborated on in Chapter 10.

The McClellan Summation Index has a number of different calculations. The one that is used by the most analysts is probably also the one that is not as good as at least one of the others. The use of exponential moving averages (percent of trend) for calculating the summation index is

Advance Decline Difference Indicators

Chart 4-39 McClellan Summation Index—Traditional.

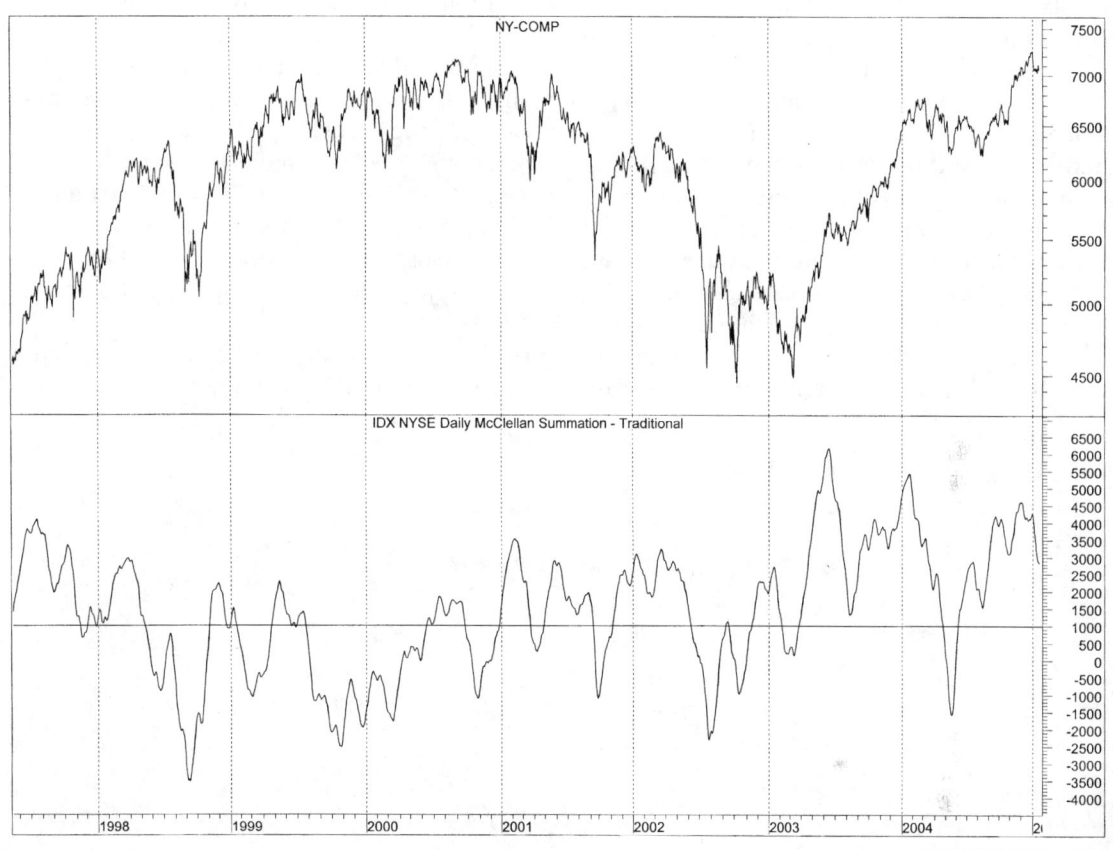

common and actually how the McClellans originally did it. However, in the early 1990s, a bright mathematician named James R. Miekka came up with a modification to the McClellan formula that is today used by the McClellans, Carl Swenlin, and most of the other purists in the field. While this modification does not affect the oscillator, it does have a significant effect on the summation index, which is derived from the oscillator.

One of the problems with the original formula was that as the summation index levels were found to also be important, it was difficult for two different analysts to have exactly the same values. If breadth values from different sources were used, if math errors were present, or if any day's data were missing anywhere in the calculation, then those differences would accumulate and remain in the Summation Index values forever.

Miekka found that the Summation Index could be calculated for any day in history, simply by knowing that day's values for the 10 percent trend and 5 percent trend. He created a calibration formula so that the levels will remain the same no matter when you begin the calculation, and any data or calculation errors would eventually be factored out of the Summation Index value just as they are factored out of the 10 percent trend and 5 percent trend. The mathematics of Miekka's calculation formula can be found in Chapter 10. In addition, Jim Miekka has offered a McClellan Summation Buy Signal report, also found in Chapter 10.

In their vast research on their indicators, the McClellans found that when the Summation Index went above +3000, it was time to pay attention. The first observation was that whenever that happened, a strong bull market was nearby. From the early 1970s until 1994 (time of their interview), there were seven instances of the summation index breaching +3000. From Chart 4-40, you can see the ones in more recent history. The rise to +6000 in April, 2003 was also telling. Looking at the same chart, it is also apparent that when the McClellan Summation Index reaches a deeply negative value on the downside, an important bottom is close at hand. Chart 4-40 shows the McClellan Summation Index using the Miekka formula adjustment (see Chapter 10 for more details) with the +3000 and −1200 thresholds.

Carl Swenlin and the McClellans also use an adjusted advance decline formula in association with the Miekka modification. This is an attempt to somewhat neutralize the growing effect of the

Chart 4-40 McClellan Summation Index—Miekka.

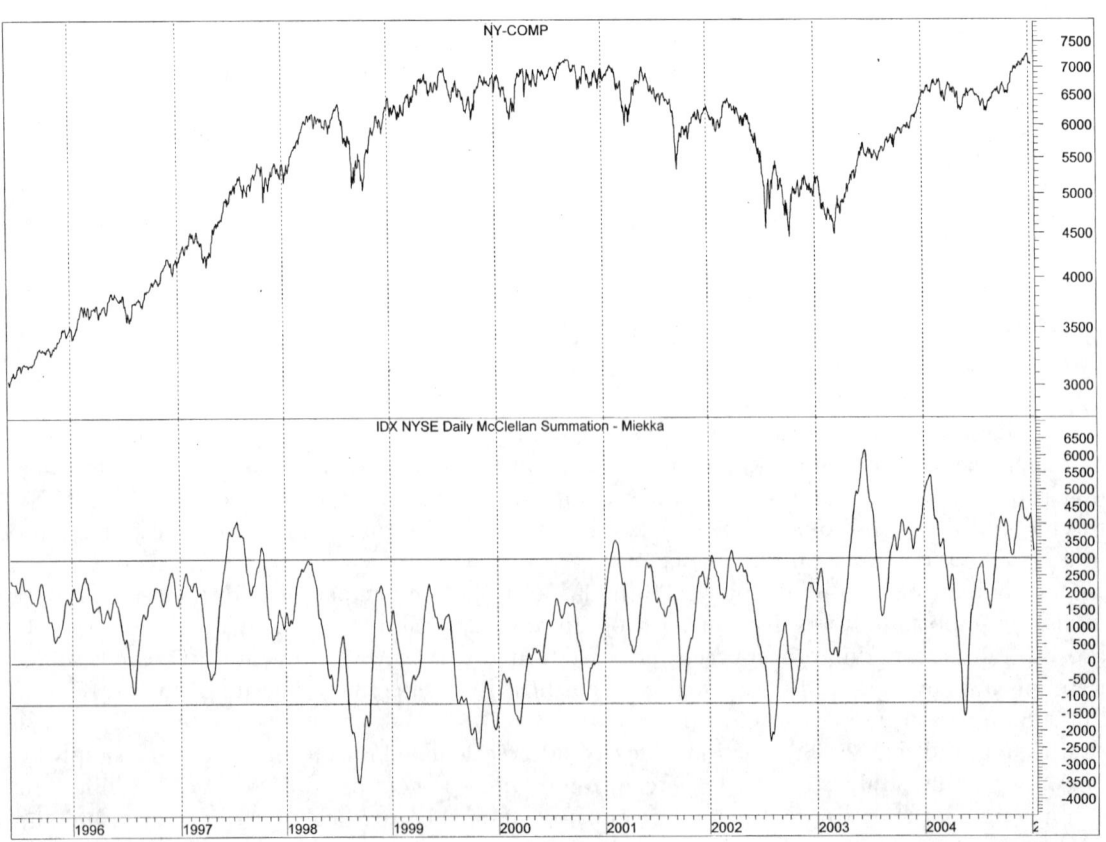

Advance Decline Difference Indicators

advance decline information on the New York exchange. The ratio used is $(A - D) / (A + D)$. Often a factor of 1000 is used to move the numbers from out of the realm of fractions and into the more normal type of numbers. Chart 4–41 shows the McClellan Summation Index using the ratio and the Miekka formula adjustment and is the version used by Carl Swenlin the McClellans today.

Tom McClellan says that when the McClellan Summation Index drops below the zero line, it is a precursor for a bear market. At much deeper levels, the Summation Index can reveal when enough of a decline has taken place, and when traders should begin to look for a strong up move out of that deep bottom. As the market moves up out of a deeply oversold bottom, the Summation Index comes into play again when it either confirms or refutes the strength of the new up move. A move from a deeply oversold level to a very high level within a 5-month period can confirm that a new bull market has been established. Failure to achieve a high enough Summation Index reading after a bear market decline can reveal that the bears are still in control, and the price low needs to be retested or exceeded to the downside.

Chart 4–41 McClellan Summation Index—Swenlin.

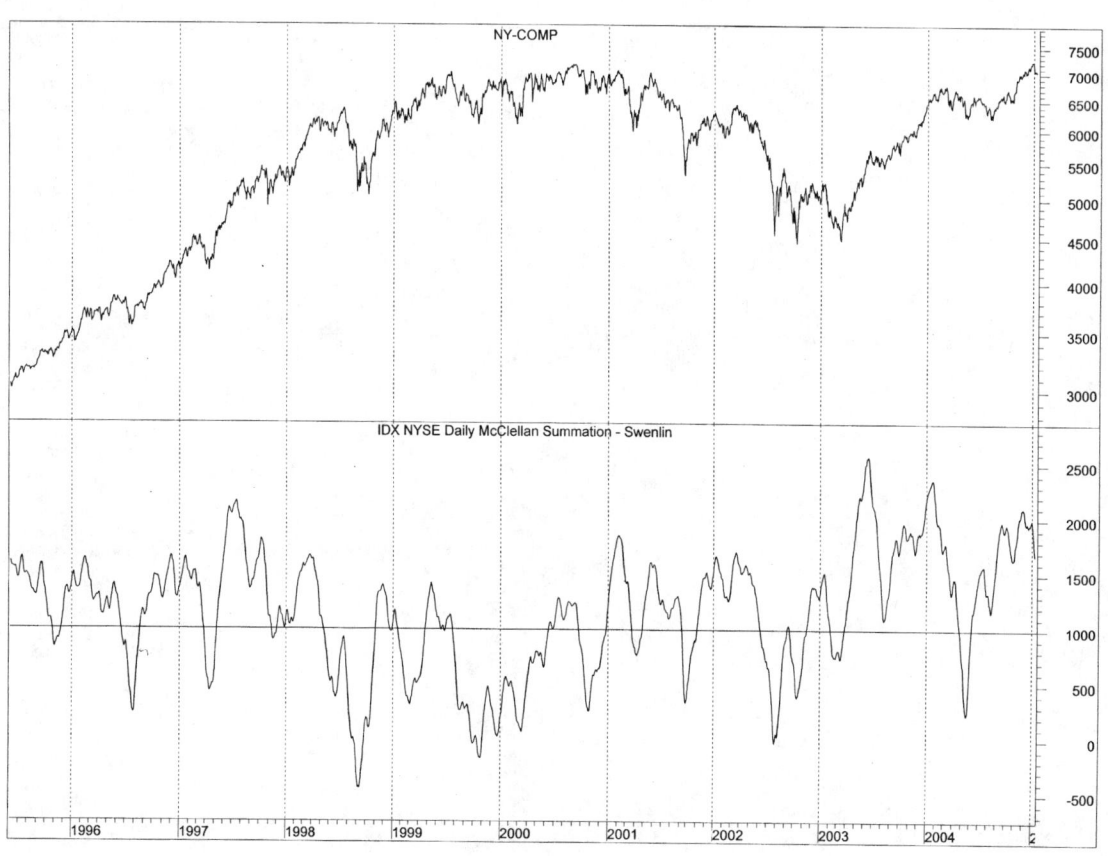

Another analysis method the McClellans used was to overlay past summation index charts based on significant market bottoms or low summation readings. This technique helps to anticipate market movements.

Martin Pring claims that using the Summation Index with a 35-day simple moving average crossover offers good results. He also states that using normal trendline analysis on the summation index can lead to changes in market direction. Chart 4–42 shows Pring's use of the McClellan Summation Index with a 35-day moving average.

Formula: This is the accumulation of the McClellan Oscillator. *SI* today = *SI* yesterday + *McO* today

References

McClellan, Sherman and Marian. *Patterns for Profit*. Lakewood, WA: McClellan Financial Publications, Inc., 1989. This book was originally published by Trade Levels in 1970.

Chart 4–42 McClellan Summation Index—Pring.

McClellan Family Interview, "It's All In the Family: Sherman, Marian, and Tom McClellan." *Stocks and Commodities*, Volume 12, June 1994, pp. 264–273.

Pring, Martin, "Internal Market Momentum." *Stocks and Commodities*, Volume 11, July 1993, pp. 298–305.

Miekka, James, *The Sudbury Bull and Bear Report*, St. Petersburg, FL.

Merriman Breadth Model

Author/Creator: Paul Merriman
Data components required: Advances (A), Declines (D), Market Index (MKT)

Description

This indicator uses the advance decline line and the New York Composite Index. It utilizes a relationship between the two in a manner not as complex as the advance decline divergence oscillator, but one that is effective.

Interpretation

A buy signal is given when the advance decline line is 2 percent or more above its 150-day moving average and when the index is 2 percent or more above its 150-day moving average. A sell signal is given when the advance decline line is 2 percent or more below its 150-day moving average or the index is 2 percent or more below its 150-day moving average. In Chart 4–43, a buy signal is when the indicator is at +1 and a sell signal is when it is at −1. Multiple signals should be ignored.

Author Comments

This is a simple but quite good concept. It offers double confirmation in order to get into the market where only one of the two components can get you out. I'm not sure how he measures the percentages because the numerical values of the advance decline line can get quite large, depending on where the calculation was started. However, if he is looking at the percentage relative to a moving average of the same values, this would self-adjust over time.

References

Merriman, Paul, www.fundadvice.com/modelsexplained.html.

Swenlin IT Breadth Momentum Oscillator

Also known as: ITBM
Author/Creator: Carl Swenlin
Data components required: Advances (A), Declines (D).

Chart 4-43 Merriman NYSE Breadth Model.

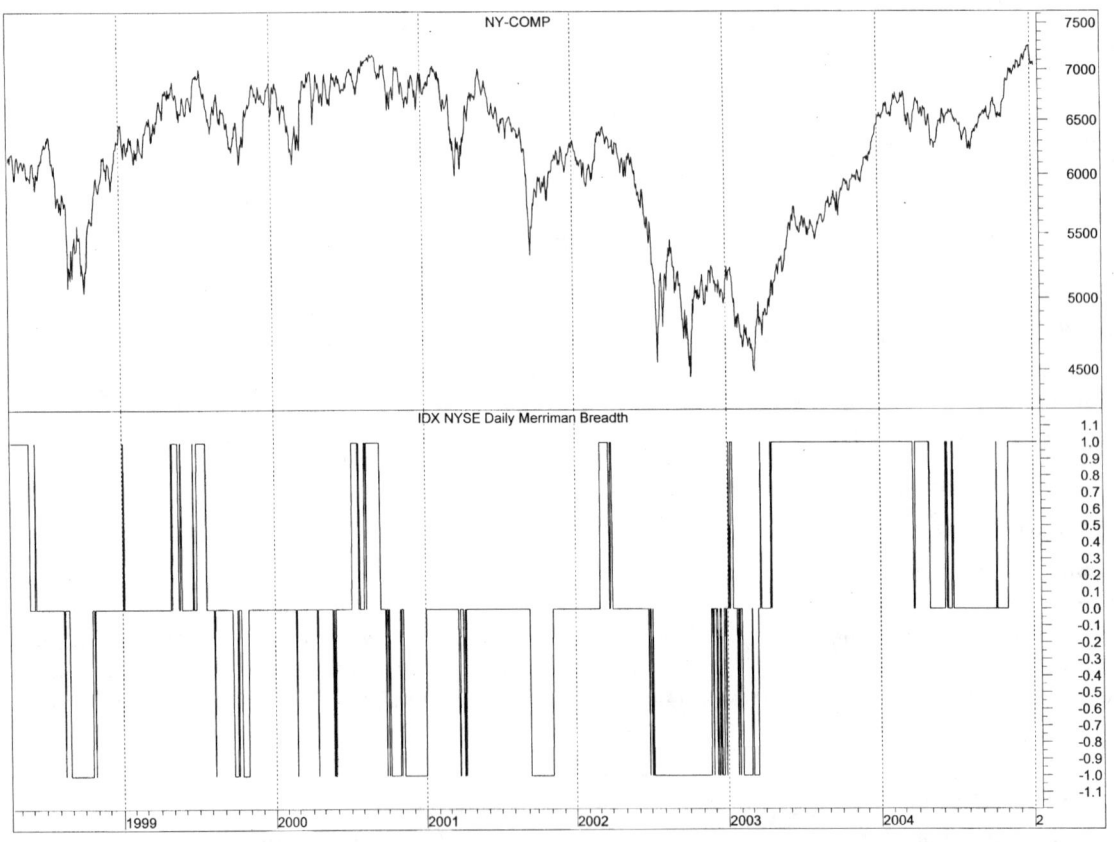

Description

The Intermediate Term Breadth Momentum Oscillator is a barometer of breadth. To calculate the ITBM, add the daily McClellan Oscillator (ratio adjusted) to the daily 39-day exponential average, then calculate a 20-day exponential average of the result.

Interpretation

Carl offers this short bit of advice on his indicator: It is better if this indicator is above the zero line and rising. Below the zero line and falling is the worst scenario. Rising is better than falling, even if below the zero line. Above the zero line and rising is best. The absolute value indicates how overbought/oversold the market is. Direction is most important because it indicates whether the market is getting stronger (rising) or weaker (falling). The best condition is for the ITBM to be rising above its 10-EMA (exponential moving average), and the worst is falling below its 10-EMA.

Chart 4-44 Swenlin IT Breadth Momentum Oscillator.

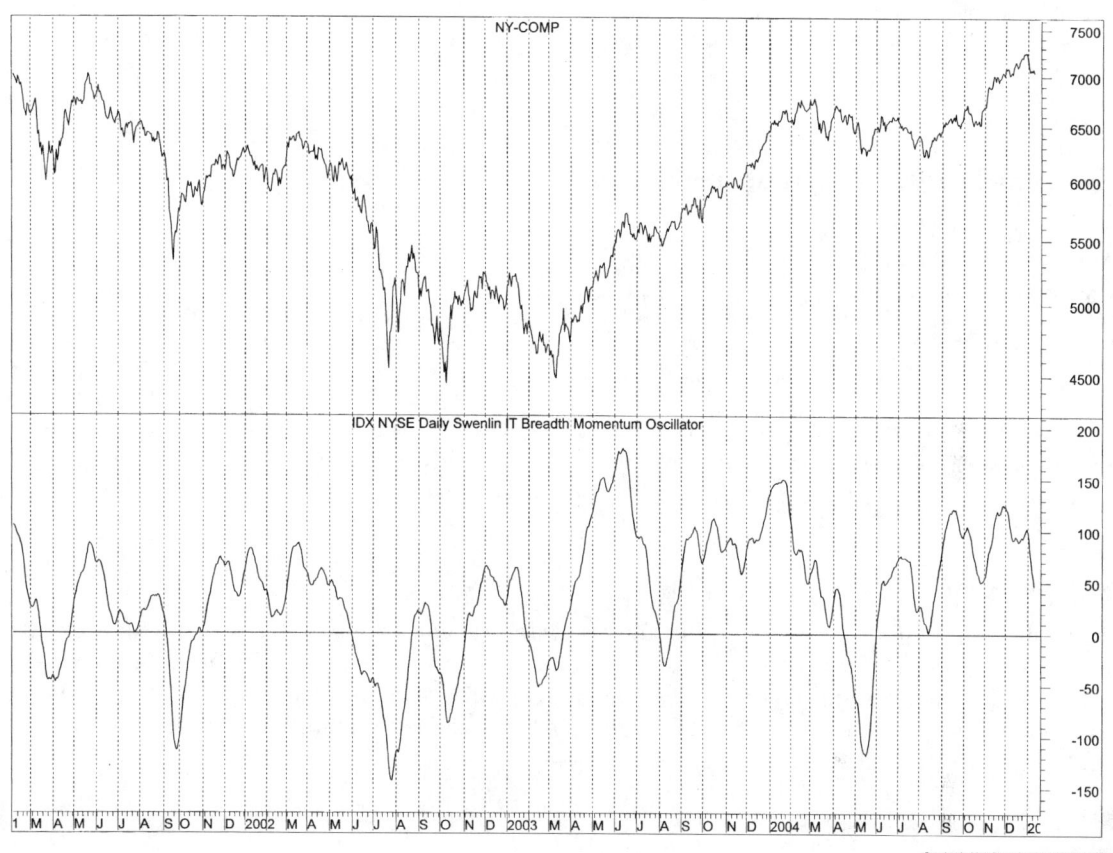

It is extremely negative if the ITBM tops below its 10-EMA and below the zero line. Chart 4-44 shows the Swenlin IT Breadth Momentum Oscillator.

Author Comments

Carl Swenlin's Web site at www.decisionpoint.com is something technical analysts should not miss. Carl has created a number of breadth-based indicators over the years. Carl uses the difference of advances and declines divided by the sum of them for his ratio-adjusted version of the McClellan formula. He wanted to develop this indicator so that it would incorporate both the McClellan Oscillator and its components. Carl's version certainly lets you know when to take negative readings seriously.

> Formula: To calculate the ITBM add the daily McClellan Oscillator (Ratio-Adjusted) to the daily 10 percent exponential average (Ratio-Adjusted), then calculate a 20-day exponential average (0.10 exponent) of the result.

References

Swenlin, Carl, www.decisionpoint.com.

McClellan, Sherman and Marian. *Patterns for Profit.* Lakewood, WA: McClellan Financial Publications, Inc., 1976.

Swenlin Trading Oscillator—Breadth

Also known as: STO-B
Author/Creator: Carl Swenlin
Data components required: Advances (A), Declines (D)

Description

The Swenlin Trading Oscillator—Breadth was designed for short-term trading. It is a 5-day simple moving average of a 4-day exponential average of the daily advances minus declines divided by the total daily advances and declines times 1000. This is the ratio that is common in Swenlin's work.

Interpretation

The double smoothing of the short-term data results in a reliable oscillator that persists in one direction, usually tops near short-term market tops, and bottoms near short-term market bottoms. As with most indicators, the primary trend of the market will determine how you will use the indicator. In a bull market, the tops will not be very reliable. In a bear market, the bottoms will not be very reliable. The indicator is shown in Chart 4–45.

Author Comments

Carl Swenlin has created a good trading vehicle with his Swenlin Trading Oscillator.

> Formula: The STO is a 5-day simple moving average of a 4-day exponential moving average of the daily advances minus declines divided by the total daily advances and declines times 1000. $(A - D)/(A + D)*1000$. First you must calculate the average value of $(A - D)/(A + D)*1000$ for the last 4 days before you can begin the exponential weighting. Next you can begin calculating the exponential average. The following is a key for the symbols in the formula. *pdEMA* = Prior Day's Average (Begin with simple *MA*, thereafter *pdEMA* is an exponential average.) $(A - D)/(A + D)*1000$ = Current day's advances minus declines divided by the total advances and declines times 1000. The formula for the *EMA* is: $((A - D)/(A + D)*1000)*0.5) + pdEMA$ All that remains is simple moving average of the *EMA*.

References

Swenlin, Carl, www.decisionpoint.com.

Advance Decline Difference Indicators

Chart 4-45 Swenlin Trading Oscillator—Breadth.

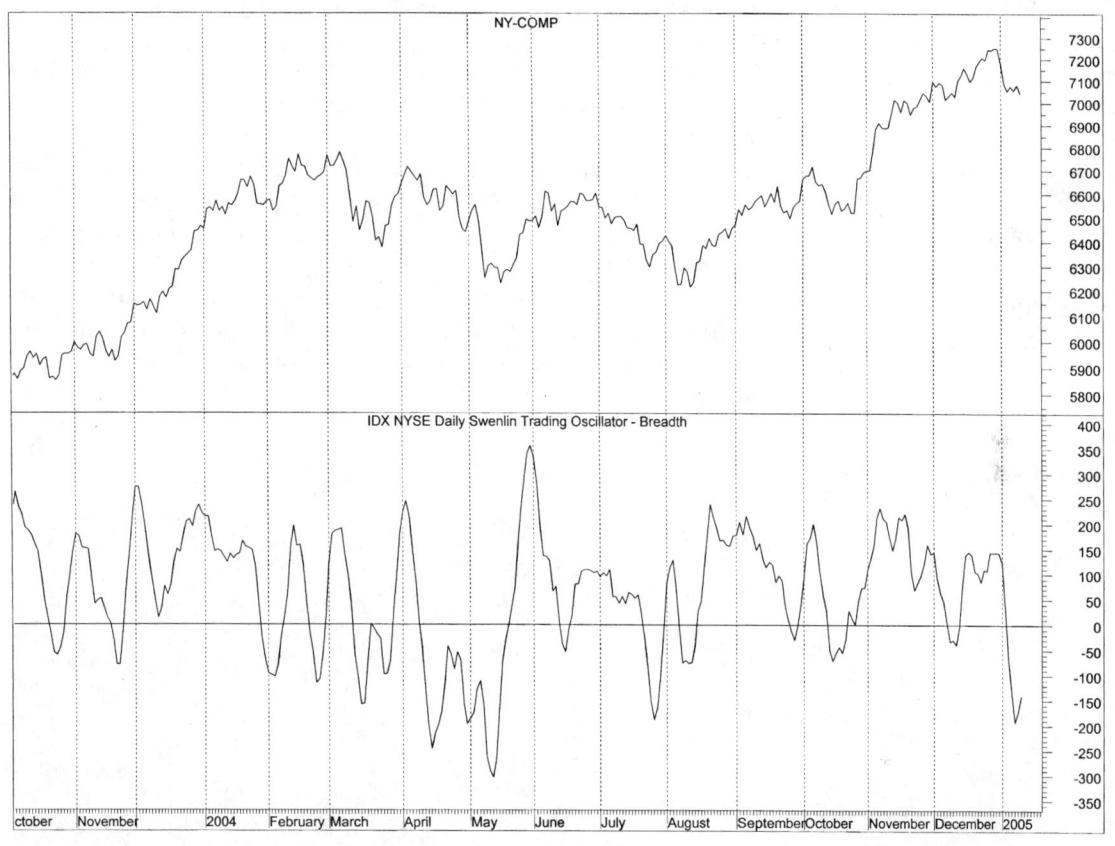

Zahorchak Method

Author/Creator: Michael G. Zahorchak
Data components required: Advances (A), Declines (D), Market Index (MKT).

Description

In his 1977 book, *The Art of Low Risk Investing*, Michael Zahorchak lays out a complete investing and analysis plan using moving averages on the New York Composite Index and the advance decline line. Zahorchak, who was assistant vice-president of the American Stock Exchange, developed this methodology using only weekly data. Basically you must maintain a 5-, 15-, and 40-week moving average on the advance decline line, the New York composite index (Zahorchak used the Dow Industrial Average), and any stocks that you wish to analyze and invest in.

Interpretation

Zahorchak defines how to move from a down trend to an up trend and also talks about periods of indecision. Basically, when the advance decline line and the market average are both above their 40-week (200-day) moving averages, the market is in an up trend. Identification of a market top is when a combination of the 5- and 15-period averages begin to break down. Similarly, a bottom occurs when they start to rise. Chart 4–46 below was developed using daily data, substituting the appropriate number of days for the weeks used by Zahorchak (15 weeks = 75 days). Daily data has more oscillations, but the method works just the same.

The indicator in Chart 4–46 is scaled from −10 to +10. As various components of this method take effect, the indicator rises or falls based on the sum of all of its components. The most bullish is +10 and the most bearish is −10. Using the zero line crossing for signals seems to work well. One could also develop more extravagant signals using various levels to enhance the timing. Always keep in mind that this was a long-term approach to identifying trends and is not for trading.

Chart 4–46 *Zahorchak Method—Daily.*

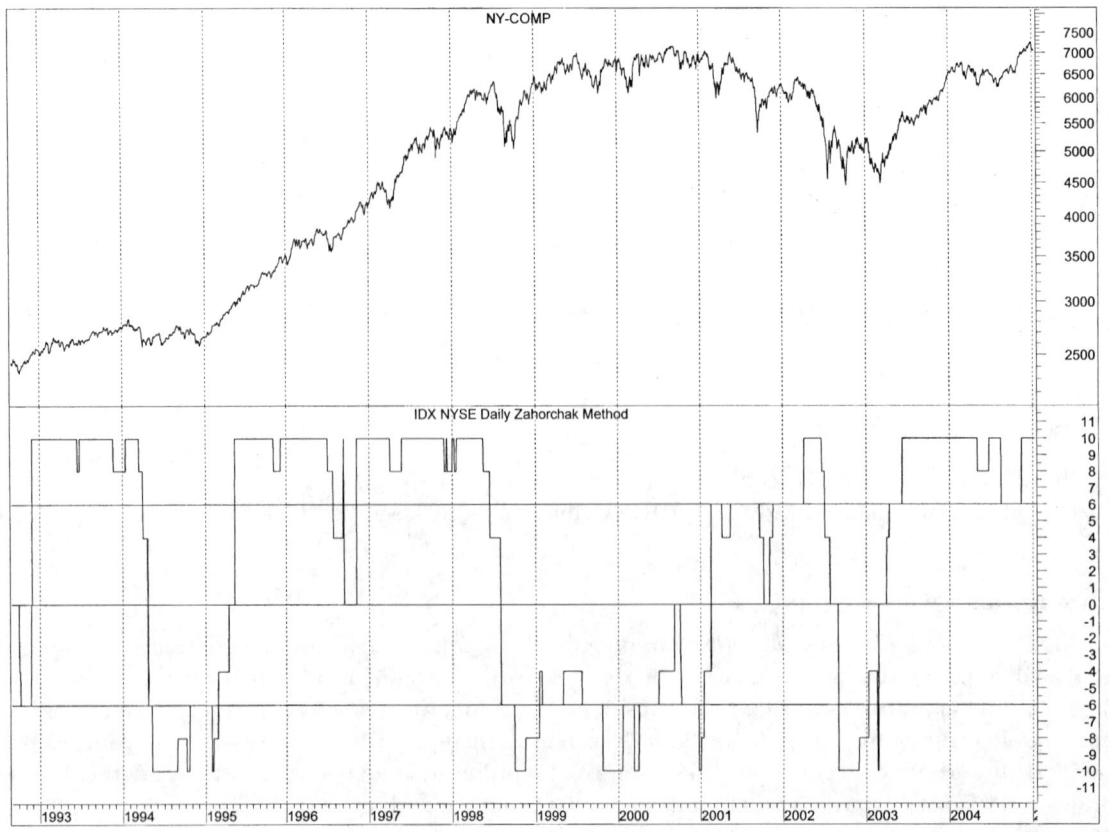

Advance Decline Difference Indicators

Chart 4-47 Zahorchak Method—Weekly.

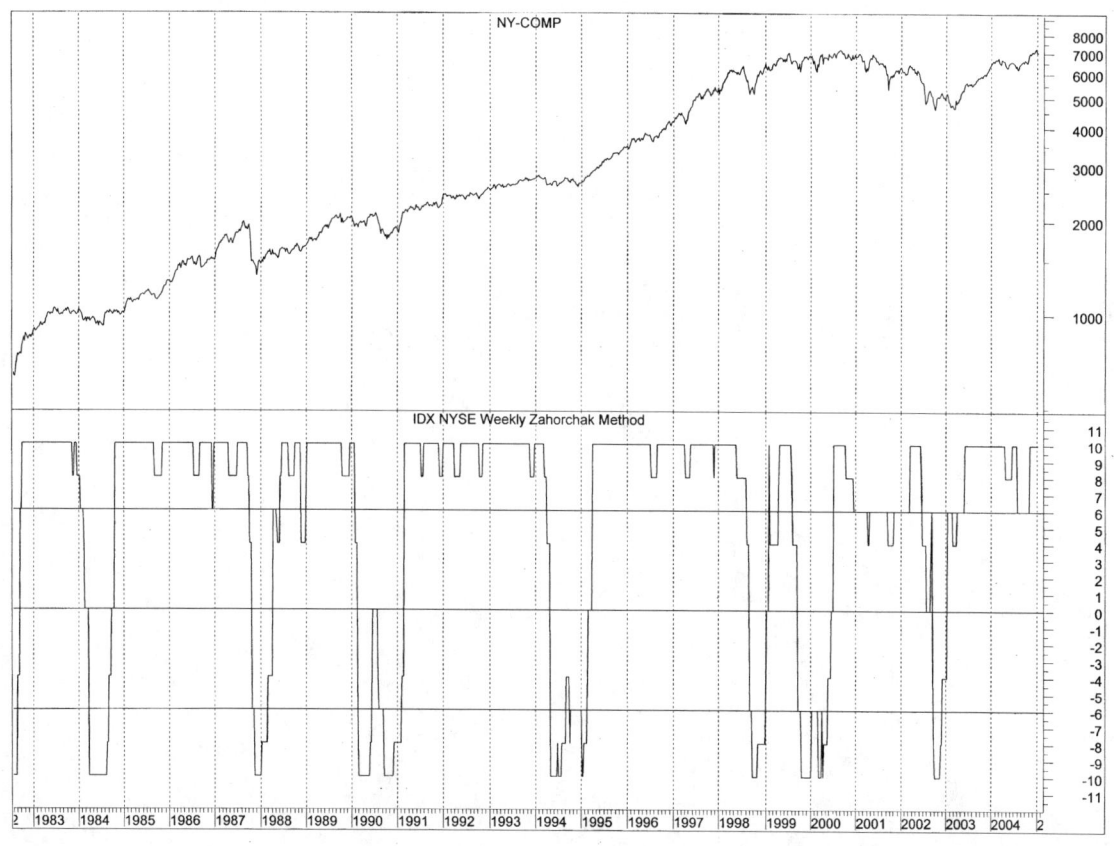

Author Comments

This was one of the first books that cemented my thinking into taking a technical approach to investing and market analysis. It is a shame the book is out of print. Zahorchak covers all the basics, from emotions, to Wall Street myths, to how to control all the outside influences that can cause you to make bad decisions in the market. I would do this method injustice if I did not include the signals using weekly data. On the weekly chart (Chart 4–47), one can see that whenever the indicator is above +6, the market is rising and when below −6 it is not. Note that the indicator dropped to +4 the first week in October, 1987. This is a good methodology for keeping yourself on the right side of the market. It is not for trading.

Formula: $(A - D)$ weekly

References

Zahorchak, Michael G. *The Art of Low Risk Investing*. Van Nostrand Reinhold Company, 1977. This book is out of print and difficult to find. If you uncover one, buy it.

5
Advance Decline Ratio Indicators

Advances / Declines

The breadth indicators in this section utilize the ratio of the advancing issues and the declining issues as their primary relationship.

Advance Decline Ratio Indicators

Advance / Decline Ratio
Breadth Thrust
Breadth Thrust Continuation
Duarte Market Thrust Indicator

Eliades Sign of the Bear
Hughes Breadth Momentum Oscillator
Panic Thrust
STIX—Short Term Trading Index

Advance / Decline Ratio

Data components required: Advances (A), Declines (D)

Description

This is the ratio of advancing issues and declining issues (Advances divided by Declines).

Interpretation

Martin Zweig liked to watch this ratio over a 10-day period. He said it was very rare for the 10-day ratio to reach 2-to-1 (2.0) or more. It seems that the level of 1.8 is better with more recent data. Both levels are shown on Chart 5–1.

Author Comments

Ratios and differences account for many different variations of technical indicators. If you take the 10-day difference of price and plot it next to the 10-day ratio of price, you will get a similarly shaped line, only the values are different. Another interesting discovery was that the ratio of advances and declines was called the overbought oversold index by Norman Fosback (Steve Achelis used the difference of advances and declines for the overbought oversold index). Fosback says that the 10-day

Chart 5-1 Advance Decline Ratio—1965–2004.

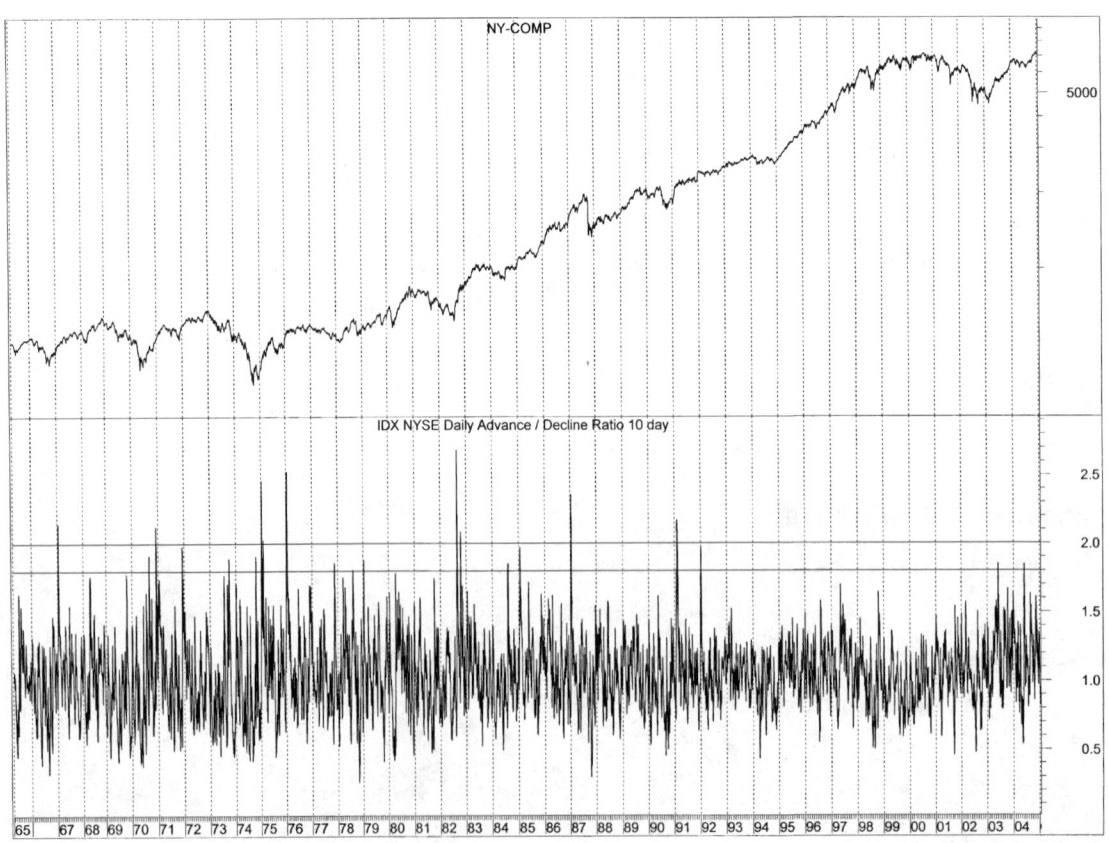

average of the ratio is good for determining overbought and oversold areas in the market. He says that the market is oversold when the advances are at least 25 percent fewer than the declines (0.75 on Chart 5–2). The market is overbought when the ratio shows that the number of advances is at least 25 percent more than the declines (1.25 on Chart 5–2). Fosback states that this indicator has not tested well and is probably overrated. I added a line at 1.70, which means advances outnumber declines by about 58 percent. Chart 5–2 shows that the Advance Decline Ratio seems to better reflect overbought with today's breadth numbers.

$$\text{Formula: } (A \ / \ D)$$

References

Fosback, Norman G. *Stock Market Logic*, Fort Lauderdale, FL: The Institute for Economic Research, Inc., 1976.

Chart 5–2 Advance Decline Ratio—1996–2004.

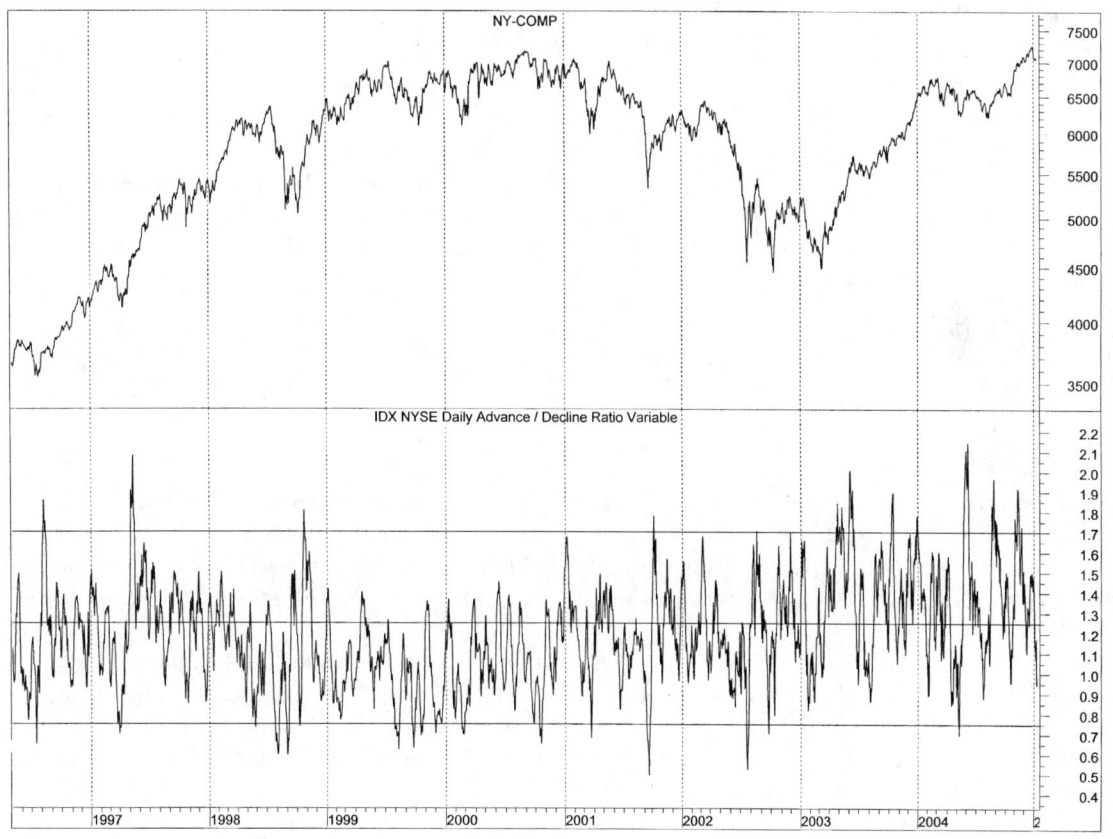

Breadth Thrust

Author/Creator: Martin Zweig
Data components required: Advances (A), Declines (D)

Description

Breadth Thrust is a 10-day exponential average of the advances divided by the sum of the advances plus the declines. A Breadth Thrust signal occurs when this indicator goes from under 0.40 to above 0.615 within a 10-day time period or less.

Interpretation

Between 1945 and 2000 there were 14 thrusts. Martin Zweig says that strength does indeed tend to lead to greater strength. He goes on to say that when people miss the first move of an explosive rally by waiting for a correction, they often miss most of the action. Chart 5–3 shows the Breadth Thrust signals (tall vertical lines that begin at zero) since 1965.

Author Comments

I wish I had a dime for every time I have seen this indicator misquoted or used incorrectly. The component that is usually overlooked is that it must go from oversold to overbought within 10 days. Since 1965 there have been only five Breadth Thrust signals as shown in Chart 5–3. Here are the dates:

October 14, 1974
January 8, 1975
August 20, 1982
August 6, 1984
May 25, 2004

Those intimately familiar with the market over the last 30 years will recognize the first two dates as the first bottom of the giant 1973–74 bear market, the 1982 date as within a week of the beginning of the biggest bull market in history, and the 1984 date as one that coincides with a good market bottom. The May, 2004, breadth thrust was about 2–3 months before the market began to rise significantly.

Robert Colby tested this indicator with 62 years of data and found that using 0.659 for a buy signal and dropping below 0.366 for a sell signal worked well. However, he used a simple moving average instead of an exponential one, and it appears he did not use the 10 periods for the signal to occur. However, that does not detract from the importance of his results and further offers another use of the breadth thrust concept.

Advance Decline Ratio Indicators

Chart 5-3 Breadth Thrust.

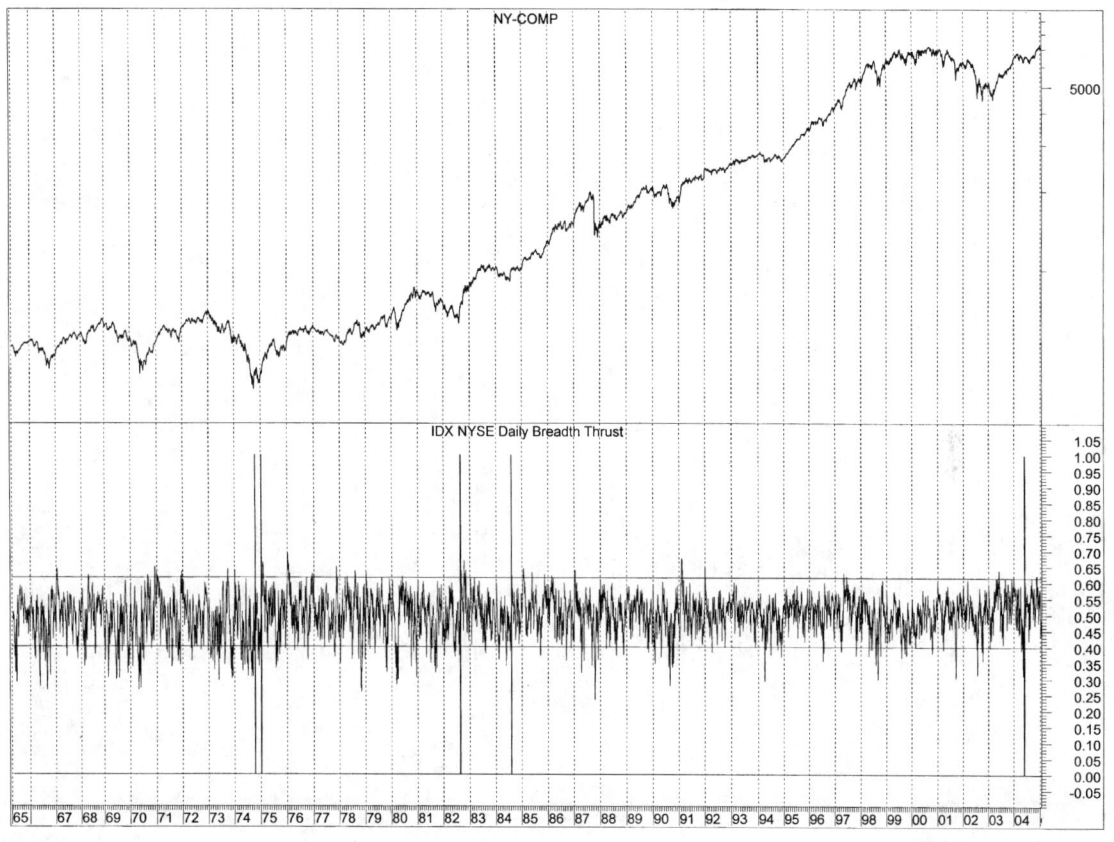

As I always do, I ask what I can do to this indicator to improve it. I can increase the days to give a signal, say to 15 days. This would give the indicator more time to reach its goal of going above 0.615. I can change the smoothing from 10 to 8 (to make it faster), and even change the type of smoothing from exponential to arithmetic (to make it slower). All of these may or may not yield better results. The problem here is that one is deviating from the initial concept and trying to build a better mousetrap. Martin Zweig's concept was that the market sometimes launches like a rocket, and he attempted to define that with his Breadth Thrust. You can see in Charts 5–4 and 5–6 that it didn't change much. Chart 5–4 uses an arithmetic smoothing instead of an exponential one, and Chart 5–5 uses an 8-day period to allow a signal to generate.

Formula: $(A / A + D)$

Chart 5-4 Breadth Thrust with Simple 10-Day Smooth.

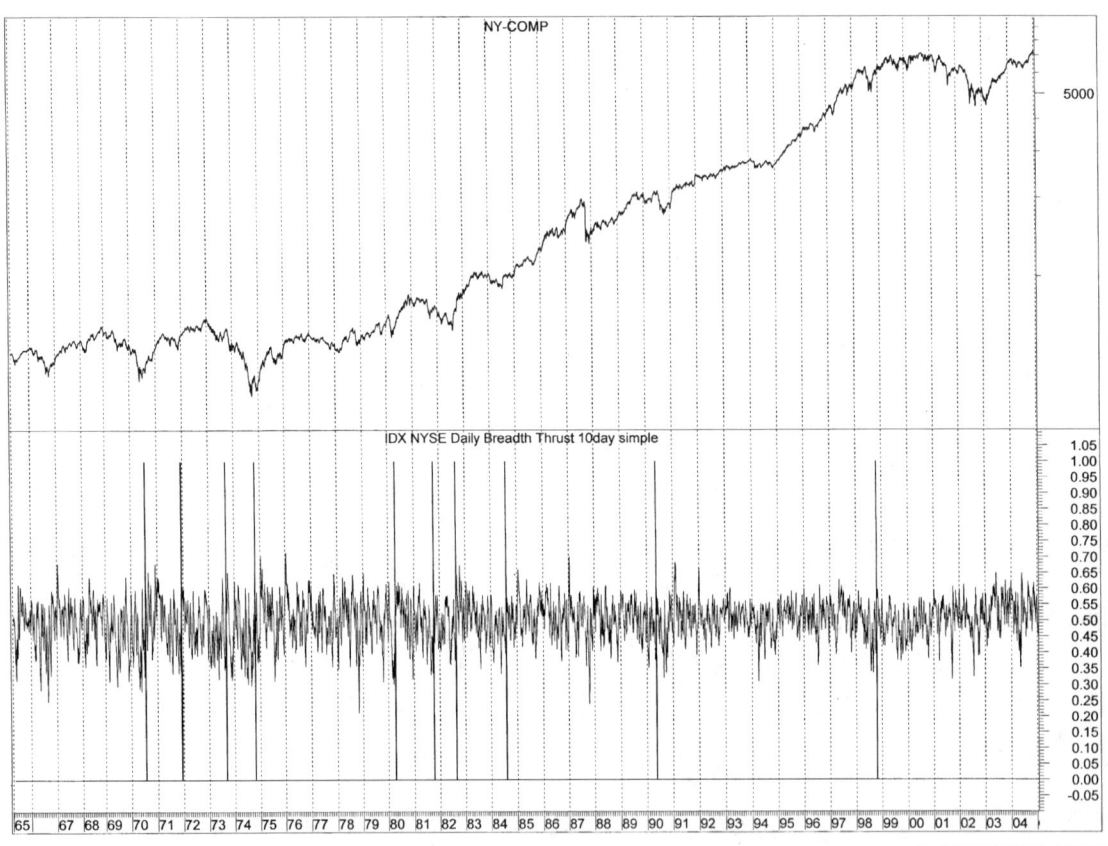

References

Achelis, Steven B. *Technical Analysis from A to Z.* New York: McGraw-Hill, 1995.
Colby, Robert W. *The Encyclopedia of Technical Market Indicators.* New York: McGraw-Hill, 2003.

Breadth Thrust Continuation

Author/Creator: Gerald Appel
Data components required: Advances (A), Declines (D)

Chart 5-5   Breadth Thrust with Exponential 8-Day Smooth.

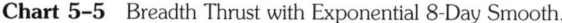

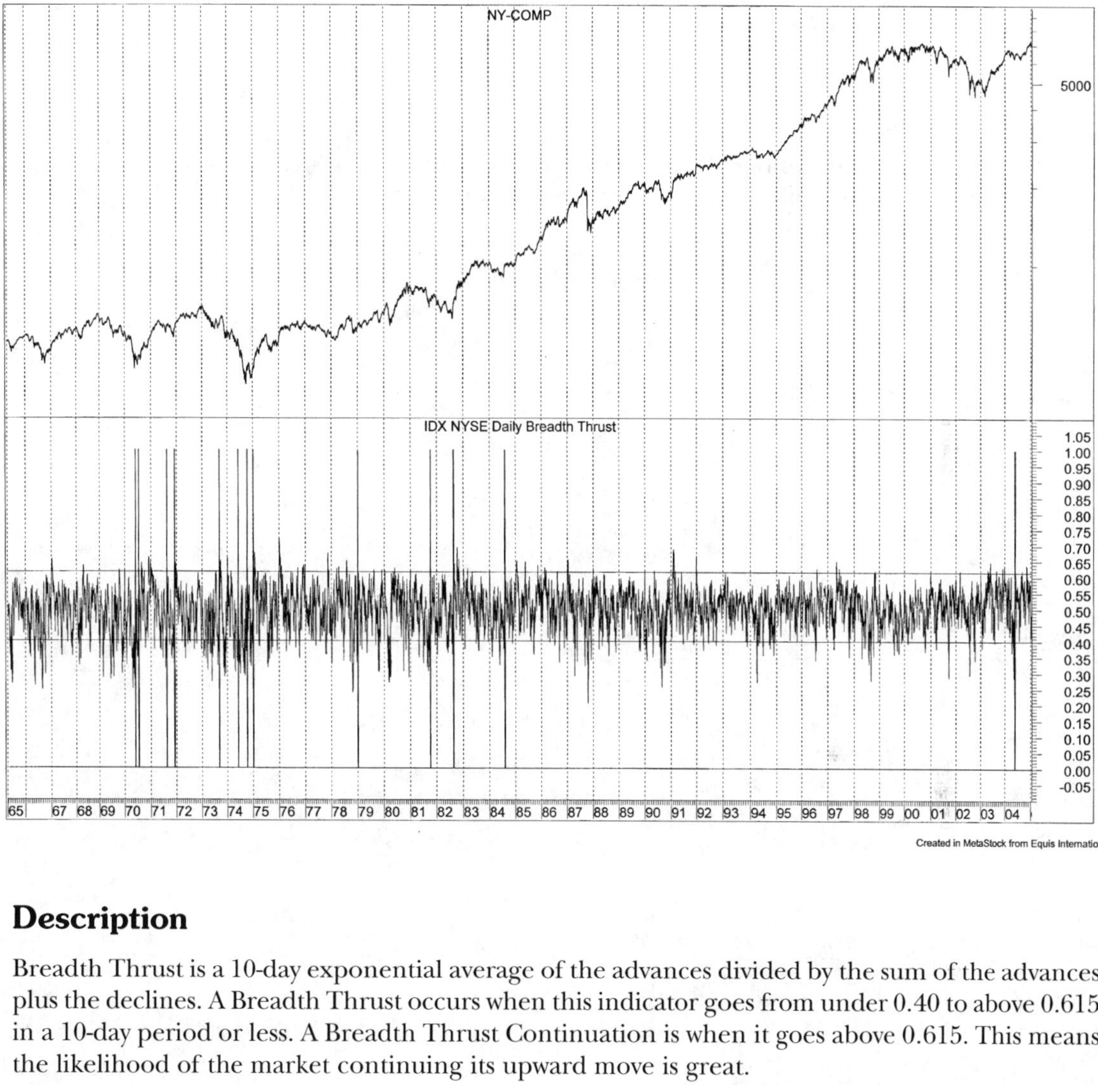

Description

Breadth Thrust is a 10-day exponential average of the advances divided by the sum of the advances plus the declines. A Breadth Thrust occurs when this indicator goes from under 0.40 to above 0.615 in a 10-day period or less. A Breadth Thrust Continuation is when it goes above 0.615. This means the likelihood of the market continuing its upward move is great.

Interpretation

A Breadth Thrust Continuation signal is given whenever it goes above 0.615 without the requirement for it to come from below 0.40 in 10 days. That continuation signal is good until it then drops below 0.50. On Chart 5-6, the upward spikes denote the Breadth Thrust Continuation signals, with the sell signals being the downward spikes. Subsequent sell spikes should be ignored. They only come into play after an upward buy spike.

Author Comments

Tom McClellan added an additional rule stating that the continuation signal expires after 50 days, but can restart that timing (50 days) with any subsequent move above 0.615. Since 1965 there have been 31 Breadth Thrust Continuation signals.

$$\text{Formula: } (A / A + D)$$

Chart 5-6 Breadth Thrust Continuation.

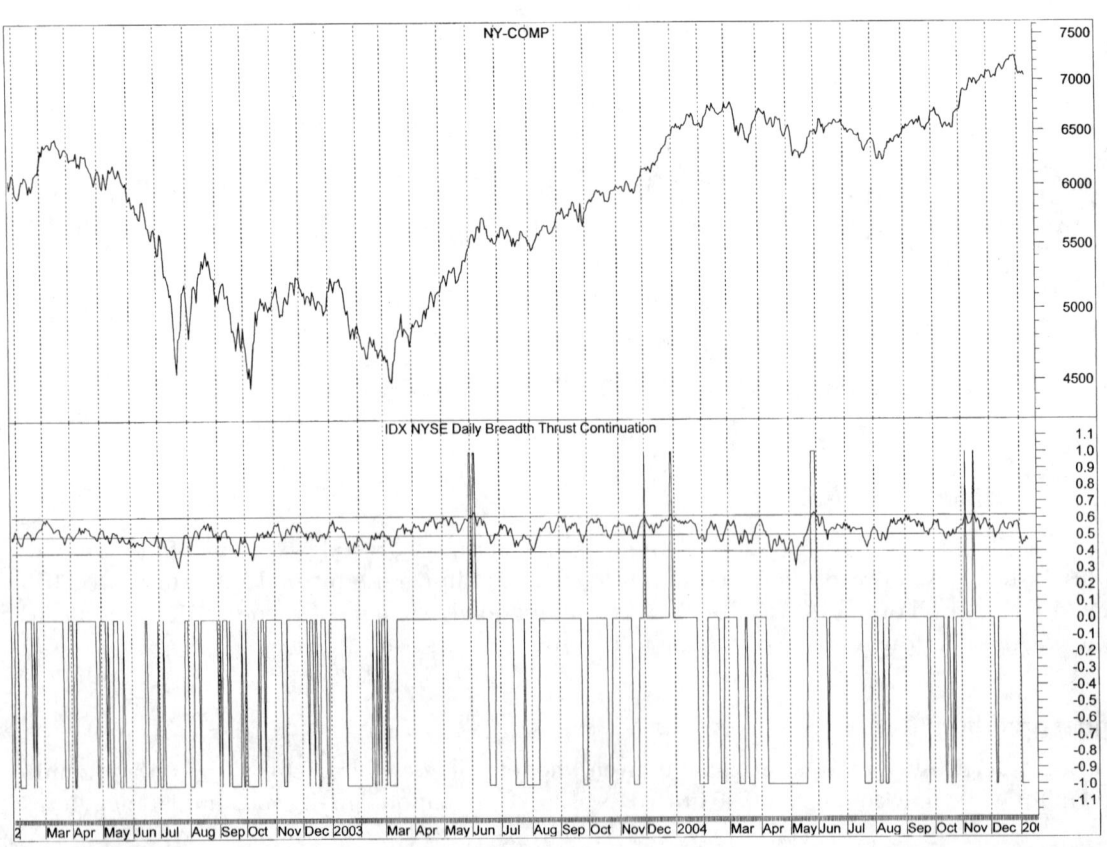

References

McClellan, Tom, "The McClellan Market Report," November 19, 2004.
Achelis, Steven B. *Technical Analysis from A to Z*. New York: McGraw-Hill, 1995.
Colby, Robert W. *The Encyclopedia of Technical Market Indicators*. New York : McGraw-Hill, 2003.

Duarte Market Thrust Indicator

Also Known As: Bi-weekly Market Thrust Indicator (BMTI)
Author/Creator: Dr. Joe Duarte
Data components required: Weekly Data, Advances (A), Declines (D).

Description

The Bi-weekly Market Thrust Indicator (BMTI) is a measure of market momentum and is based on the often-overlooked weekly variation of the advance decline line. It is a predictor of stock prices over the 6 months after a signal occurs. Based on Martin Zweig's Ten Day Advance Decline Ratio, BMTI uses weekly data, as opposed to Zweig's daily data. The difference is that Zweig captured the market's advance decline ratio for 10 straight days, looking for a two to one ratio of advancing over declining stocks on a rolling basis, while BMTI focuses on weekly data. To calculate BMTI, take the weekly advance-decline data and add the advances and the declines for two weeks.

Interpretation

Using this weekly indicator, signals are generated for buying only whenever the ratio is equal to two or greater. If you bought a market average on one of these signals and held for at least 6 months, your return would be good. Chart 5–7 shows the Duarte Market Thrust Indicator.

Author Comments

One of the important concepts that Dr. Duarte identified with this indicator is what he calls a super cluster. This is when the BMTI gives several consecutive signals. It means that upside momentum is huge and the market can stay bullish for up to a year. The super clusters in Chart 5–7 are denoted by the wider spikes. The wider the spike on the chart, the more consecutive signals, and the better the indication.

$$\text{Formula: } (A / D) \text{ (weekly values)}$$

References

Duarte, Joe, www.joe-duarte.com.
Zweig, Martin E. *Winning on Wall Street*. New York: Warner Books, 1986.

Chart 5-7 Duarte Market Thrust—Weekly.

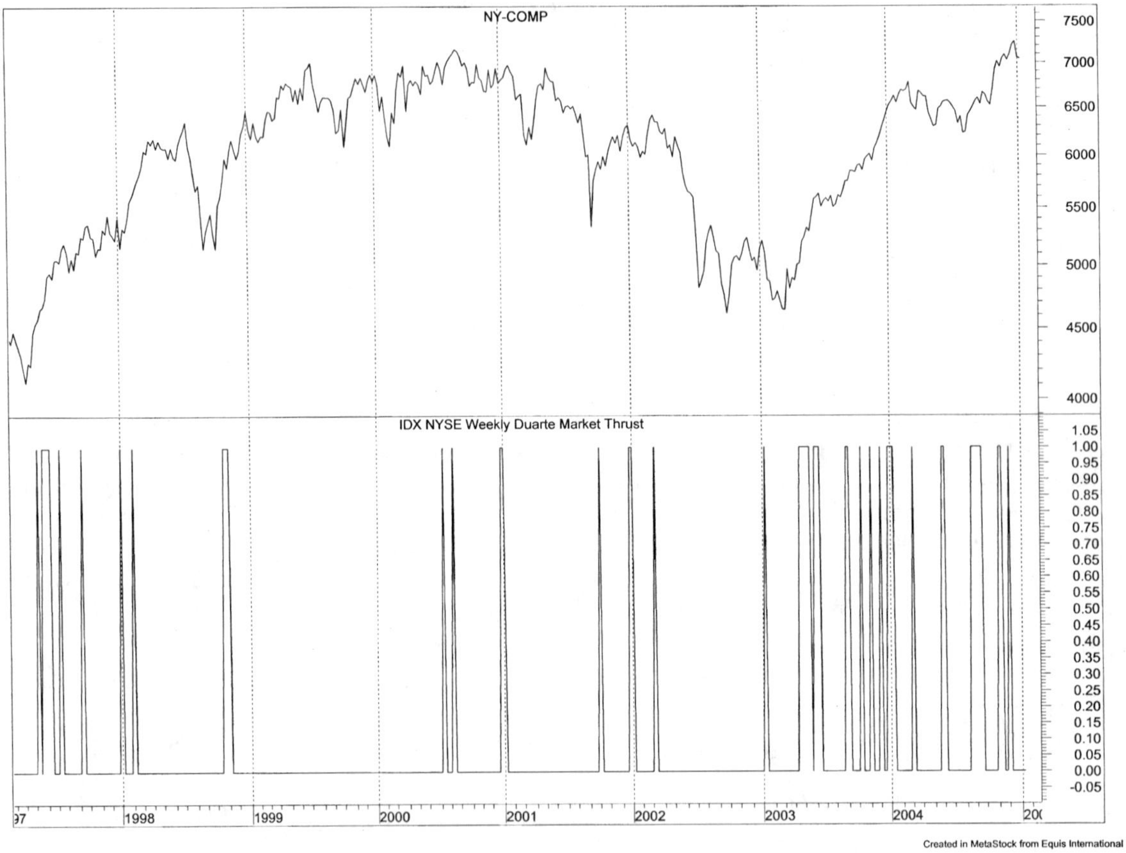

Eliades Sign of the Bear

Author/Creator: Peter Eliades
Data components required: Advances (*A*), Declines (*D*).

Description

Peter Eliades first wrote about this in 1992 after noting a lack of volatility in the advance decline numbers. After apparently much research, back to 1940, he came up with three rules required to identify the "sign of the bear."

A. There must be a streak of 21–27 consecutive days (trading) where the daily advance/decline ratio remains above 0.65 and below 1.95.

Advance Decline Ratio Indicators

B. That streak mentioned above must end with a downside break, which means the advance/decline ratio is less than 0.65.
C. The downside break must be confirmed by either a 2-day average advance/decline ratio or a 3-day average advance/decline ratio following the end of the streak being below 0.75.

Interpretation

This is not an indicator that gives many signals. In the paper that Eliades has on his Web site, www.stockmarketcycles.com, there have only been seven "sign of the bear" signals since the late 1920s. Yes, that is right, over the last 70+ years. April, 1998 and September, 2000 were the last two signals. Chart 5–8 shows all the signals prior to implementing the third parameter above. The third

Chart 5–8 Eliades Sign of the Bear.

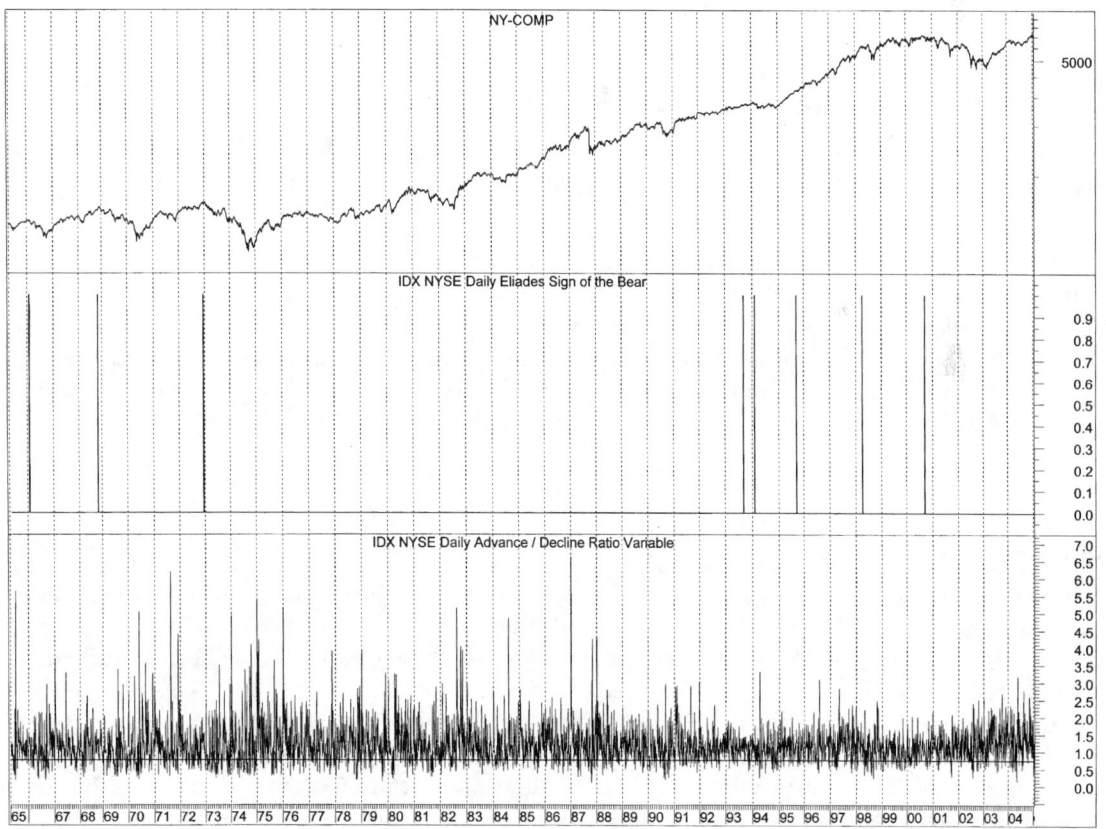

parameter is shown at the bottom of the chart and can be used for verification. When you consider that parameter, the early signals in the 1990s will go away, leaving only the 1998 and 2000 signals.

Author Comments

The first rule (A) addresses the lack of volatility that he first noticed when deriving this indicator. Originally it was just 21 days. The second rule (B) requires for a day to have at least 1.5 times more declines than advances. The third rule (C) is a way to give the breakout some time for confirmation. This is an indicator that one needs to be aware of. Visit his Web site and read the paper he wrote on "the sign of the bear."

References

Eliades, Peter, *www.StockMarketCycles.com,*

Hughes Breadth Momentum Oscillator

Author/Creator: James F. Hughes
Data components required: Advances (*A*), Declines (*D*), Unchanged (*U*).

Description

This ratio indicator uses all the breadth movement (advances, declines, unchanged) issues in its formula. It is the difference of advances and declines as the numerator and the sum of the advances, declines, and unchanged as the denominator. This sum is also the total issues. Hughes defined selling climaxes as when the declines were over 70 percent of total issues while advances were less than 15 percent of total issues.

Interpretation

This is an oscillator that utilizes all components of issue-oriented breadth. Putting overbought and oversold zones on the chart will make this a good short-term oscillator. The shorter the term that you want to work with, the shorter the smoothing you should use. Chart 5–9 uses 21 days and would be good for intermediate-term analysis.

Hughes Breadth Momentum % Oscillator was a creation of Robert Colby as an attempt to avoid using negative numbers and fractions and have it oscillate around 100. Overbought and oversold zones at 87 and 110 seem to work well. Colby's modification, while not changing the concept of the indicator, is an improvement. Chart 5–10 is that modification further smoothed by 21 days.

Advance Decline Ratio Indicators

Chart 5-9 Hughes Breadth Momentum Oscillator.

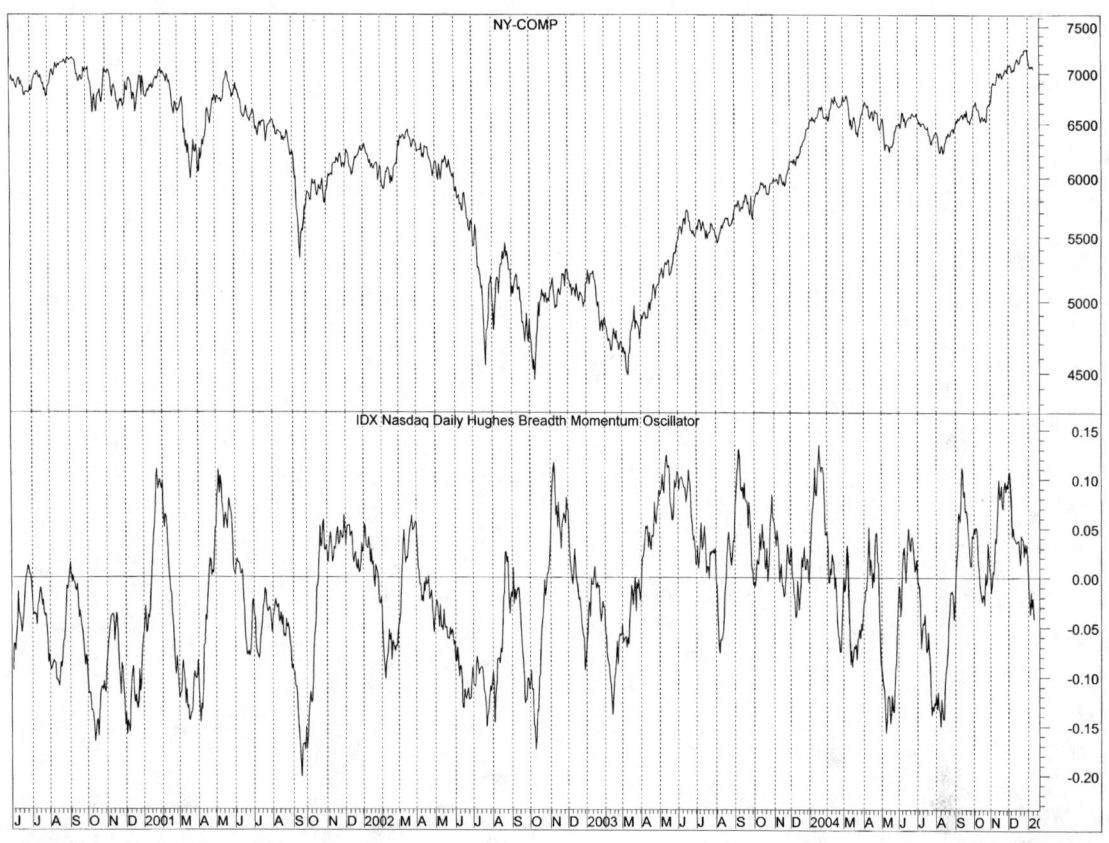

Author Comments

The sum of the advances, declines, and unchanged issues is nothing more than the total issues. This is yet another way to derive a ratio that should use the same overbought and oversold zones over time. If Total Issues traded is available, and one is entering this data manually, one could use that as the denominator instead.

Formula: $(A - D) / (A + D + U)$ or $(A - D) / TI$

References

Colby, Robert W. *The Encyclopedia of Technical Market Indicators.* New York : McGraw-Hill, 2003.
Dworkin, Fay H., "Defining Advance/Decline Issues," *Stocks and Commodities*, Volume 8, July 1990, pp. 274–278.

Chart 5-10 Hughes Breadth Momentum % Oscillator.

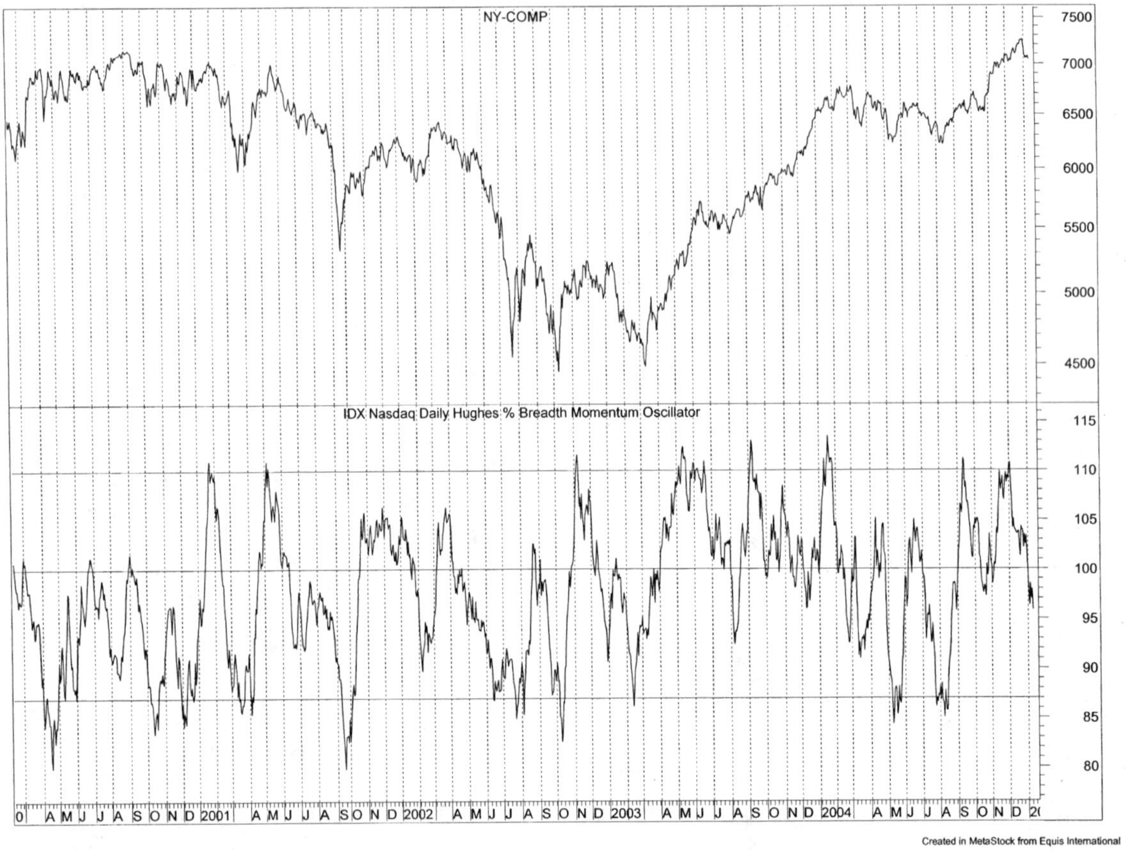

Panic Thrust

Data components required: Advances (*A*), Declines (*D*).

Description

This indicator is a method to determine overreaction to market extremes. Simple to calculate and, while not always accurate, will certainly alert you to those extremes.

Interpretation

Whenever the ratio of advances to declines is greater than 4, a buy signal is given. This means that there were more than 4 times as many advancing issues as there were declining issues. Chart 5-11 shows all instances where the advances outnumbered the declines by 4 to 1.

Advance Decline Ratio Indicators

Chart 5-11 Panic Thrust.

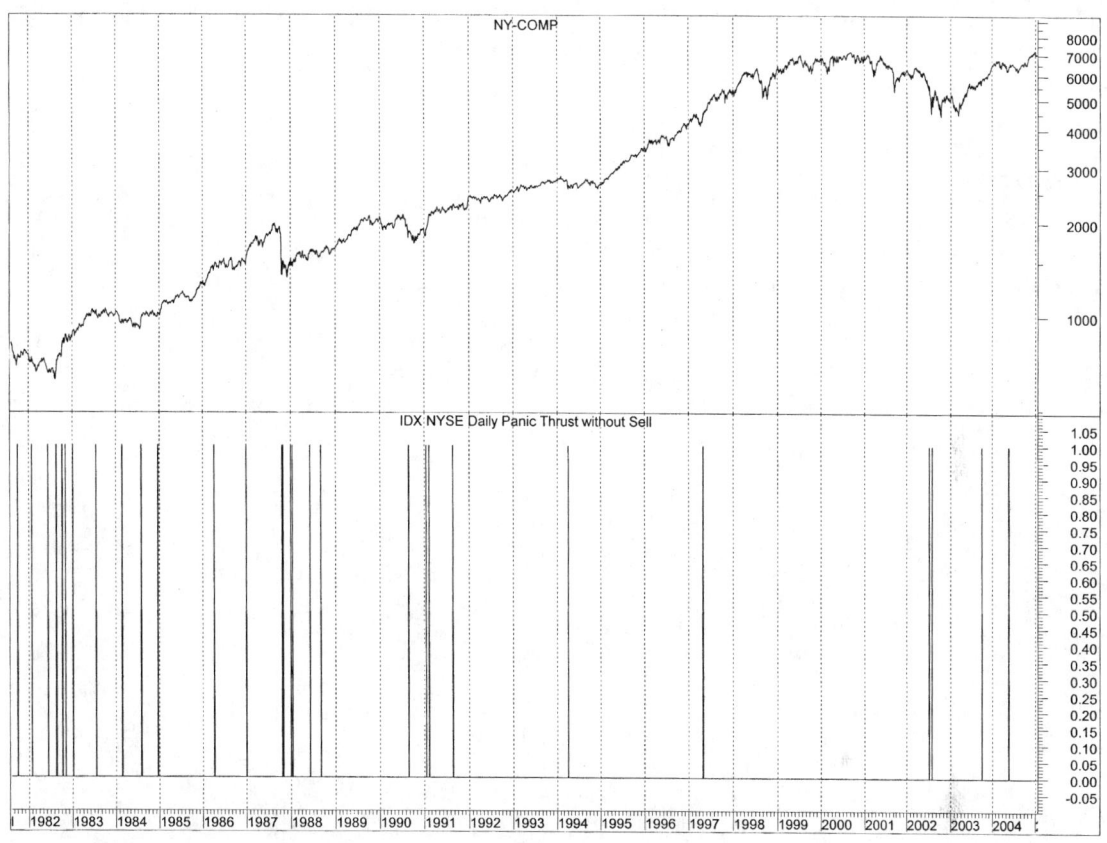

Author Comments

There is no doubt that when markets go to extremes, people react differently. In this case, the attempt to pick a bottom based on an extremely oversold condition is identified. This indicator was created after experimenting with a number of different ratios. Four to one is reliable.

$$\text{Formula: } (A / D) > 4$$

STIX

Author/Creator: The Polymetric Report
Data components required: Advances (A), Declines (D).

Description

STIX is an acronym for Short Term Trading Index. It is the advances divided by the sum of the advances and declines. Then you exponentially smooth it with a 21-day moving average to get STIX.

Interpretation

Low STIX readings are bearish and high readings are bullish. STIX has a normal range in the 42 percent and 58 percent range. Somewhat overbought is in the range of 56 percent to 58 percent and oversold in the range of 42 percent and 44 percent. Chart 5–12 shows STIX with the above mentioned thresholds.

Chart 5-12 STIX—Short-Term Trading Index.

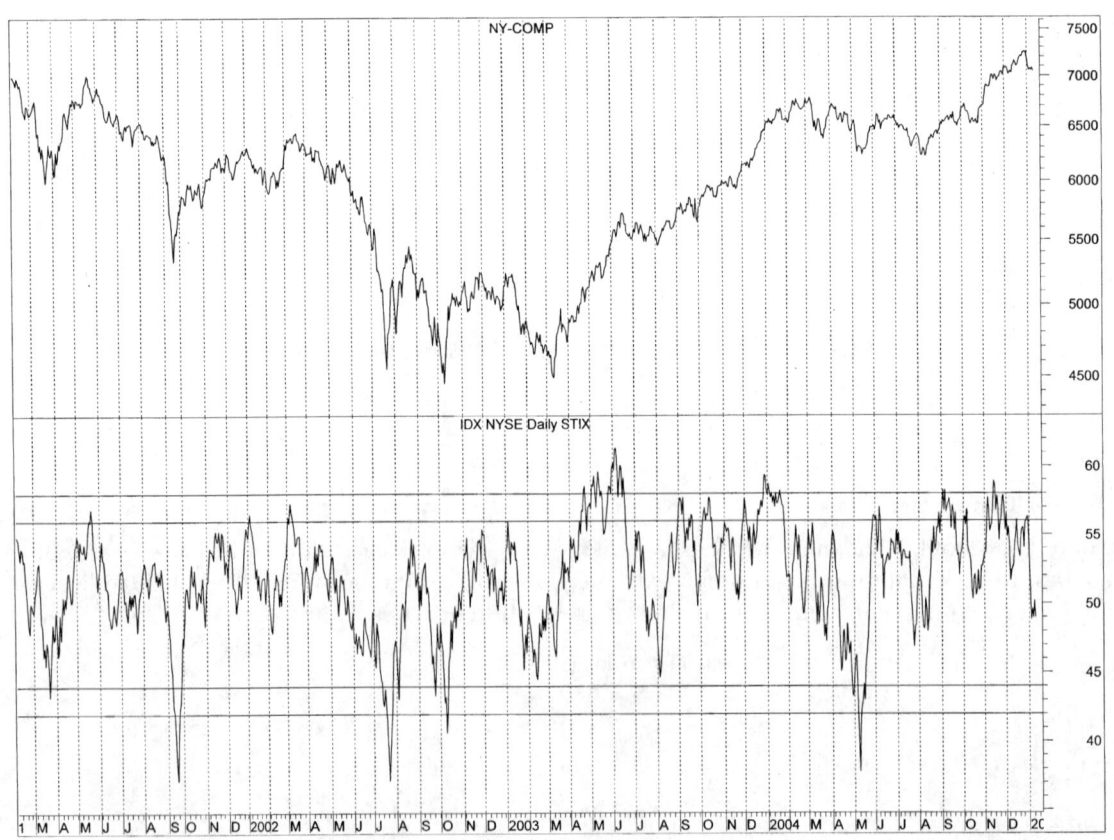

Author Comments

Because this is a ratio of advances to the sum of advances plus declines, the overbought and oversold zones mentioned by Fay Dworkin in his 1990 article still appear to be good ones. A slight further enhancement might be to additionally smooth STIX with a simple 10-day average. Chart 5–13 shows the 10-day simple average (dark line) of STIX. One can see that the additional smoothing removed many of the signals and kept the really good ones.

$$\text{Formula: } (A / (A + D)) * 100$$

References

Dworkin, Fay H., "Defining Advance/Decline Issues," *Stocks and Commodities*, Volume 8, July 1990, pp. 274–278.

Chande, Tushar, "Breadth Stix and Other Tricks," *Stocks and Commodities*, Volume 12, May 1994, pp. 211–214.

Chart 5-13 STIX—With 10-Day Smooth.

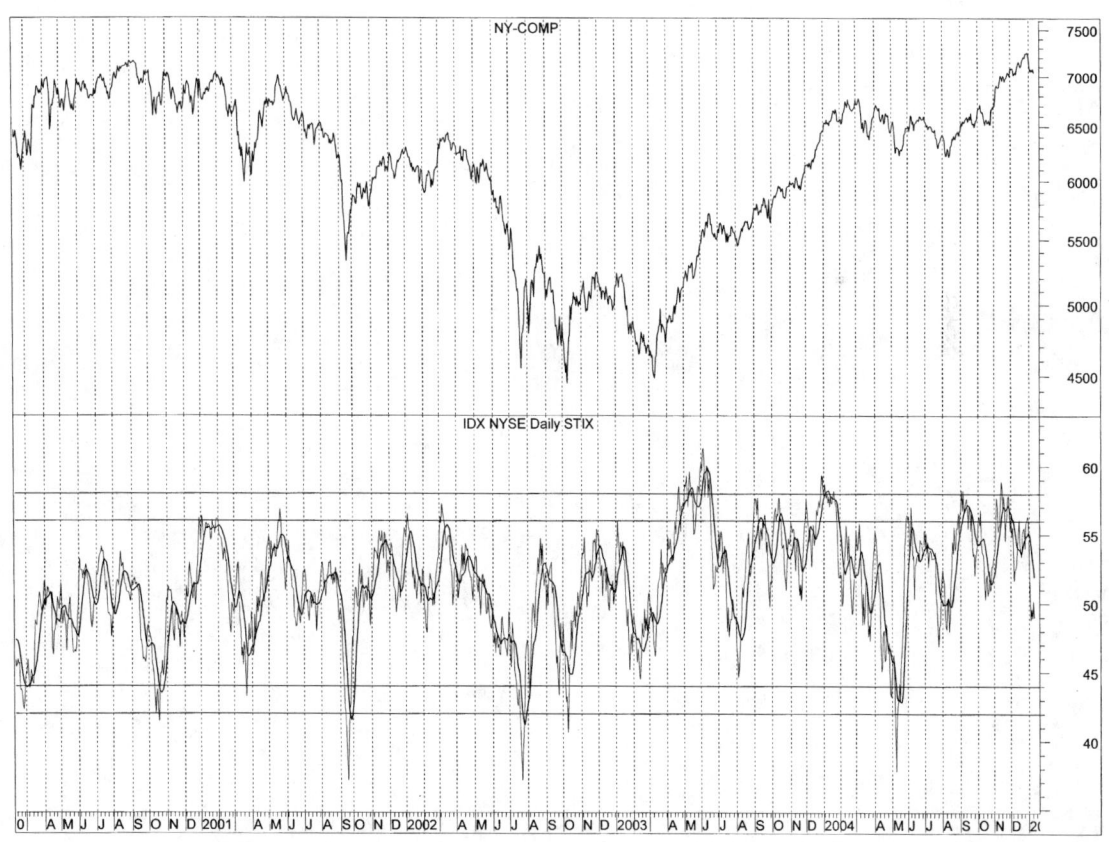

6

Advance Decline Miscellaneous Indicators

The breadth indicators in the section could not be categorized as using the difference or the ratio of the advances and declines, so they are in the miscellaneous section.

Advance Decline Miscellaneous Indicators

Advances / Issues Traded
Advance Decline Divergence Oscillator
Advance Decline Diffusion Index
Breadth Climax
Declining Issues TRIX

Disparity Index
Dynamic Synthesis
Unchanged Issues
Velocity Index

Advances / Issues Traded

Also known as: Schultz AT
Author/Creator: Schultz
Data components required: Advances (A), Total Issues (TI)

Description
This indicator looks at only the advancing issues relative to the total issues, calculated as a ratio.

Interpretation
Schultz did not use total issues, but summed the advances, declines, and unchanged issues, which would yield the same result. Chart 6–1 shows that in its raw from (unsmoothed), this would be a

Chart 6-1 Schultz Advances / Issues Traded Ratio.

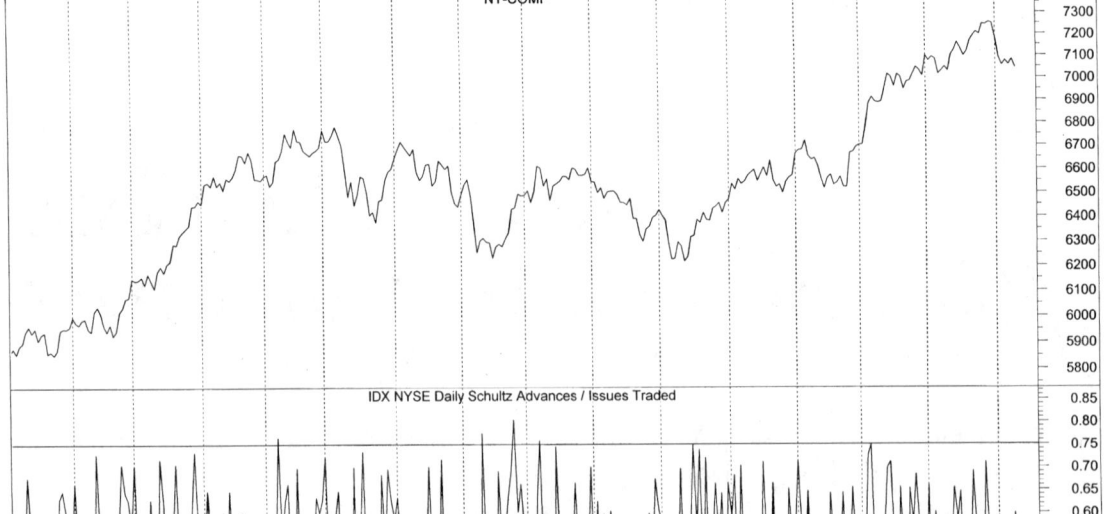

difficult indicator to use. However, if you put threshold values on the oscillator, you can see it helps identify the spikes relative to market action.

Author Comments

Other than a brief reference in a very old CompuTrac software manual, I have not been able to find out any more about this indicator or about Mr./Mrs. Schultz. I spoke with Tim Slater, the founder of CompuTrac, and he was gracious enough to look through his old files to see if he could find any reference. Tim called me back a few weeks later and was of the belief that the indicator was obtained from Dunn and Hargitt; however, he could not uncover any further information.

Chart 6–2 Schultz Advance/Total Issues—Smoothed.

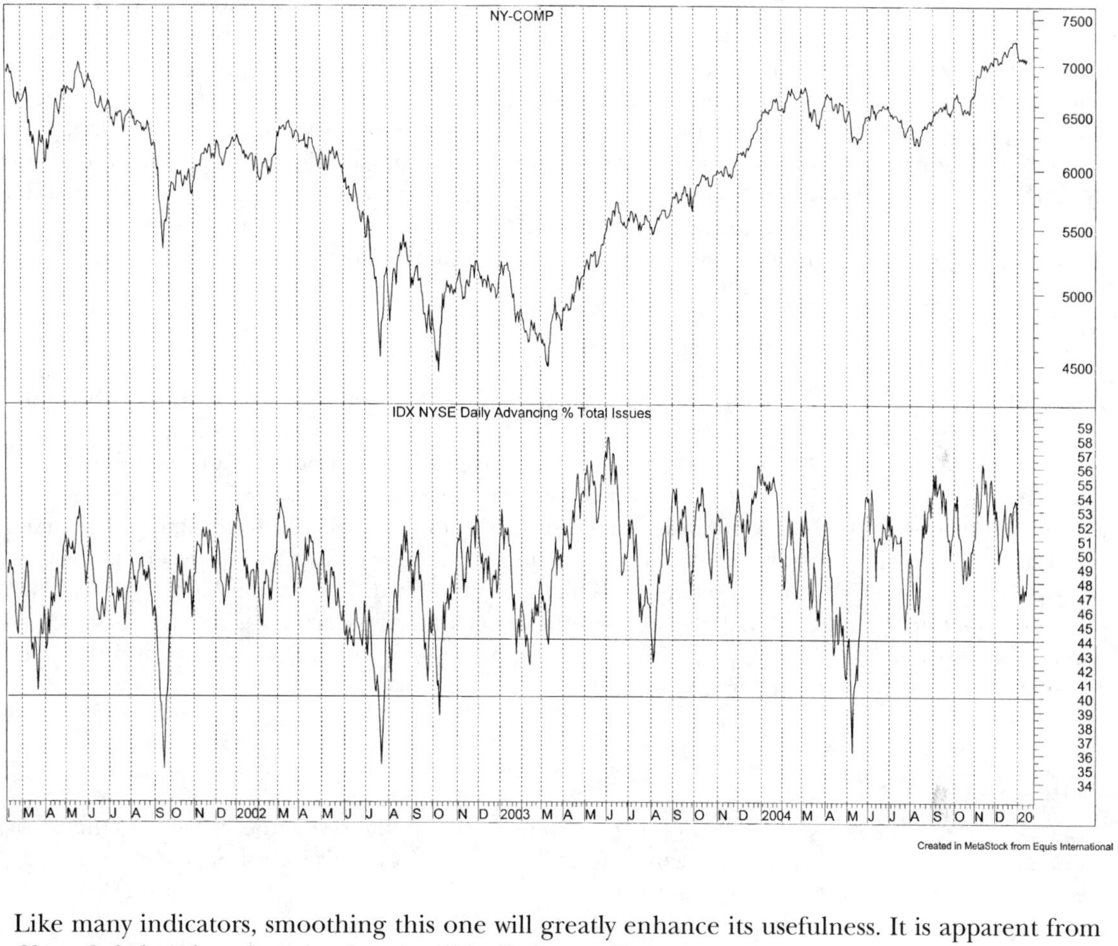

Like many indicators, smoothing this one will greatly enhance its usefulness. It is apparent from Chart 6–2 that the advancing issues will lead almost all market up moves.

$$\text{Formula: } (A / TI)$$

References

1984 CompuTrac software manual.

Advance Decline Divergence Oscillator

Author/Creator: Arthur Merrill
Data components required: Advances (A), Declines (D), Unchanged (U) Market Index (MKT).

Description

This was Arthur Merrill's Disparity Index, an attempt to see how a breadth indicator performed relative to a market index. He stated that he did not like the subjectivity of visually looking at a chart of each one. Here is what he said: "The comparison isn't easy, since the market average is in dollars, and the advance decline line is an accumulation which could start anywhere." He made the comparison into an oscillator. Rather than subtracting one index from the other, he calculated a simple least squares regression line. The calculation is the same as a least squares trend, except the ordinal statistics are the Dow Jones Industrial Average, and the abscissa statistics are the advance decline accumulation (advance decline line). To make the oscillator, he compared the Dow with the least squares line, and then calculated the percentage that the Dow was above or below the line.

Interpretation

If the Advance Decline Divergence Oscillator is positive, the Dow Industrials are pulling ahead of the Advance decline Line. Assuming a better breadth indicator over prices, a positive value is bearish and a negative value is bullish. Art Merrill also used signals based upon 2/3 of a standard deviation. It was bullish when it was below −0.7 and bearish was when it was above +5.4. Chart 6–3 is a modified version of Art Merrill's Advance Decline Divergence Oscillator. It normalizes the market price data and also the advance decline data, then looks at the difference between the two. A period for normalization of 1 year was used. While considerably different than Merrill's work, the concept is identical. Chart 6–3 clearly shows the concept that Art Merrill was talking about. The top plot is the Dow Industrial Average, the middle plot is the advance decline line, and the bottom plot is the AD Divergence Oscillator.

Author Comments

You can see from Chart 6–3 that whenever the advance decline line is stronger relative to the Dow Industrials, the oscillator is above the zero line. It is apparent from this indicator that the advance decline line is a very early warning indicator of future market direction, especially at market tops. And this is good because most indicators are better at identifying market bottoms.

Arthur Merrill also included in the advance decline calculation Edmund Tabell's adjusted *AD* value by dividing the difference between advances and declines by the unchanged issues. Edmund Tabell figured that if the unchanged issues were low, then there was a great deal of conviction in the market.

$$\text{Formula:} \quad ((A - D) / U) / MKT$$

References

Merrill, Arthur, "More Trend Direction." *Stocks and Commodities*, Volume 6, June, 1988, pp. 218.
Merrill, Arthur, "Fitting a Trendline by Least Squares." *Stocks and Commodities*, Volume 6, July, 1988, pp. 254.
Merrill, Arthur, "Advance Decline divergence as an oscillator." *Stocks and Commodities*, Volume 6, September, 1988, pp. 354.

Advance Decline Miscellaneous Indicators 113

Chart 6-3 Advance Decline Divergence Oscillator.

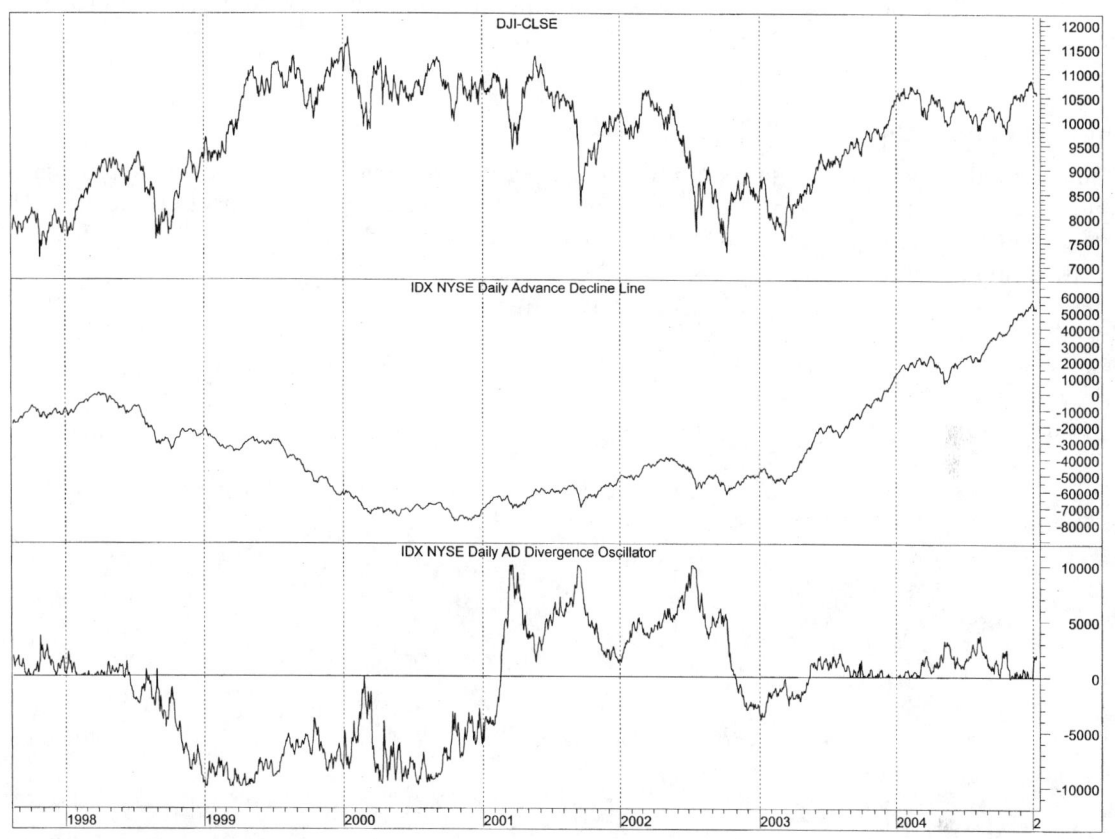

Advance Decline Diffusion Index

Author/Creator: Richard Carlin
Data components required: Advances (*A*), Declines (*D*), Total Issues.

Description

This is a 10-day moving average of the percentage of advancing issues over total issues.

Interpretation

According to Carlin, simply watch for change in direction ahead of the appropriate market. This is not unlike the advance decline line interpretation, but much shorter term in nature. Carlin also says that when it descends from a high level while the market continues to rise, a sell signal is at hand. Complementarily, when it rises ahead of the market, a buy signal is given. He also suggests using it with weekly data. Chart 6–4 shows the AD Diffusion Index.

Author Comments

I'm confused at the name for his relatively simple indicator. Where do the declines come into play and what does it diffuse? There was only a single source of information on this indicator that I could find. Because a good bull market will have ever-expanding advancing issues, this could offer a divergent indicator for long up moves.

$$\text{Formula: } (A \, / \, TI) * 100 \text{ for 10 days}$$

Chart 6–4 Advance Decline Diffusion Index.

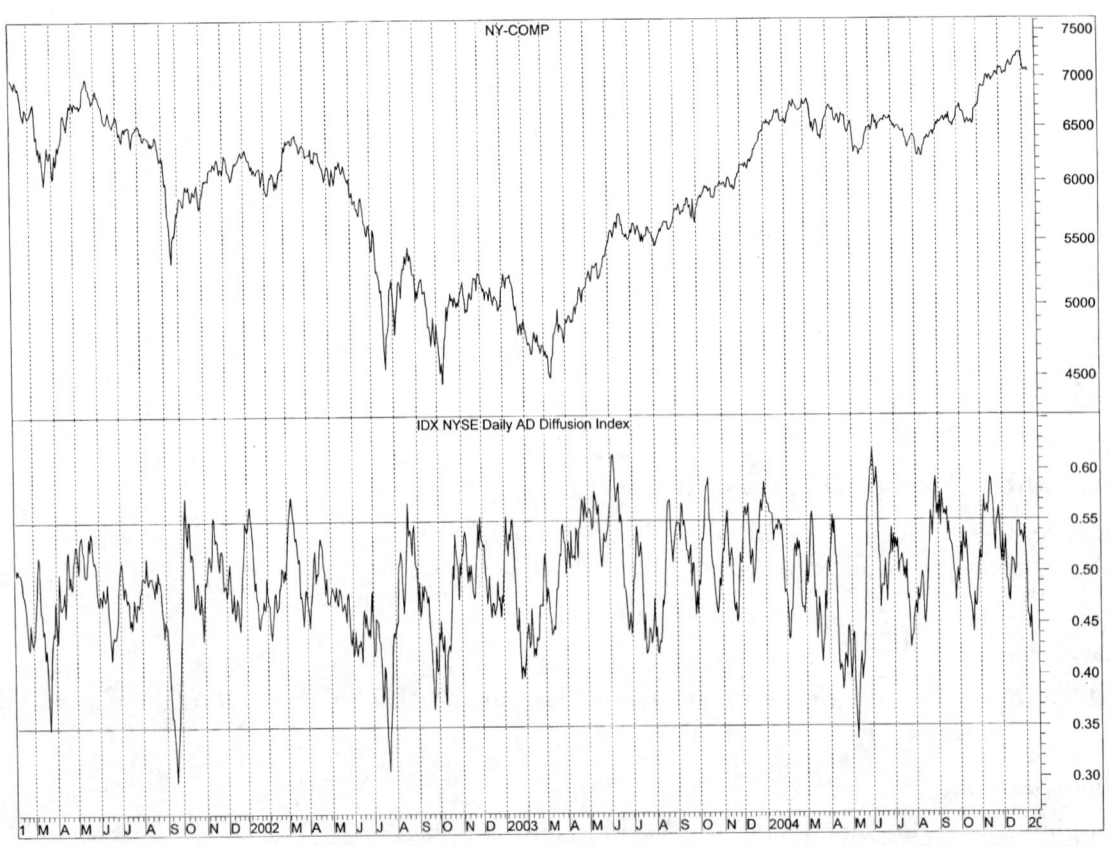

References

Carlin, Richard K., PhD, "Technical analysis of industry groups." *Stocks & Commodities*. Volume 6, November, 1988, pp. 408–410.

Breadth Climax

Author/Creator: Gerald Appel
Data components required: Advances (A), Declines (D), Unchanged (U).

Description

A buying climax is when the market puts together no more than two consecutive days having 1000 or more advancing issues. A selling climax is when the following conditions are met:

1. At least 70% of the total issues are declines.
2. No more than 15% of the total issues are advances.
3. Less than 150 issues are unchanged.

Interpretation

When either the buy criteria or the sell criteria are met, a Breadth Climax has occurred. This means that the buying or selling has reached an excess and the market should reverse its previous trend.

Author Comments

Gerald Appel developed this system over 30 years ago. The breadth numbers have changed dramatically since then. I took the basic concept he was using and found a better set of parameters. A buying climax occurs when there are two consecutive days where the advances are greater than 65 percent of the total issues. A selling climax is when the following conditions are met (only slightly different that Appel's):

1. At least 75% of the total issues are declines.
2. No more than 15% of the issues are advances.
3. There are less than 150 issues unchanged.

Chart 6–5 shows the buying climaxes as upward spikes and the selling climaxes as downward spikes.

Chart 6–5 fairly well identifies periods in the market when sharp declines or advances have occurred. The long period between 1988 and 2001, without any buying climaxes, falls in line with a number of other indicators similar to this one, such as Martin Zweig's Breadth Thrust. In a bull market, after it gets underway, there are few, if any, buying climaxes.

References

Appel, Gerald. *Winning Market Systems*. Greenville, SC: Traders Press, 1973.

Chart 6-5 Breadth Climax.

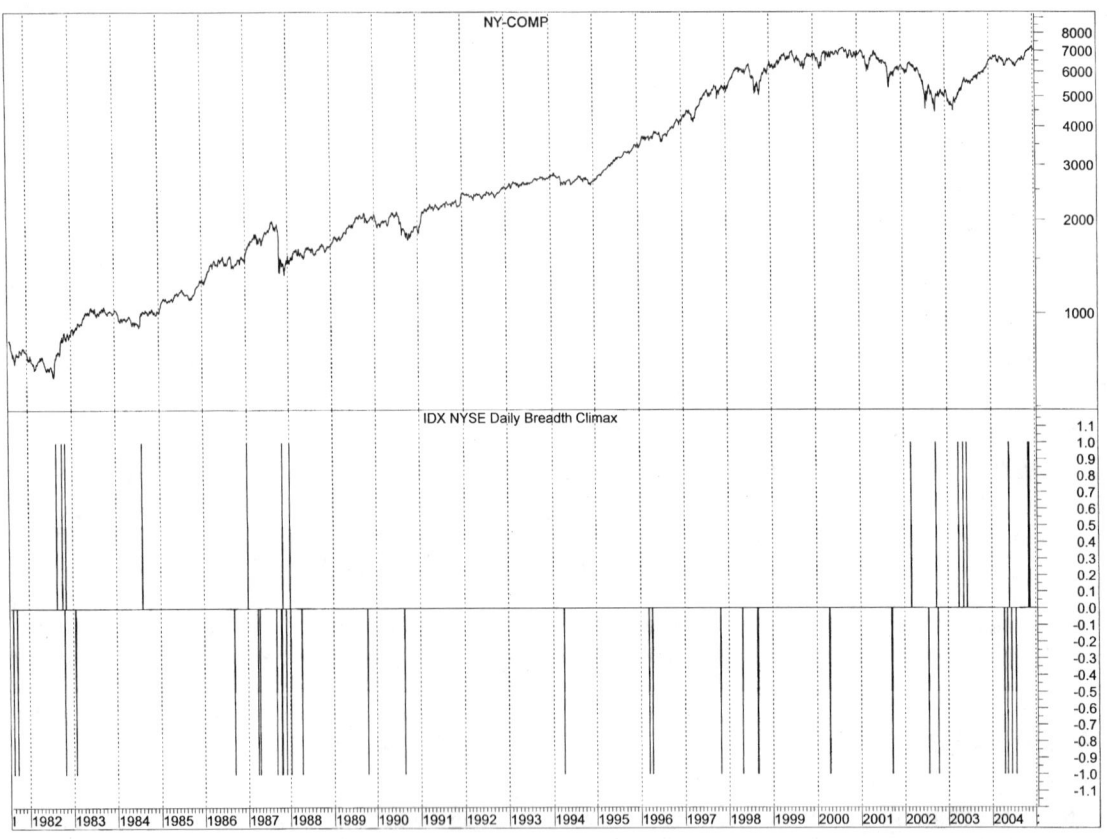

Declining Issues Trix

Author/Creator: Gilbert Raff
Data components required: Declines (*D*)

Description

The Trix indicator was developed by Jack Hutson, publisher of *Stocks and Commodities* magazine. Trix is defined as the one-period percent change of an *x*-period exponential moving average of an *x*-period exponential moving average of an *x*-period exponential moving average of price. Or it is also known as triple exponential smoothing. Gilbert Raff has taken the daily number of declining issues and applied the Trix smoothing using a 35-day period.

Interpretation

Chart 6–6 shows the Declining Issues Trix indicator. When the indicator goes from positive to negative (crosses the zero line from above to below), it is a positive signal for the market. Similarly, when it rises above the zero line, it is a negative sign for the market. This is an inverted indicator in that regard because it uses declining issues.

Author Comments

This seems to work fairly well when the market is trending well. However, it has many whipsaws during sideways market action. The extremes in this indicator seem to identify market tops and bottoms. Using this with a short-term simple moving average might generate some good signals.

Chart 6–6 Declining Issues TRIX.

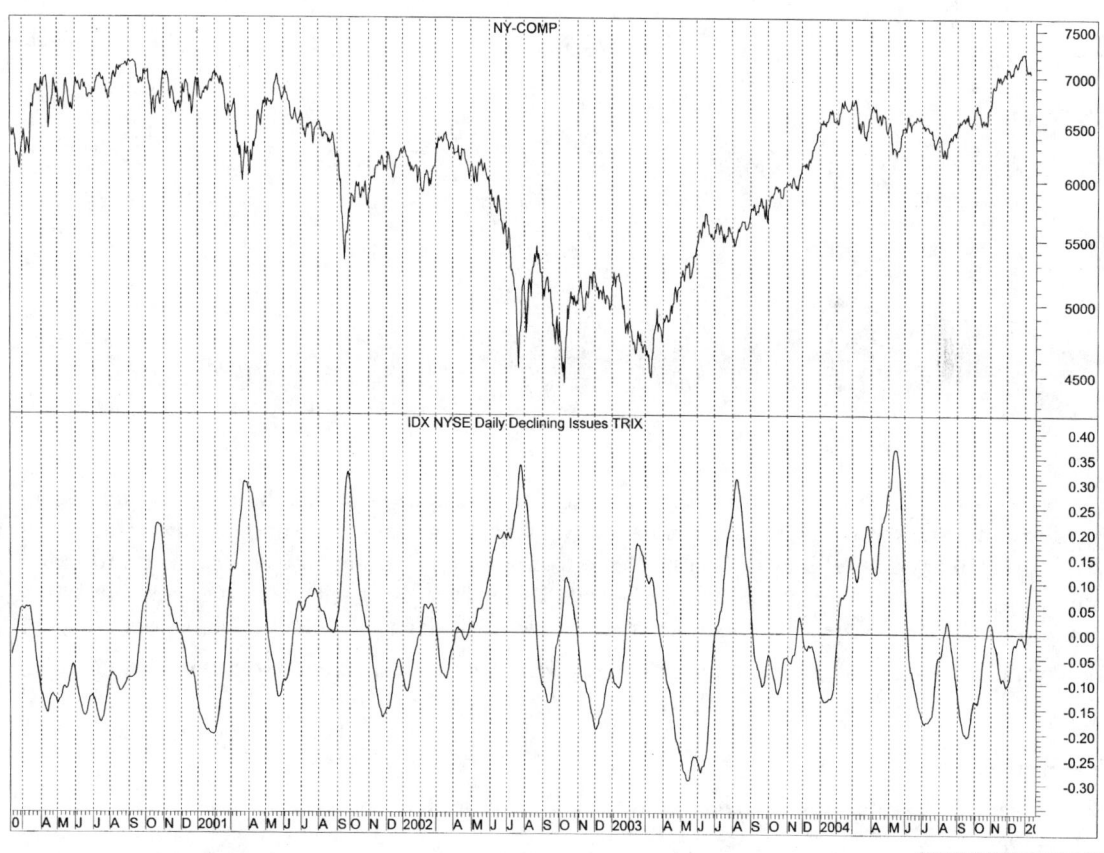

Chart 6-7 Advancing Issues TRIX.

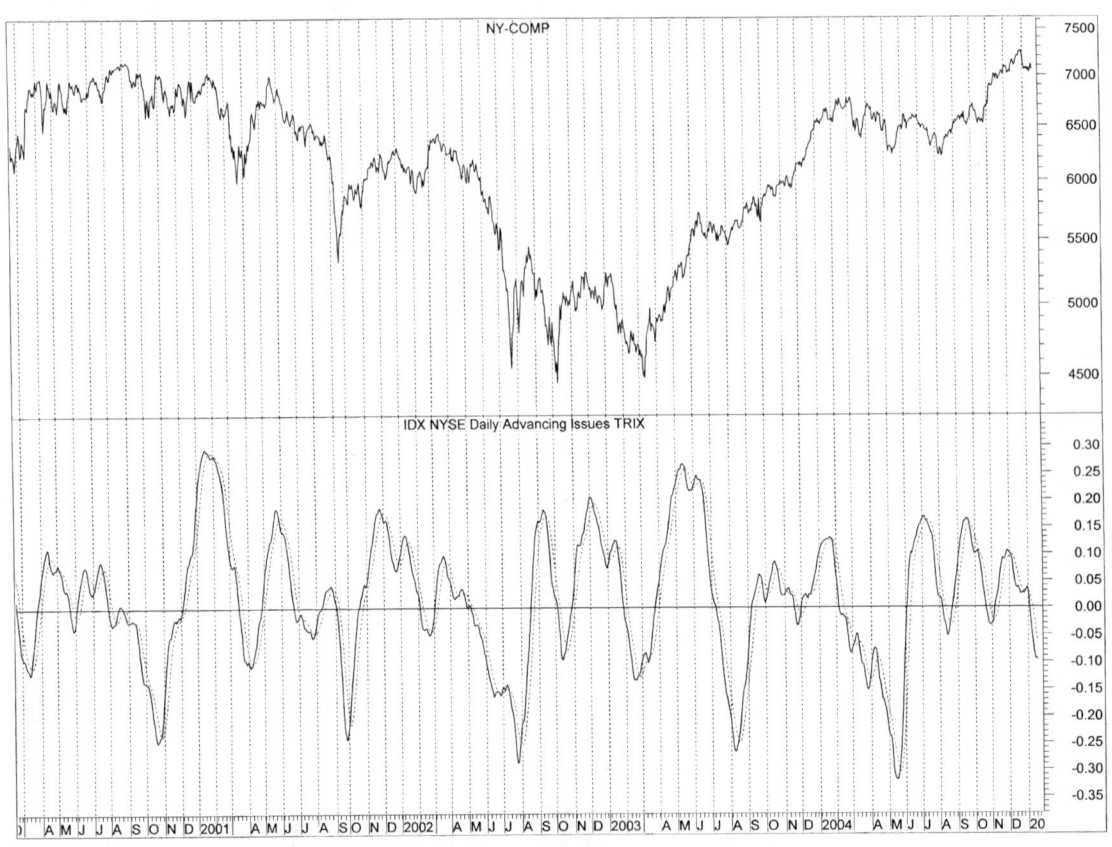

Chart 6–7 is the Advancing Issues TRIX. At first glance it appears to just be the complement of the declining issues trix, but closer examination will reveal that it is not. Using the Advancing Issues Trix with a 10-day smoothing (dotted line) seems to give a good way to use this. When the indicator is above the zero line and it drops below its 10-day average, a sell signal is generated. When the indicator is below the zero line and it rises above its 10-day average, a buy signal occurs.

Formula: Exponentially smooth the declines 3 times and then take a one day rate of change.

References

Raff, Gilbert, "Exponentially Smoothing the Daily Number of Declines." *Stocks and Commodities*, January 1992, pp. 15–18.
MetaStock Professional, Equis International, Salt Lake City, UT.

Disparity Index

Also known as: Advance Decline Divergence Oscillator

Author/Creator: James Alphier, in an October, 1988 article said that James Hughes had written on the subject of the divergence between the advance decline line and the market indices. Hughes was the first person to whom Col. Leonard P. Ayres showed this new idea of counting the number of advances and declines in 1926. Charles Dow may have been first, as he did so in a 1901 market commentary (see Introduction).

Data components required: Advances (A), Declines (D), Market Index (MKT).

Description

This is an attempt to spot the divergence of the advance decline line and a market index. It is well documented that such divergences can be leading indications; however, the lead time is the issue that seems to be the most difficult to deal with.

Interpretation

Like many technical indicators, looking for a divergence with the price-based counterpart is the purpose of the Disparity Index. One of the best ways of doing this is to put both indicators on the same chart and visually determine when they were diverging. In fact, this is how it is done most of the time because of the visual capabilities. Chart 6–8 shows the New York Composite index on the top plot and the Advance Decline Line on the bottom plot.

Author Comments

I have attempted to create an indicator that shows the divergence between the advance decline line and the market index. The concept was to first normalize the components over the long term. This would give them equal weighting in the overall calculation. Secondly, I then smoothed, exponentially, the difference over a 10-day period. I worked with a number of different smoothing values, but the 10-day period was long enough to give the divergence I wanted to see, and short enough to be timely. The longer the value used, the better the divergence showed up, but it was almost too late to be beneficial. Very similar to the divergence indicator Art Merrill created, Chart 6–9 shows positive whenever the breadth (Advance Decline Line) is outperforming the price (market index). The top plot is both the New York Composite Index (solid line) and the Advance Decline Line (dotted line).

$$\text{Formula: (Previous Value} + (A - D)) / MKT$$

References:

Alphier, James, "The Tragic Neglect of the Old Masters." *Stocks and Commodities*, Volume 6, October, 1988, pp. 395–396.

Chart 6-8 Disparity Between NYSE Index and Advance Decline Line.

Dynamic Synthesis

Author/Creator: Walter A. Heiby

Data components required: Advances (*A*), Declines (*D*), Unchanged Issues (*U*), Market Index (*MKT*).

Description

In 1965, Walter Heiby wrote about a method to help determine market tops and bottoms. To use his technique, one has to take the 10-day average of advancing issues, the 10-day average of declining issues, and the 10-day average of unchanged issues, each plotted separately. The plots need to further divide the plots into quarters, starting over every 50 days. Said a different way, we are look-

Advance Decline Miscellaneous Indicators

Chart 6-9 Disparity Index.

ing for new 10-day highs or lows in the advances, declines, and unchanged. The new highs or lows are based upon the last 50 days.

Interpretation

Heiby states that the unchanged issues normally move in the same manner as the advancing issues, and opposite that of the declining issues. There is a strong tendency on the part of the unchanged issues to be low at good buying opportunities and to be high near rally tops. Chart 6–10 shows the New York Index and the components of Heiby's Dynamic Synthesis. You can see that September, 2001 gave a good buying opportunity based upon Heiby's analysis. Similarly, October, 2002 did also. Remember that the issues plot must be in the top or bottom quartile in order for the signal to be

Chart 6-10 Walter Heiby Dynamic Synthesis.

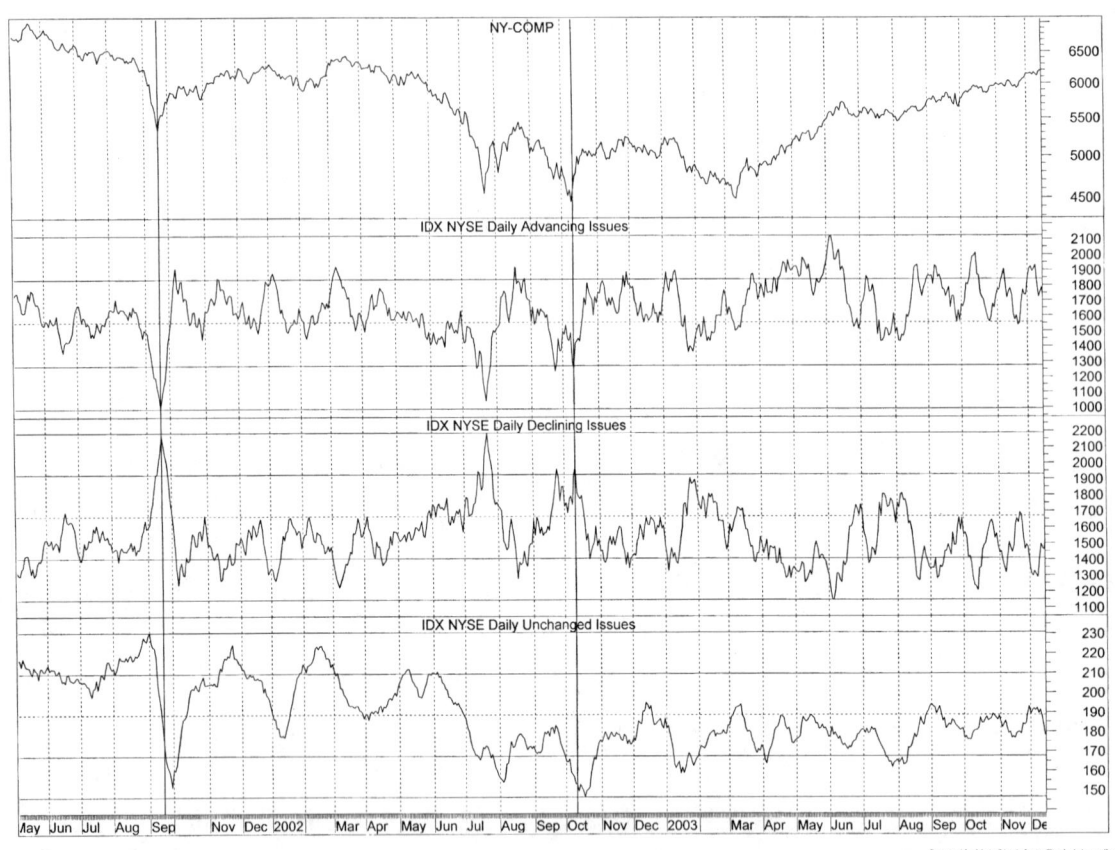

generated. These plots did not adhere to Heiby's desire to look at new highs and lows only over the last 50 days, as there did not seem to be many signals.

Buy Signal Criteria

1. The market index must be in the bottom quartile.
2. The advances index must be in the top quartile.
3. The advances index must be greater than the declines index.
4. The unchanged issues must be in the top quartile.

Sell Signal Criteria

1. The market index must be in the top quartile.
2. The advances index must be in the bottom quartile.

Advance Decline Miscellaneous Indicators

3. The decline index must be in the top quartile.
4. The advances index must be less than the declines index.
5. The unchanged index must not be in the lowest quartile.

Author Comments

With the big changes in pricing on the New York Stock Exchange in 1997 (pricing went to sixteenths from eighths) and early 2001 (went to decimal pricing—cents), the unchanged issues are distorted, so ensure that you are viewing like data, even when adjusting the individual issues on a percentage of total issues. This is especially true with the unchanged issues because they were the most affected by the pricing changes. Chart 6–11 shows the three components adjusted for total issues during a 6-year period of exceptional market volatility. One can spot numerous occurrences of Heiby's theory.

Chart 6–11 Walter Heiby Dynamic Synthesis as a Percentage of Total Issues.

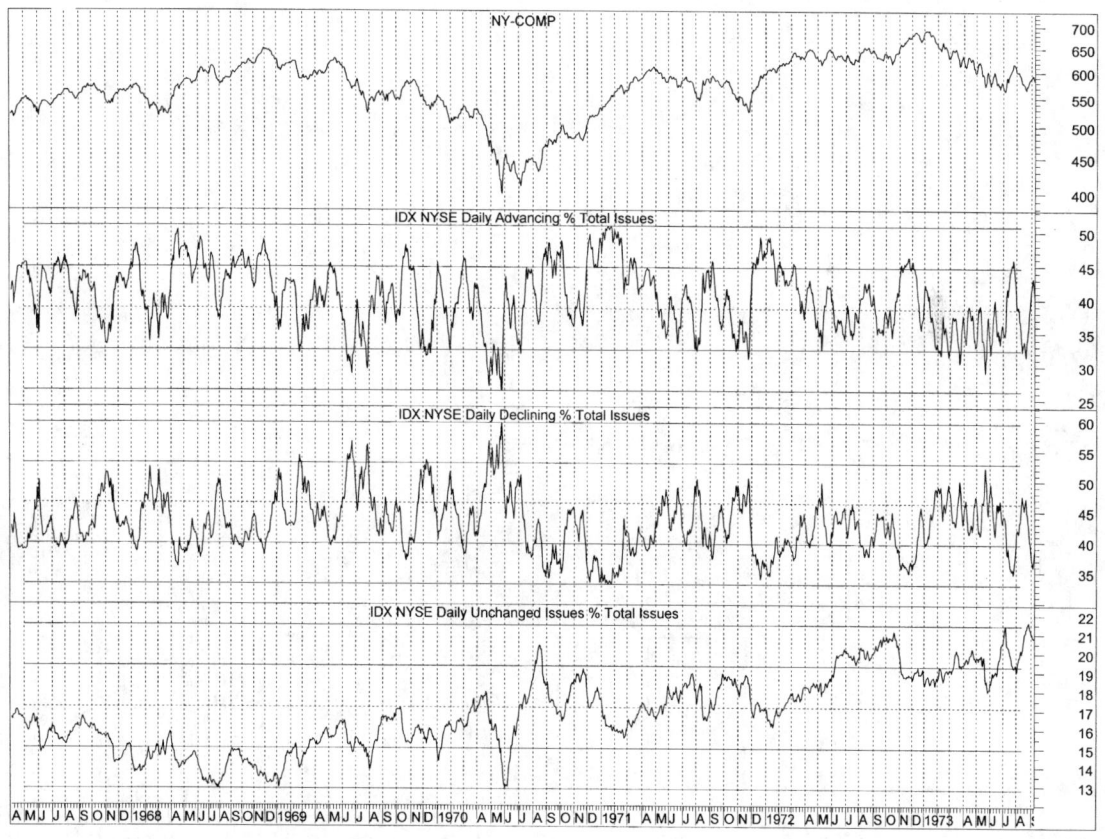

Normalizing the various components of the Heiby dynamic synthesis over a 50-day period and creating buy and sell signals based upon the parameters above takes out the visual chart subjectivity. Chart 6–12 shows Heiby's signals with the up spikes being buy signals and the down spikes being sell signals.

Formula: This is a charting method using a market index (*MKT*), advances (*A*), declines (*D*), and unchanged issues (*U*).

References

Heiby, Walter. *Stock Market Profits through Dynamic Synthesis*. Chicago : The Institute of Dynamic Synthesis, 1965.

Unchanged Issues

Data components required: Unchanged (*U*)

Chart 6–12 Walter Heiby Dynamic Synthesis Indicator.

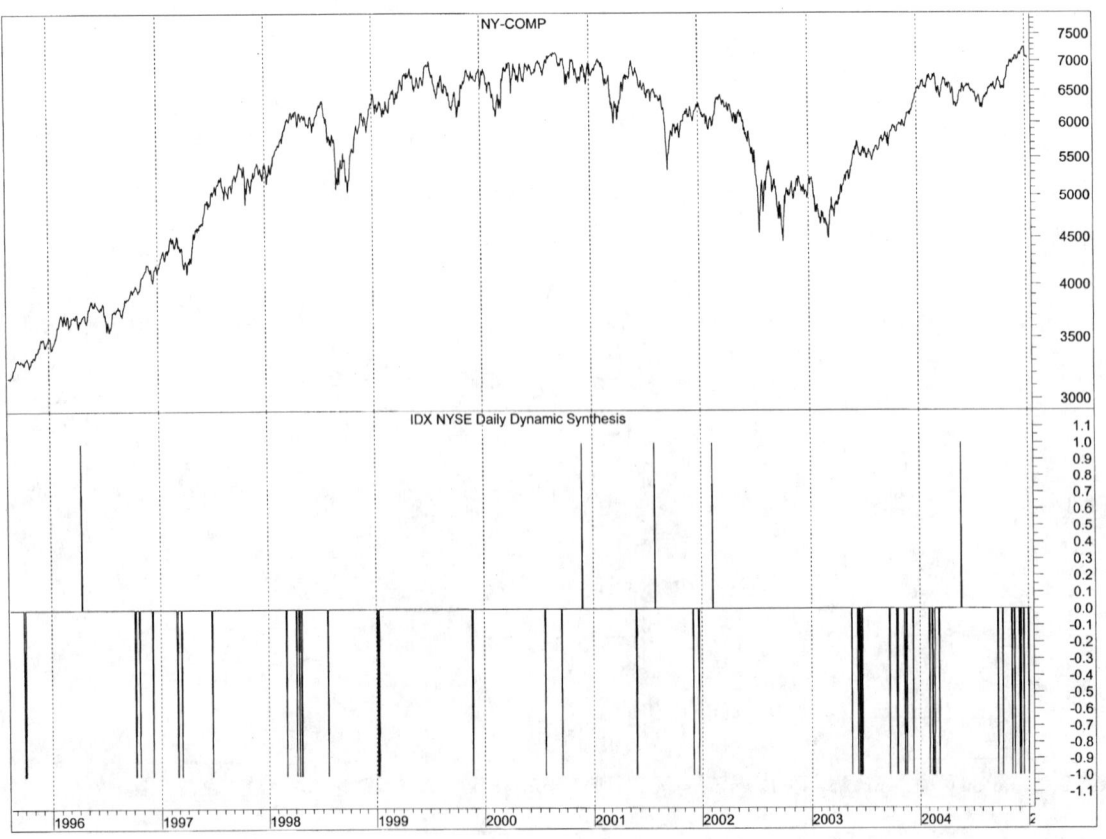

Advance Decline Miscellaneous Indicators

Description

Looking at the unchanged issues that traded is a new twist and researched by Anthony Tabell. Earlier writings were by Walter Heiby in 1965.

Interpretation

On days with a high number of unchanged issues, and the market was up based on breadth, there had to be fewer advances, and even fewer declines than normal. This could mean that a market top is being put into place as issues refuse to advance further. In fact, it is normal for the number of unchanged issues to increase as the market peaks. During a market decline, a low number of unchanged issues usually indicates that the decline will continue. Because of the usual quick and sharp patterns generated at market bottoms, the unchanged issues will tend to be low, initially, as the decrease in the number of declines is overtaken by the rapid rise in advancing issues. Tabell says that the low number of unchanged issues is generally bullish over a 1-year period. Chart 6–13 shows the raw unchanged data.

Chart 6–13 Unchanged Issues.

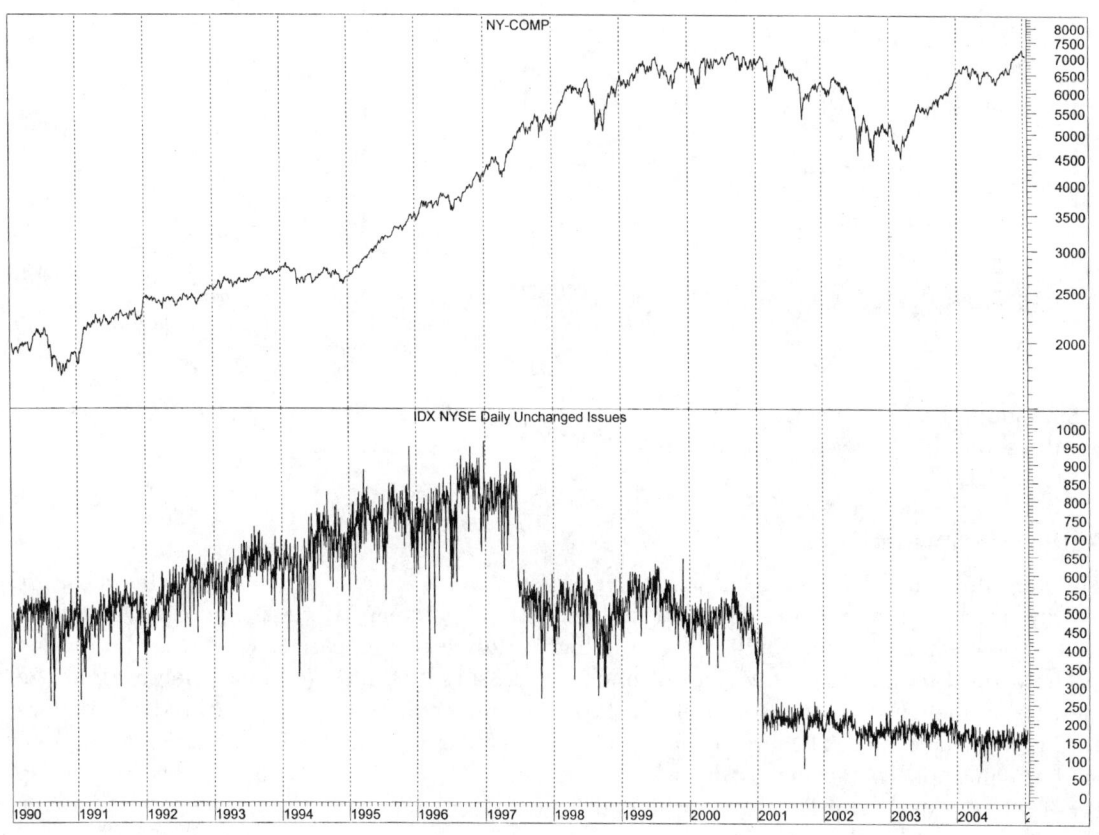

Chart 6-14 Unchanged Issues—21-Day Smooth.

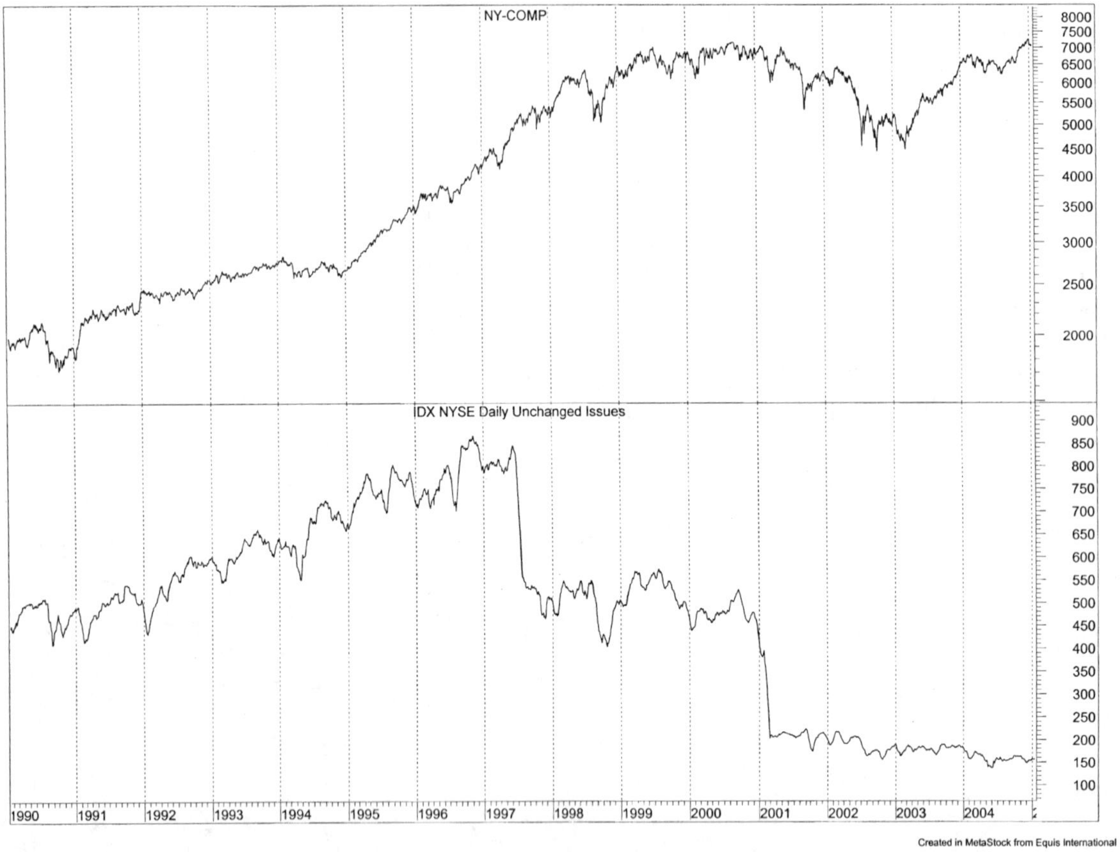

Smoothing the raw unchanged issues by 21 days presents a similar-shaped chart (Chart 6–14), but it is somewhat easier to read and use.

Author Comments

Theoretically, when there are a large number of issues not advancing or declining, the market is usually in the process of topping. Looking at the chart of unchanged issues as a percentage of total issues, a low reading is more bullish, with the high readings being bearish.

There are three things on the chart of unchanged issues that bothered me. One was the large increase in unchanged issues from 1991 to 1997. The other two were the significant drops in mid-1997 and January, 2002. The large drop in unchanged issues in June, 1997 was the beginning step to decimalization by moving to the use of sixteenths (1/16) or about 6.25 cents in pricing. Previously, the smallest price move was in eighths (1/8) or 12.5 cents. The large drop in January,

Advance Decline Miscellaneous Indicators

2002 was when the New York Exchange changed from using fractions to using decimals. A stock can now be an advancing or a declining issue with only a 1-cent move.

If you look at the chart of unchanged issues above, you will quickly notice that the unchanged issues continue to climb as the market rallied during the period from 1991 to 1997. Why is this? It is because of the large growth in overall issues on the New York Stock Exchange during that time period. This is why many single-breadth components must be used as a ratio. I divided the unchanged issues by the total issues and then smoothed it by 21 days. Notice in Chart 6–15 that the increase in the period from 1991 to 1997 went away. Yes there was growth in the number of issues, but not in just the unchanged issues.

Because of the two steps in the middle of 1997 and early 2001 to get to the decimalization of minimum price changes in trading, using the unchanged issues by themselves should be done in steps to eliminate the two significant drops in unchanged issues. Chart 6–15b shows the unchanged issues as a percentage of total issues over a 2-year period starting in early 1987. You can see that as

Chart 6–15 Unchanged Issues as a Percentage of Total Issues.

the market rallied off of the low set in October, 1987, the unchanged issues continued to climb. This seems to follow the logic of the unchanged issues talked about earlier in this section.

Formula: (U).

References

Jaffe, Charles A., "Unchanged Stocks." *Stocks & Commodities*, Volume 8, January 1990, p. 44.

Velocity Index

Data components required: Advances (A), Declines (D), Unchanged (U)

Chart 6-15b Unchanged Issues/Total Issues—1987.

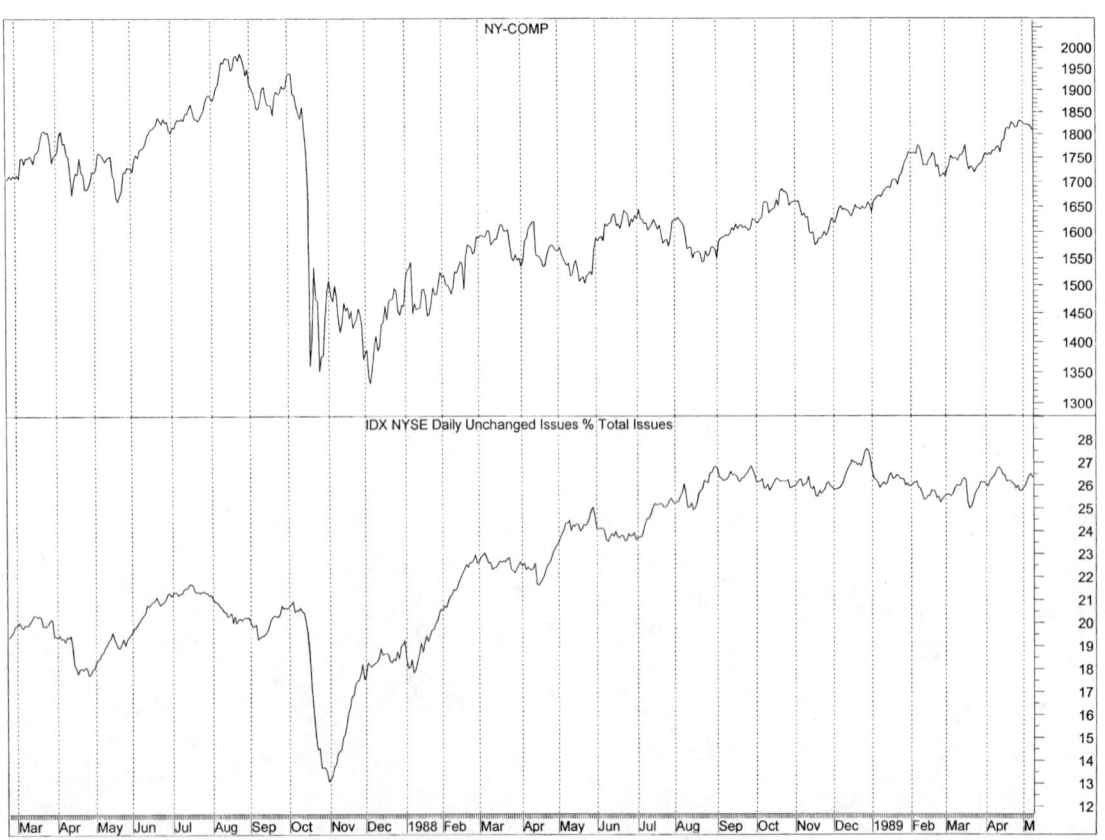

Description

This indicator measures the unchanged issues and advancing issues relative to total issues. It takes one-half of the unchanged issues and the advancing issues and then divides that sum by the total issues.

Interpretation

Moves in the Velocity Index greater than +10 and −12 normally indicate continued movement in that direction. Keep in mind that this is not much different than the advances as a percent of total issues. The addition of using one-half of the unchanged issues would imply that this indicator would be coincident at market tops as the advancing issues dry up. Chart 6–16 shows the Velocity Index.

Chart 6-16 Velocity Index.

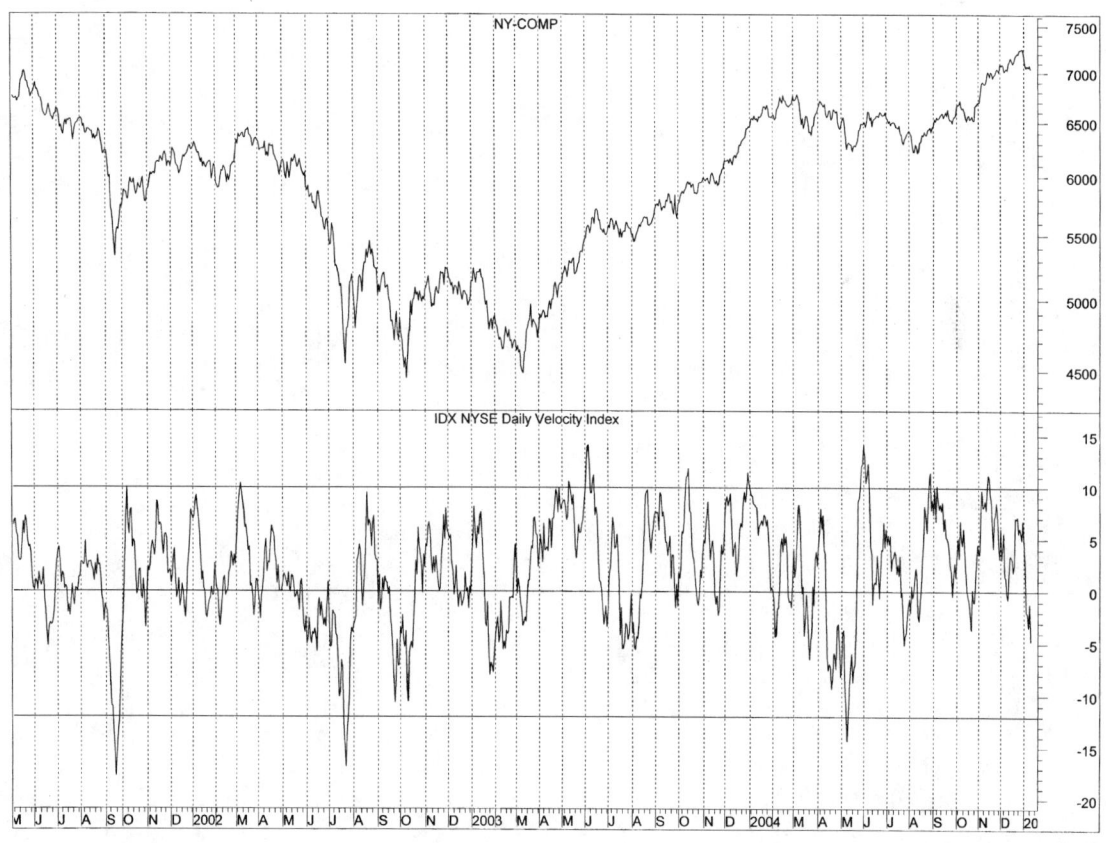

Author Comments

I put his indicator into a breadth formula package I created over 10 years ago. I cannot find any additional information on it or who created it. It wasn't me.

$$\text{Formula: } (U/2 + A) / (A + D + U)$$

References

Morris, Greg, "Indicators and Trading Systems Software," G. Morris Corporation, Dallas, TX.

7
New High, New Low Indicators

This chapter contains all the indicators that are dedicated to using new highs and/or new lows.

High Low Difference

New Highs − New Lows
New High New Low Line

New Highs and New Lows Oscillator
New Highs and New Lows Derivations

High Low Ratio

New Highs / New Lows Ratio

High Low Miscellaneous

New Highs and New Lows
New Highs % Total Issues
New Lows % Total Issues

High Low Logic Index
High Low Validation

High Low Difference
New Highs − New Lows

Data components required: New Highs (H), New Lows (L).

Description

This is the difference between the daily new highs and new lows. If the new highs outnumber the new lows, the indicator will be above the zero line. If the new lows outnumber the new highs, it will be below the zero line. Without some sort of smoothing or rate of change, it is a very noisy oscillator.

Interpretation

Basically it can be used as an overbought oversold oscillator, similar to the advance decline overbought oversold indicator. Chart 7–1 shows that smoothing it by 21 days takes out much of the noise, and then it can be used for bullish and bearish signals as it crosses the zero line.

Chart 7–1 New Highs − New Lows—21-Day Smooth.

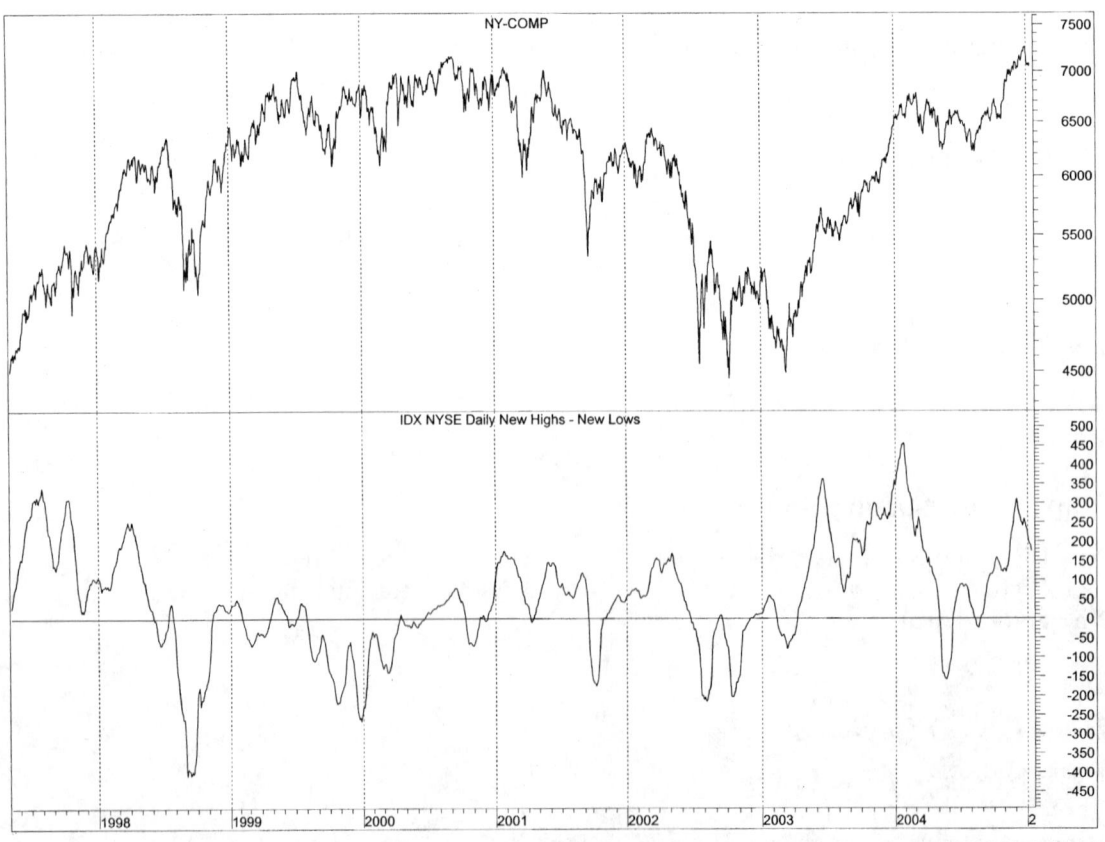

New High, New Low Indicators

Author Comments

In its raw form this is not useable other than to get a feel for the number of new highs relative to the number of new lows. A better derivation for this would be to look at the difference as a percentage of total issues. Tim Hayes of Ned Davis Research gives the following information using weekly data. When this weekly indicator is above 8.8 percent it is bullish and when it is below −3.6 percent it is bearish. Chart 7-2 shows Hayes' thresholds, along with an overlay for identifying buy and sell signals. Whenever the difference is above the upper (8.8 percent) threshold the value is +30 and when below the lower (−3.6 percent) threshold it is −30.

Formula: $(H - L)$

Chart 7-2 New Highs, New Lows Percent Total Issues—Hayes.

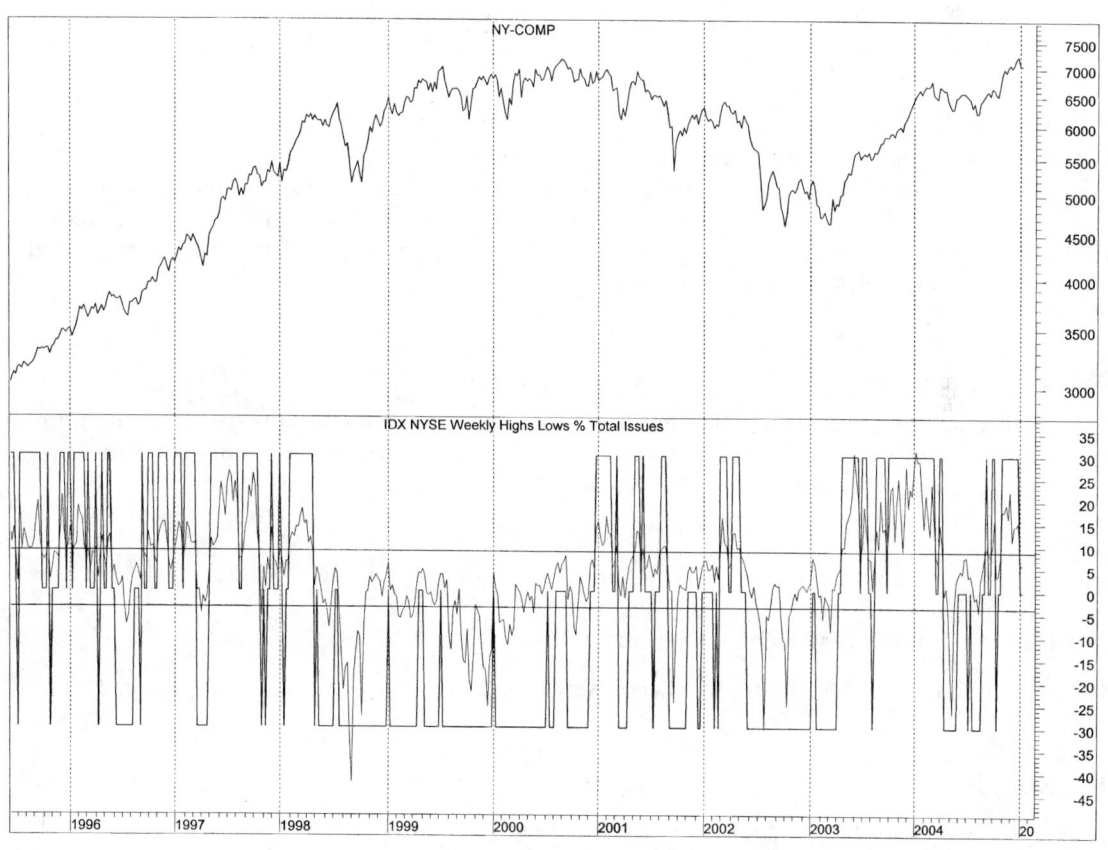

References

Hayes, Timothy. *The Research Driven Investor.* McGraw-Hill, 2001.
Author Note: This is a great book, but unfortunately it is out of print. I strongly recommend it if you can find a copy.

New High New Low Line

Data components required: New Highs (H), New Lows (L).

Description

The New High New Low Line plots the difference between the number of stocks hitting new 52- week highs and those hitting 52-week lows and then adds that difference to the value from the previous day. It is constructed like the advance-decline line and can be interpreted in a similar way.

Interpretation

When the spread between the number of new highs and lows is widening, the New High New Low line is rising, which is positive. Any serious divergence between the NH-NL line and the stock average can be an early warning of a possible trend change. Whenever this cumulative line (shown in Chart 7–3) changes direction, it is an important move in the market that cannot be ignored. Divergence of this indicator with price is also a good technique.

Author Comments

If this indicator changes direction, it is important. To remove some small whipsaws, one can smooth it with a 21-day arithmetic average. Again, when this indicator changes direction, you should pay attention because the market is also changing direction, as shown in Chart 7–4.

$$\text{Formula:} \quad (H - L).$$

New Highs and New Lows Oscillator

Data components required: New Highs (H), New Lows (L).

Description

This is the difference between the new highs and new lows, then put into a relationship like the advances and declines are with the McClellan Oscillator.

Chart 7-3 New Highs, New Lows Line.

Interpretation

Chart 7-5 shows that the crossing of the zero line seems to be very effective. However, it does produce too many whipsaws to be used for anything other than short-term trading.

Author Comments

I like the McClellan concept of looking at the difference between two different smoothings, and I tend to like highs and lows a little better than advances and declines. Keep in mind that the new highs and new lows have a much different relationship with each other than the advances and declines do. This is because a new high or new low is based on data over the last year, and advance

Chart 7-4 New Highs, New Lows Line—21-Day Smooth.

or decline is based on yesterday's data. This is a good indicator. Gerald Appel likes to smooth it by 10 days. Smoothing it by 15 days makes it work very well, as shown in Chart 7–6.

While creating Chart 7–6, I accidentally put the wrong formula in the MetaStock indicator builder and created a chart of the 19-day exponential average of new highs minus the 39-day exponential average of new lows. There seems to be some merit in this; observe in Chart 7–7 how it works as it crosses the zero line.

Formula: 19-day exp average $(H - L)$ − 39-day exp average $(H - L)$.

Chart 7-5 New Highs and New Lows Oscillator.

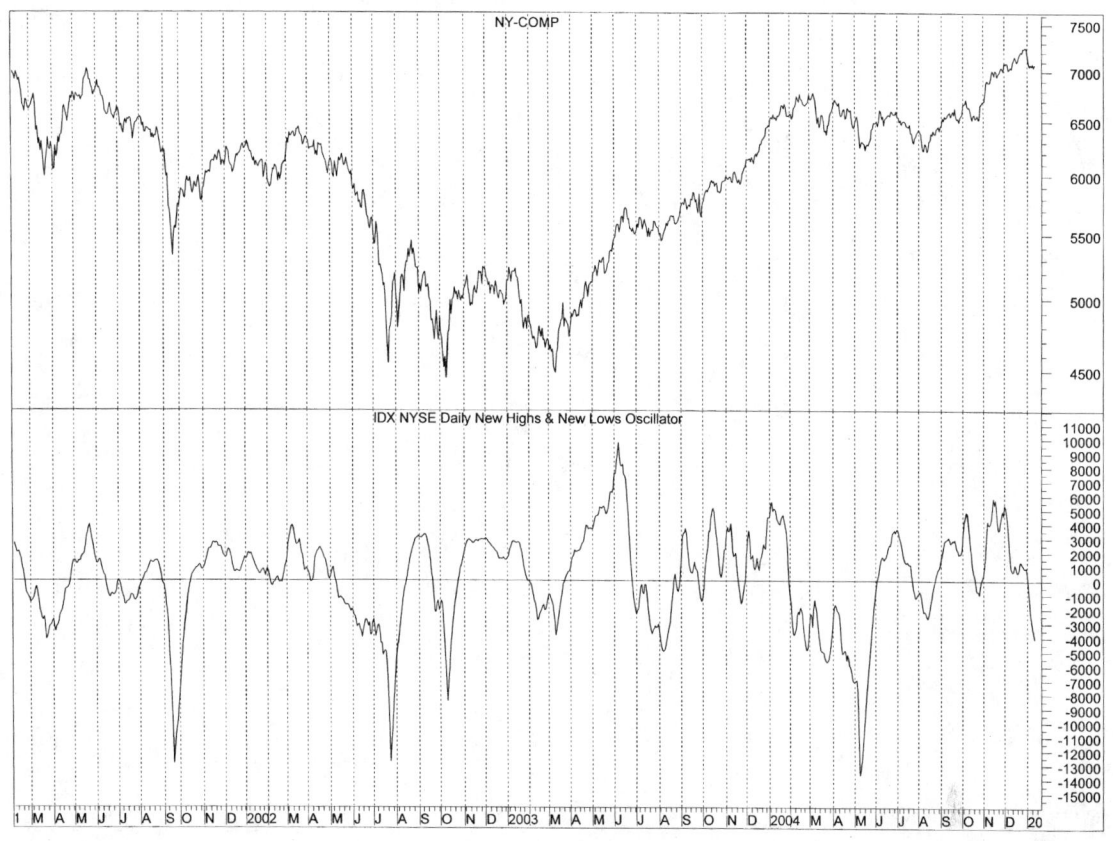

References

Appel, Gerald, "Gerald Appel, with Systems and Forecasts." *Stocks & Commodities*, Volume 12, March 1994, pp. 98–105.

New Highs and New Lows Derivations

Data components required: New Highs (H), New Lows (L).

Chart 7-6 New Highs and New Lows Oscillator—Appel.

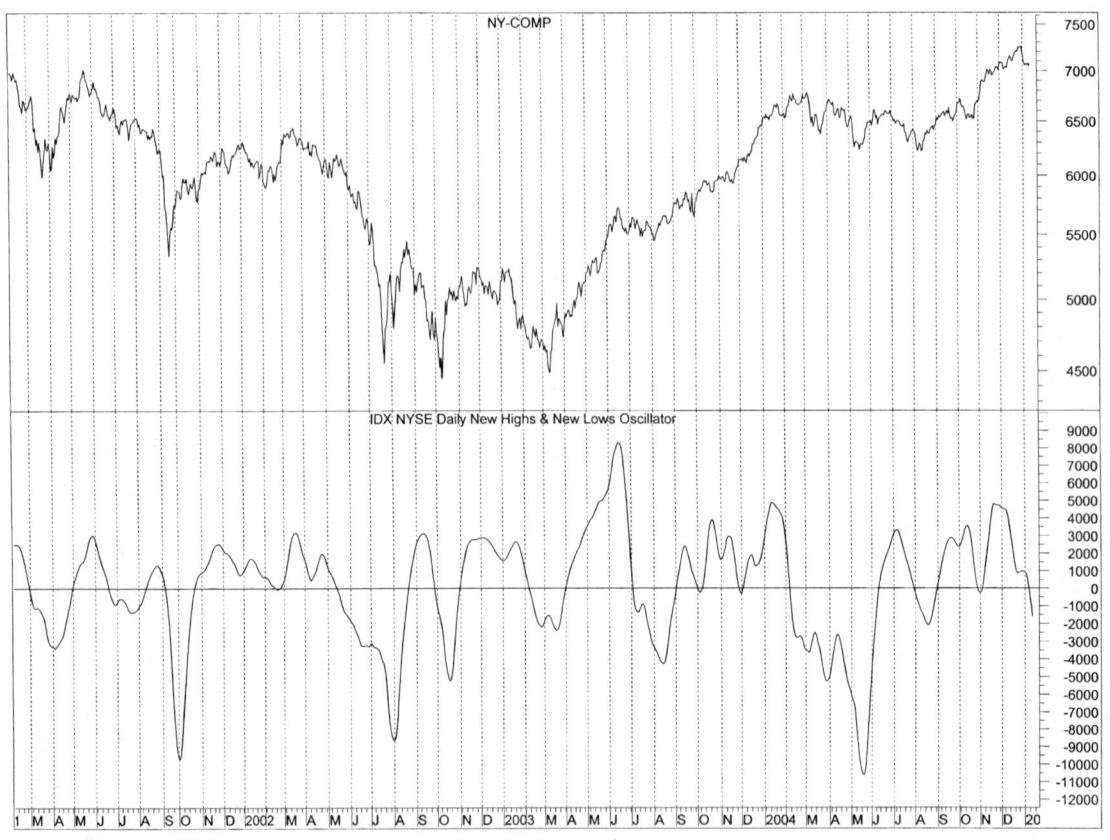

Description

These are two indicators based on two popular price-based technical indicators, Welles Wilder's relative strength index (RSI), and George Lane's Stochastics (%K). While those indicators used price, these derivations use the difference between the new highs and new lows.

Interpretation

The RSI version uses the difference between the RSI of new highs and the RSI of new lows. Like the price-based RSI, in trending markets, this indicator is not telling us much. From Chart 7–8 we can see that crossing the zero line seems to work best. There is a zero line here since this is the

New High, New Low Indicators

Chart 7-7 New Highs, New Lows—Morris.

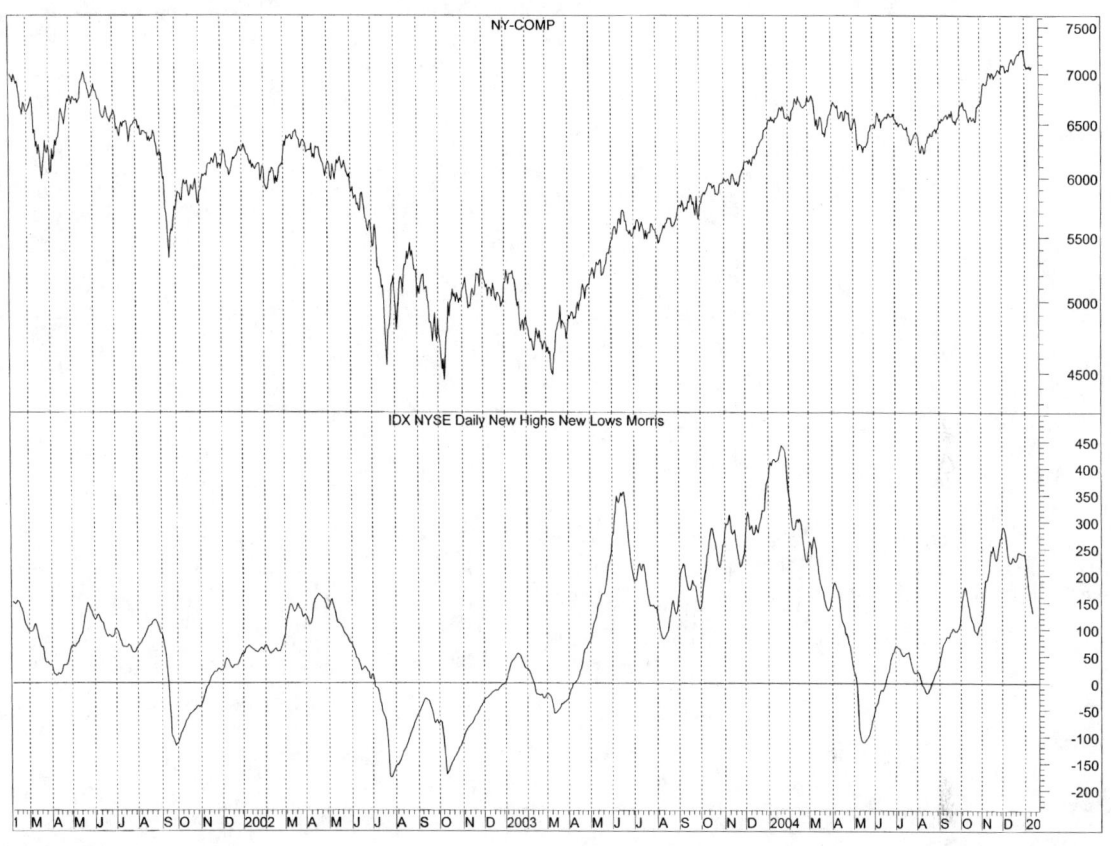

difference between two RSI calculations. The more common price-based RSI oscillated between zero and 100.

The Stochastic version of the high low difference was created the same way as the RSI version. Basically a difference between the stochastic of the new highs minus the stochastic of the new lows. Chart 7–9 is using a 65-day period for the stochastics.

Author Comments

I'm not sure I have added anything to the arsenal of breadth indicators already in existence. However, the concept could certainly be further refined.

Chart 7-8 High Low RSI.

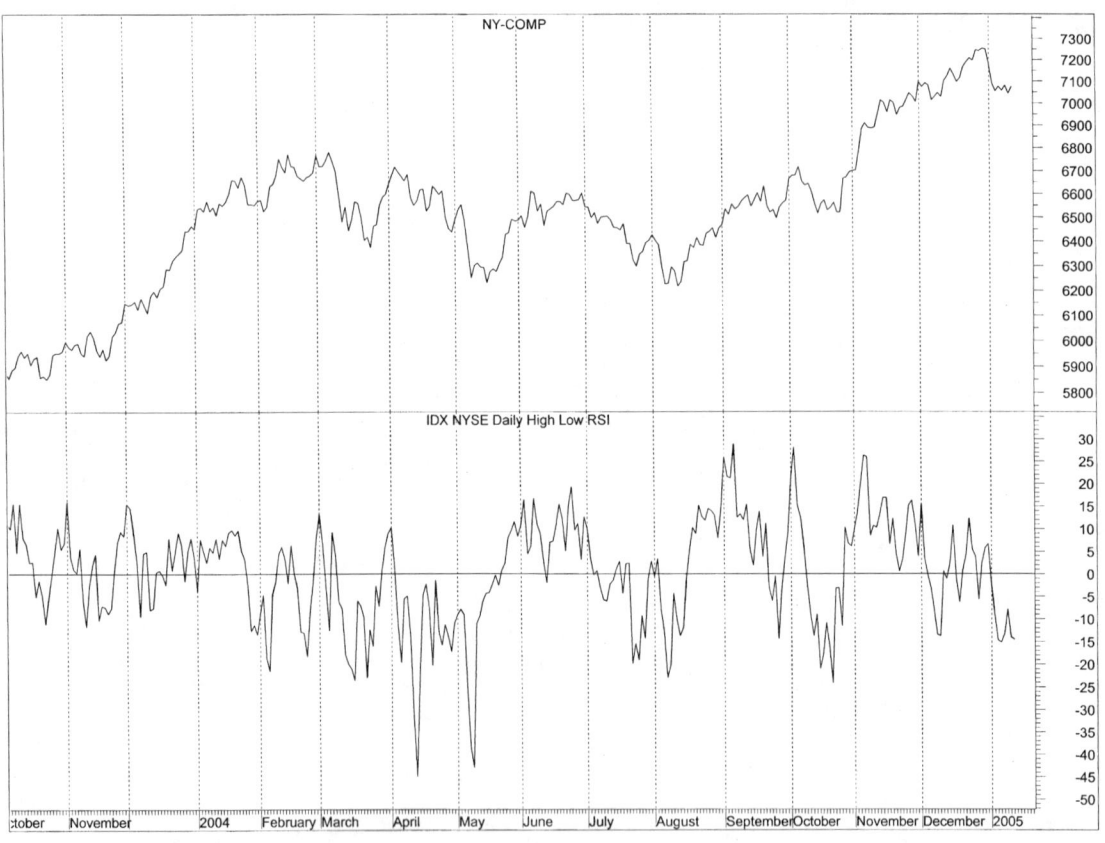

High Low Ratio
New Highs / New Lows Ratio

Data components required: New Highs (H), New Lows (L).

Description

This is the new highs divided by the new lows. Because there is the possibility of a day with zero new lows (you cannot divide by zero—it is undefined), the individual components must be smoothed before doing the division.

Chart 7-9 High Low Stochastic.

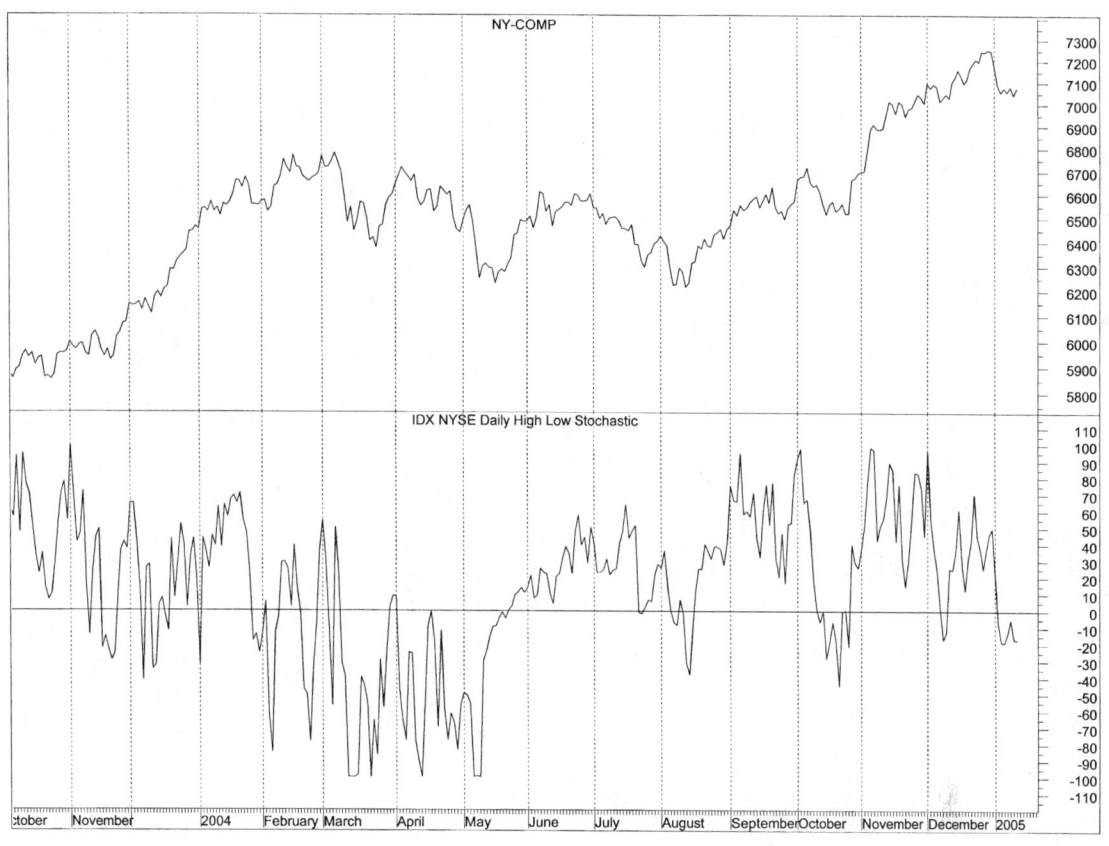

Interpretation

Chart 7–10 shows this ratio smoothed with a 21-day simple average. Most of the down spikes are just after market lows. When the market is declining, there are not many new highs being made, but once it starts to rally, new highs come quickly. Watching the upward moves for a reversal can assist in identifying tops. Also, Chart 7–10 uses semilogarithmic scaling for the indicator to better reflect the changes over such a long time.

Gerald Appel uses a 10-day smoothing as shown in Chart 7–11. He states that when this indicator falls to 30 and turns up, it is a buy signal. When it gets above 90, the market is strong and will continue for some time. He says anytime the indicator stays over 70, you can stay in the market.

Chart 7-10 New Highs, New Lows Ratio—21-Day Smooth.

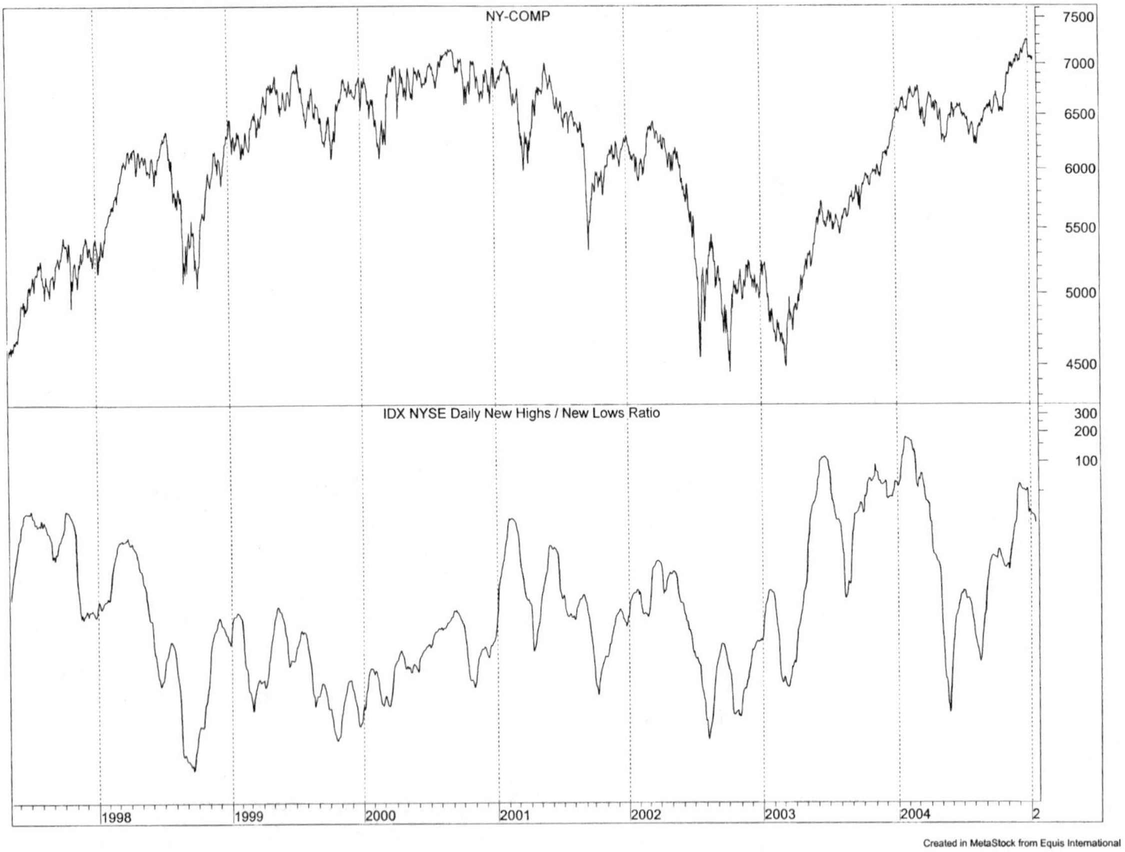

Author Comments

On Chart 7–11, notice the period near the 1987 crash and how this indicator did not register much movement. Why? The crash in October was sharp and quick and recovered quickly. New highs and new lows data covers the preceding year. There was a strong market up move from 1984 until the crash, preventing any new highs to occur off of the 1987 crash bottom. Said a little differently to ensure that you understand it, as the market rallied off of that October bottom, the action did not produce new highs because the drop was so sharp and quick.

Abraham Cohen, from Investor's Intelligence, used a 10-day average of new highs divided by the sum of new highs and new lows. This was also a stable part of Art Merrill's and John McGinley's Technical Trends service. Chart 7–12 shows Cohen's version.

New High, New Low Indicators

Chart 7-11 New Highs, New Lows Ratio—10-Day Smooth.

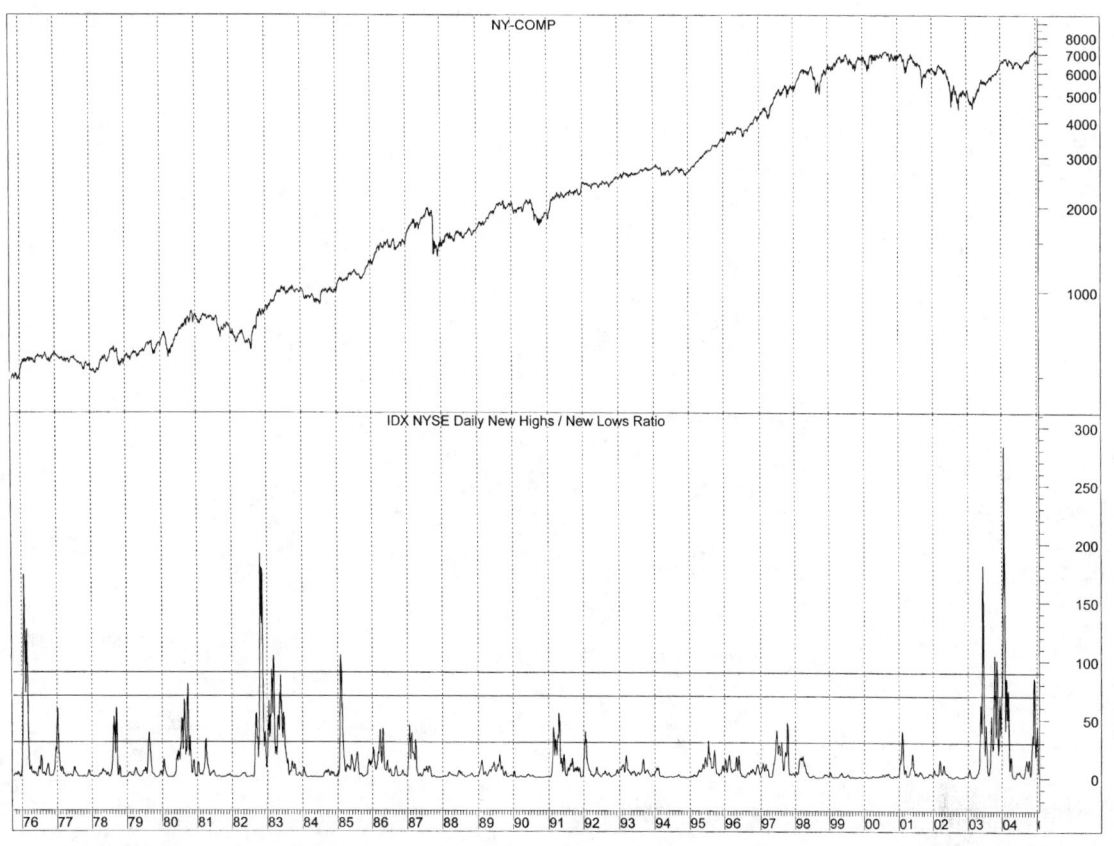

Arthur Merrill tested an indicator that used new highs divided by the sum of new highs and new lows using a percentage over a 10-day period. With the usual Arthur Merrill thoroughness, testing was done over a 10-year period using this indicator and the Dow Industrial Average. It turned out that the indicator worked well as an overbought and oversold indication, showing that an excess of new highs is bearish and an excess of new lows is bullish. Chart 7–13 shows this, but also shows that long periods of extended moves will keep the indicator in an overbought or oversold area. This is to be expected because up moves that are longer than 52 weeks will continue to generate new highs with each up day, and similarly for down moves and new lows. I have attempted to identify the validity of this thinking with the High Low Validation Index later in this section.

Chart 7-12   New High, New Low—Cohen.

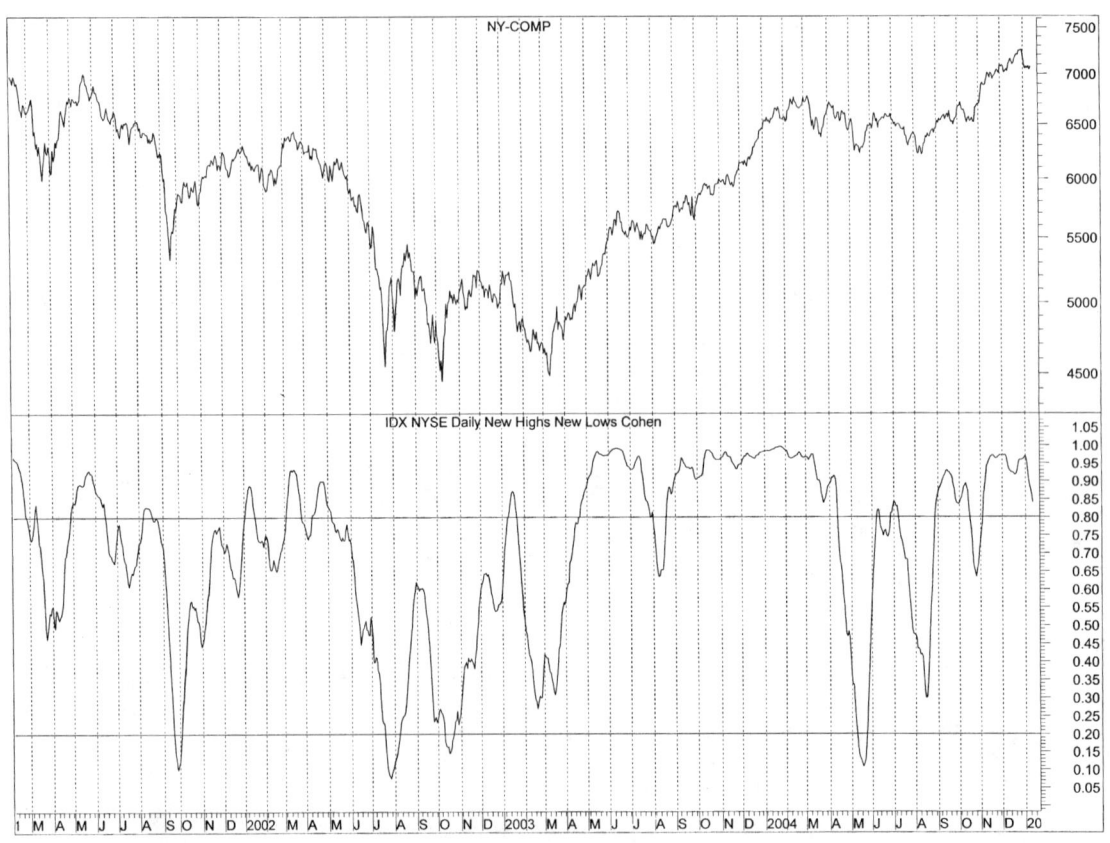

In 1993, Tim Hayes of Ned Davis Research said that using weekly new highs is a very good leading indicator for a market top. As of late 1993, out of 14 indicators this was the second best in his testing. He states that the weekly new highs indicator was 100 percent successful in leading nine bull markets, doing so by a median of 34 weeks and with a range of 71 weeks. It appears that this simple indicator continues to do well. Chart 7–14 shows this. This is not an indicator using the ratio, but just the weekly new highs.

The third best indicator out of the Tim Hayes' study mentioned above was a daily ratio of new highs to the sum of new highs and new lows, smoothed by 55 days. Hayes claims it has a better record than the advance decline indicators. Determination of it signaling a market top

New High, New Low Indicators

Chart 7-13 New Highs, New Lows Ratio—Merrill.

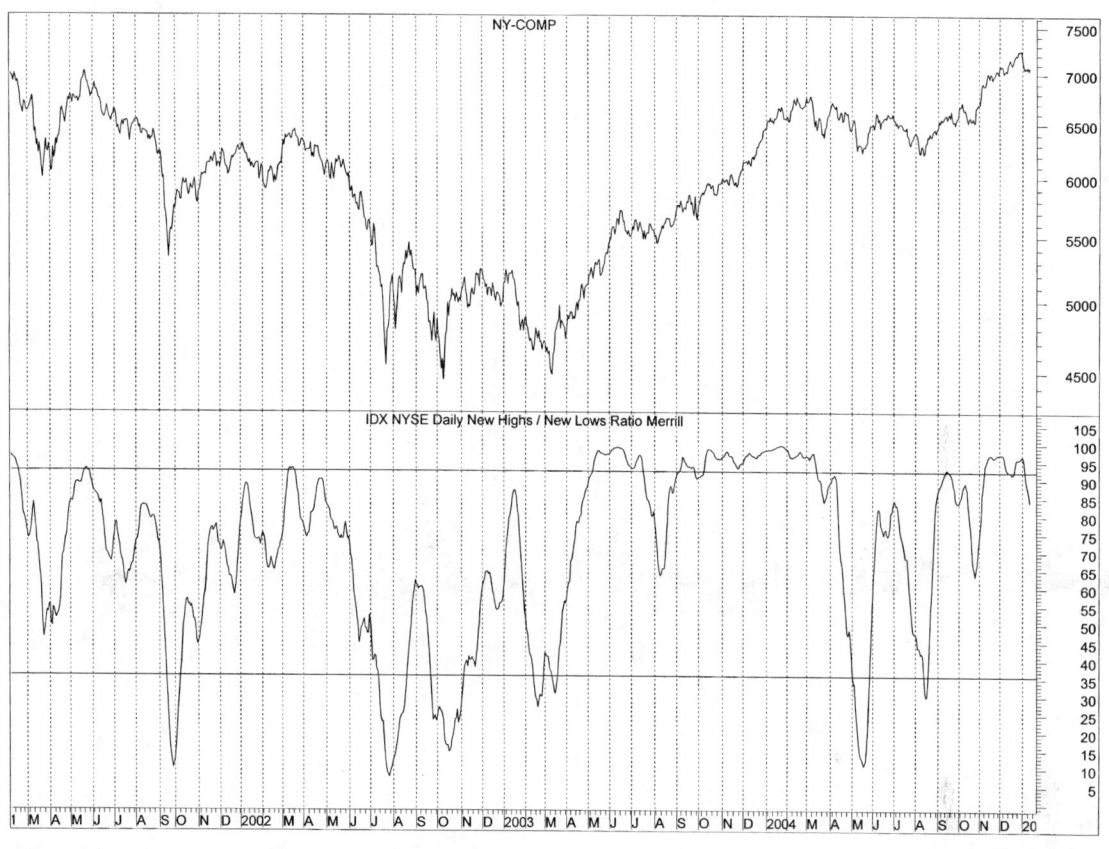

is done by a divergence in the indicator. All divergences have been identified in Chart 7–15. Also, Hayes says that when it is below .21, the market is oversold, again, as shown by the line in Chart 7–15.

$$\text{Formula: } (H/L), (H/(H+L))$$

References

Appel, Gerald, "Gerald Appel, with Systems and Forecasts." *Stocks and Commodities*, Volume 12, March 1994, pp. 98–105.

Chart 7-14 Weekly New Highs—Hayes.

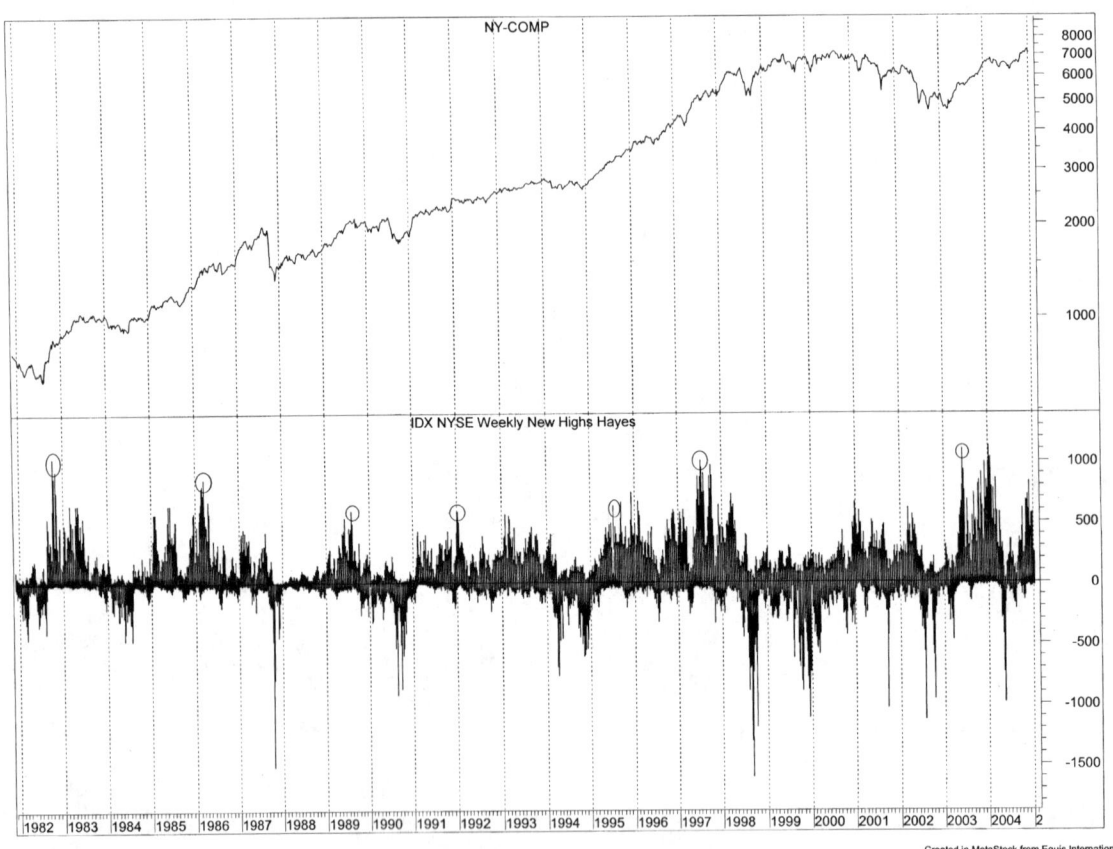

Merrill, Arthur, 1985, *Technical Trends*, Merrill Analysis.
Merrill, Arthur, "New Highs / New Lows." *Stocks and Commodities*, Volume 8, June 1990, pp. 228- 229.
Hayes, Tim, "Leading Indices at Bull Market Peaks." *Stocks and Commodities*, Volume 11, December 1993, pp. 483–488.

High Low Miscellaneous
New Highs and New Lows

Data components required: New Highs (H), New Lows (L).

New High, New Low Indicators

Chart 7-15 New Highs—Hayes.

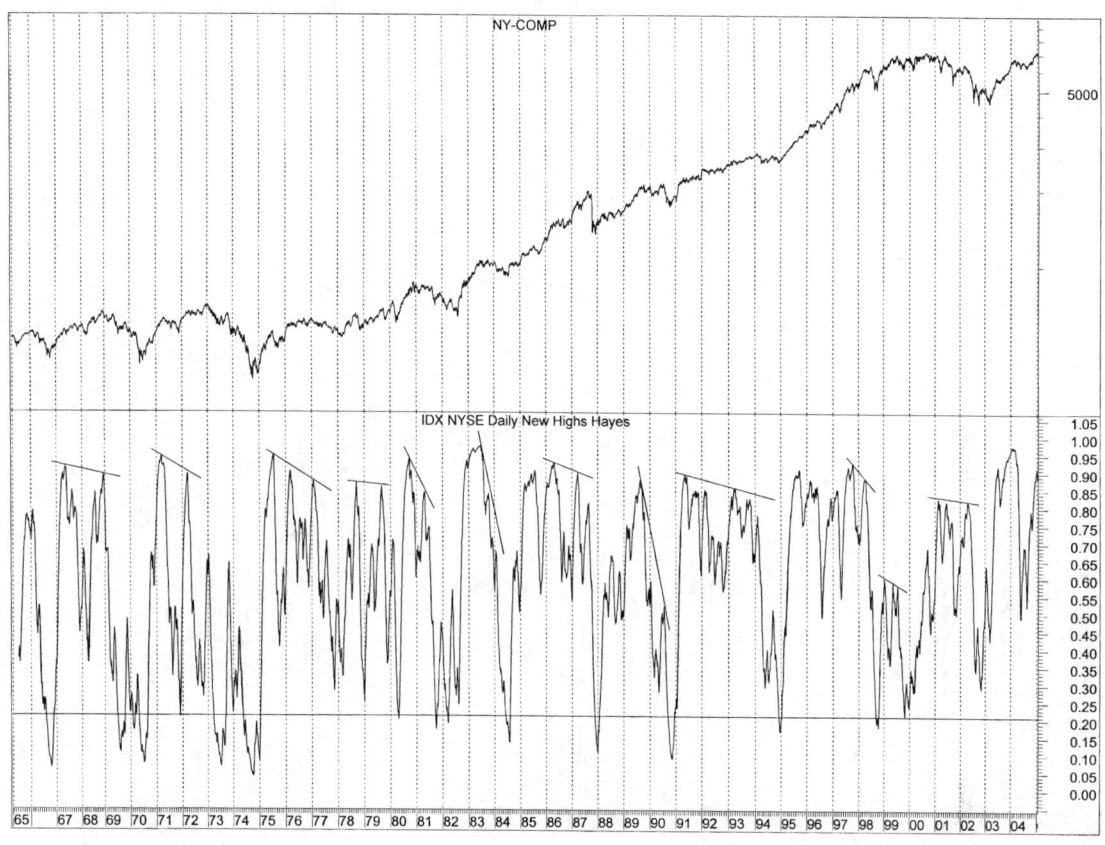

Description

This is merely the act of displaying both the new highs and new lows as separate lines, each arithmetically smoothed by 10 days. This makes it somewhat subjective and not good for detailed analysis, but good for a general picture of the breadth of the market in accordance with new highs and new lows.

Interpretation

From Chart 7–16 you can see that in normal times, the new highs are above the new lows during market rises and below the new lows during market declines. This is as one would expect, so looking for the early reversal of this would possibly lead to turns in the market. The two plots in the

Chart 7-16 New Highs and New Lows Cross.

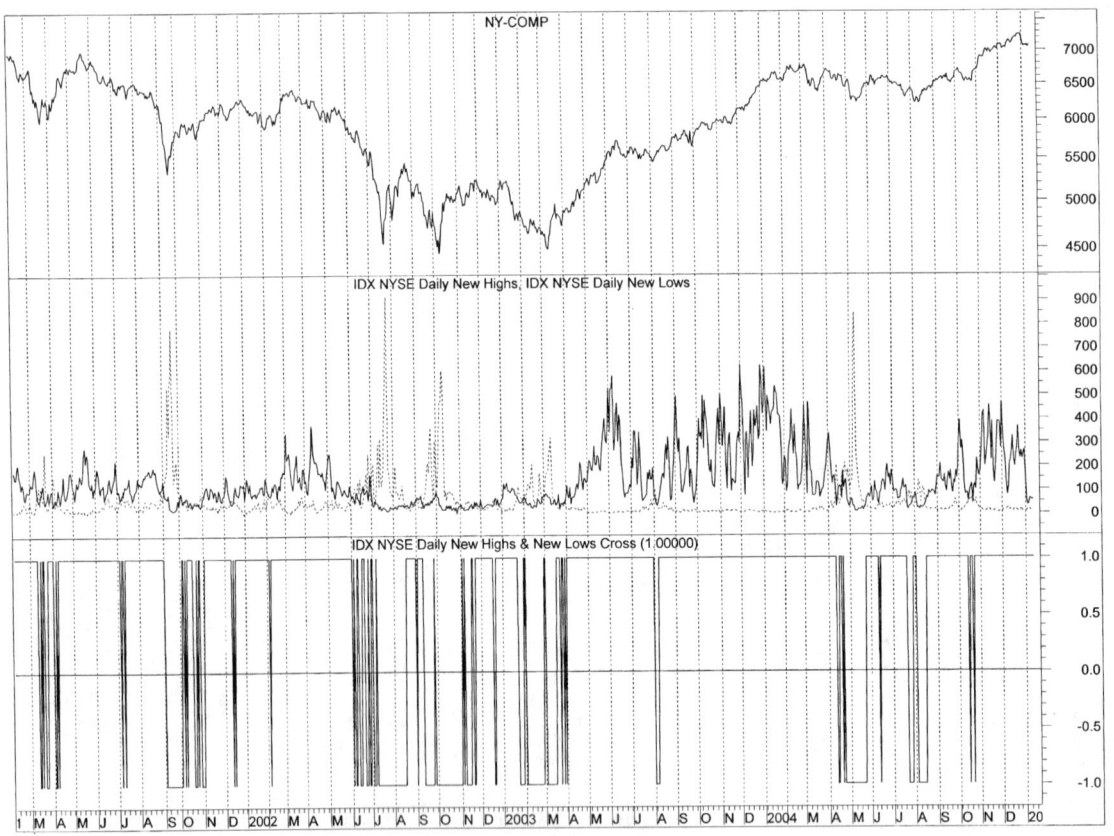

middle show this, the new lows being the dotted line and the new highs being the solid line. In the bottom plot, when the line is above zero, it shows a value of +1 and means the new highs are greater than the new lows. If below the zero line at −1, the new lows are above the new highs.

Author Comments

An awareness of the number of stocks making new highs and new lows is an important part of breadth analysis. I prefer to remove as much subjectivity from the analysis as possible. Chart 7–17 is a chart showing the new highs and new lows each smoothed by a 10-period average, then showing it as +1 when the new high average is above the new low average, and −1 when the new high average is below the new low average.

Chart 7-17 New High, New Low Cross—10-Day Smooth.

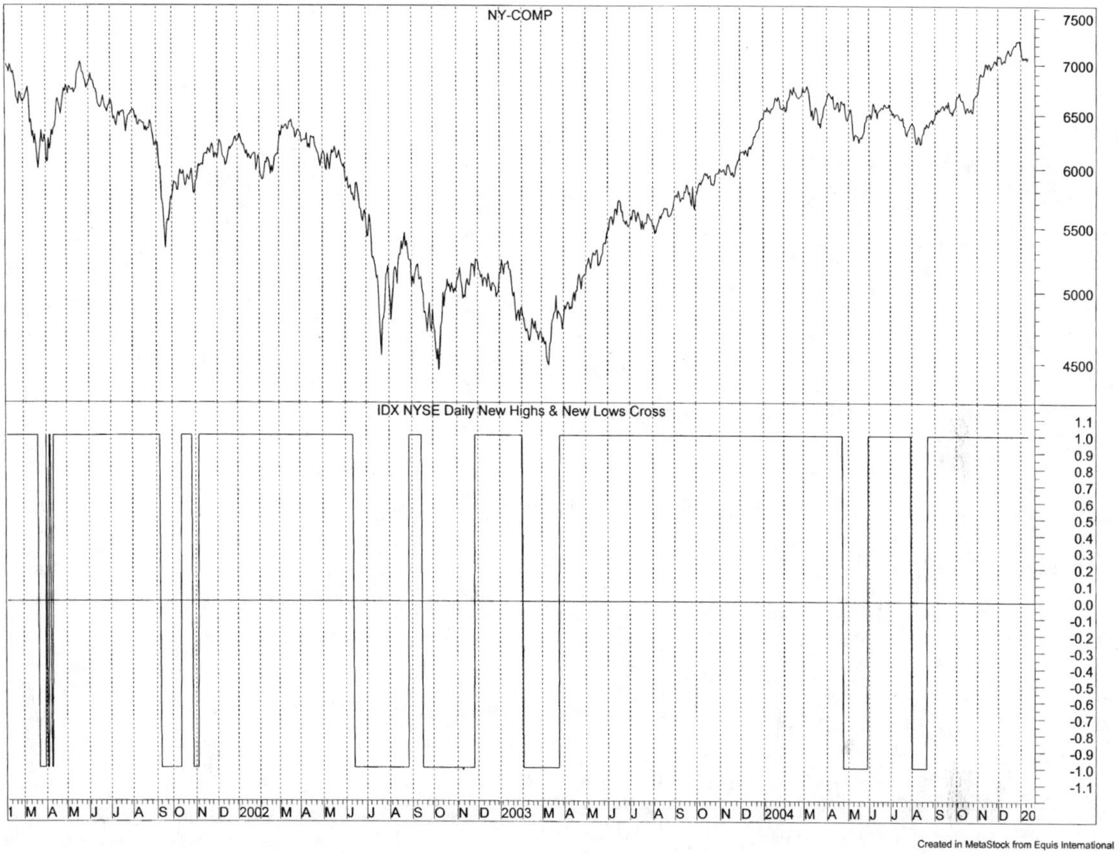

Mike Burk shows an unusual way to display the new high and new low data. New highs were shown as a 19-period smoothing and normalized on a scale from zero to 100. The new lows were shown similarly but with an inverted scale. This meant that as new lows increased, they would descend from the top of the chart. They share a common high value, whether it is new highs or new lows. Also, the normalizations are for periods of about 100 trading days.

Chart 7–18 shows Burk's charting convention. The number of new lows (dotted line) relative to the range of new lows over the last 100 days helps identify market bottoms with fairly good accuracy. The number of new highs, again relative to the range of new highs over the last 100 days shows market tops, but only after the number of new highs starts to drop.

Formula: $(H + L)$

Chart 7-18 New Highs, New Lows—Burk.

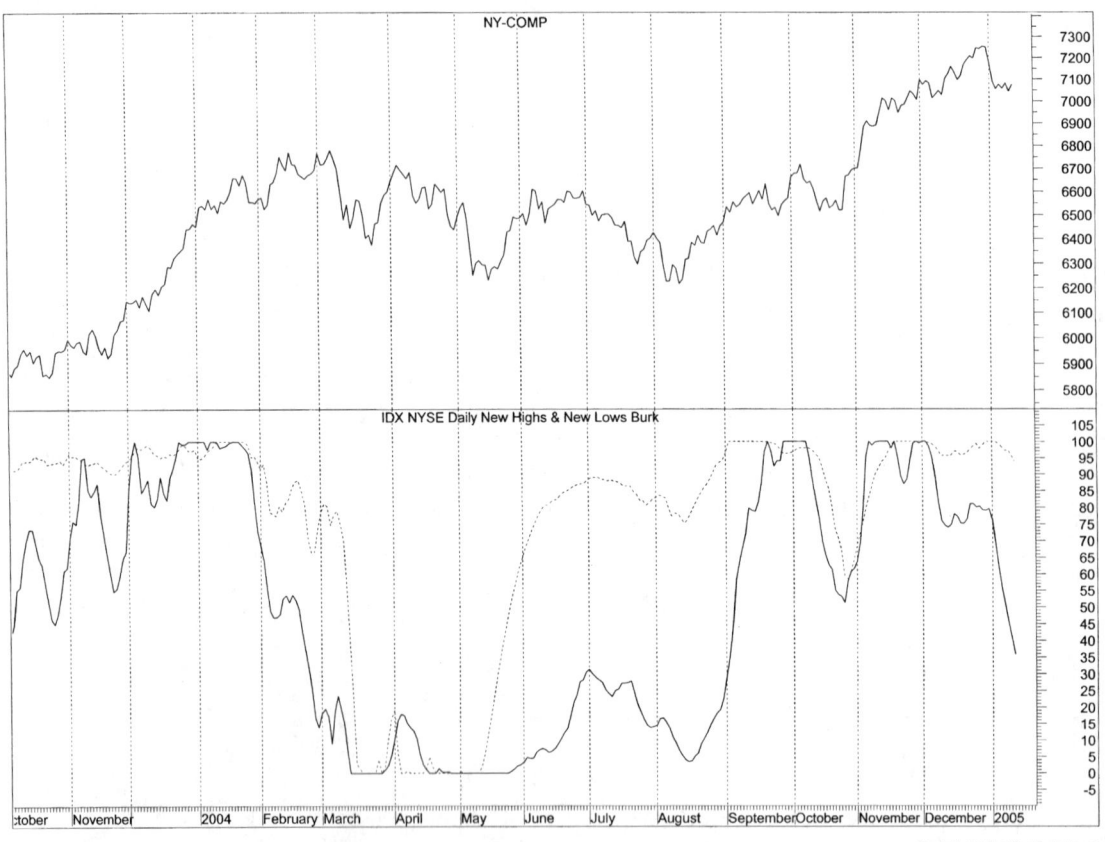

References

Burk, Mike, "New High and New Low Indicators." *Stocks and Commodities*, Volume 8, May 1990, pp. 197–198.

New Highs % Total Issues

Data components required: New Highs (*NH*), Total Issues (*TI*).

Description

Probably the best way to look at a single data component is to put it into perspective with a related, but more global, breadth component. Here we take the new highs as a percentage of total issues.

Interpretation

Leading up to a market top, the number of new highs is considerably more than the number of new lows. The first warning sign is when they start to become equal. This is because as a top is formed, many stocks stop making new highs, and there is a churning of issues making new highs, which keeps the total number of them from declining. Once the top is in full swing, the stocks that peaked at the beginning of the top are now dropping and soon will be making new lows. Much of this is based on how long of a topping process it has been. When the number of new highs and new lows are about equal, but still have numbers around 100 or more of each, look out. Chart 7–19 shows this percentage smoothed by 21 days.

Author Comments

At times I believe that new high and new low data is better than the advance decline data for identifying market trends and turning points. New highs, like advances, will drive the market higher.

Chart 7–19 New Highs Percent Total Issues.

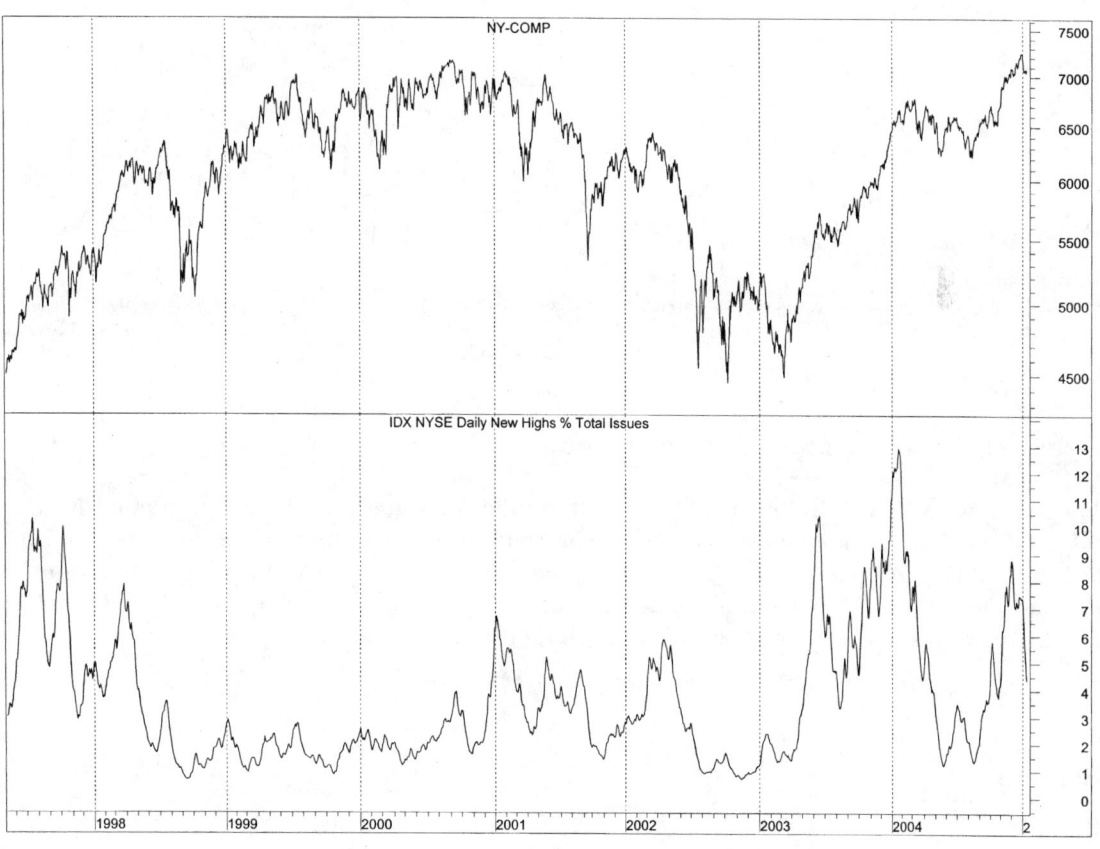

Chart 7-20 New Highs Percent Total Issues Rate of Change.

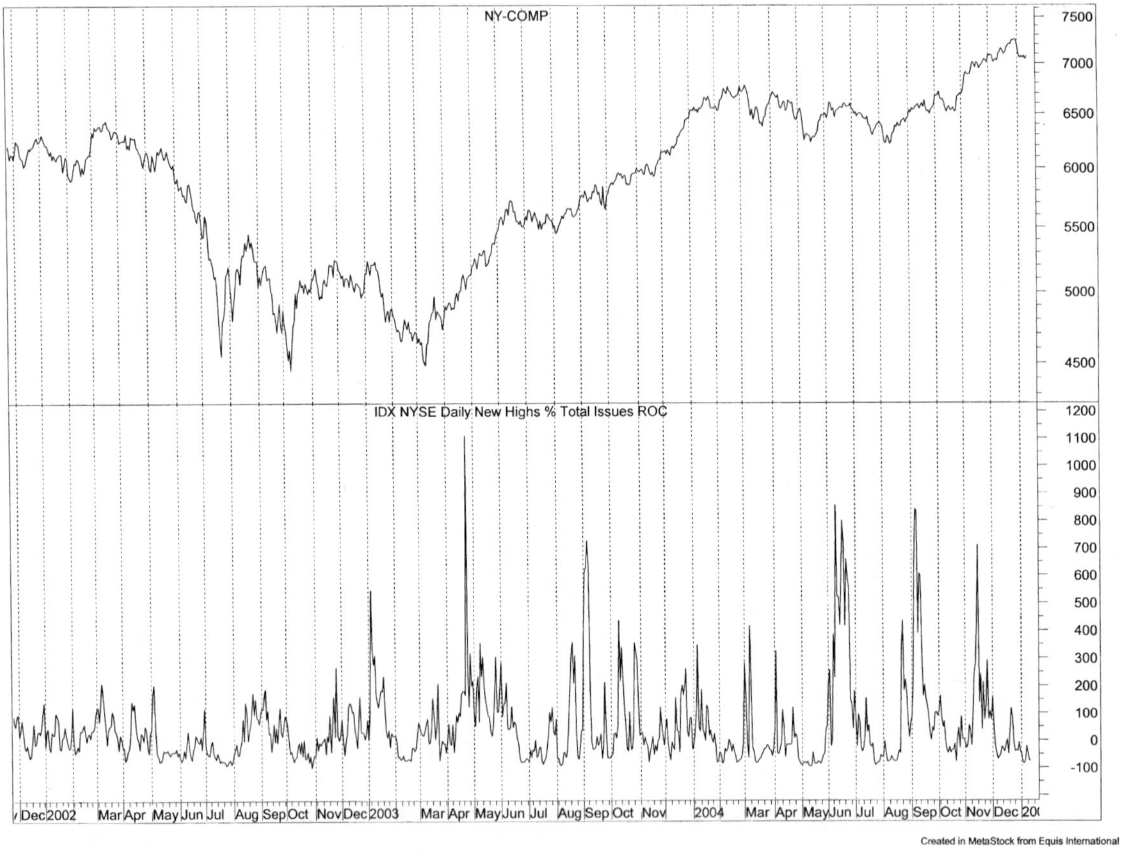

Chart 7-20 shows the percentage of new highs viewed as a rate of change, and again, smoothed by 21 days.

Tim Hayes, of Ned Davis Research, looks at this indicator and claims that when the weekly new highs as a percentage of total issues exceed 30 percent for the first time in a new year, it is bullish. Similarly, when the weekly new lows, as a percentage of total issues, is below 1.95 percent, it is bullish, and when above 7.2 percent it is bearish. Chart 7-21 shows the new highs in the middle plot and the new lows in the bottom plot with the Hayes thresholds shown.

Formula: $(H / TI) *100$

References

Davis, Ned. *Being Right or Making Money*. Ned Davis Research, 1991.

New High, New Low Indicators 153

Chart 7-21 Weekly New Highs, New Lows—Hayes.

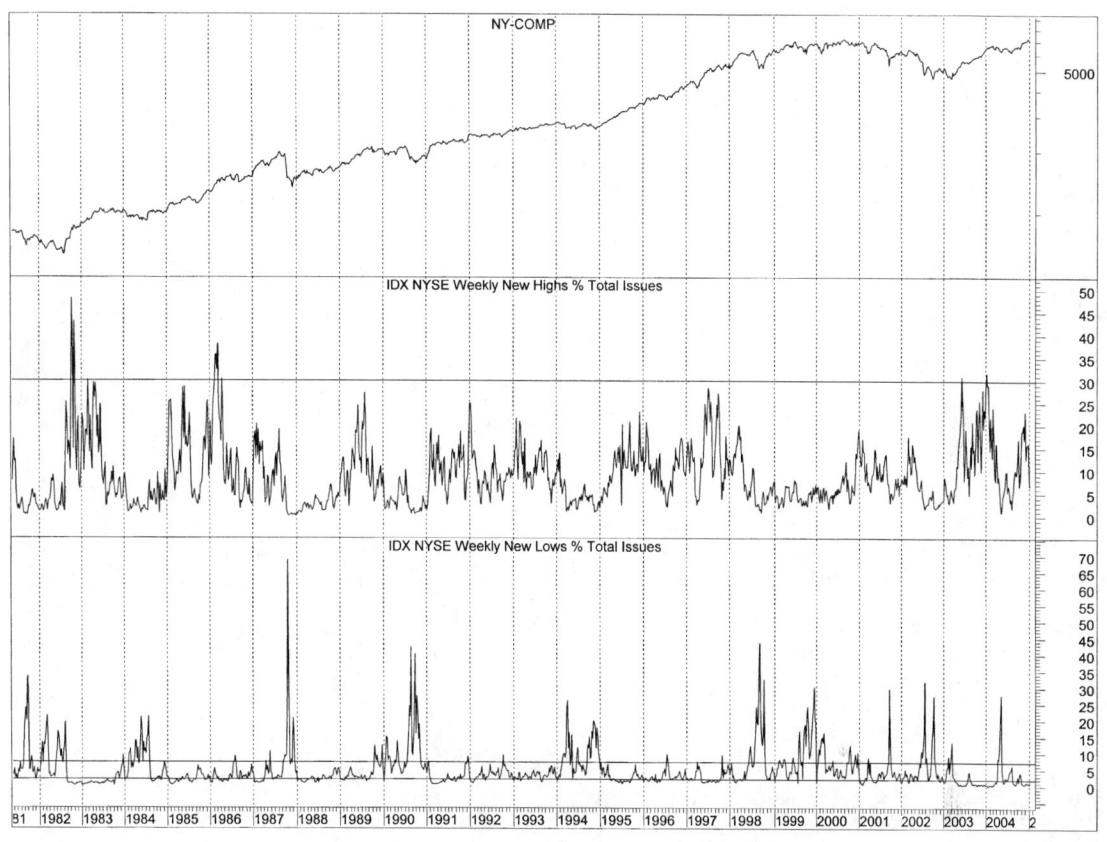

New Lows % Total Issues

Data components required: New Lows (NL), Total Issues (TI).

Description

This is the number of stocks hitting a new low for the first time in the last 52 weeks relative to the total issues traded.

Interpretation

New lows will show you additional information about the health of the market. Chart 7-22 shows this with the percentage smoothed over 21 days. As expected because of the sharp tendency of the markets at bottoms, the new lows usually spike at or very near to those bottoms.

Chart 7-22 New Lows Percent Total Issues.

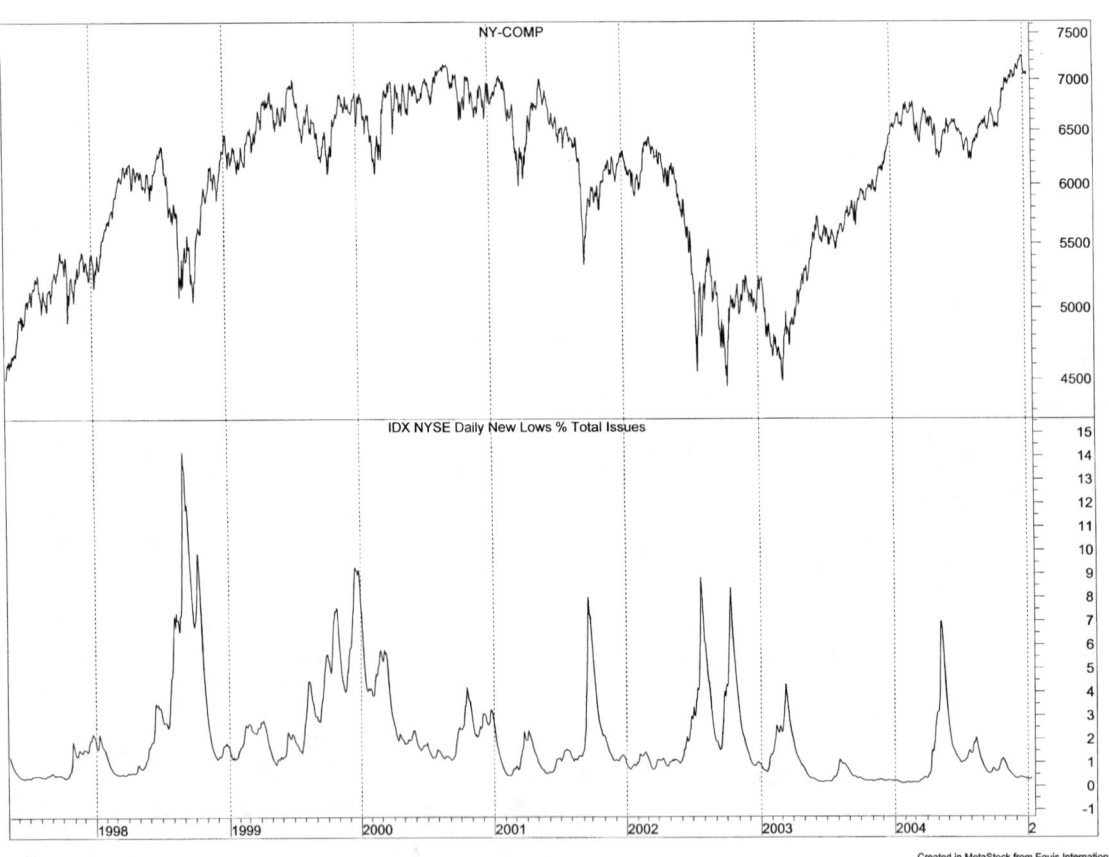

Author Comments

Mike Burk claims that the new lows are best at defining cycles in the market, and not particularly useful for day-to-day trading. Chart 7-23 is the rate of change chart similar to that used in the new high-percentage section. The dashed vertical lines represent a 60-day cycle anchored near the March, 2003 low point in the market. It seems that the cycle lines fall fairly regularly on the peaks in the New Low rate of charge indicator.

Tim Hayes of Ned Davis Research offers buy and sell information on the weekly new lows as a percentage of total issues. Look under New Highs % Total Issues earlier in this section.

$$\text{Formula: } (L / TI) * 100$$

References

Burk, Mike, "New High and New Low Indicators." *Stocks and Commodities*, Volume 8, May 1990, pp. 197–198.

New High, New Low Indicators

Chart 7-23 New Lows Percent Total Issues Rate of Change.

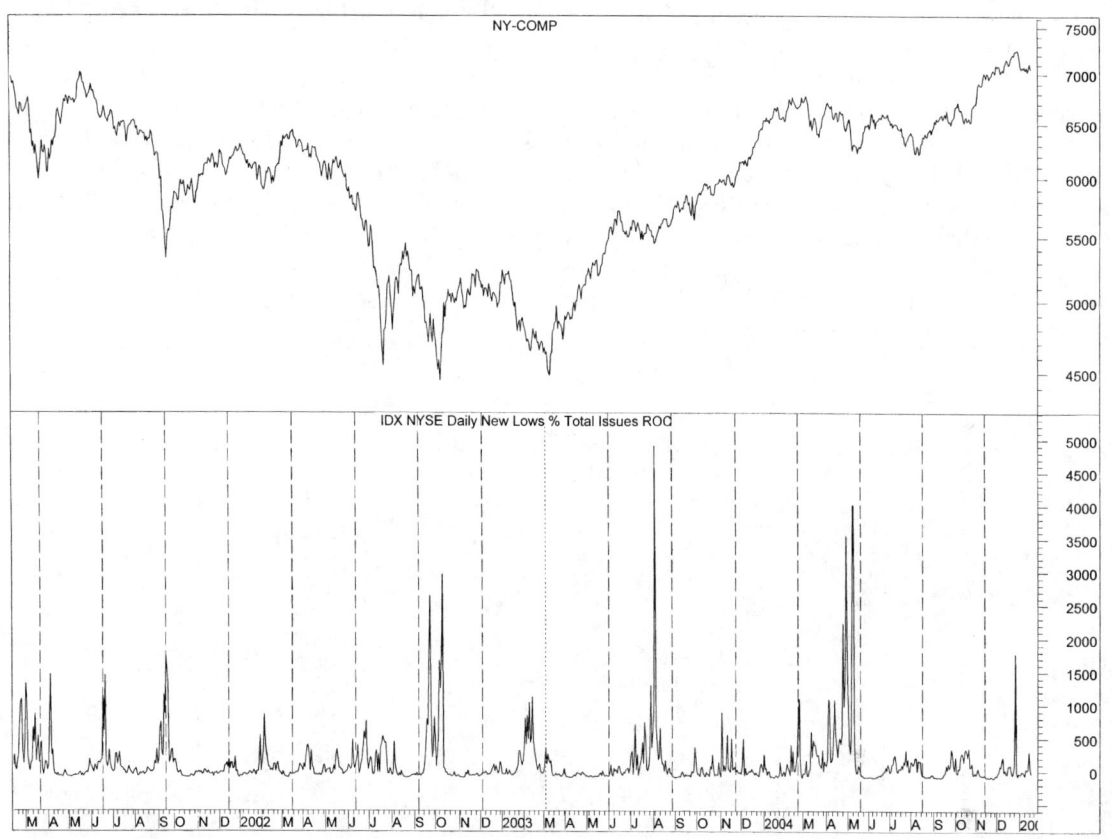

High Low Logic Index

Author/Creator: Norman Fosback
Data components required: New Highs (H), New Lows (L)

Description

This is an indicator that uses two ratios: the new highs divided by the total issues, and the new lows divided by the total issues. The High Low Logic Index uses the lesser of the two ratios on any given day and then exponentially smoothes it by 50 days. Note: Fosback used weekly data for this indicator with a 10-day smoothing.

Interpretation

The concept is that either a large number of issues will reach new highs or will reach new lows, but normally not at the same time. Because the indicator uses the lower of new highs or new lows, a low reading on this indicator could indicate a strong trend. If you think about it, it is somewhat of a consensus indicator based on new highs and new lows. When it reaches a high reading, it means that there is something inconsistent about the market and it is not a good sign. Chart 7–24 also shows the individual new highs and new lows (dotted line) in the middle and the high low logic index on the bottom. This chart uses daily data adjusted for Fosback's parameters. You can see in Chart 7–24 that when the market is trending, the indicator is at its low points.

Chart 7–25 uses weekly data as preferred by Norman Fosback. Close examination of the daily and weekly versions does not yield much difference. This is because new high and new low data is based on a much larger time frame.

Chart 7–24 High Low Logic Index.

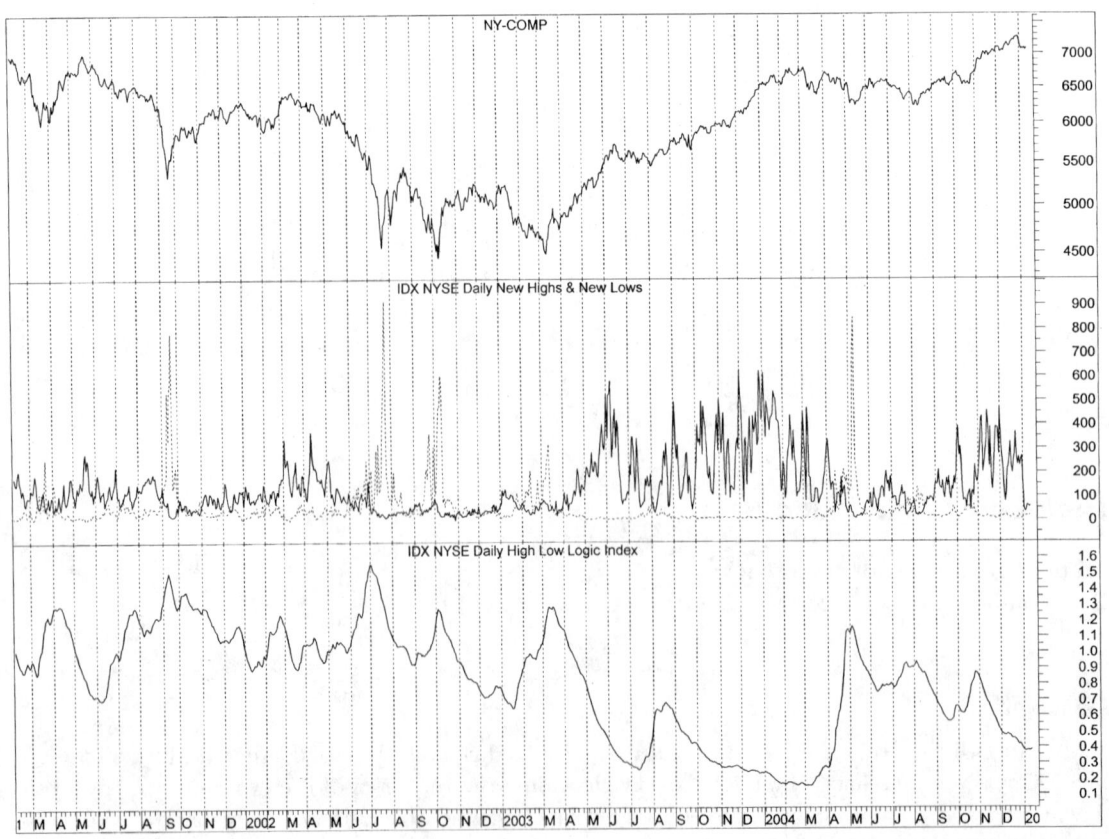

New High, New Low Indicators

Chart 7-25 High Low Logic Index—Weekly.

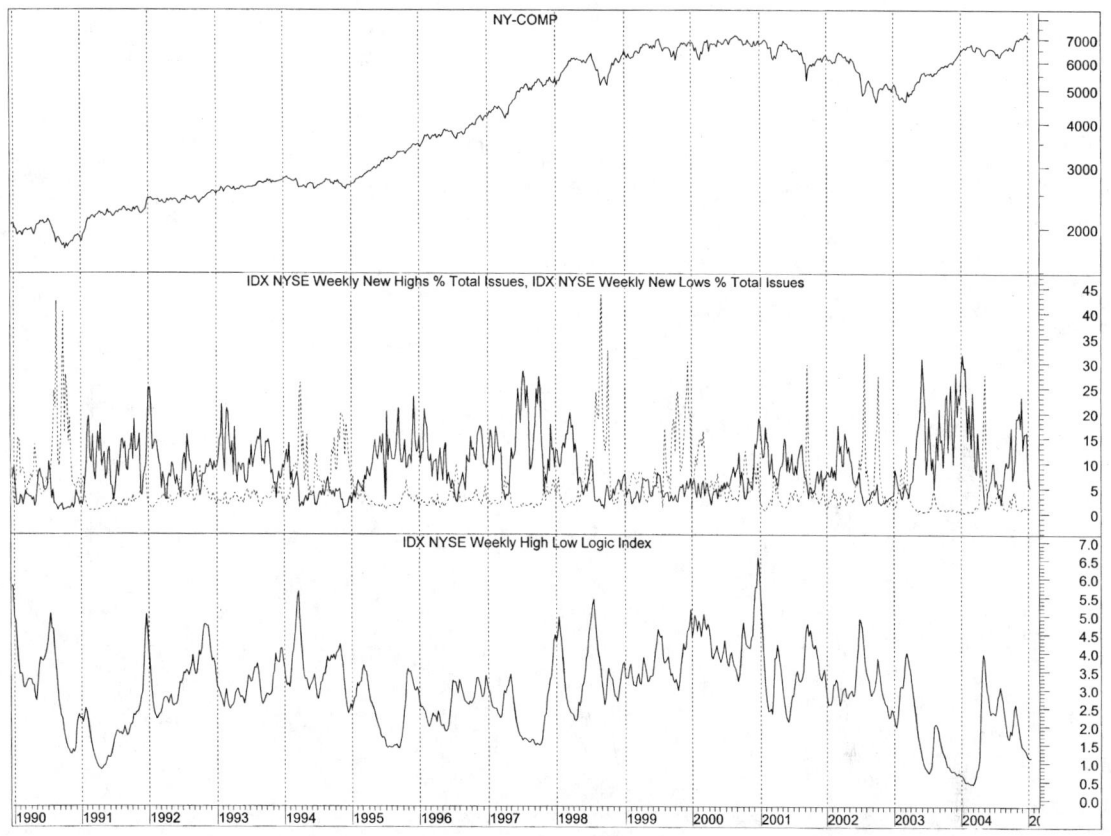

Gerald Appel uses a slight modification to this indicator. He uses the lesser of the two ratios of new highs to total issues and new lows to total issues. Because he also used weekly data for the new highs and new lows, I adjusted his sell parameter to 2.4 as shown in Chart 7-26. This version seems to identify tops when it rises above 2.4.

Author Comments

I think that the weekly data was easier to work with when there were no personal computers, and that accounts for its use in some of these older indicators. I also believe there isn't much difference in using weekly data versus daily data in regard to new highs and new lows because they are based on prices 52 weeks (252 days) ago. If an issue reaches a new high on Monday, it means it is

Chart 7-26 High Low Logic—Appel.

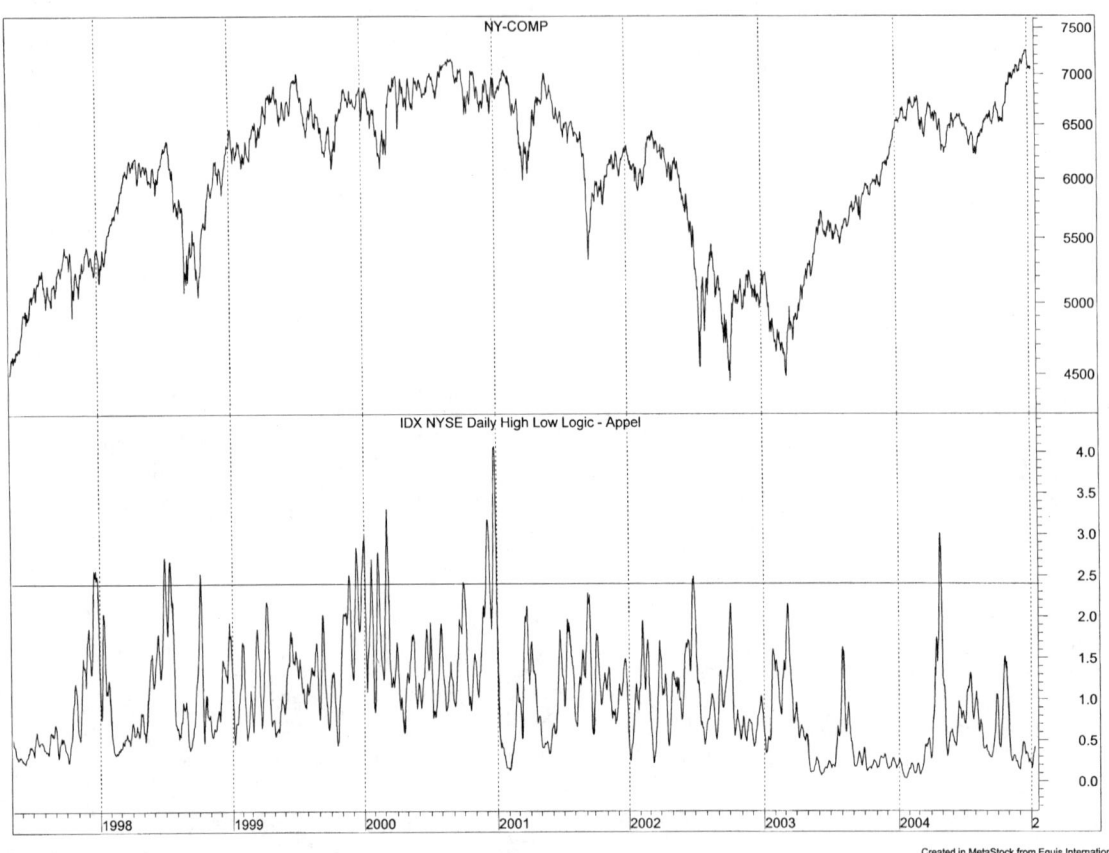

the highest high value for that issue in a year. If the weekly new highs (Friday close) also reflect that, it is within less than 2 percent of representing the time of the new high. And that is the worst-case scenario. The other days of the week are even closer, with Friday being the same as the weekly.

This unique concept is somewhat similar to Wilder's Directional Movement. The steady moves of the indicator either up or down can represent good trending markets. Look at the period between 1992 and 1997 (Chart 7-25), a time of continuous market upwards movement. The high low logic index stayed at low readings much of the time, indicating there were many new highs (or new lows) being made.

I figured I would reverse the concept and created the Low High Logic Index as shown in Chart 7-27. This is the opposite of Fosback's indicator in that it uses the higher of the two ratios mentioned above instead of the lower. Setting a decision zone at 10 tells us that we are either at a new

New High, New Low Indicators

Chart 7-27 Low High Logic Index.

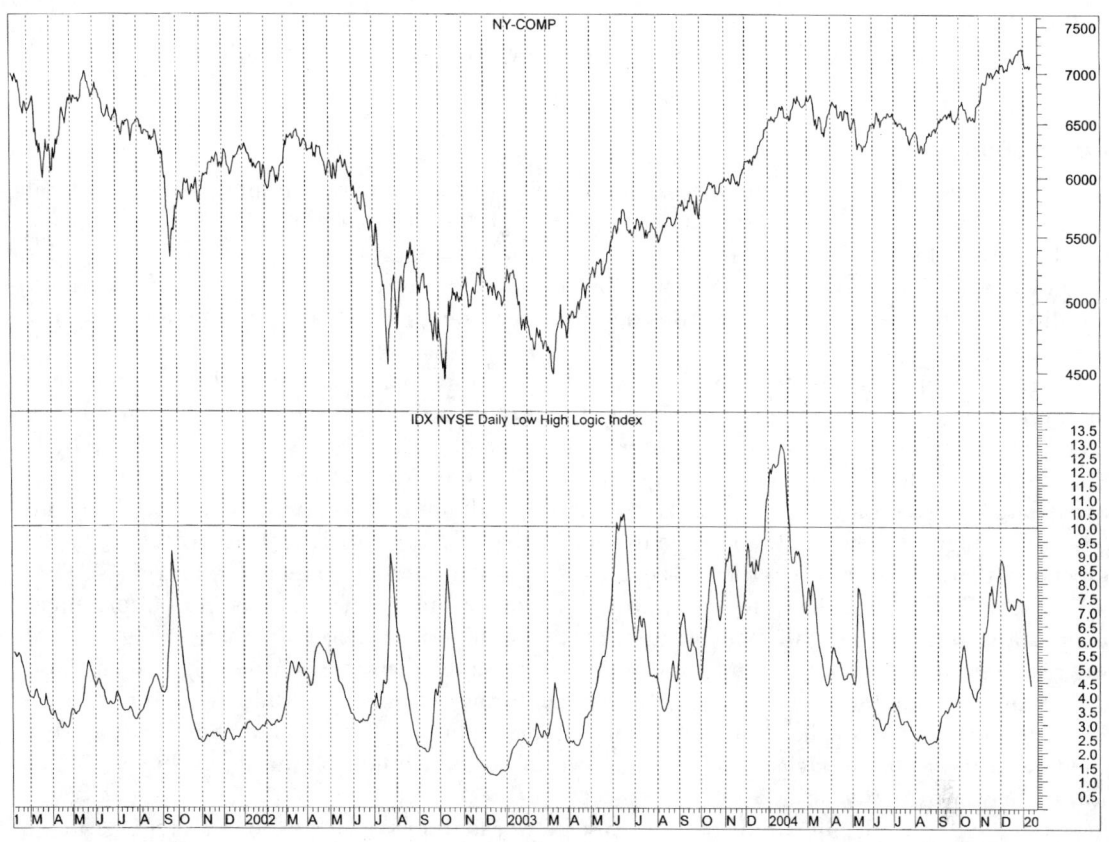

market top or a market bottom. The good news is that the trend of the market up to that point should tell us which it will be. Like its complement, the high low logic index, it stays at low values during strong trending markets.

Formula: Previous Value + $((H / TI)$ or $(L / TI))$ (exponentially smoothed by 50 days).

References

Fosback, Norman G. *Stock Market Logic*, Fort Lauderdale, FL: The Institute for Economic Research, Inc., 1976.

Appel, Gerald, "Gerald Appel with Systems and Forecasts." *Stocks and Commodities*, Volume 12, March 1994, pp. 98–105.

High Low Validation

Author/Creator: Greg Morris
Data components required: New Highs (H), New Lows (L), Market Index (MKT)

Description

This is an attempt to help validate new high and new low data and, to be honest, is still a "work in progress." If you consider the facts relating to new highs and new lows, you will see the necessity for this. A new high means that the closing price reached a high that it had not seen in the last year (52 weeks). Similarly, a new low is at a low not seen for at least a year. This indicator tries to identify when the new high or new low is determined to be good or bad using the following line of thinking.

Consider that prices have been in a narrow range for more than a year. Something then triggers an event that causes the market to move out of that trading range to the upside. This will immediately cause almost every stock that moves with the market to also become a new high. New highs are generally the force that keeps good up moves going. The new lows in this scenario will dry up, as expected. Now consider that the market has had a steady advance for quite some time. The number of new highs will generally continue to remain high, as most stocks will rise with the market. Of course there will be drops as the market makes it corrections on its path to higher prices. When the number of new highs starts to dry up, you will probably notice that the number of unchanged issues starts to increase slightly because a lot of stocks will just cease to participate in the continuing rise. New lows will not happen for some time because the market is just starting to form a top. The number of new lows will increase as the market forms its broad top, while the number of new highs gets smaller and smaller. It will be the time frame of this topping action that determines when the new lows will start to kick in. Remember, you cannot have a new low until an issue is at a new low price over the last year.

When the market declines and you start to see fewer new lows, it means the market is losing its downside momentum. Why is this so? It is because some issues have already bottomed and are not continuing to make new lows. This is tied to the rotational effect, sometimes caused by various market sectors hitting bottoms at different times.

Interpretation

Chart 7–28 is an attempt to show this visually. Up spikes (solid line) equal to +2 represent good new highs. Up spikes (dashed line) equal to +1 represent bad new highs. Similarly, down spikes (solid line) at −2 equates to good new lows and −1 (dotted line) equates to bad new lows. You might read that again since it is not obvious. I wanted to keep the new highs as the up spikes and the new lows as the down spikes. Short up spikes are bad new highs and short down spikes are bad new lows. Bad, in this case, means they did not conform to the theory talked about above.

New High, New Low Indicators

Chart 7-28 High Low Validation Index.

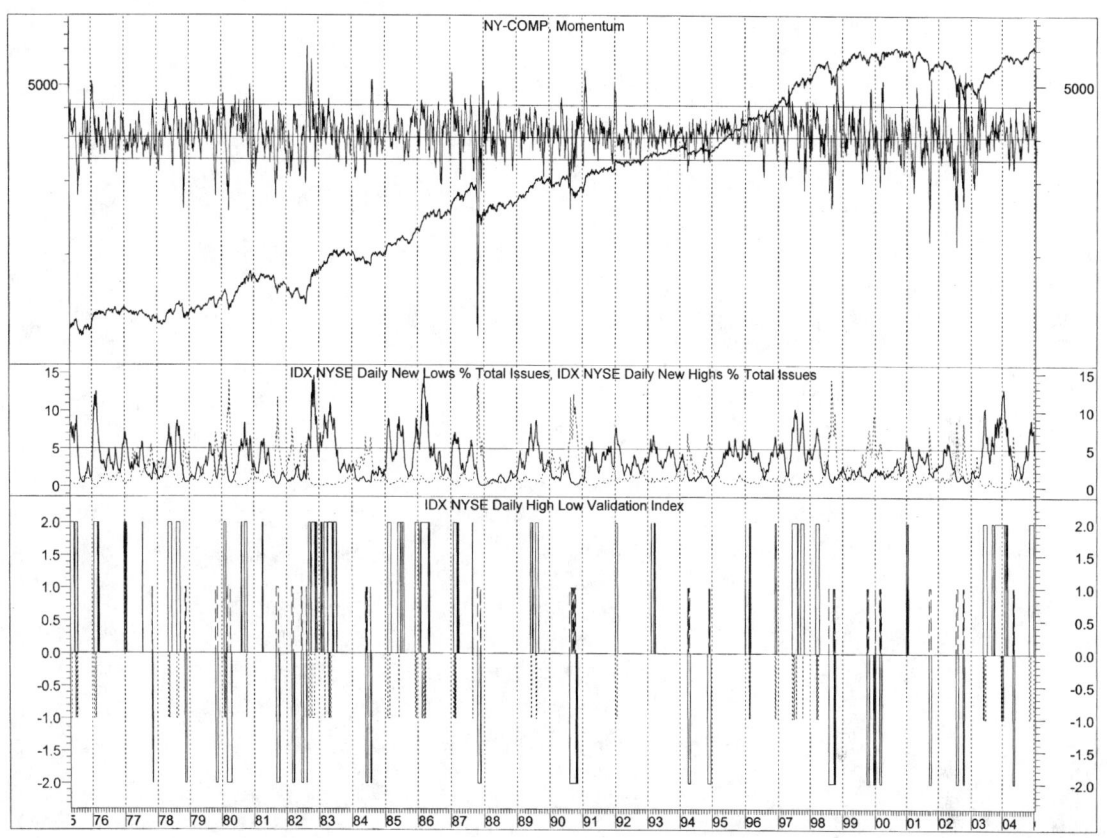

Author Comments

This method of trying to determine when the new highs and new lows are truly good ones involves the rate of change of the market, a smoothed value of each component relative to the total issues traded, and their relationship with each other. For example, if the market is in a rally (rate of change high) and the new highs are increasing, any new lows that appear are not good ones.

8

Up Volume, Down Volume Indicators

The breadth indicators in this section utilize either up volume, down volume, or both in their calculation. Please do not confuse this with the plethora of technical indicators that use total volume.

Up Volume and Down Volume Indicators

Up Volume
Down Volume
Changed Volume
Up and Down Volume
McClellan Oscillator—Volume
McClellan Summation Index—Volume
Merriman Volume Model
Swenlin IT Volume Momentum Oscillator

Swenlin Trading Oscillator—Volume
Up Volume, Down Volume Line
Cumulative Volume Ratio
Up Down On Balance Volume (OBV)
Volume Percentage Ratio
Upside − Downside Volume
Upside / Downside Volume Ratio
Zweig Up Volume Indicator

Up Volume

Data components required: Up Volume (UV)

Description

This is the total amount of volume that is in the advancing issues on a daily basis.

Interpretation

By itself, it is a noisy number and almost unusable, however, smoothing it by 21 days gives some interesting information about the market. Volume generally precedes market highs. Many say that the up volume fuels the market's rise. If this smoothed indicator is not making new highs with the market, be on the alert. Chart 8–1 is the 21-day smooth of the up volume.

Gerald Appel likes to look at up volume smoothed over 10 days. He says that if the market makes a new high and the up volume (10-day average) does not also make a new high within about 6 weeks, be alert for a market top. Leigh Stevens says that up volume is a true test of buying interest. He also uses a 10-day average of up volume for his analysis. He watches a baseline in up volume, which is at 525–550 million shares. The midpoint of his range (537m) is shown on Chart 8–2.

Author Comments

John McGinley liked to use up volume as a percentage of total volume with a 3-week average. His reason was that up volume was the motor of the market; without it the market will drop. In order for the market to just remain even, it must have up volume.

Chart 8-1 Up Volume—21-Day Smooth.

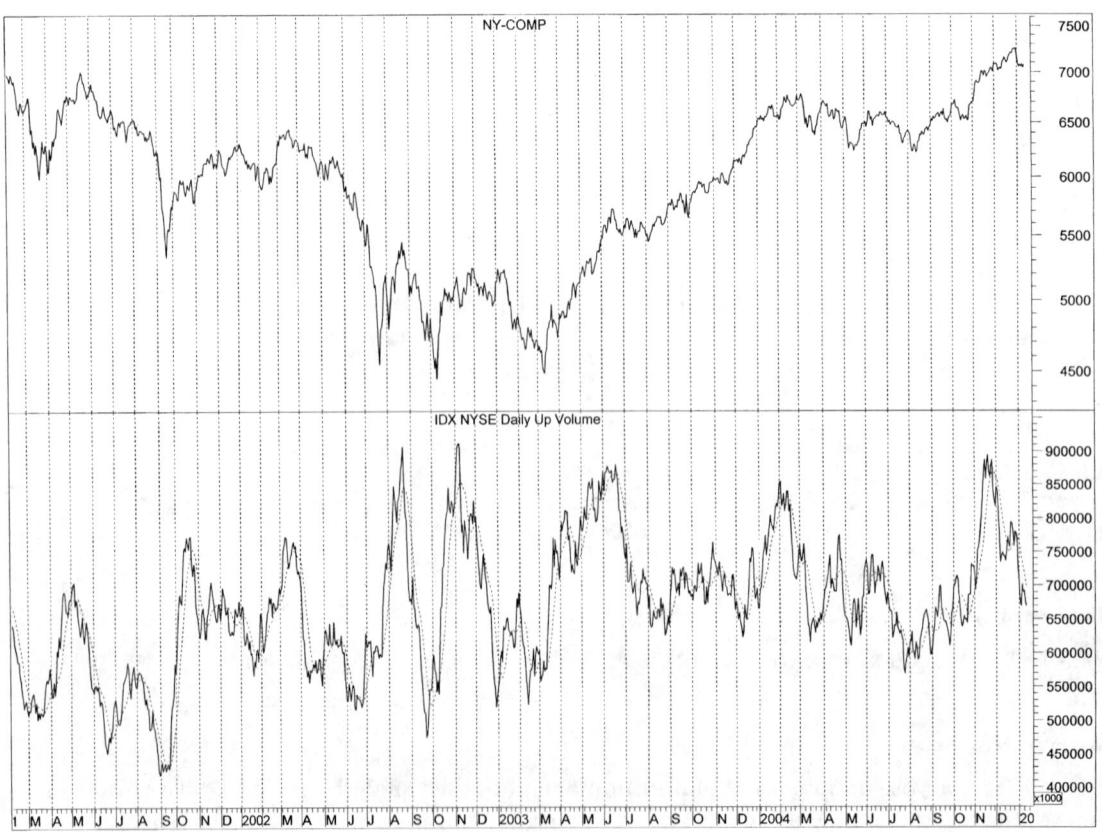

Chart 8-2 Up Volume—10-Day Smooth.

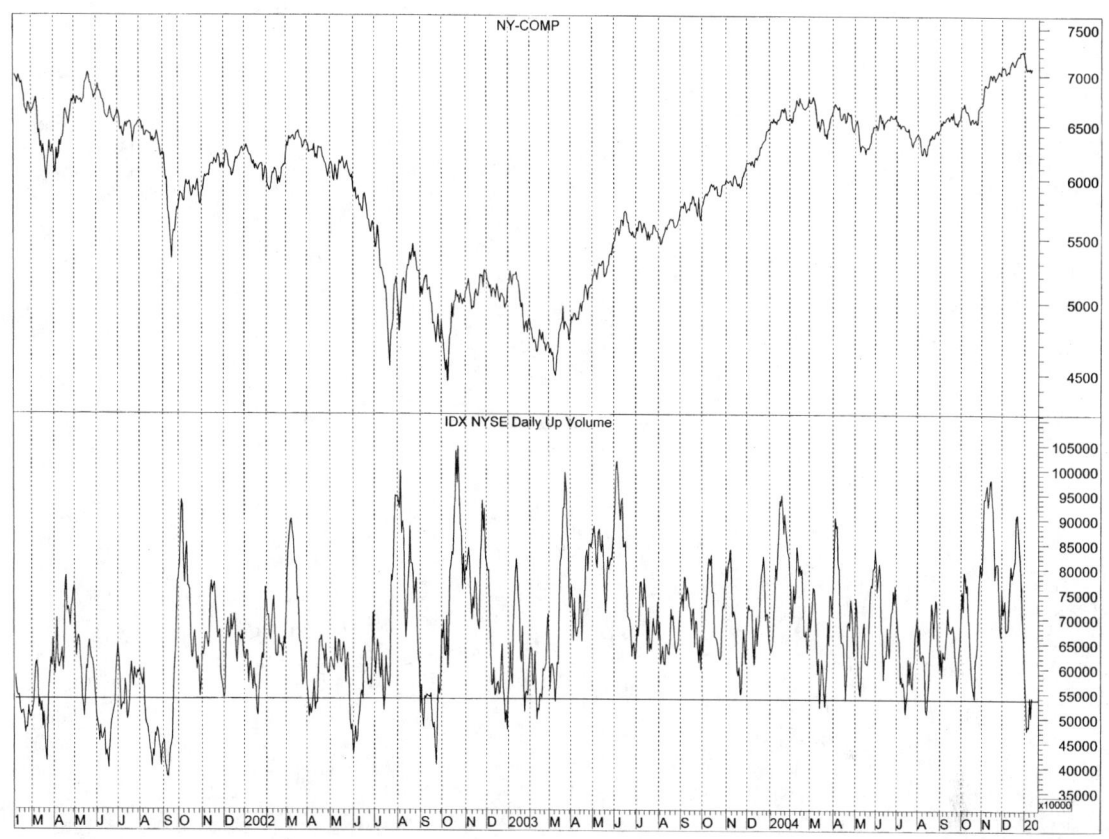

I think detrending a data set such as this is better than looking at the raw data, even if it is smoothed as in the example prior to this. Chart 8–3 shows the up volume relative to its 21-day average, with the results further smoothed by 10 days. You can spot periods of strong up volume associated with good up market moves. However, once the market starts to weaken, this indicator turns around quickly. It does not mean the up move is over, but the good strong up volume associated with its initial launch is no longer present. Keep in mind that as long as this indicator is above the zero line, the up volume is still above is moving average. A longer term moving average would avoid many of the whipsaws but would reduce the timing.

Formula: *UV*

References

Appel, Gerald, "Gerald Appel, with Systems and Forecasts." *Stocks and Commodities*, Volume 12, March 1994, 98–105.

Stevens, Leigh, "Spotting Index Tops and Bottoms." *Stocks and Commodities*, August 2004, pp. 23–26.

Chart 8-3 Up Volume—21-Day Detrended.

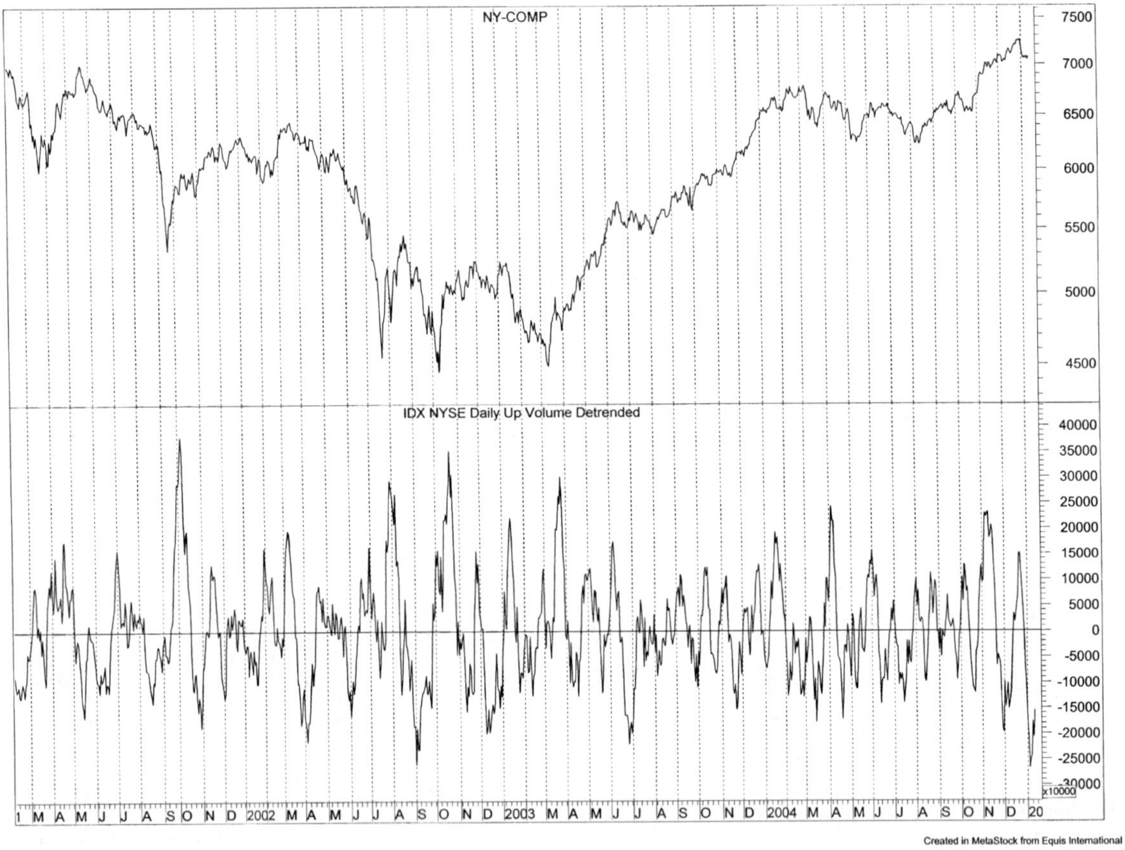

Down Volume

Data components required: Down Volume (*DV*).

Description

This is the total volume of all issues that declined in price for the day.

Interpretation

While there are no popular ways to use this, it seems that it should be used when the market is in a down trend, as it will assist you in identifying when that down trend might end. The down volume should start to decrease as the selling abates. As a market starts to bottom, the down volume

Up Volume, Down Volume Indicators

Chart 8–4 Down Volume—21-Day Smooth.

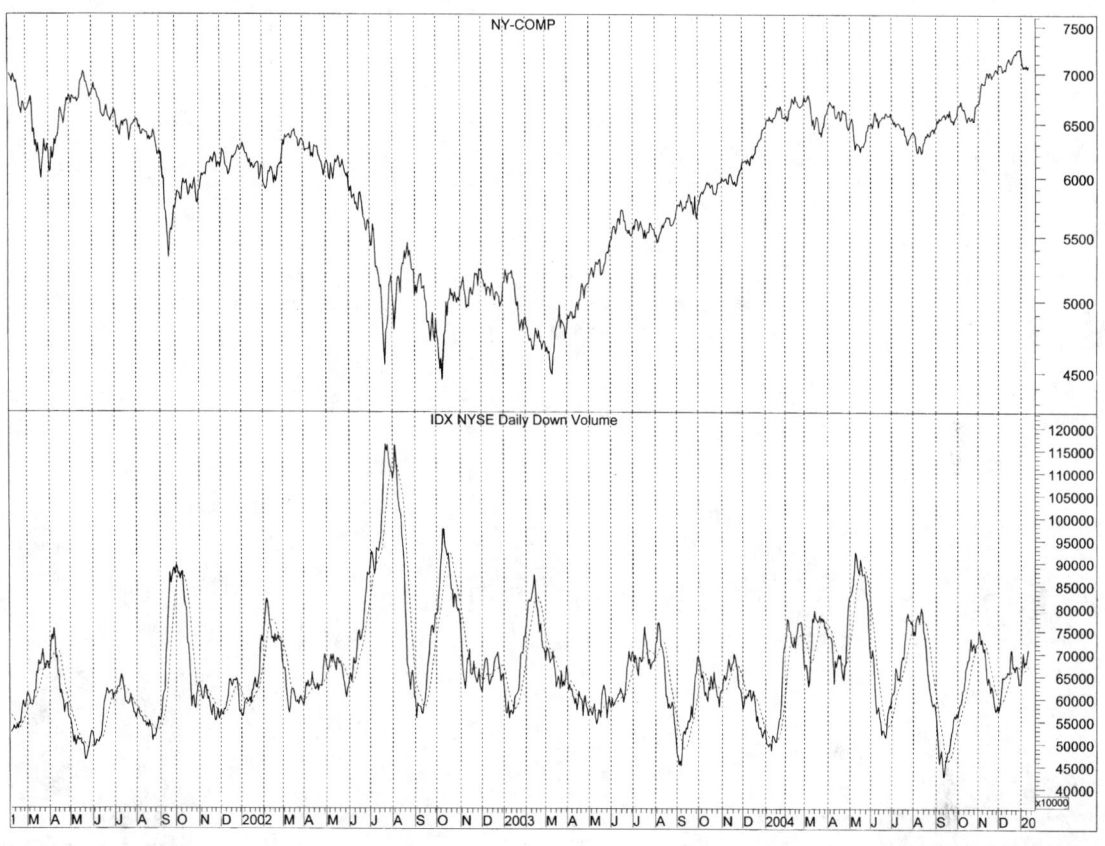

will decrease relative to total volume. Chart 8–4 shows the down volume smoothed by a 10-day average (dotted line). The peaks in this indicator point out most of the market bottoms.

Author Comments

Using raw data, even though it is smoothed, is not as good as using the raw data relative to a smoothed value of it. This is called detrending. Chart 8–5 is showing the down volume relative to its 21-day average, with the result further smoothed by 10 days (the same thing that was done with the up volume in the previous section).

$$\text{Formula: } (DV)$$

Changed Volume

Data components required: Up Volume (UV), Down Volume (DV).

Chart 8-5 Down Volume—21-Day Detrended.

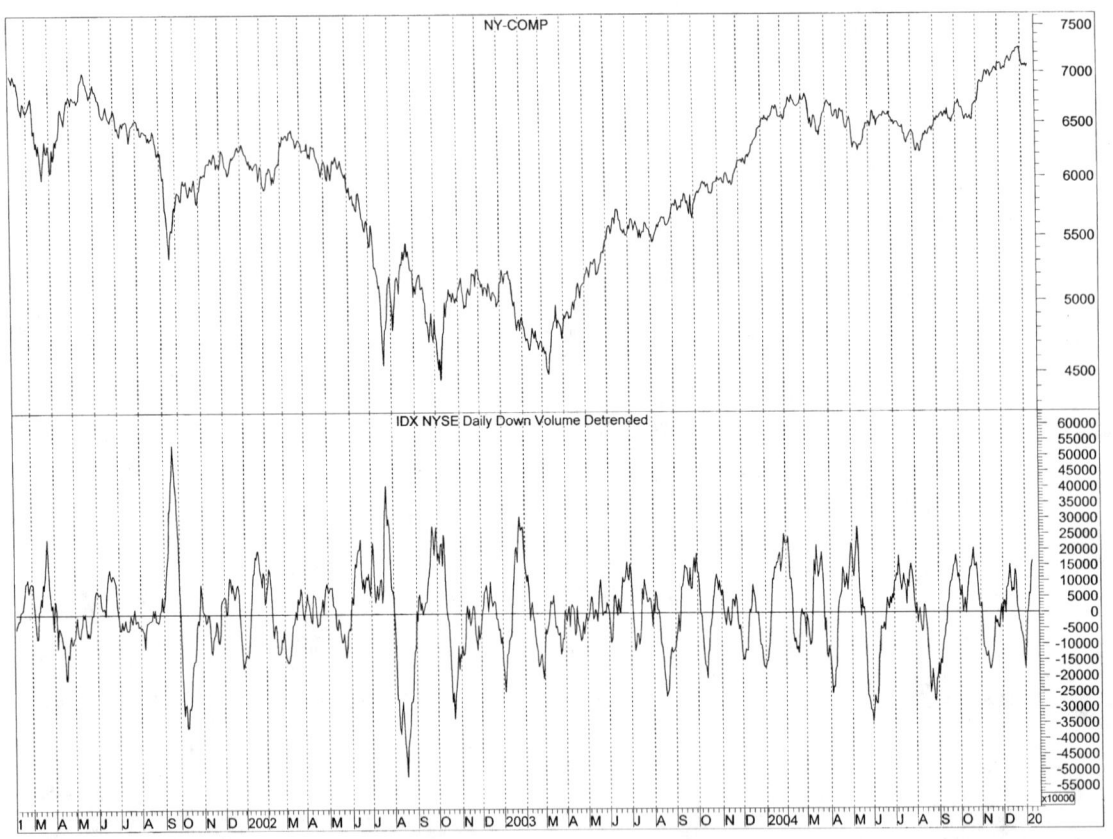

Description

This represents all the shares on an particular exchange that changed in price for the day. It includes the up volume and the down volume. Total volume is different, in that it includes the unchanged issues volume. You could also subtract the unchanged volume from the total volume to arrive at the same value.

Interpretation

The volume used here is the active volume for the day. Because of decimalization, this indicator needs to be looked at in stages, similar to the unchanged issues. Decimalization caused a giant decrease in unchanged issues, so this would cause a giant increase in the changed or active issues. Chart 8–6 shows this indicator since the decimalization that occurred in January, 2001.

Up Volume, Down Volume Indicators

Chart 8-6 Changed Volume—21-Day Smooth.

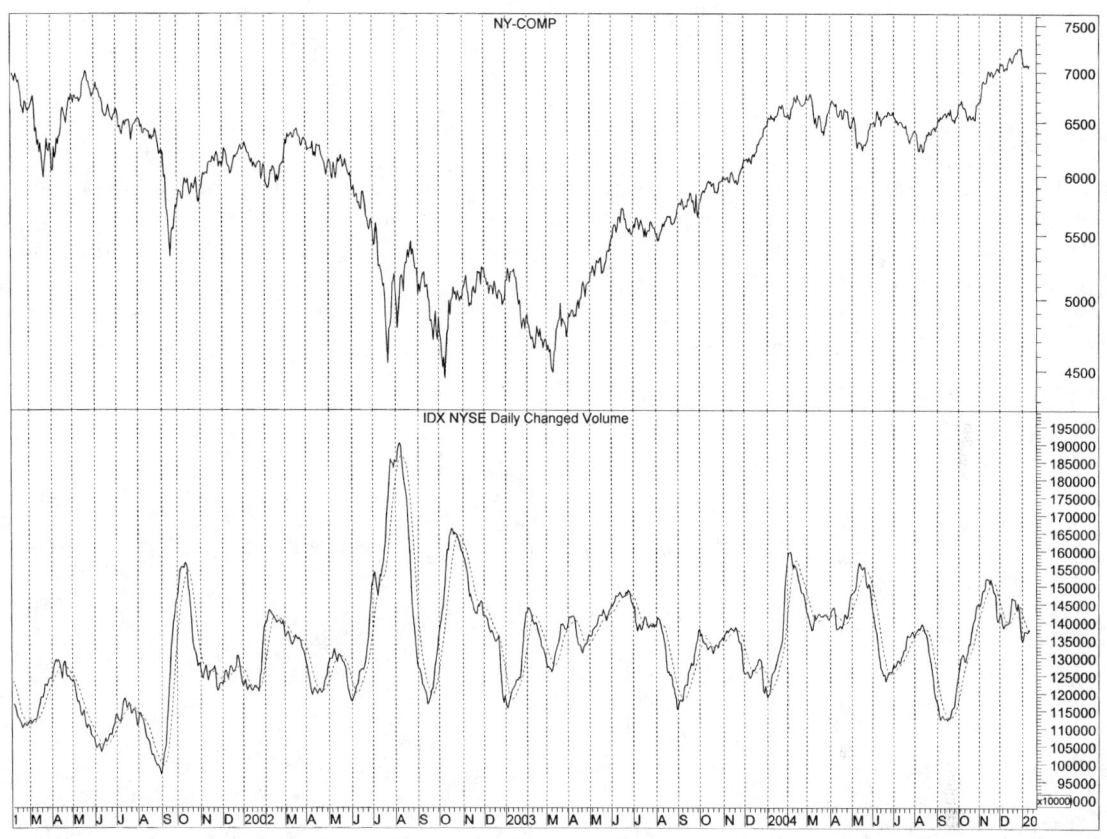

Author Comments

One might be able to tie this to the fact that as markets start their topping process, the number of unchanged issues should start to increase. If the unchanged volume increases, this would assist and also help to confirm it. Therefore, if the changed volume were to decrease, this might offer the same interpretation. This could be construed to be more important than total volume by some.

$$\text{Formula: } (UV + DV).$$

Up and Down Volume

Data components required: Up Volume (UV), Down Volume (DV).

Description

A chart showing the up volume and down volume on the same plot will tell a lot about where volume is flowing. Smoothing each of them will make it much easier to use and interpret.

Interpretation

In Chart 8–7, the up volume is the solid line and the down volume is the dotted line. You can see how the up volume generally increases during up moves and the down volume increases during down moves. This is normal market action and is to be expected. It is the deviation from this that you need to watch for.

Chart 8-7 Up Volume and Down Volume.

Author Comments

You can see that as a market drops in price, the down volume steadily increases and peaks right at the market bottom. Just after the market bottom, up volume rises quickly and continues to dominate throughout the upward move. You can also see that even small corrections in the market will cause the up and down volume to react significantly. Trends in the market are shown when one of the lines remains above or below the other for extended periods of time.

$$\text{Formula: } (UV), (DV)$$

McClellan Oscillator—Volume

Author/Creator: Sherman and Marian McClellan
Data components required: Up Volume (UV), Down Volume (DV).

Description

This is the McClellan Oscillator, but instead of using advances and declines data, up volume and down volume data are used. The calculation is exactly the same, only the data components are changed.

Interpretation

Using the analogy that volume precedes price, the McClellan Oscillator using up and down volume should be used in the same manner as the advance-decline-based McClellan Oscillator. Look for extreme readings to warn against market turning points. Keep this in mind: the market cannot go up in a healthy way without good accompanying up volume. It can certainly fall much easier. Trendline analysis of the McClellan Oscillator—Volume is also a good technique when using this indicator. Chart 8–8 shows the McClellan Oscillator—Volume.

Author Comments

From Chart 8–8, it appears that watching this indicator as it crosses from below to above the zero line will almost nail the market bottoms, including those that are just trading rallies. This is probably because changes in the market are more quickly reflected in the up and down volume.

The McClellan Volume Oscillator also has importance when one compares it to the McClellan Advance Decline Oscillator. When the two disagree, such as if one moves above the zero line while the other does not, it is usually the Volume Oscillator that tells the truer story. Volume is not always the correct one, but that is the tendency, and any disagreement is a sign for the analyst to be concerned.

Volume also differs from Advance Decline numbers in that Volume numbers are theoretically limitless, whereas the difference between Advances and Declines can never be greater than the

Chart 8-8 McClellan Oscillator—Volume.

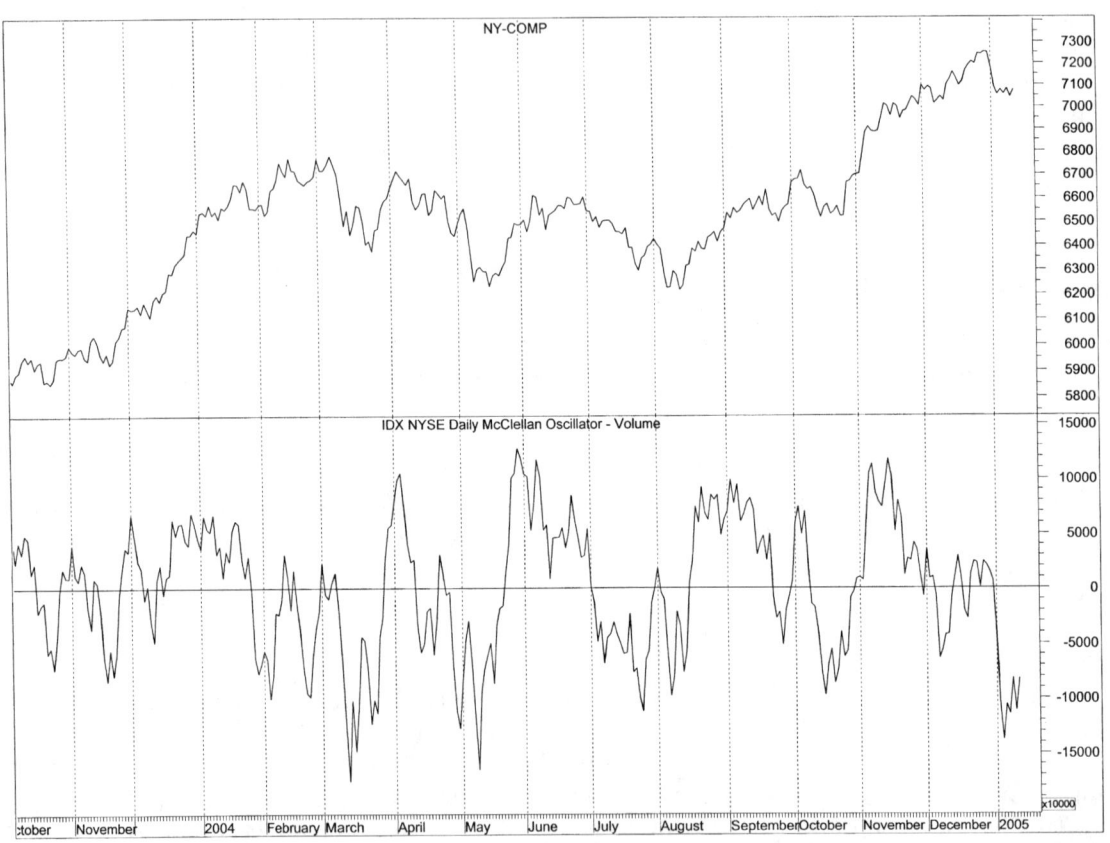

number of issues traded. Big volume trading days can therefore have a bigger impact on volume breadth indicators like the McClellan Volume Oscillator. Conversely, small volume days like the day after Thanksgiving can have only a minimal contribution to changing the volume-based oscillator, while the Advance Decline Oscillator does not know the difference. My thanks go to Tom McClellan who reviewed this section and the following one on the McClellan Summation Index—Volume.

Formula: (Today's 19 exp average of (UV − DV)) − (Today's 39 exp average of (UV − DV))

References

McClellan, Sherman and Marian. *Patterns for Profit.* Lakewood, WA: McClellan Financial Publications, Inc., 1989. This book was originally published by Trade Levels in 1970.

McClellan Family Interview, "It's All In the Family: Sherman, Marian, and Tom McClellan." *Stocks and Commodities*, Volume 12, June 1994, pp. 264–273.

McClellan Summation Index—Volume

Author/Creator: Sherman and Marian McClellan
Data components required: Up Volume (UV), Down Volume (DV)

Description

Like the McClellan Oscillator that uses volume, this is the McClellan Summation Index using up volume and down volume instead of the advances and declines. The calculations are identical, just the breadth components have changed.

Interpretation

As with the McClellan Advance Decline Summation Index, the Volume Summation Index indicates the prevailing trend for the market based on its direction of movement. It also makes for a nice intermediate-term overbought/oversold indicator when it reaches extreme values. The McClellan Volume Summation Index is shown in Chart 8–9.

Author Comments

Because of the large increases in daily trading volume over the years, making a ratio adjustment of the daily Up and Down Volume figures is even more important than for the A − D numbers when trying to make long-term historical comparisons. The McClellans do this adjustment in the same way for Volume that they do for Advance Decline, by dividing the Up Down Volume difference by the total of Up plus Down Volume. The one drawback is that this equalizes all trading days, so big or small volume days do not have the same impact that they would in the raw calculations.

Formula: This is the accumulation of the volume based McClellan Oscillator.

$$VOLSUM_{TODAY} = VOLSUM_{YESTERDAY} + VOLOSC_{TODAY}$$

References

McClellan, Sherman and Marian. *Patterns for Profit*. Lakewood, WA: McClellan Financial Publications, Inc., 1989. This book was originally published by Trade Levels in 1970.

McClellan Family Interview, "It's All In the Family: Sherman, Marian, and Tom McClellan." *Stocks and Commodities*, Volume 12, June 1994, pp. 264–273.

Merriman Volume Model

Author/Creator: Paul Merriman
Data components required: Up Volume (UV), Down Volume (DV).

Chart 8-9 McClellan Summation—Volume.

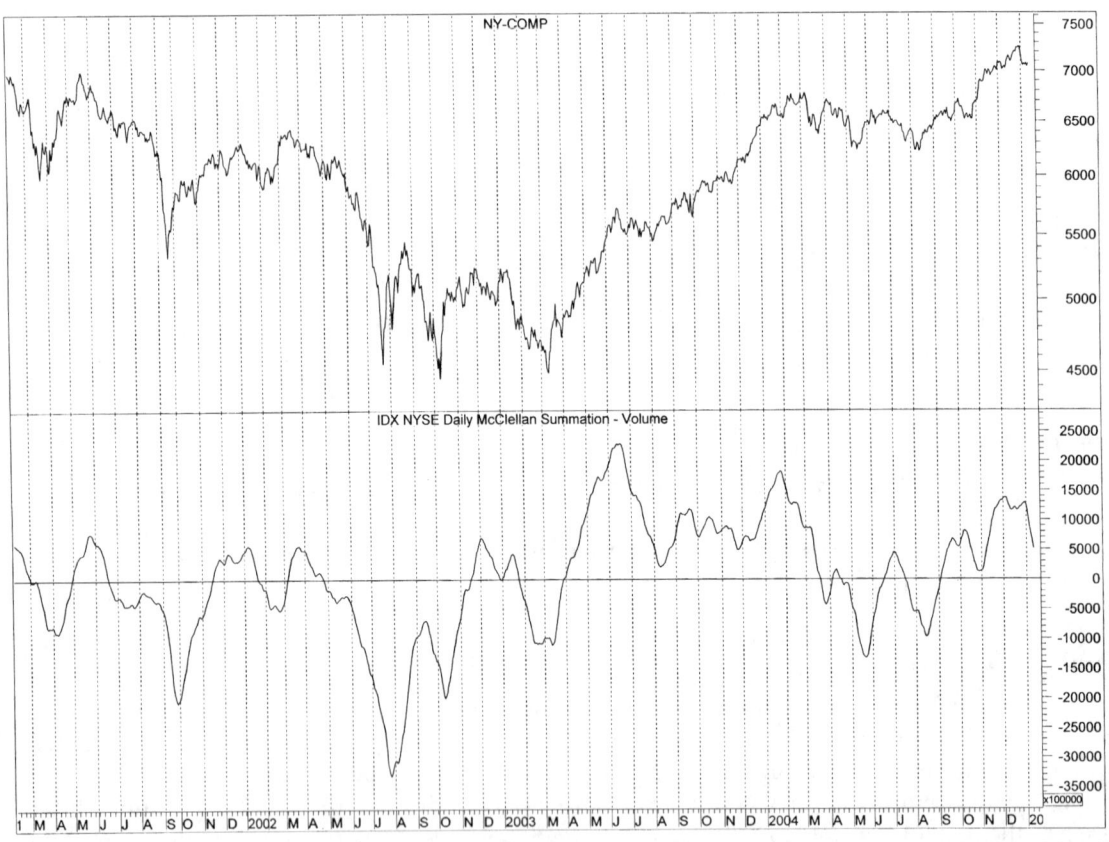

Description

This is a simple but effective indicator that uses the up and down volume as a ratio. One looks for extreme levels to determine market strength or weakness. Merriman initially created this indicator using the up and down volume from the Nasdaq market.

Interpretation

When the sum of the up volume over the last eight trading days divided by the sum of the down volume over the last eight days is greater than 1.5, a buy signal is generated. A sell signal is when the eight-day ratio of the sums is equal to 0.8. Merriman's logic is simple; in an up market you can expect more up volume and in a down market you can expect more down volume. Chart 8–10 is the indicator using New York breadth data. Ignore repetitive signals in the chart.

Chart 8-10 Merriman NYSE Volume.

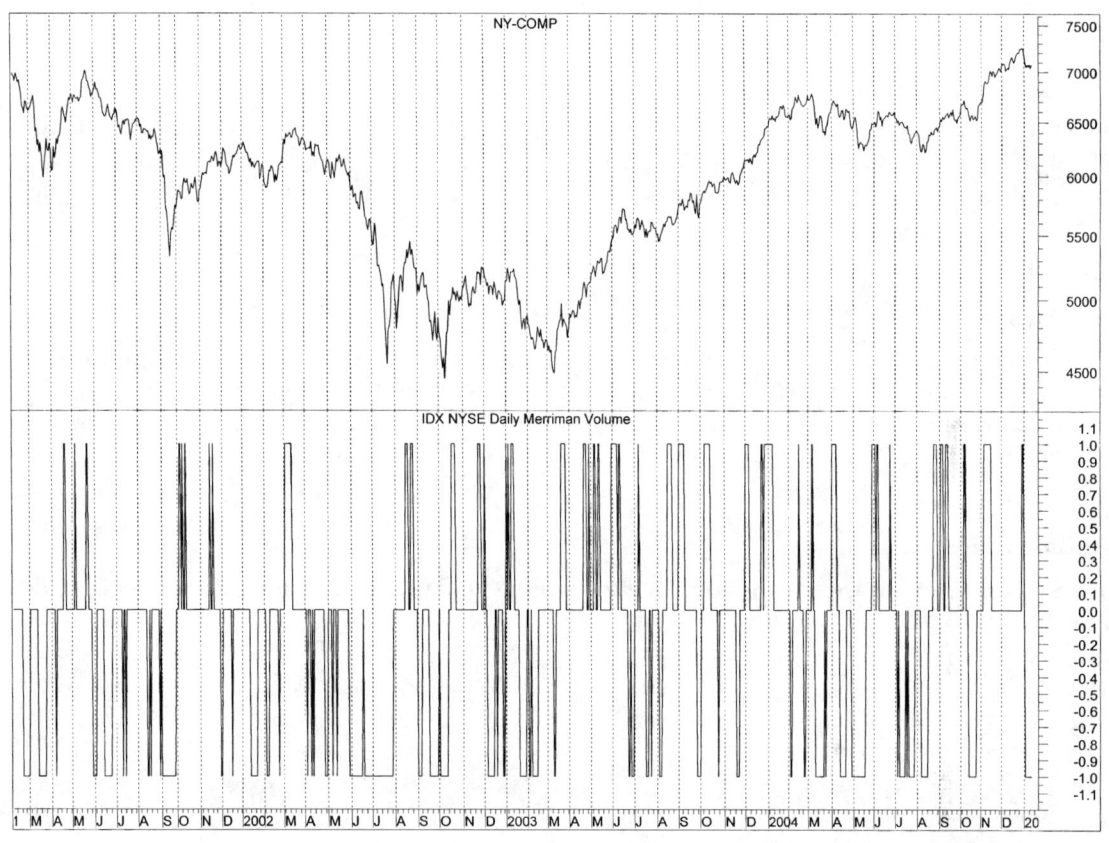

Author Comments

Paul Merriman has created a fairly simple but reliable indicator for determining market turns based on volume. While he originally used Nasdaq data, the use of New York data seems to work just as well.

Formula: 8 day sum of UV / 8 day sum of DV

References

Merriman, Paul, www.fundadvice.com/modelsexplained.html.

Swenlin IT Volume Momentum Oscillator

Also known as: ITVM

Author/Creator: Carl Swenlin
Data components required: Up Volume (UV), Down Volume (DV), Total Volume (V).

Description

The Intermediate Term Volume Momentum Oscillator is a barometer of breadth. To calculate the ITVM add the daily McClellan Oscillator—Volume (ratio adjusted using the difference of up and down volume divided by the total volume) to the daily 39-day exponential average, then calculate a 20-day exponential average of the result.

Interpretation

Carl Swenlin offers the following comments: It is better if this indicator is above zero line and rising. Below the zero line and falling is the worst scenario. Rising is better than falling, even if below the zero line. Just like the McClellan's version with volume, this is Carl's volume version of his Intermediate Term Breadth Momentum Oscillator. Chart 8–11 shows the ITVM.

Author Comments

The indicator troughs seem to pinpoint market bottoms, and the peaks point out the loss of upside momentum.

References

Swenlin, Carl, www.decisionpoint.com.

Swenlin Trading Oscillator—Volume

Also known as: *STO-V*
Author/Creator: Carl Swenlin
Data components required: Up Volume (UV), Down Volume (DV), Total Volume (V).

Description

The Swenlin Trading Oscillator—Volume was designed for short-term trading. It is a 5-day simple moving average of a 4-day exponential average of the daily up volume minus down volume divided by the total daily volume times 1000.

Interpretation

Carl Swenlin offers these comments: The double smoothing of the short-term data results in a reliable oscillator that persists in one direction, usually tops near short-term market tops, and bottoms

Up Volume, Down Volume Indicators

Chart 8-11 Swenlin IT Volume Momentum Oscillator.

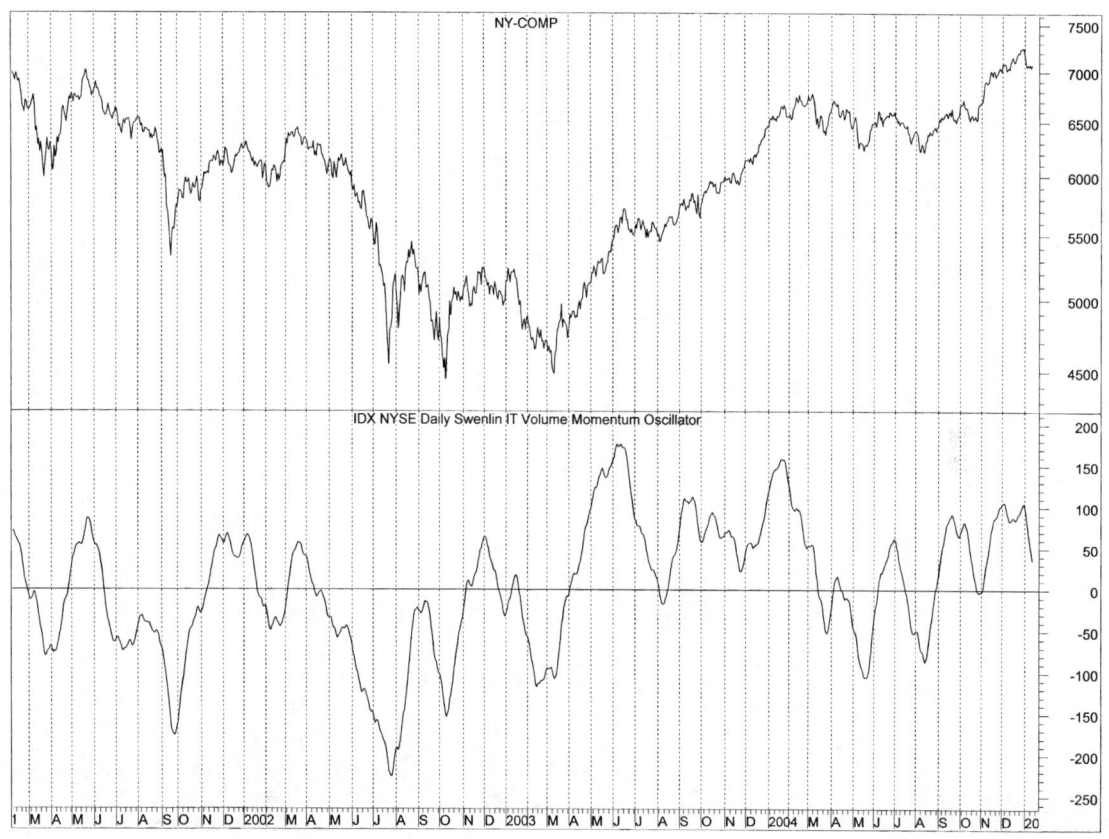

near short-term market bottoms. As with most indicators, the primary trend of the market will determine how you will use the indicator. In a bull market, the tops will not be very reliable. In a bear market, the bottoms will not be very reliable. Chart 8–12 shows the Swenlin Trading Oscillator for Volume.

Author Comments

You can see that this indicator will generally cross the zero line after a market makes a top or bottom, but will not be far behind it.

References

Swenlin, Carl, www.decisionpoint.com.

Chart 8-12 Swenlin Trading Oscillator—Volume.

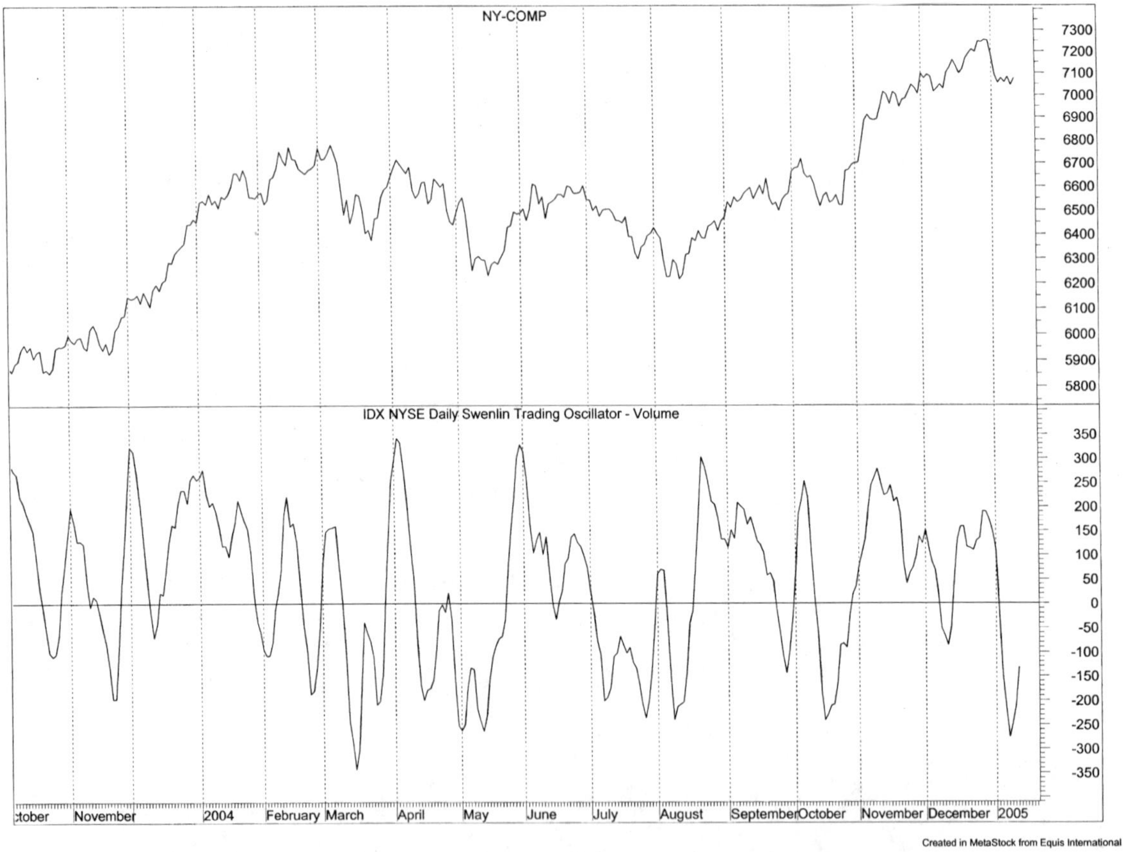

Up Volume, Down Volume Line

Data components required: Up Volume (UV), Down Volume (DV)

Description

The Up Volume, Down Volume Line is a variation of the advance decline line concept, except that it uses up and down volume instead of advances and declines.

Interpretation

This indicator can be used the same way as the advance decline line. Look for divergence patterns with the market. Using trendline analysis will also help you identify market turning points. Chart 8–13 shows the Up Volume, Down Volume Line.

Author Comments

Dick Arms would tell you that this is a much better advance decline line because it incorporates volume. Volume drives the market and this indicator will certainly hint at when a bullish run is ending.

$$\text{Formula:} \quad (UV - DV).$$

Cumulative Volume Ratio

Author/Creator: John C. Lawlor
Data components required: Up Volume (UV), Down Volume (DV)

Description

This is an indicator that sums the up volume for the last 50 days and divides it by the sum of the down volume over the last 50 days.

Chart 8-13 Up Volume, Down Volume Line.

Interpretation

This will indicate the momentum of volume over a predetermined time period. For example, if the number of days used is 50, and the ratio is equal to 4, it means there was an average of 4 times as much up volume as there was down volume over the last 50 days. Likewise, if the value of the ratio (up volume/down volume) over 50 days, is −3, it means that 3 times more down volume than up volume occurred during that time frame. One can also see from Chart 8–14 that divergence with price seems to be an early indicator of market direction.

Author Comments

Lawlor developed a methodology in which he identified cyclicality in the Cumulative Volume Ratio. This seemed to be more prevalent when using the ratio over a 10-day period. While not precise in

Chart 8–14 Cumulative Volume Ratio.

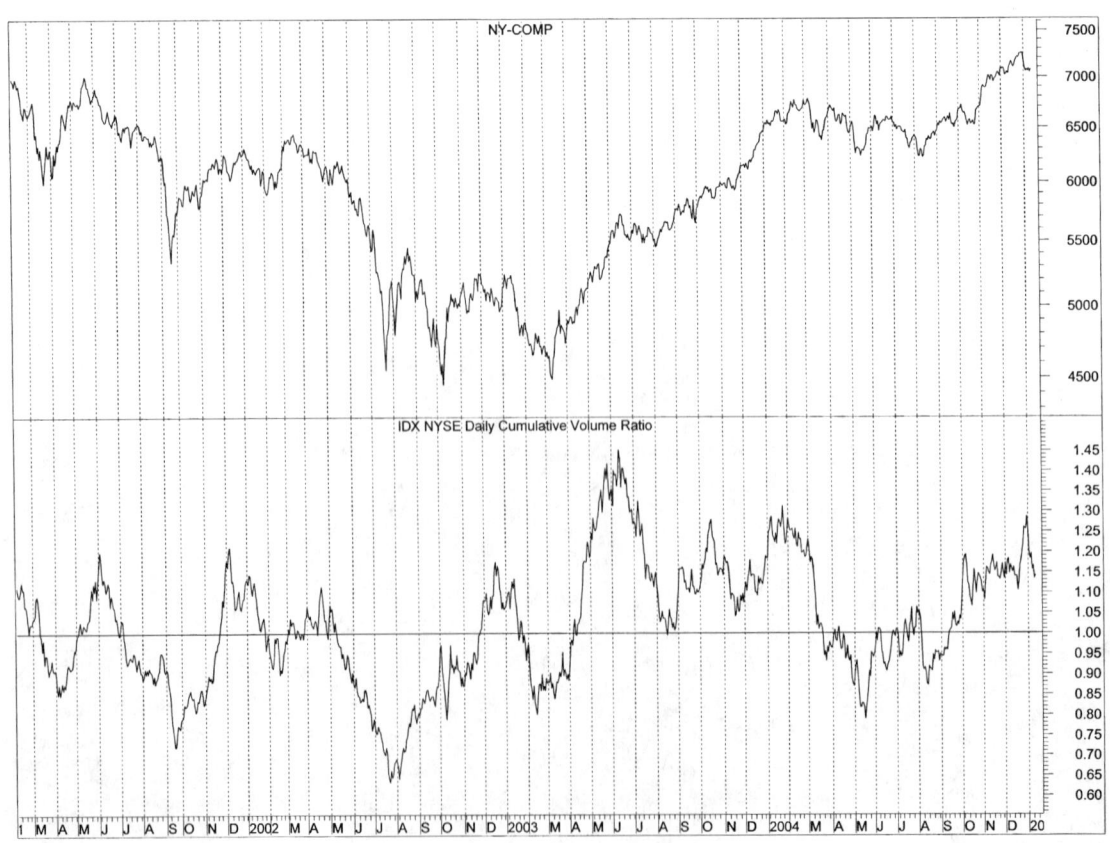

identifying significant tops and bottoms, it did seem to show short-term price peaks with some consistency. Chart 8–15 is shown with a 10-period ratio and its 10-period cyclicality (dotted sine wave).

Formula: Previous Value + (UV for 50 days / DV for 50 days)

References

Lawlor, John, "Cumulative Volume and Momentum." *Stocks and Commodities*, February 1988, pp. 67–69.

Up Down OBV

Author/Creator: Greg Morris
Data components required: Up Volume (UV), Down Volume (DV) Market Index (MKT).

Chart 8–15 Cumulative Volume Ratio—10-Day Smooth.

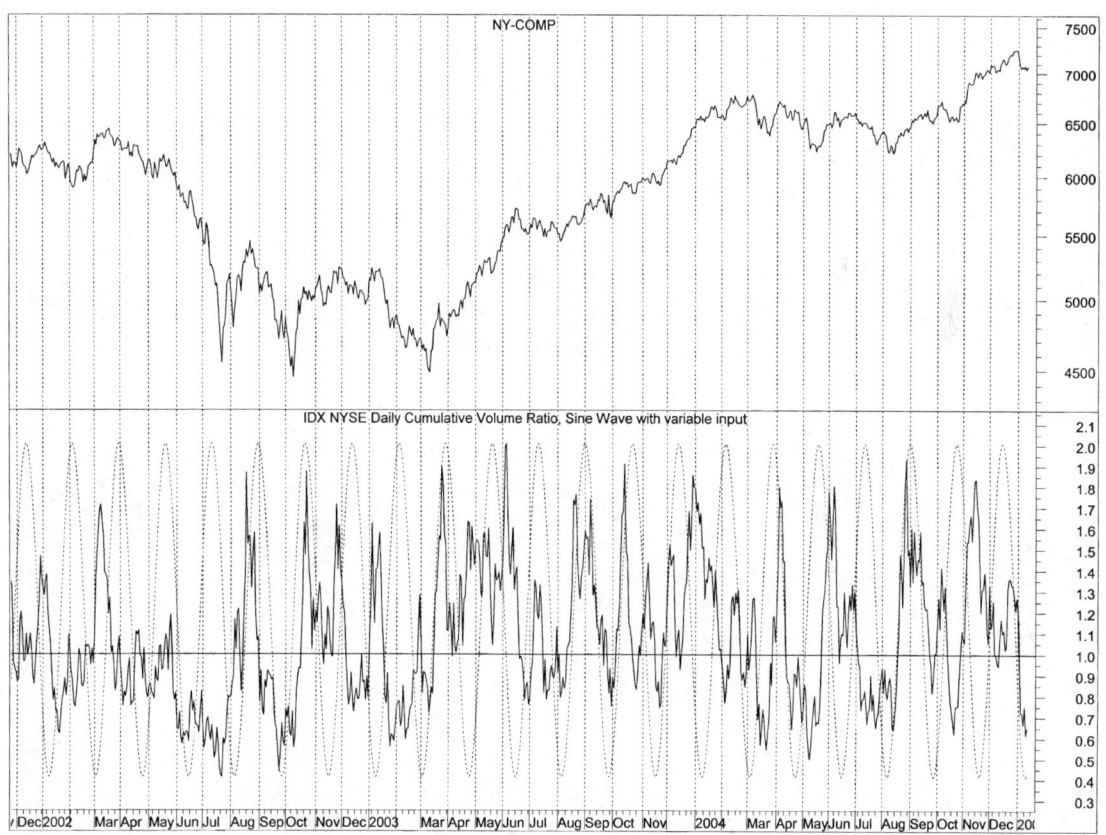

Description

This is a unique take off from Joseph Granville's On Balance Volume (OBV). On Balance Volume added the day's total volume when the closing price was higher than the previous day and subtracted the total volume for the day when the closing price was lower than that of the previous day. The Up Down OBV uses a similar concept of determining the change in closing prices, but uses Up Volume if the close is higher and Down Volume if the close is lower. The daily values are accumulated similar to the way the advance decline line is calculated.

Interpretation

It would seem that increases in Up Volume associated with the price closing up would cause this indicator to reflect moves in the market in an exaggerated sense, and similarly on down moves. Chart 8–16 shows that it seems to reflect market action much like Granville's OBV.

Chart 8–16 ADOBV with OBV Similarity.

Up Volume, Down Volume Indicators

Author Comments

This is a difficult one to interpret, and one has to be careful not to read too much into these types of indicators. In Chart 8–17 you can see that, similar to Granvilles' OBV, you can spot divergences with price.

I think using this as an oscillator would produce better results and offer more interpretive value. Chart 8–18 is the Up Down OBV Oscillator, and when referring to the peaks and troughs, it aligns well with the market. This is the Up Down OBV with a 21-day rate of change. Up markets will keep the indicator above the zero line and down markets will keep it below zero.

Volume Percentage Ratio

Author/Creator: Mike Burk
Data components required: Up Volume (UV), Down Volume (DV) Total Volume (V)

Chart 8–17 ADOBV with Trendline Divergence.

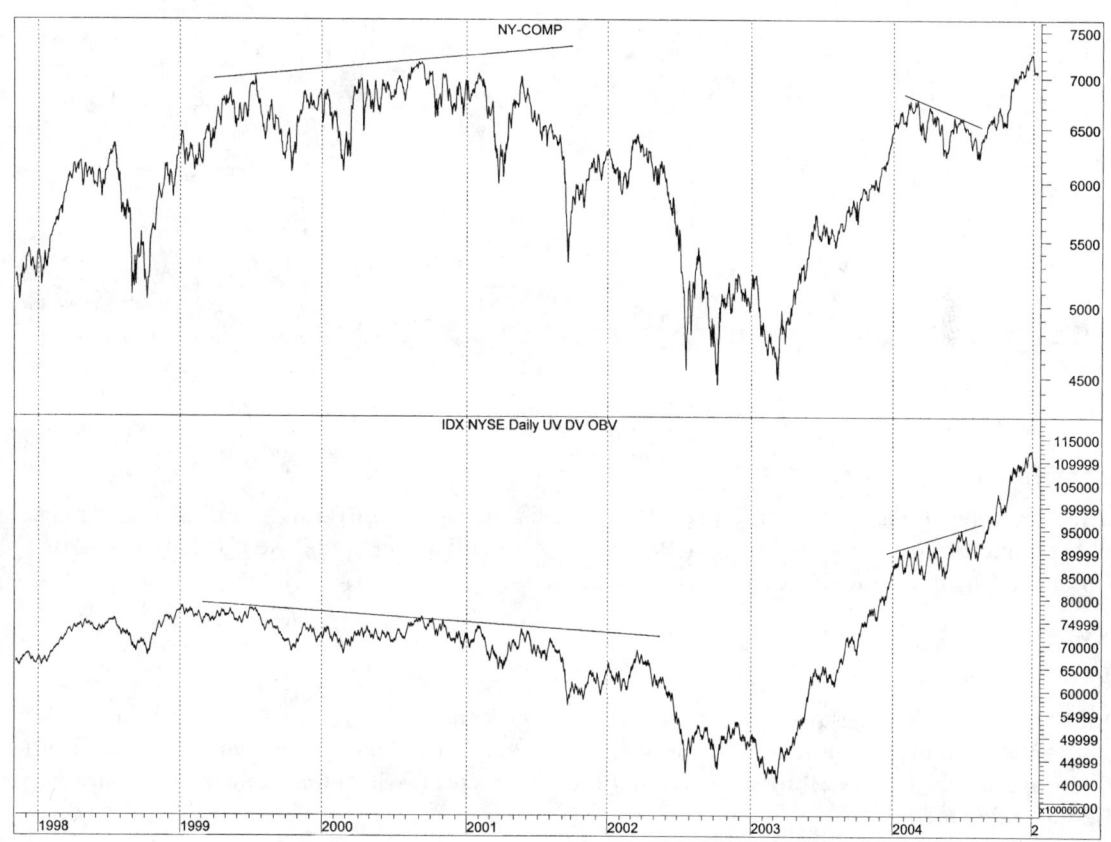

Chart 8-18 ADOBV Oscillator.

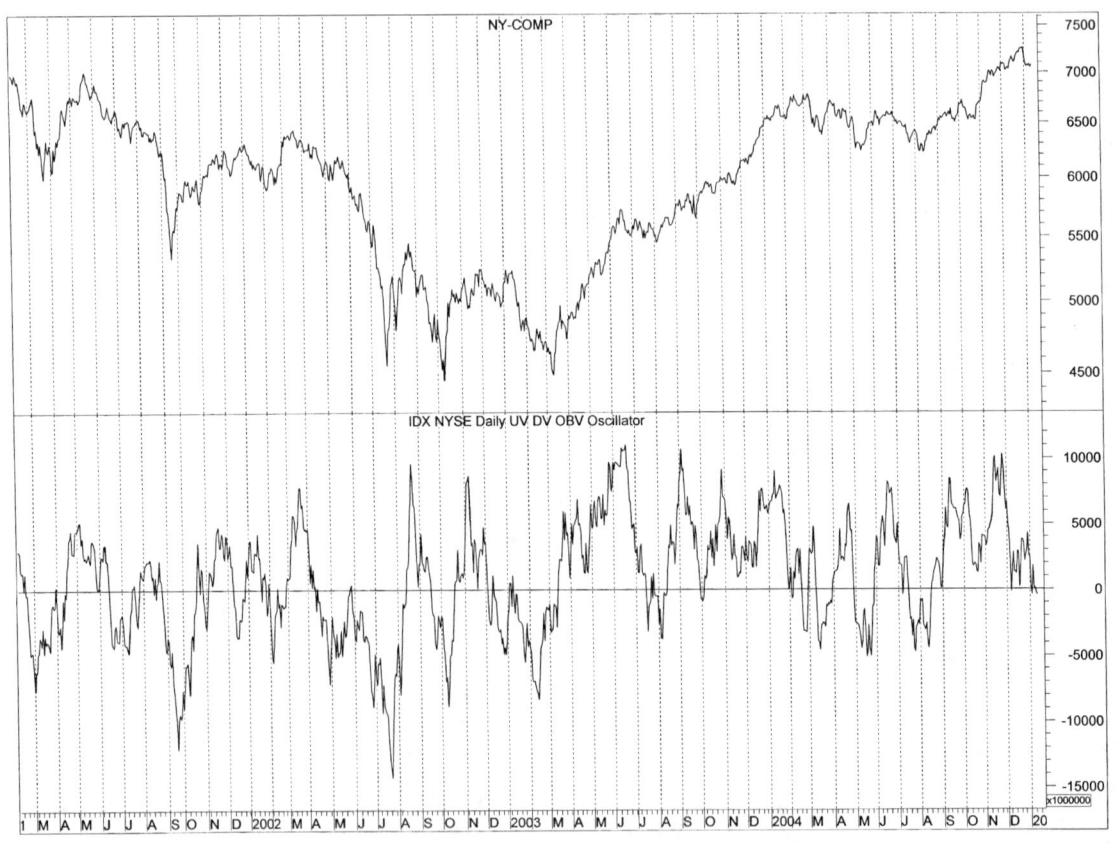

Description

The volume percentage ratio is a 19-period exponential average of the down volume as a percentage of the total volume subtracted from a 19-period exponential average of the up volume as a percentage of the total volume.

Interpretation

Burk states that volume is best used as a confirming indication of the market. When viewing a plot of the Volume Percentage Ratio such as in Chart 8–19, it is the relative position that is important and not the actual values. Burk also says that it is best used as a short-term indicator, usually over periods of 50 to 75 days.

Chart 8-19 Volume Percent Ratio.

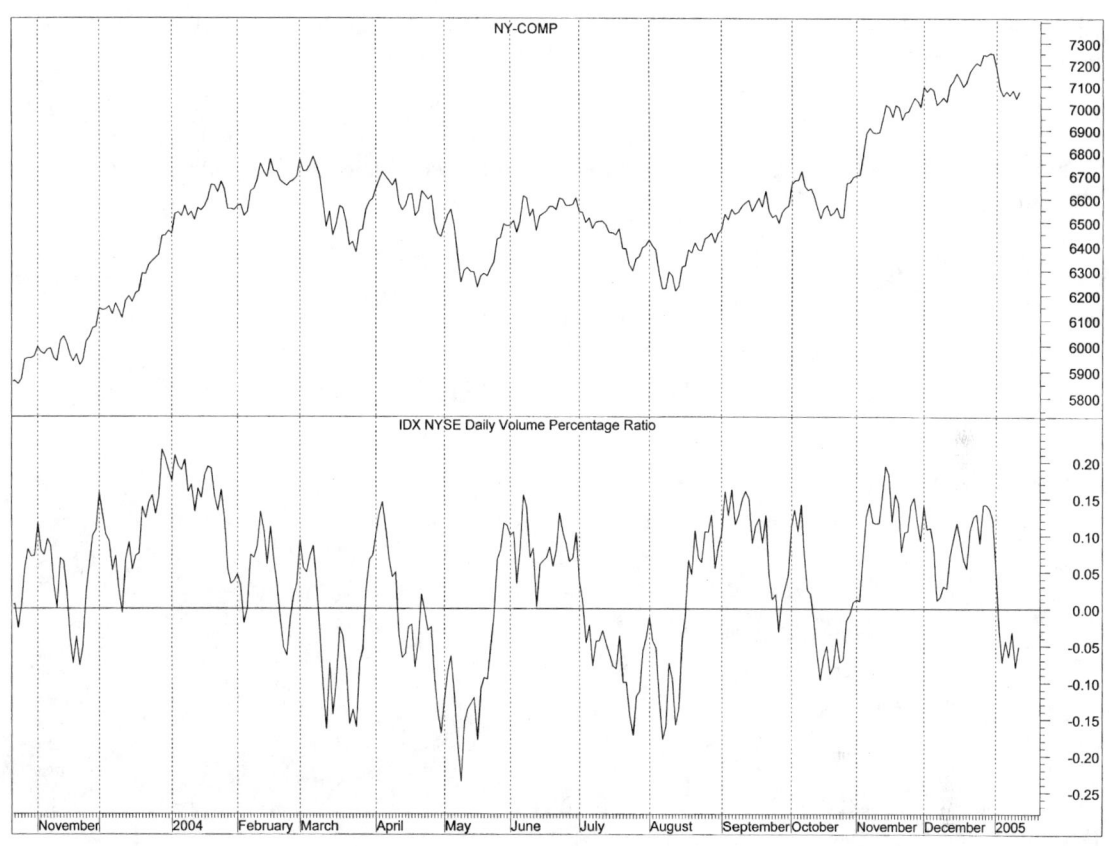

Author Comments

It seems that the Volume Percentage Ratio is fairly good at calling market bottoms, but offers little in calling tops. Of course, that falls in line with most short-term indicators and is not surprising.

$$\text{Formula: } 19 \; exp \; avg \; (UV\% \; TV) - 19 \; exp \; avg \; (DV\% \; TV)$$

References

Burk, Mike, "Volume Percentage Ratio." *Stocks and Commodities*, Volume 7, December 1989, pp. 453–455.

Upside − Downside Volume

Data components required: Up Volume (UV), Down Volume (DV).

Description

This is calculated the same as the advances minus declines except using up volume and down volume. Also, any variations of those indicators would apply here.

Interpretation

Chart 8–20 shows that it is generally best if smoothed and used as it crosses the zero line. In Chart 8–20, the up down volume difference is smoothed by 21 days.

Author Comments

To be honest, I do not find much in the way of importance of difference with this one. Because this book is the complete guide, it has to be here.

$$\text{Formula: } (UV - DV)$$

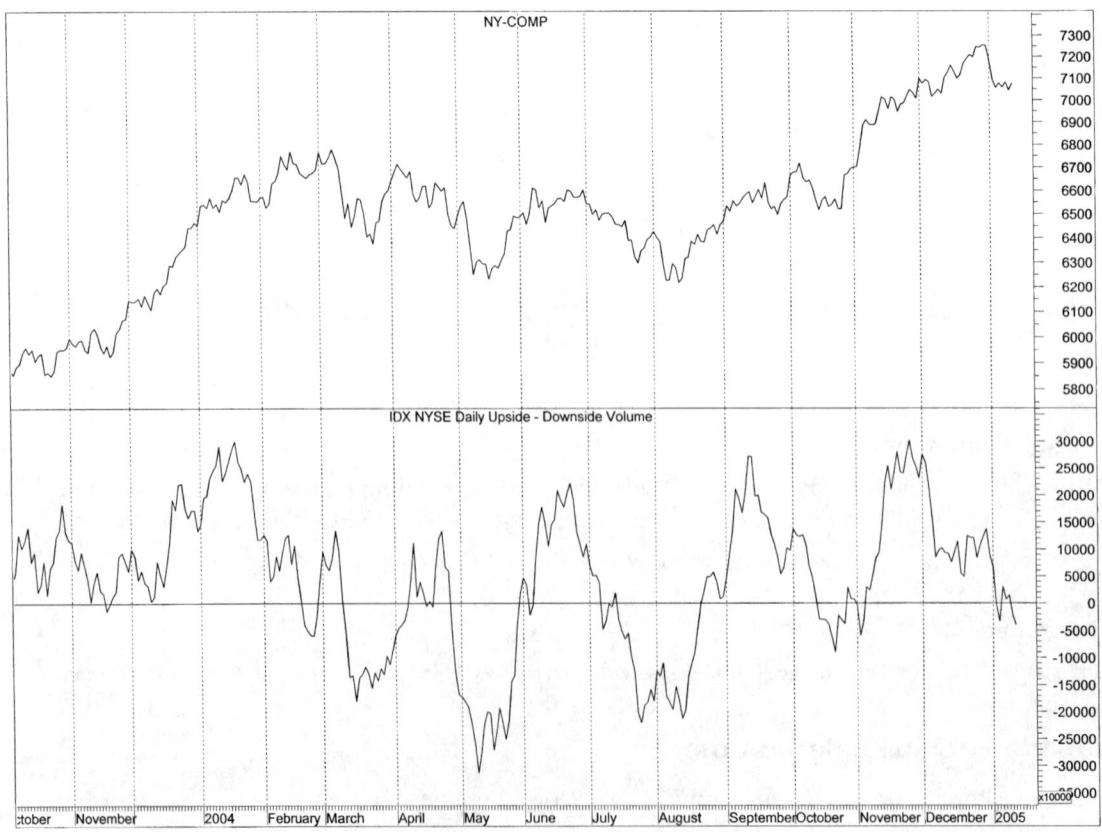

Chart 8-20 Up Volume − Down Volume.

Upside / Downside Volume Ratio

Data components required: Up Volume (UV), Down Volume (DV)

Description

This is the ratio of up volume to down volume (up volume divided by down volume).

Interpretation

Chart 8–21 shows that spikes to the upside represent up volume that is significantly more than down volume. Remember that a ratio of positive numbers will always yield a positive number.

Chart 8–21   Upside Downside Volume Ratio.

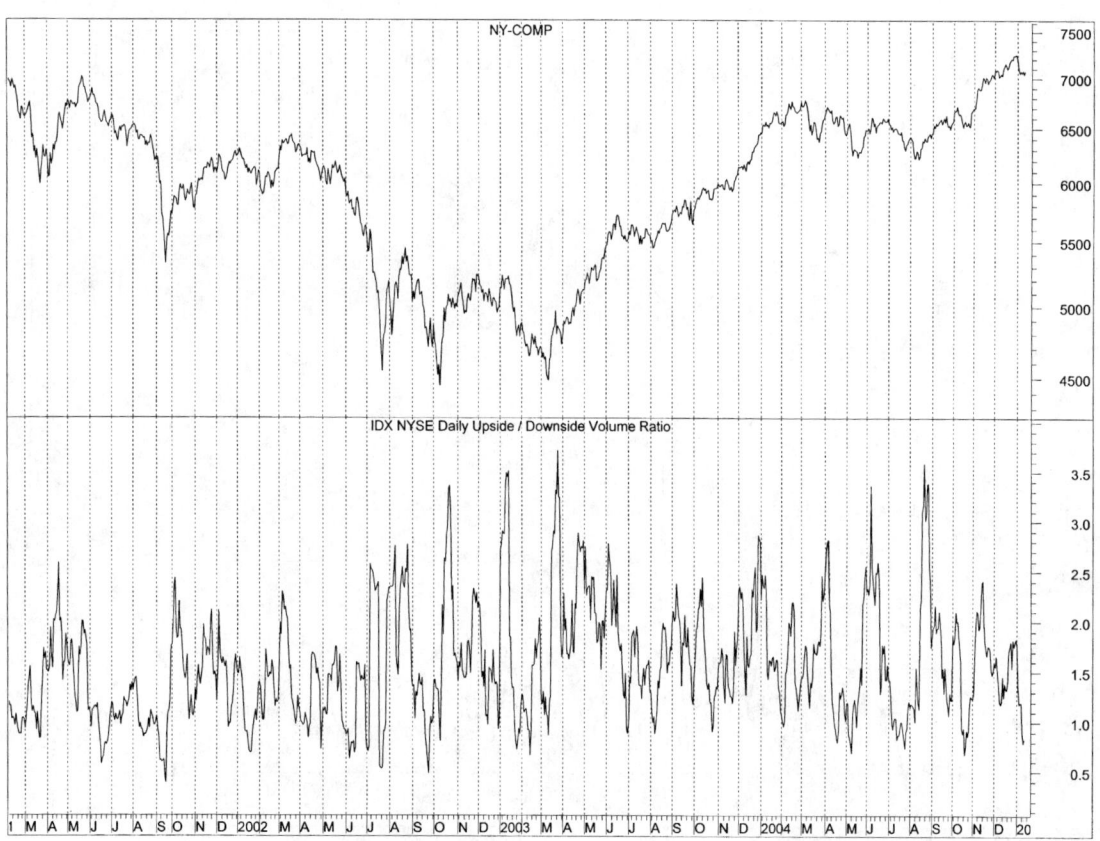

Author Comments

William O'Neil, founder and publisher of *Investor's Business Daily*, mentions the upside/downside volume indicator in his book, *How to Make Money in Stocks*. He states that an impending up turn in the market occurs when, after a decline of 10–12 percent, while the market continues to drop, the upside/downside volume starts to shift.

Larry McMillan, author of numerous books on options, uses a 50-day sum of up volume divided by a 50-day sum of down volume. Larry says that if the ratio is greater than 3.0, it is excellent volume, if greater than 2.0, it is very good volume, 1.0 is neutral, less than 0.8 is poor, and less than 0.5 is terrible. This ratio attempts to measure whether stock traders are participating with good buying volume on days that the market is up. While Larry uses this primarily on individual stocks, Chart 8-22 shows the upside downside volume using the data from the New York Stock Exchange.

Another version of up and down volume was written about by Dennis Peterson, a frequent contributor to *Stocks and Commodities* magazine. This version uses a 3-day sum of the ratio of up volume to changed volume (up volume plus down volume) and then divided by 3. The division serves

Chart 8-22 Upside Downside Volume—McMillan.

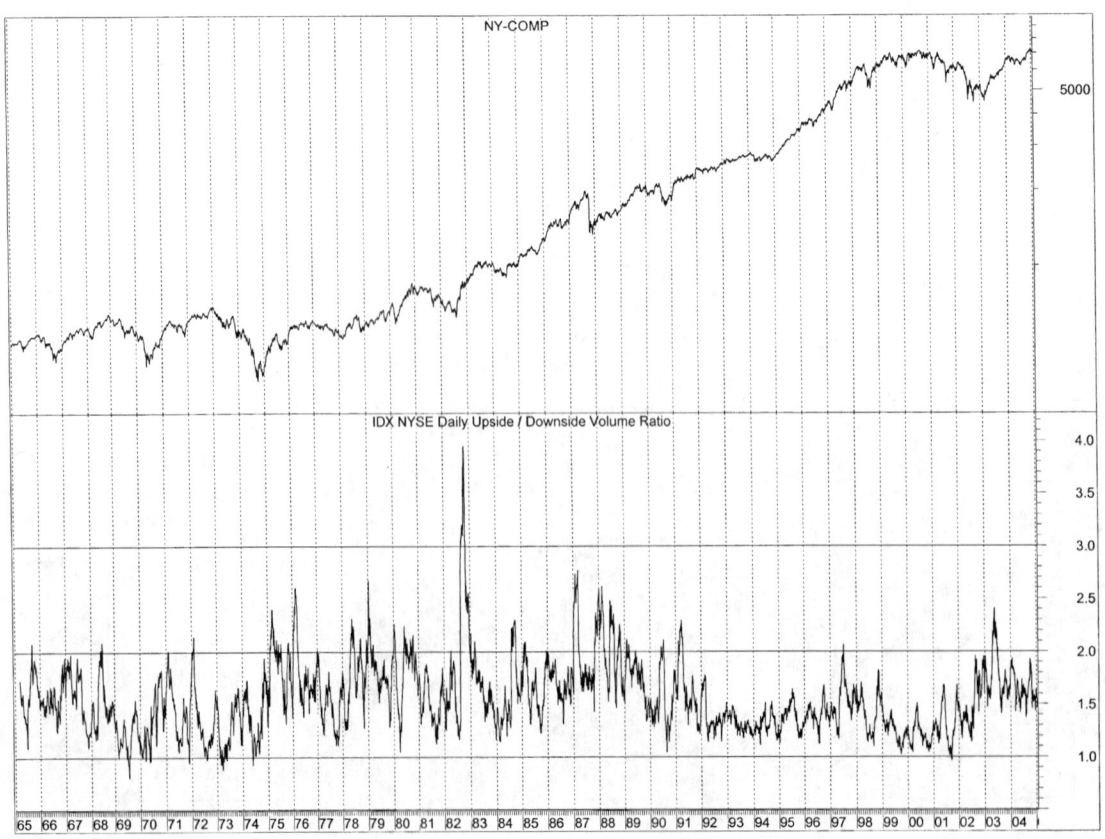

no real purpose other than to reduce the large scaling numbers. Peterson's version is shown in Chart 8–23.

$$\text{Formula: } (UV / DV)$$

References

O'Neil, William J., *How to Make Money in Stocks*. McGraw-Hill, 1988.
McMillan, Larry. www.theoptionstrategist.com.
Peterson, Dennis, "Market Breadth: Volume." *Stocks and Commodities*, Volume 19, February 2001, pp. 57–60.

Zweig Up Volume Indicator

Author/Creator: Martin Zweig
Data components required: Up Volume (UV), Down Volume (DV).

Chart 8–23 Peterson Up Down.

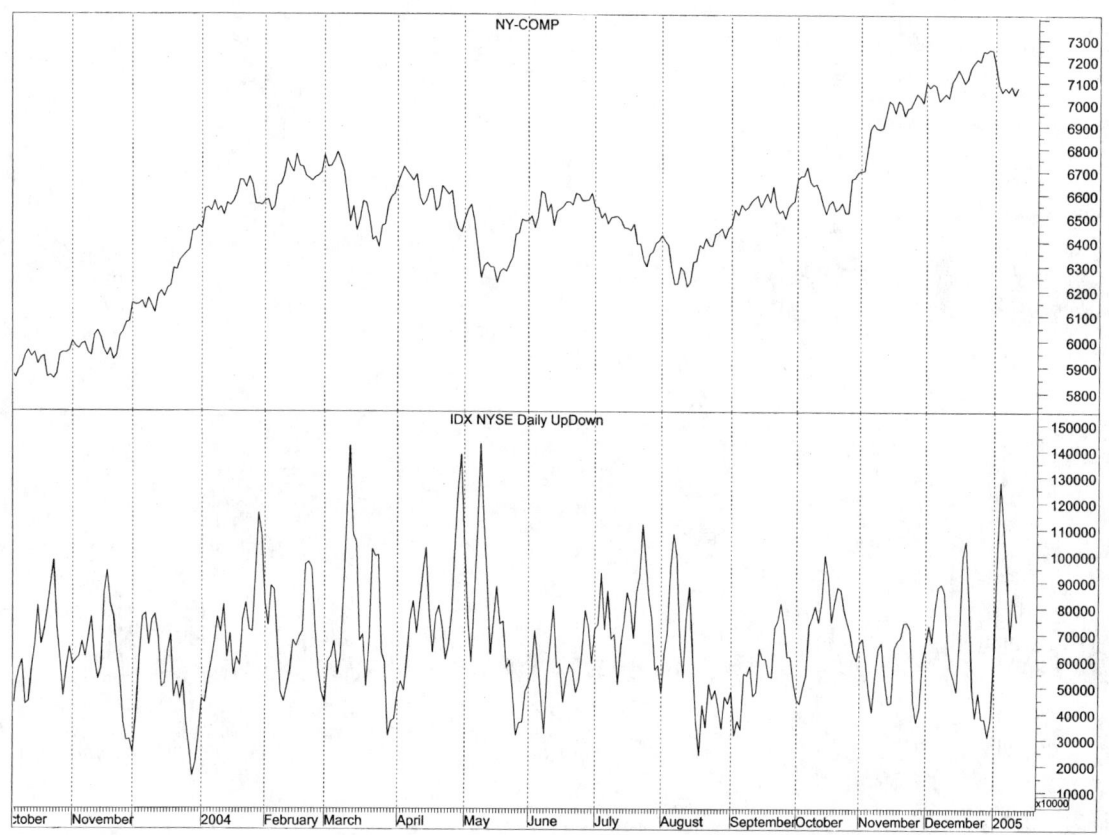

Description

This is another of Dr. Martin Zweig's momentum indicators. This one uses a ratio of up volume and down volume. This ratio shows the powerful thrust of the market and cannot be ignored.

Interpretation

Whenever the ratio reaches 9 to 1, a good buying opportunity exists. There have been 53 signals given since 1965. The biggest ratio ever was on August 17, 1982, the beginning of an 18-year bull market. Chart 8–24 shows each occurrence of the 9-to-1 up volume ratio since 1965, identified by the down spikes that go down to −9. You will notice in Chart 8–24 that they generally happen near significant, certainly tradable, market bottoms.

A further concept from Dr. Zweig is to expand the 9-to-1 ratio of up volume to down volume to state that anytime there are two signals in any 3-month period, the evidence suggests a strong market to follow. Since 1965 there have been 21 of these "double nine" signals. Here are the dates:

Chart 8–24 Zweig Up Volume.

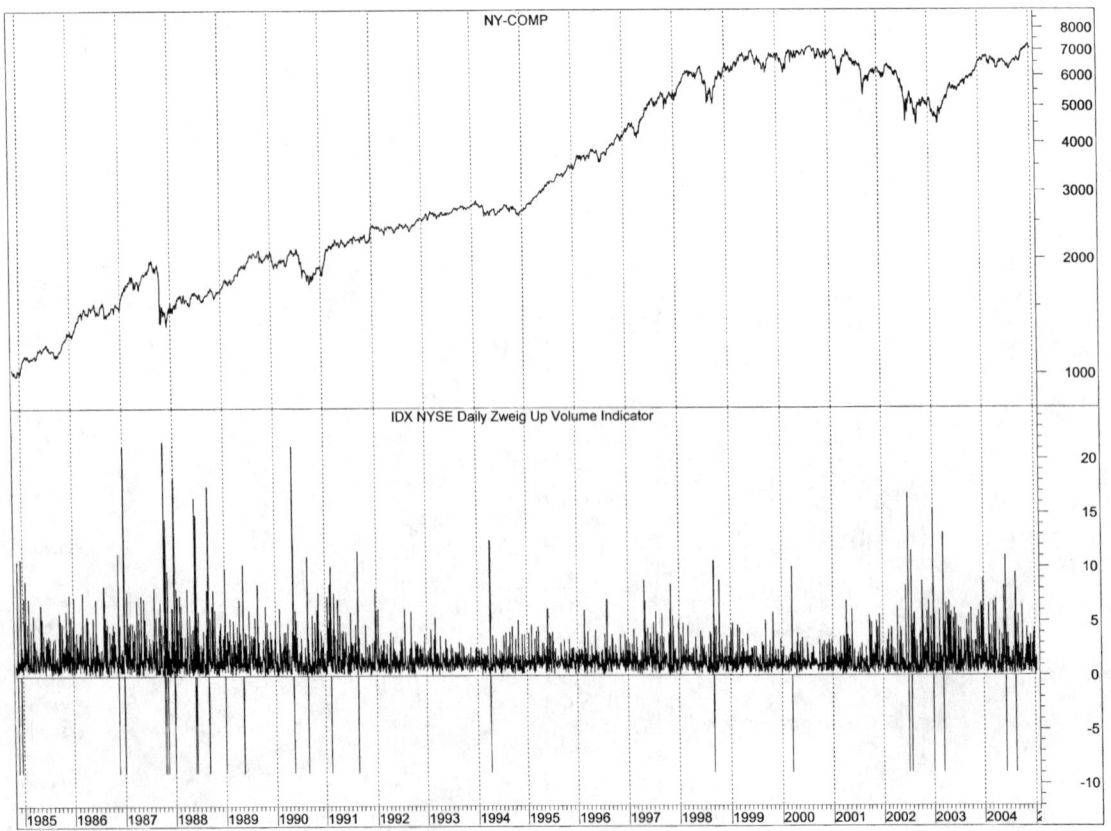

Up Volume, Down Volume Indicators

October 12, 1966	August 9, 1984
May 27, 1970	September 13, 1984
November 29, 1971	November 23, 1984
September 19, 1975	December 18, 1984
October 3, 1975	January 2, 1987
January 5, 1976	October 29, 1987
April 22, 1980	November 12, 1987
March 22, 1982	January 4, 1988
August 20, 1982	June 8, 1988
October 6, 1982	September 2, 1988
November 3, 1982	July 29, 2002
January 6, 1983	March 17, 2003
August 2, 1984	August 16, 2004

Chart 8–25 Zweig Double 9 Up Volume.

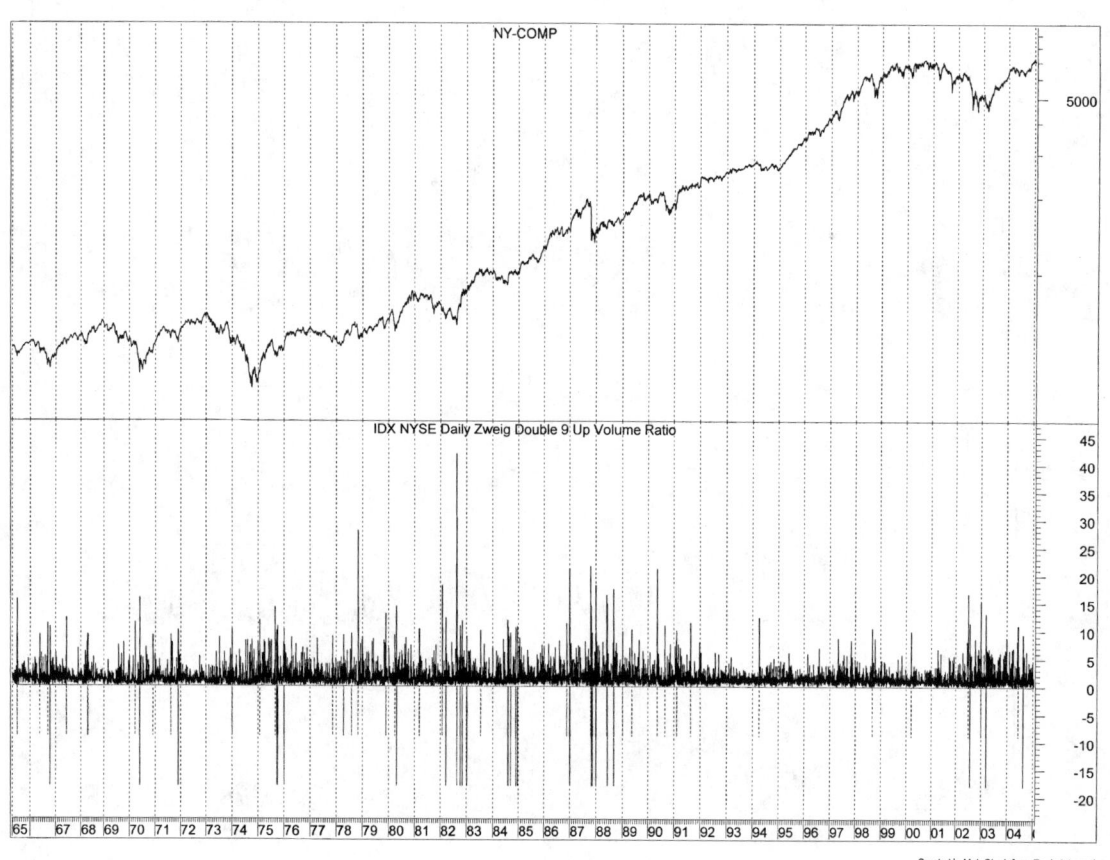

Notice in Chart 8–25 that these "double nine" signals are after the market bottoms. They are identified as the longer of the down spikes and go down to −18, whereas the down spikes that go down only to −9 are the regular ones mentioned earlier. The longer down spikes are the second of the 9-to-1 ratios to occur in a 3-month period. They won't be good market bottom signals, but will give you an opportunity to get onboard a strong market. They are almost confirmation that a good upward move is underway and considered as a continuation of the first 9-to 1 down spike.

Author Comments

I took his concept one step further and identified all the down volume days in which the down volume was 9 times greater than the up volume. There were many more signals for both the regular 9 to 1 ratio and also the "double nine" signals. Chart 8–26 shows the double nine signals as the down spikes that go down to −18, and the regular nine-to-one ratios are the shorter down spikes

Chart 8-26 Zweig Double 9 Down Volume.

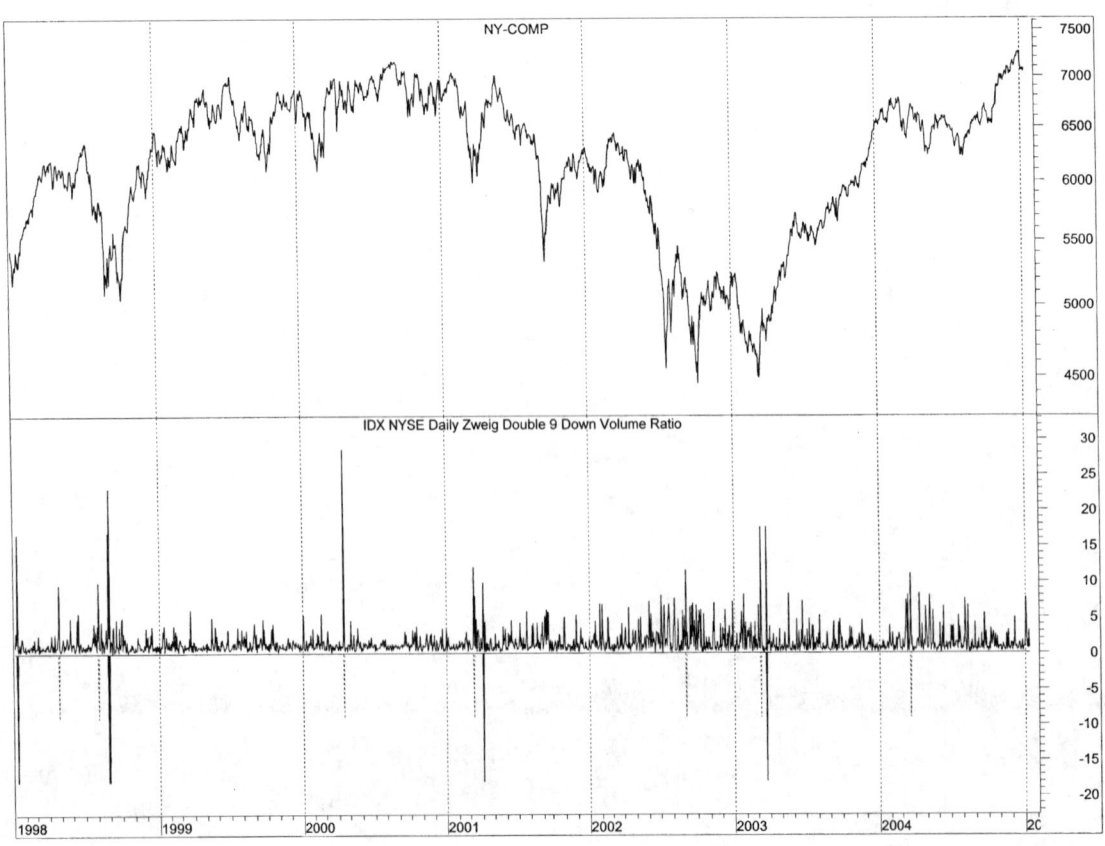

(dotted lines). The October 19, 1987 "Black Monday" market plunge distorts the chart because there was over 500 times more down volume than up volume on that day. That is the reason chart 8–26 does not display data back to that date. After studying this data for some time, I think it is best to keep it in the "nice to know" category. I do not see any trading opportunities or investing strategies that can make use of this. When you think about it, down volume in excess is usually from panic situations. Many times they are near market bottoms as it is during capitulation, but mostly during only 1-day panics. The down volume 9-to 1 ratios could be the first indication that the ensuing rally might be a good one.

References

Zweig, Martin E. *Winning on Wall Street*. New York: Warner Books, 1986.

9
Composite Indicators

The breadth indicators in this section utilize different categories of breadth components for their calculation. Some use all breadth components, and some use only two or three components.

Composite Indicators

Arms Index
Arms Open Index
Bretz TRIN-5
Cash Flow Index
Composite Tape Index
Dysart Positive Negative Volume
Eliades New TRIN
Haller Theory
Hindenburg Omen

Market Thrust
McClellan Oscillator with Volume
McClellan Summation Index with Volume
Meyers Systems
Moving Balance Indicator
Technical Index
Titanic Syndrome
Trend Exhaustion Index

Arms Index

Also known as: TRIN and MKDS
Author/Creator: Richard W. Arms
Data components required: Advances (A), Declines (D), Up Volume (UV), Down Volume (DV)

Description

The Arms Index (TRIN) is the ratio between advancing issues and declining issues divided by the ratio between the up volume and the down volume. Said differently, it is the ratio of the volume of declining stocks divided by the volume of advancing stocks. A rising line above 1.0 reflects more volume in declining issues and is negative. A falling line below 1.0 reflects more volume in rising stocks and is positive. The Arms index trends in the opposite direction of the market and is considered an inverse indicator.

TRIN came from its original name of Short Term TRading INdex. When computers came along and everyone started attaching their names to their creations (appropriately so), it was changed to Arms Index. The first known writing on it appeared in Barrons in 1967.

Interpretation

Newton Zinder, of E. F. Hutton and Co. has identified the bullishness of the Arms Index when two consecutive days had readings of 2.0 or greater. To produce levels like this, there must be a large number of declines compared to advances, plus those declines must garner most of the volume for that day. It represents almost a panic type of selling for the day.

Chart 9–1 is the Arms Index in its basic form. A line is drawn at an Arms Index value of 2.0, showing the extreme levels of large volume going into declining stocks. Remember that this is an inverse (upside down) indicator. You can quickly see that it is volatile and difficult to interpret in

Chart 9–1 Arms Index.

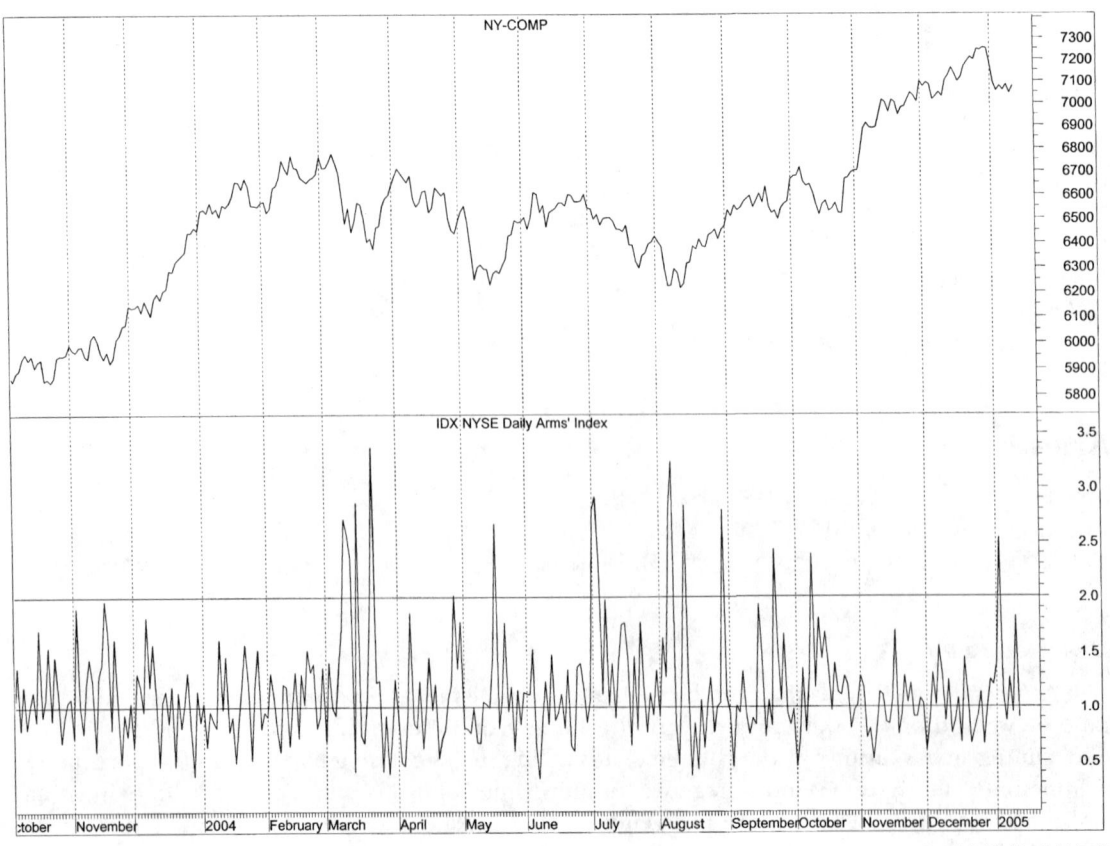

this basic form. The following (Chart 9–2) shows different ways to chart and use the Arms Index and will add significantly to its merit.

Richard Arms has stated that he uses a 21-day smoothing for intermediate forecasts and 55 days for longer term use. In 1991, Richard Arms talked about an oscillator using the 21-day smoothing and the 55-day smoothing of the Arms Index. Whenever the 21-day average dropped below the 55-day average, it was giving a buy signal (remember, this is an inverted indicator), and whenever the 21-day average went above the 55-day average, a sell signal was generated. Richard Arms called this indicator the "Cross Your Arms" indicator. Arms further refined his use of this indicator by suggesting that you use it as an intermediate-term market direction indicator, and when it is bullish look for buys only. Likewise, if it is bearish, look only for selling opportunities. A lot like the old saying—don't fight the tape. A little known fact is that Richard Arms preferred exponential smoothing instead of arithmetic. Thomas Aspray wrote about such an oscillator but used a 10-day average and a 30-day average for his indicator. The "cross your arms" indicator is shown in Chart 9–2.

Chart 9–2 Arms Index Oscillator 21–55.

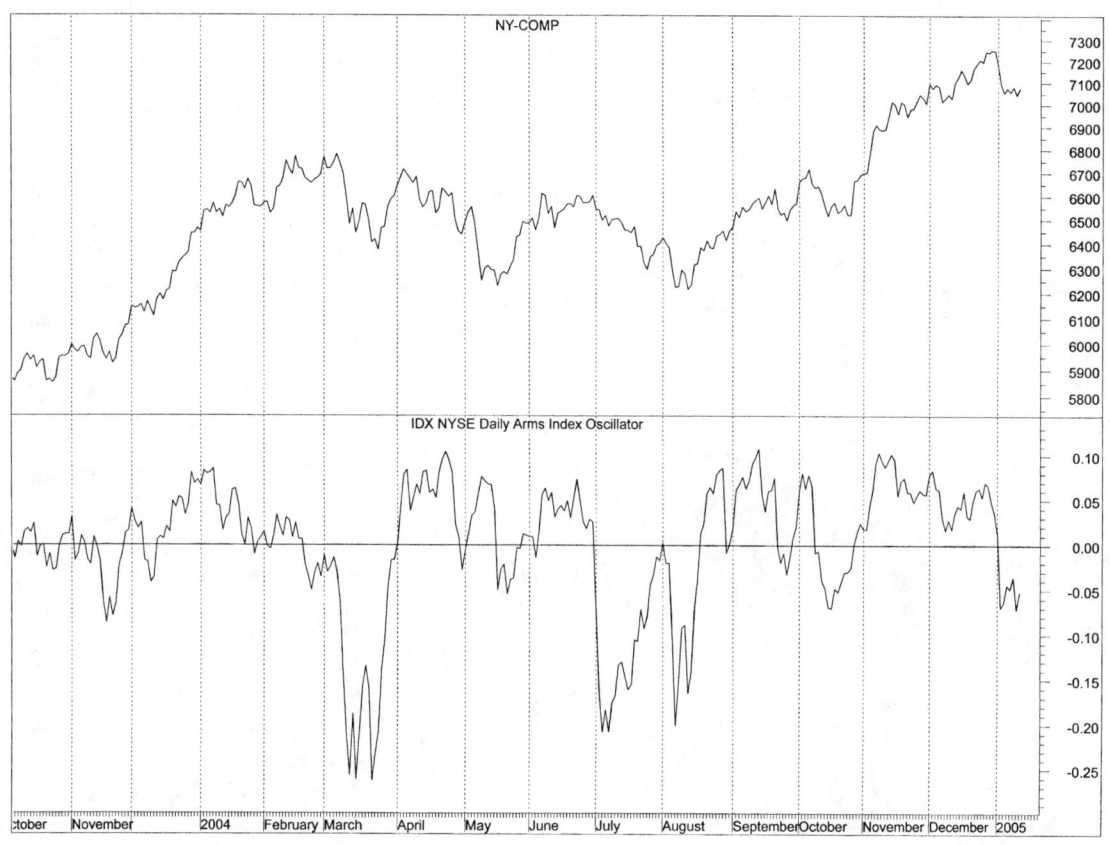

of Arms' uses of his indicator, the Arms Index, is to plot a 4-day average of it and put 15 percent bands around a 13-day simple average. He states that it is very short term and only used for trading. When it moves outside the bands, a signal is given. Again, keep in mind that this is an inverse indicator, so when it breaks out of the top band a buy signal is given and when it breaks out below the bottom band, a sell signal is given. Chart 9–3 shows this method, with the 15 percent bands being the dotted lines.

Steven Achelis, founder of Equis International, suggests using a 4-day moving average for short-term work, a 21-day moving average for intermediate-term work, and a 55-day moving average for long term work. These values are inline with Arms' suggestions. You can see a plot of the Arms Index with a 21-day smoothing in Chart 9–4. Trendlines are shown pointing out some obvious divergences with the market.

Notice in Chart 9–4 how it builds higher and higher during the topping process of the market. This is because the Arms Index is not a true ratio, in that it theoretically has no limit to the upside,

Chart 9–3 Arms Index—4 Day with Bands.

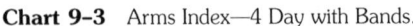

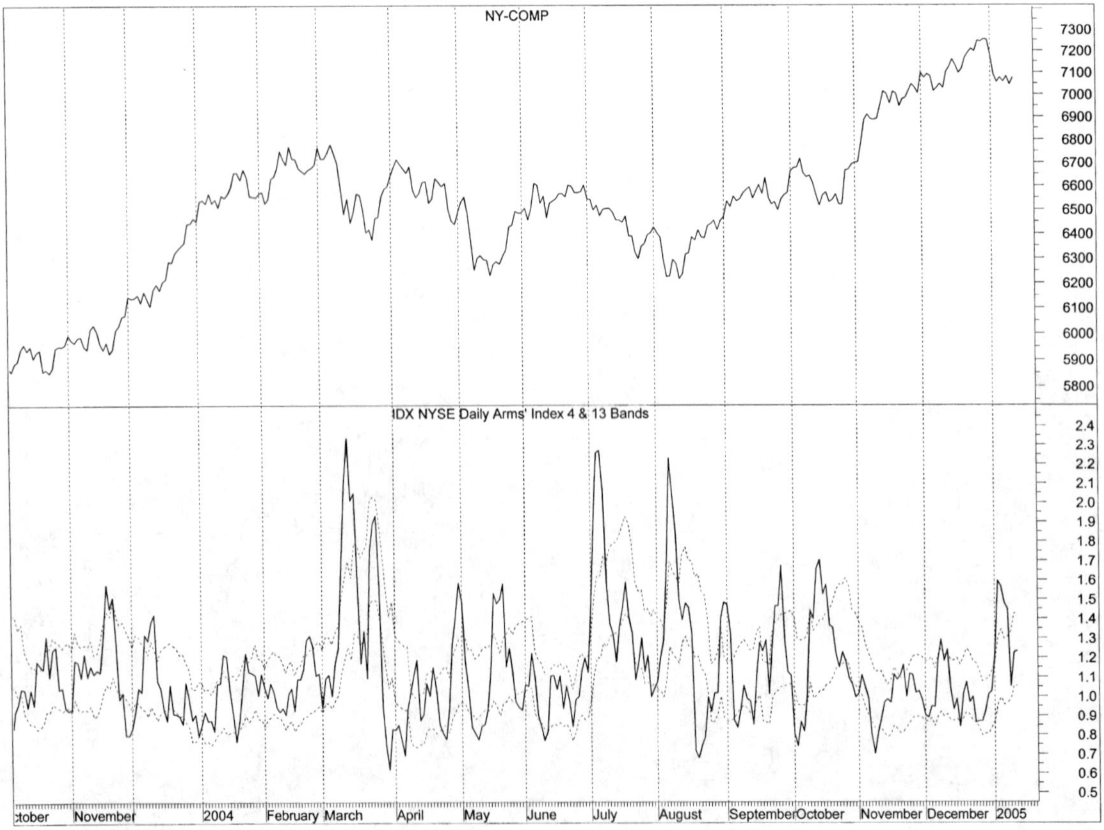

Created in MetaStock from Equis International

Chart 9-4 Arms Index—21-Day Smooth with Divergence.

but cannot go below zero on the downside, giving it an upside bias. Smoothing it will not change this bias. Another popular way to interpret this indicator is to construct a 10-day moving average of its daily values. A 10-day Arms Index over 1.20 is oversold; a 10-day Arms index below .80 is overbought, as shown in Chart 9–5. A further enhancement, which is strictly visual appeal, is to invert the indicator so that up is bullish and down is bearish, which is more inline with most indicators. This can easily be accomplished by dividing 1 by the indicator. If you do this, then the Arms Index over 1.20 is overbought, and when below. 80, it is oversold. You can quickly see that using this as a trading tool will generate entirely too many false signals. I just prefer to monitor it to keep a mental focus on where the volume is going, into advancing stocks or declining stocks. In general, because of swings in market sentiment, the Arms Index can be bullish when either overbought or oversold. It is the rapid change in sentiment that forces the Arms Index to swing to extremes.

In 1987, James Alphier and Bill Kuhn wrote an article in *Stocks and Commodities* magazine after a comprehensive study of the market using a daily Arms Index reading of 2.65 or greater. They

Chart 9-5 Arms Index—10-Day Smooth Inverted.

showed the performance of the S&P 500 Index 3, 6, 9, and 12 months after the Arms Index gave a 2.65 reading. A cursory glance at their table revealed that the market was usually higher over different time periods after the big selling day when the Arms Index went above 2.65. The question they wanted to answer was: "Does it pay to go along and panic with the herd?" Their answer: "It does not." Remember that when the Arms Index is at a high, it means that most of the volume is going into the declining issues. Many times this extreme selling can be a form of panic and a selling climax. Another very interesting note that they made was that after a 2.65 reading, a key trading low came a short time later. Chart 9–6 shows the Arms Index when values are greater than 2.65. Each down spike at the bottom of Chart 9–6 identifies a day when the Arms Index is greater than 2.65.

Tim Hayes at Ned Davis Research uses a 40-day average of the Arms Index for their intermediate-term work. He says that the Arms Index is a good measure of the quality of volume in the market, more on an intermediate to short-term basis. Buy signals occur when the indicator increases

Chart 9-6 Arms Index—2.65 Days Shown.

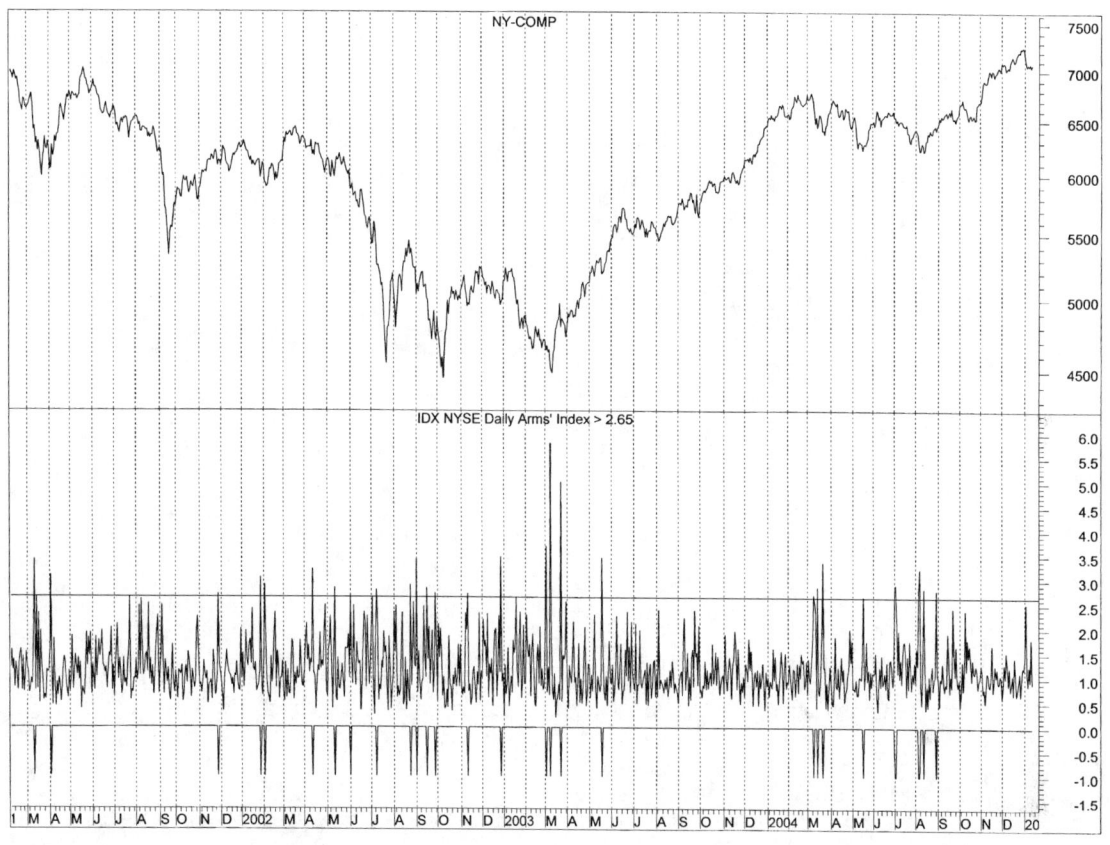

to 1.12 or at least to .968 and then reverses. Sell indications are readings below .798 or a decrease to at least .928 and then back above the level. Chart 9–7 is a plot of the 40-day average of the Arms Index (TRIN).

In 1992, Arthur Merrill said that the simple daily closing Arms Index seems to be useful in forecasting the direction of the market of the following day only at very high readings above 2.3, or very low readings below 0.4. This occurs only rarely. Arthur was using the prices of the Dow Jones Industrial Average for this analysis and only 435 days (less than 2 years) of market data.

Author Comments

The Arms Index and the Advance Decline Line are the two most overanalyzed breadth indicators I know of. That is certainly a measure of their popularity. There are many derivations of the Arms Index, some good, some not so good. This section has presented most of them. One thing that

Chart 9-7 Arms Index—40 Average.

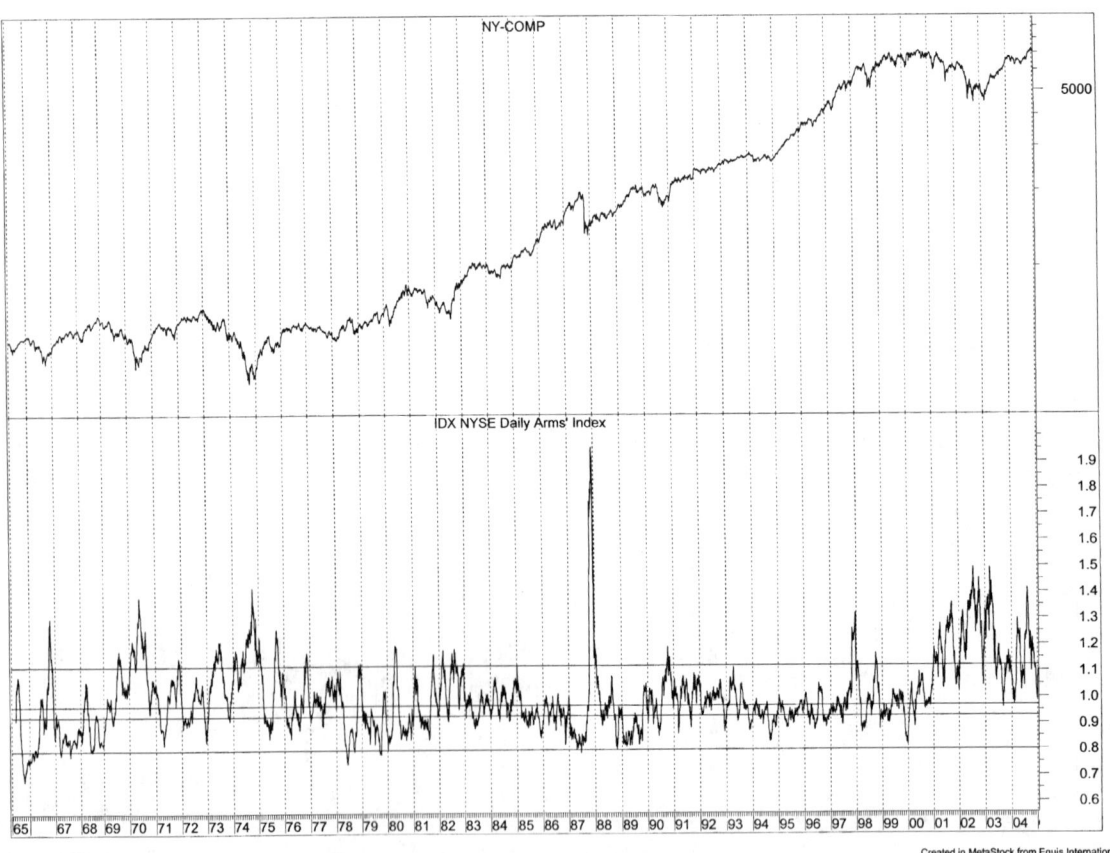

stands out is that the bullishness of the Arms Index is related to the number of declining issues. This is a little hard to grasp until you study the formula.

I have always found the raw Arms Index difficult to use for trading, other than a quick picture of where volume is flowing, either into advancing stocks or declining stocks. I much prefer to invert it, smooth it, and set up zones for bullish and bearish readings. Richard Arms told me at a technical analysis conference in Dallas, Texas, in the early 1990s, that he wished he had inverted it in the beginning because of the interpretation problems most folks had with using an inverted indicator. Inverting it does not affect its interpretation in any way; it just uses the more popular "up is bullish and down is bearish" convention. Also, Richard Arms is of the belief that volume is the most important component of the market. To make his point during his presentation, Dick made the comment that when he left his office to go to lunch, he told his secretary that he would be back in about 35 million shares. He also said in a 1991 interview for *Stocks and Commodities* magazine that if the market were a wristwatch, it would be divided into shares, not hours.

In reference to Arms 4-day average of the Arms Index and the 15 percent bands around the 13-day average shown in Chart 9–3, it looks to me that the concept is quite good, but even better if you wait until the 4-day smoothed value returns within the bands before generating a signal. In other words, a buy signal is given after the 4-day average goes above the upper band and then drops below it. Likewise, a sell signal is given when it comes from below to above the lower band. This interpretation was done by using a cursor and visually looking at the data from 1965 to early 2005.

Robert Nurock, the chief elf on the *Wall Street Week* television show, who created the Wall Street Week Index, used the Arms Index as one of that index's components. A bullish signal was given when the 10-day average of the Arms Index was above 1.2 and bearish when below 0.8.

$$\text{Formula: } (A / D) / (UV / DV)$$

References

Arms, Richard W. Jr. *The Arms Index (TRIN)*. Dow Jones-Irwin, 1989.
Arms, Richard W., "Cross Your Arms." *Stocks and Commodities*, Volume 9, May 1991, pp. 177–179.
Achelis, Steven B. *Technical Analysis from A to Z*. New York: McGraw-Hill, 1995.
Alphier, James and Kuhn, Bill, "A Helping Hand from the Arms Index." *Stocks and Commodities*, Volume 5, April 1987, pp. 142–143.
Aspray, Thomas, "NYSE technical indicators: diagnosing market bottoms." *Stocks and Commodities*, Volume 6, June 1987, pp. 227–231.
Merrill, Arthur, "Volume Indices." *Stocks and Commodities*, Volume 7, September 1989, pp. 301-303.
Hayes, Tim, "Tim Hayes: Running with the Trend." *Stocks and Commodities*, Volume 9, August 1991, pp. 310–315.
Davis, Ned. *Being Right or Making Money*. Ned Davis Research, 1991.

Arms Open Index

Author/Creator: Suggested by Harley Wilbur, recommended by John McGinley and Peter Eliades
Data components required: Advances (A), Declines (D), Up Volume (UV), Down Volume (DV).

Description

This is a smoothed version of Richard Arms' Short Term Trading Index or Arms Index, however, it smoothes the individual components prior to doing the multiple divisions. Wilbur used a 10-period moving average for the smoothing each of the components.

Interpretation

Steve Achelis states that readings above .9 are bearish and below .9 are bullish. While it seems to pick tops and bottoms at times, other times seem to not do so, as shown in Chart 9–8.

Chart 9-8 Arms Open Index—10-Day Smooth.

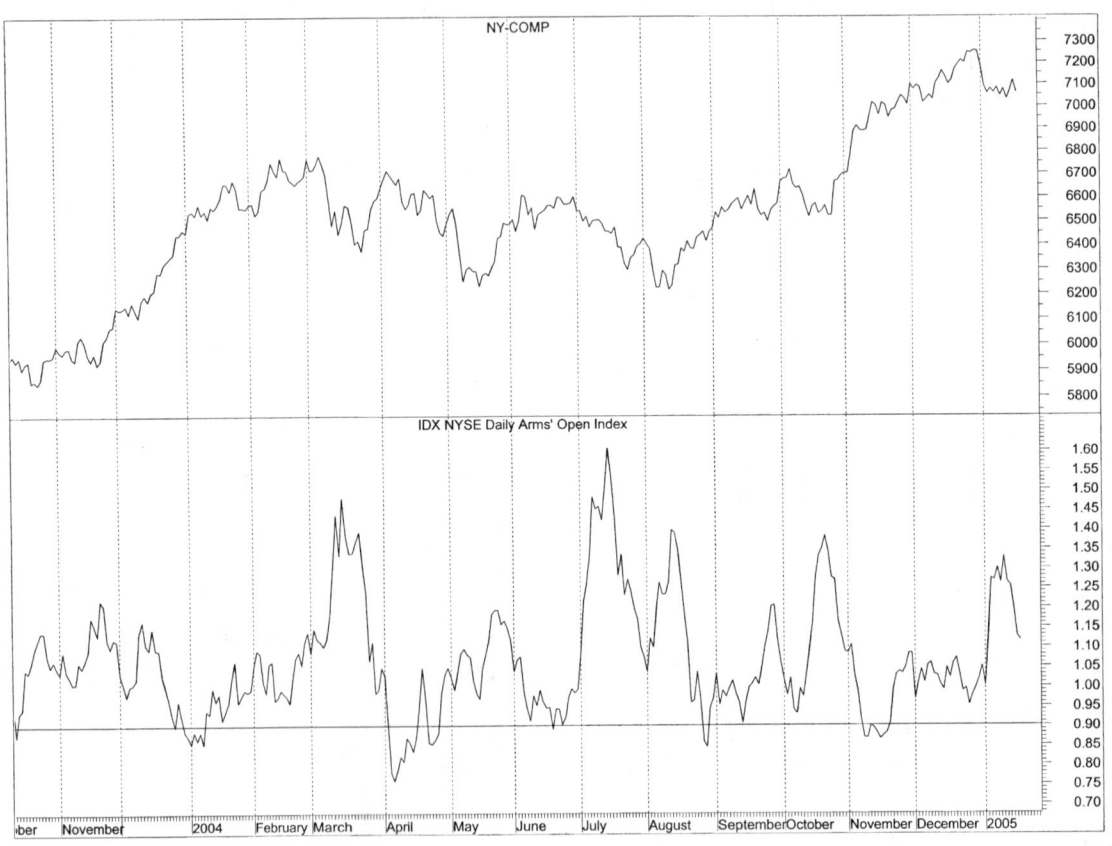

Author Comments

Personally, I'll stick with Dick Arms' original index, but display it upside down so it is more intuitive for me and then give it a 10-day smoothing. I use the Arms Index for a short-term picture of the markets, to assist in determining where the volume is going, either into advances or declines. I can see the merits of the Arms Open (prefer Open Arms—sounds more inviting), but I also prefer to just use a smoothed version of TRIN (Arms Index). However, Wilbur wasn't finished with the Arms Index and his modifications to it.

In November, 1992, Harley Wilbur presented, in my opinion, the best modification to the continuously modified Arms Index. He normalized it relative to its own volatility. First of all, he took the Arms Open Index using 10-day averages, took a 10-day average of that, and then normalized it with typical two standard deviation Bollinger bands. This made the indicator oscillate essentially between zero and 100, with zero being the lower Bollinger band and 100 representing the upper

Chart 9-9 Arms Open and with Bollinger Bands.

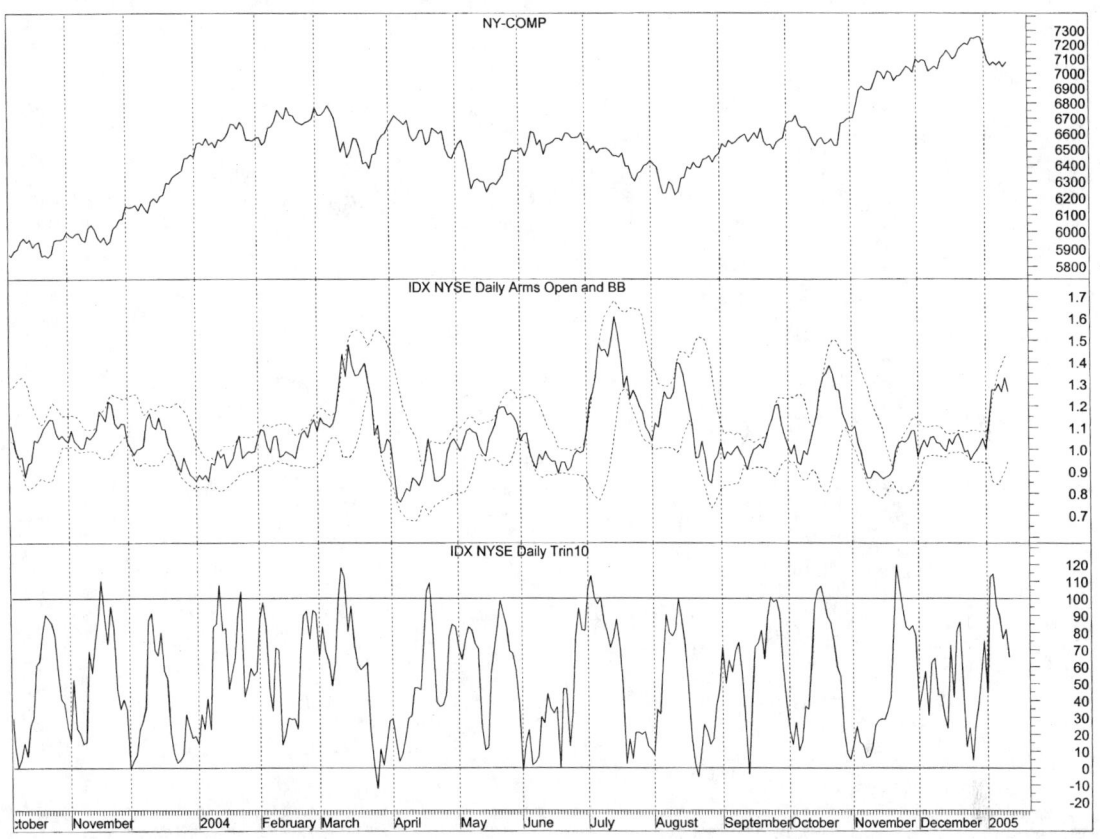

Bollinger band. He called this indicator Trin10. Chart 9–9 shows in the middle plot the Arms Open Index with Bollinger bands. If you then imagined that you took the ends of the two Bollinger bands and pulled them taught so they were parallel straight lines, the lower plot shows this. The horizontal lines at zero and 100 are in fact the Bollinger bands, and the open Arms index is displayed with its same relative position to the bands as it was in the middle plot.

Wilbur next weighted the Trin10 with a five period weighted moving average as shown in Chart 9-10. A weighted average is one that has a linear weighting, with the most recent having the greatest weight and the oldest having the least. Wilbur suggested the trading strategy was to buy on an up tick from below 20 and sell on a downtick from above 80. Wilbur readily admitted that it did not always work, but rated it good enough to keep in the technician's arsenal. I certainly agree.

Formula: $TRIN = (A / D) / (UV / DV), (TRIN - LowerBB) / (UpperBB - LowerBB)$

Chart 9-10 WTRIN10.

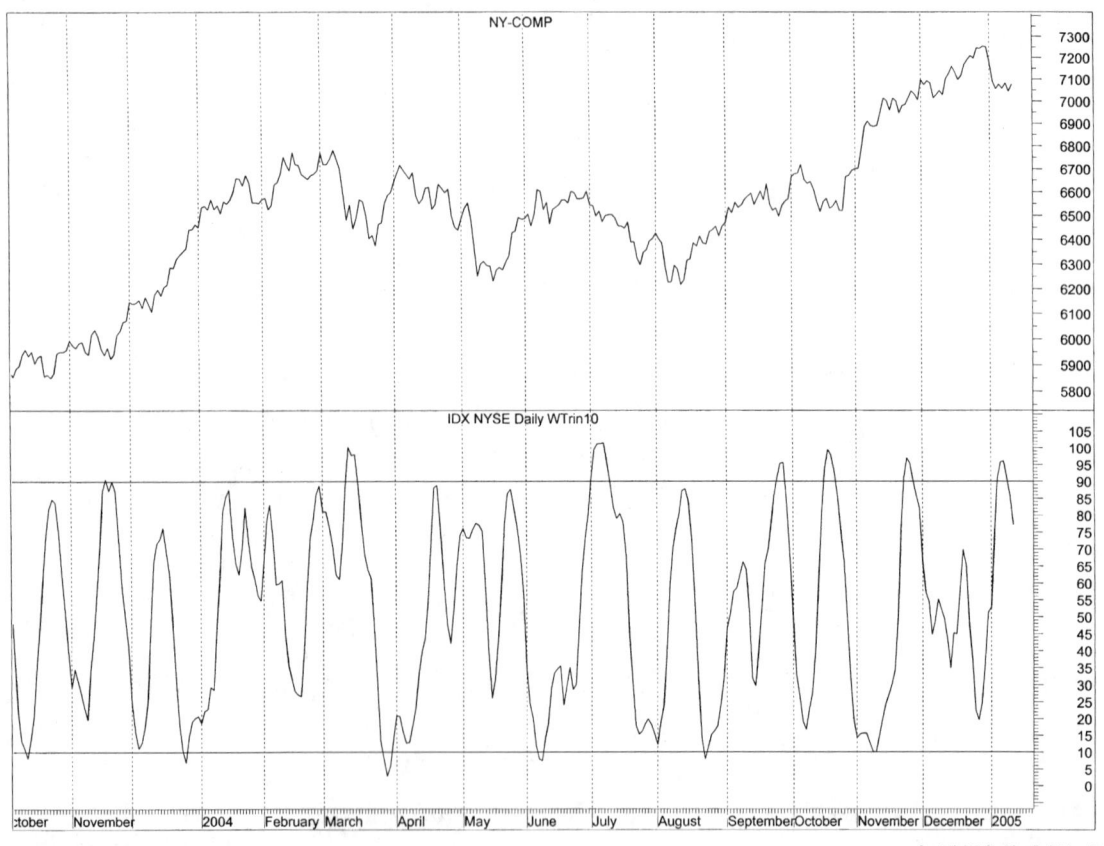

References

Achelis, Steven B. *Technical Analysis from A to Z*. New York: McGraw-Hill, 1995.
Wilbur, Harley, "A Twist on the Arms Index." *Stocks and Commodities*, Volume 10, November 1992, pp. 449–453.
Merrill, Arthur, "Closing Arms." *Stocks and Commodities*, Volume 10, April 1992, pp. 148–150.

Bretz TRIN-5

Author/Creator: W. G. Bretz
Data components required: Advances (A), Declines (D), Up Volume (UV), Down Volume (DV)

Description

The Bretz TRIN-5 Indicator was developed by W.G. Bretz, and it was dubbed the TRIN-5 by Jerry Favors, who published an article on it in *Stocks and Commodities* magazine (March 1992). Favors claimed that it is a better top picker than the other versions of the Arms Index. The calculation is simply a 5-day moving sum (not a moving average) of the Arms Index.

Interpretation

When the indicator reaches an extreme level above 6.00, then turns down, a buy signal is generated. When the indicator reaches an extreme level below 4.00, then turns up, a sell signal is generated. It appears to be as effective as or better than the 10-day TRIN at market bottoms and it is far more effective at market tops and is shown in Chart 9–11.

Author Comments

Carl Swenlin does what most of us do with Arms Index related indicators and derivations; he inverts it so that the more normal appearance of overbought and oversold are correct and more intuitive. Chart 9–12 shows it as inverted with the calculation so that overbought is up and oversold is down. The interpretation now is that when this indicator rises from below 4 and turns up, a buy signal has been generated. And when it goes from above 6 and turns down a sell signal is generated. Personally I like to see buy signals when it goes from below 4 and then goes above 6 before it generates a buy signal. Likewise, when it drops from above 6 and goes below 4, a sell signal is given.

Formula: $(A/D)/(UV/DV)$ summed over the last 5 days

References

Bretz, W.G. *Juncture Recognition in the Stock Market*. Vantage Press, 1972.
Favors, Jerry, "The Trin-5." *Stocks and Commodities*, Volume 10, March 1992, pp. 125–126.

Cash Flow Index

Also known as: see The Technical Index
Author/Creator: William Mason
Data components required: Advances (A), Declines (D), Up Volume (UV), Down Volume (DV), New Highs (H), New Lows (L), Total Issues (TI), Volume (V).

Description

The Cash Flow Index is created by taking the net difference of the advances and declines, up and down volume, and new highs and new lows; expressing them as a percentage of their respective base; combining them to get a new value; multiplying it by the volume for the day; then accumu-

Chart 9-11 Bretz TRIN-5.

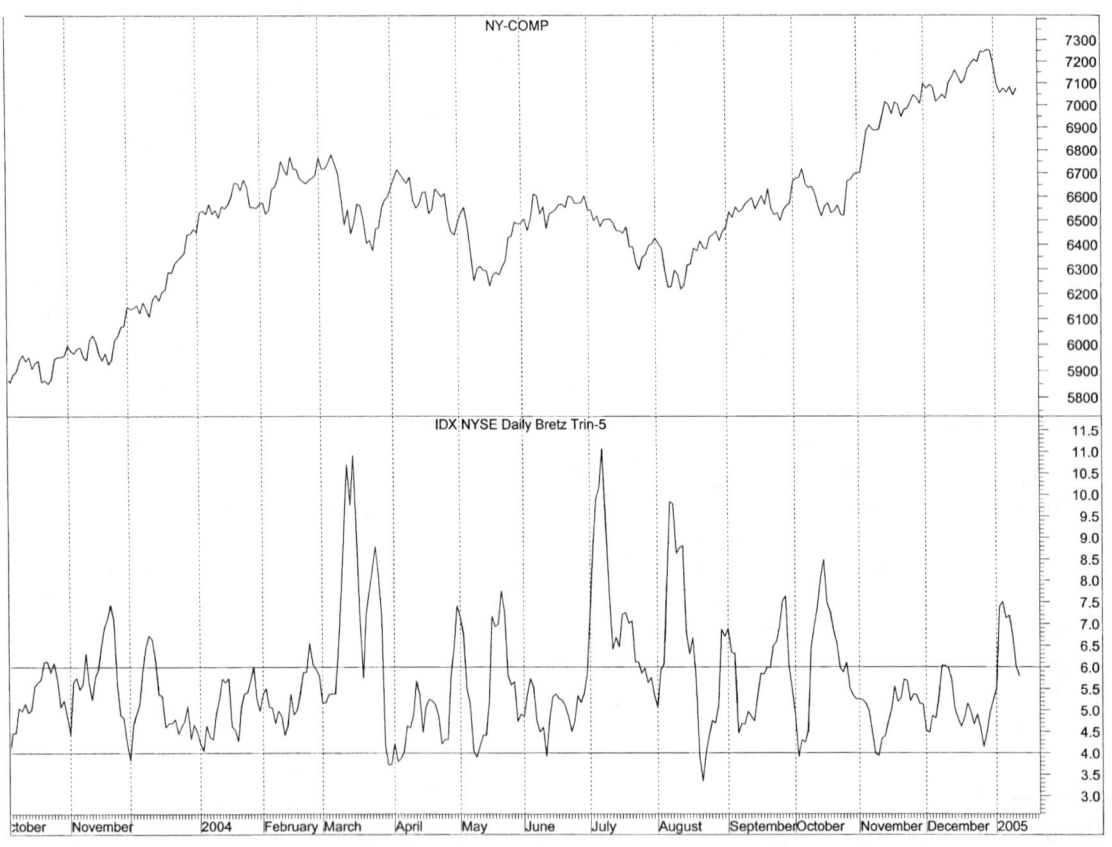

lating the daily values. Mason said that the reason for using percentages is that no single parameter will dominate.

Interpretation

Most indicators of cash flow are measuring price and volume or two nonneutralizing components of market statistics. Using it to help confirm new highs in the market would be about the only way I can think of that this would be effective. Chart 9-13 is the cash flow index developed by Mason.

Author Comments

I have only found a few sentences on this indicator by William Mason. It is a derivation of the Technical Index he developed with a daily total volume component added to it. Since one of the components in the Technical Index is the up volume, down volume difference and total volume ratio. Adding the total volume as a multiplier seems to dampen, and almost hinder, the usefulness

Chart 9-12 Bretz TRIN-5 Inverted.

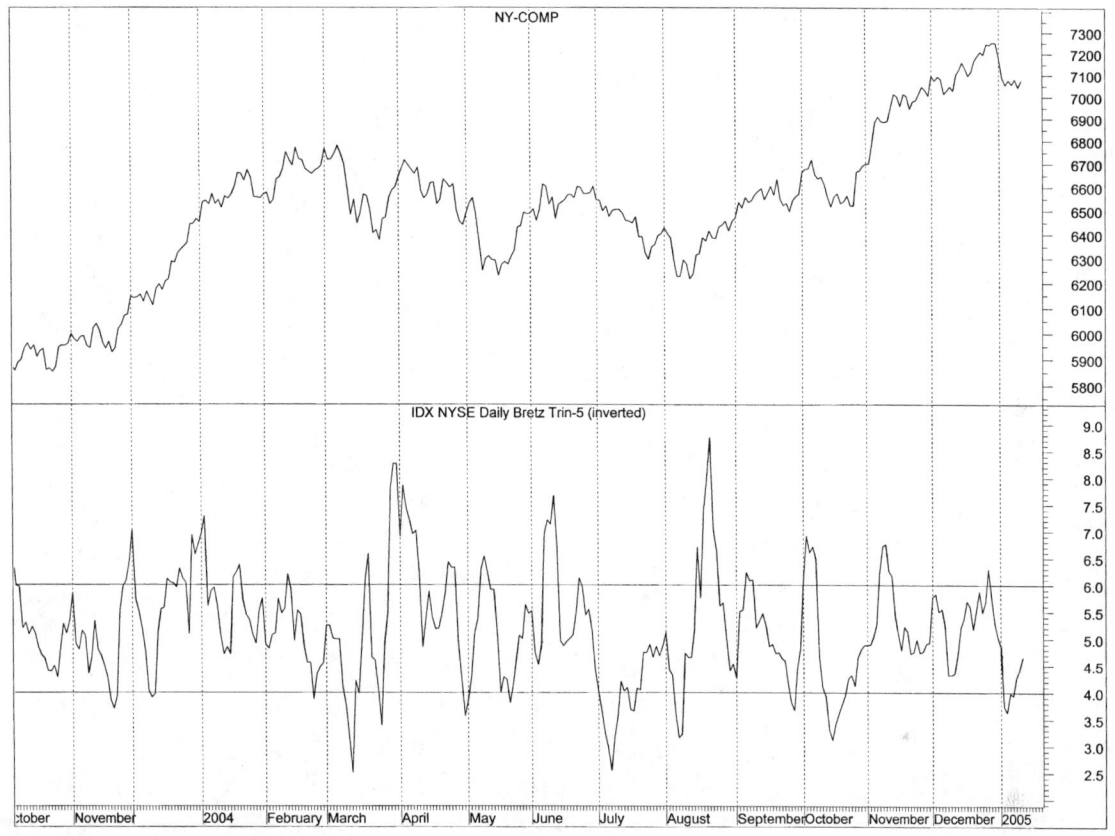

of this indicator. It renders the ratio ineffective and makes the volume contribution only that of the difference between the up and down volume. One might improve it by detrending it with a moving average of 50 days or so.

Formula: Previous Value + Today's $(V * ((A - D) / TI) + ((UV - DV) / V) + ((H - L) / TI))$

References
Mason, William, "Master Oscillator." *Stocks and Commodities*, Volume 7, April 1989, pp. 109–111.

Composite Tape Index

Author/Creator: Equis International
Data components required: Advances (A), Declines (D), New Highs (H), New Lows (L), Up Volume (UV), Down Volume (DV)

Chart 9-13 Cash Flow Index.

Description

The Composite Tape Index shows market strength and direction. Because the CTI displays market strength (momentum), it tends to be a trend-following indicator. The indicator can be used to anticipate market moves, but it is best not to "fight the tape" (a phrase Martin Zweig coined years ago). Once the Composite Tape Index forms a trend, it tends to stay in that trend for some time. And once the trend is broken, it is usually broken for good and a new trend is then established. Because the CTI is a composite of several different momentum indicators, it is not as subject to false readings and whipsaws as often as a single indicator.

Interpretation

The basic analysis of the Composite Tape Index requires determining the current trend and deciding when the trend has changed. One method of determining the trend is to wait for the indicator to enter the overbought/oversold zones and then rise/fall from these levels. Buy signals are

Composite Indicators

given when the indicator falls below −15 and then rises above −15, or any time the indicator rises above +15. Likewise, sell signals are generated when the indicator rises above +15 and then falls below +15, or any time the indicator falls below −15. Another system that works wells is to buy when CTI rises above zero and sell when it falls below zero. Chart 9–14 shows the medium-term composite tape index.

The short-term composite index uses faster parameters and is shown in Chart 9–15. In general terms, the parameters for the short-term version are about 20 percent less than the medium-term tape index. The overbought and oversold levels that seem to work well are +10 and −10. The analysis and use of the short-term composite is the same as the medium-term composite.

Author Comments

These are great indicators and I know they come from Steven Achelis, the founder of Equis International. Years ago, Steve had a software program called The Technician, which was

Chart 9–14 *Composite Tape Index—Medium.*

Chart 9-15 Composite Tape Index—Short.

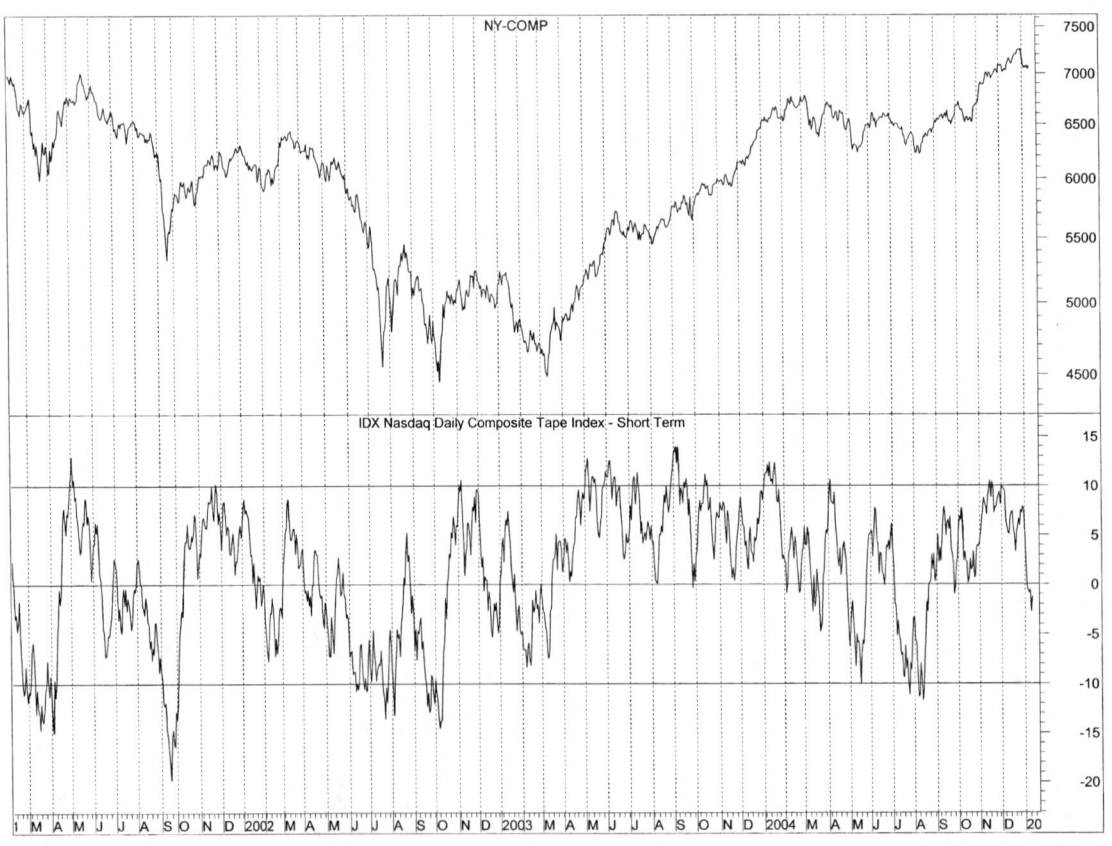

MS-DOS based and I'm sure the pressure from users to come out with a MS-Windows based version was high. Therefore it has essentially been incorporated into the latest version (9.0) of MetaStock.

I prefer to use this indicator for signals that occur when it crosses above and below the zero line. They seem to work better and avoid the often subjective nature of overbought and oversold.

If there is a short- and medium-term version, why not a long-term version? For this, I just doubled the value of the default parameters of the medium version to get Chart 9–16. Here is how I would use this version: It does a great job of identifying tops and bottoms using +30 for overbought and -20 for oversold. It also seems to be good using the zero line crossover. One can begin to leg in on the oversold crossing from below to above the −20 line, then take more positions after crossing the zero line. Selling can be done the same way. Partially exit positions when it comes from above to below the +30 line, then exit all when it drops below the zero line. Chart 9–16 is my version of the long-term composite tape indicator.

Chart 9-16 Composite Tape Index—Long.

References
MetaStock Professional 9.0, Equis International, Salt Lake City, UT.

Dysart Positive Negative Volume

Author/Creator: Paul Dysart
Data components required: Advances (A), Declines (D) Volume (V)

Description

Paul Dysart used a similar concept to Granville's On Balance Volume with his Positive and Negative Issues Traded Indexes. The positive version was the summation of advances minus declines only on days when the total volume of trading increases over that of the previous day. The negative version is similar in that it uses the advance decline difference when the volume decreases.

Interpretation

This would be used similar to using Joe Granville's On Balance Volume. Spotting where they do not follow the price will lead to market turns. Chart 9–17 shows both versions, with the negative version being the bolder of the two. Do not get confused with this chart, as the two indicators are displayed using totally different scales so any crossing of each other is not viable. The darker line is the positive version.

Author Comments

There is very little written about these indicators. They are takeoffs of Dysart's original Negative Volume Index.

Formula: If the close today is greater than the close yesterday, use up volume. If not, use down volume. Then accumulate the numbers.

Chart 9–17 Dysart Positive and Negative.

References

Merrill, Arthur, "Negative Volume Divergence Index." *Stocks and Commodities*, Volume 8, October 1990, pp. 396–397.

Peterson, Dennis, "Market Breadth: Volume." *Stocks and Commodities*, Volume 19, February 2001, pp. 57–60.

Eliades New TRIN

Author/Creator: Peter Eliades
Data components required: Advances (A), Declines (D), Up Volume (UV), Down Volume (DV)

Description

The Eliades New TRIN calculation is a 10-day moving average of down volume, divided by a 10-day moving average of up volume, further divided by a 10-day moving average of the Arms Index (TRIN).

Interpretation

When the indicator crosses below .8, and then moves back above .8, a sell signal is generated. Chart 9–18 shows Eliades New TRIN.

Author Comments

Once again, inverting the chart of this indicator will make it more intuitive but does not add anything to the interpretation. However, my seventh-grade algebra says that this is essentially just the ratio of declines and advances. The act of smoothing the components keeps this somewhat different than the decline advance ratio in that the levels are a little different; however, the lines are close to the same. Because Peter Eliades has made significant contributions to technical analysis, I suspect his interpretation would be better than mine.

$$\text{Formula: } (DV/AV) / ((A/D) / (UV/DV))$$

References

Swenlin, Carl, www.decisionpoint.com.
Eliades, Peter, www.stockmarketcycles.com.

Haller Theory

Author/Creator: Gilbert Haller
Data components required: Advances (A), Declines (D), New Highs (H), New Lows (L)

Chart 9-18 Eliades New TRIN.

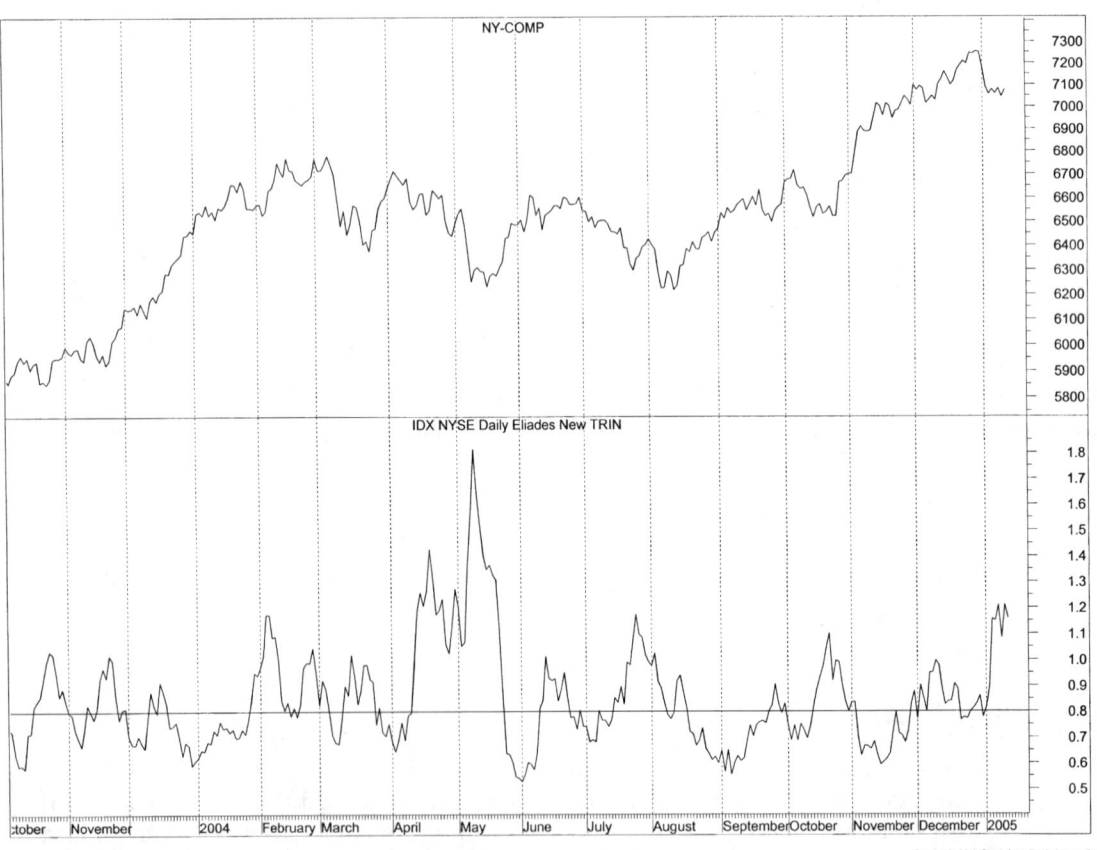

Description

The Haller Theory for determining market tops and bottoms is more than just a breadth-based method. It involves the yield on the Dow Jones Industrial Average in addition to weekly advance decline line data and weekly new high and new low data. There are essentially two types of buy signals, one which is an opportunity to buy during an identifiable trend and the other is during a selling climax. The sell signals are basically the opposite.

Interpretation

Trend Buy Signal

1. The advance decline line must turn up by 2400 points.
2. The new high, new low difference must equal a net +80 new highs.
3. There can be no Trend Buy until there has been a Trend Sell Signal.

Trend Sell Signal

1. The yield on the Dow Jones Industrial Average must be less than 5 percent.
2. The advance decline line must turn down by 2400 points.
3. The new high, new low difference must equal a net −80 new lows.
4. There can be no Trend Sell Signal until there has been a Trend Buy Signal.

Bottom Buy Signals

1. Buy the start of the fourth week after the net new lows equals −750.
2. If there is a week in which there are more new lows than the week that gave the first signal, start the 4-week timing over.
3. If there is no Bottom Buy Signal, buy at the next Trend Buy Signal.

Top Sell Signals

1. The yield on the Dow Jones Industrial Average was less than 4 percent at one time during the bull move.
2. The bull move had to last for at least a year.
3. The advance decline line must have failed, which is a move that drops below a previous low with each leg being at least 2 weeks in length.
4. The initial peak of the advance decline line is the high for the line.
5. The advance decline line must rise for 3 weeks to make a third peak.
6. The advance decline line then must drop by over 300 points.
7. The net number of new highs must be less than that at the final peak than at earlier peaks.
8. Volume must also be lower on the final peak than previously based on a 6-week moving average.

Author Comments

Haller's self-published book is an interesting read. The concept he developed is fairly simple insofar as the data relationship and is quite effective, but it is not conducive for a chart with an indicator or trading system. I spent quite a bit of time creating an indicator that would reflect this system, even to the point of paring it down to using only the breadth data. I like the idea of using trend signals along with climactic buy and sell signals. He claimed that from 1942 to 1964 there were no bad signals. However, no mention of drawdown or other risk-based analysis was offered. You can also sense his deep understanding of the difficulty of timing market tops based on the complex methodology given in the Top Sell Signals. Finally, keep in mind that this was all done over 40 years ago with columnar pad and not even a calculator, let alone a computer. Chart 9–19 shows portions of the Haller Theory. I used 200 for the Trend limits on the high low component because at the time of this indicator's development, the total of weekly new highs plus new lows plus 1000 is more than double now. The dotted upward spikes that reach +3 are the Bottom Buy Signals. The dotted downward spikes that reach −1 are the Trend Sell Signals. The solid line that reaches +1 are the Trend Buy Signals. The Top Sell Signals could not be reproduced because of the subjectivity of his rules.

Chart 9-19 Haller Theory.

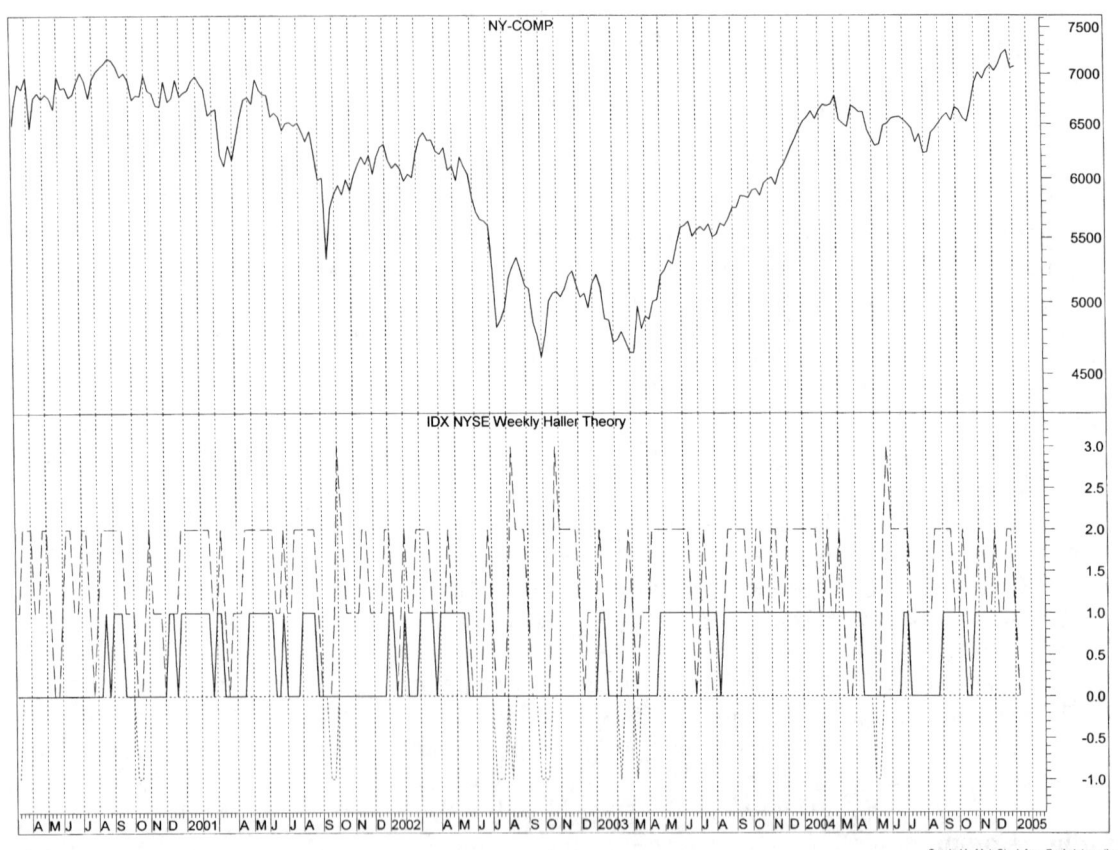

References
Haller, Gilbert. *The Haller Theory of Stock Market Trends.* West Palm Beach: Gilbert Haller, 1965.

Hindenburg Omen
Also known as: New High New Low Sell Signal
Author/Creator: James R. Miekka
Data components required: New Highs (H), New Lows (L), Advances (A), Declines (D), Total Issues (TI), Market Index (MKT).

Description
This indication of market tops was created by James R. Miekka and dubbed "the Hindenburg Omen" by Kennedy Gammage of the Richland Report. You'll recognize Kennedy as the former

provider of the McClellan Oscillator and Summation Index numbers on FNN and now, CNBC television.

The remaining material on this indicator was written by James R. Miekka, creator of the Hindenburg Omen:

The Hindenburg Omen is a sell signal that occurs when NYSE new highs and new lows each exceed 2.8 percent of advances plus declines on the same day. In addition, the NYSE index must be above the value it had 50 trading days (10 weeks) ago. Once the signal has occurred, it is valid for 30 trading days. Any additional signals given during the 30-day period should be ignored. During the 30 days, the signal is activated whenever the McClellan Oscillator (MCO) is negative, but deactivated whenever the MCO is positive. The signal starting point was originally calculated to be when NH and NL equaled or exceeded 2.4 percent of total issues traded, but was later simplified to 2.8 percent of advances plus declines. This signal was developed as an improvement upon the Split Market Sell Signal developed by Gerald Appel. Appel's signal used a fixed number of new highs and new lows (45 of each), which was not indexed for increasing numbers of shares trades, and his signal did not require validation by the MCO being negative.

Interpretation

This signal generally occurs after a rising market when the number of new lows is rising rapidly, but when new highs are still quite numerous. The large number of highs and lows suggests that the market is indecisive and probably at a turning point. Of course, a similar scenario can occur during a falling market when new lows are numerous but new highs begin to rise rapidly. The latter condition would suggest that such market indecision could be a buy signal in a falling market. This has not been studied, at least not by James Miekka, other than to note that the sell signal is not reliable when NYSE is below its 10-weeks-ago value. To utilize the Hindenburg Omen signal, Miekka suggests the following:

1. Go short the market whenever the McClellan Oscillator is negative during the 30 trading days after a valid signal has been given.
2. Exit the market for 30 days whenever the signal is given, or at least be wary of any new stock or stock index purchases while the signal is valid and especially if it is activated by a negative MCO.

By exiting the market when a signal was given on September 23, 1987, you would have avoided the crash of 1987.

Author Comments

Jim Miekka has provided a significant indicator of market danger. An indicator developed from a logical point of view is usually one that will serve you well. This one does just that. In Chart 9–20 I have tried to recreate this indicator as closely to Miekka's parameters as I can. Any difference between the chart signals and Jim's actual are a fault with my programming.

While it is not the purpose of this book to discern performance of these breadth indicators, Jim provided this for me and I want to deviate from that purpose just this once. The table below gives a history of the Hindenburg Omen from 1993 to 2004, using the old NYSE as the index. To convert to new NYSE, multiply the points by 10.78.

Chart 9-20 Hindenburg Omen.

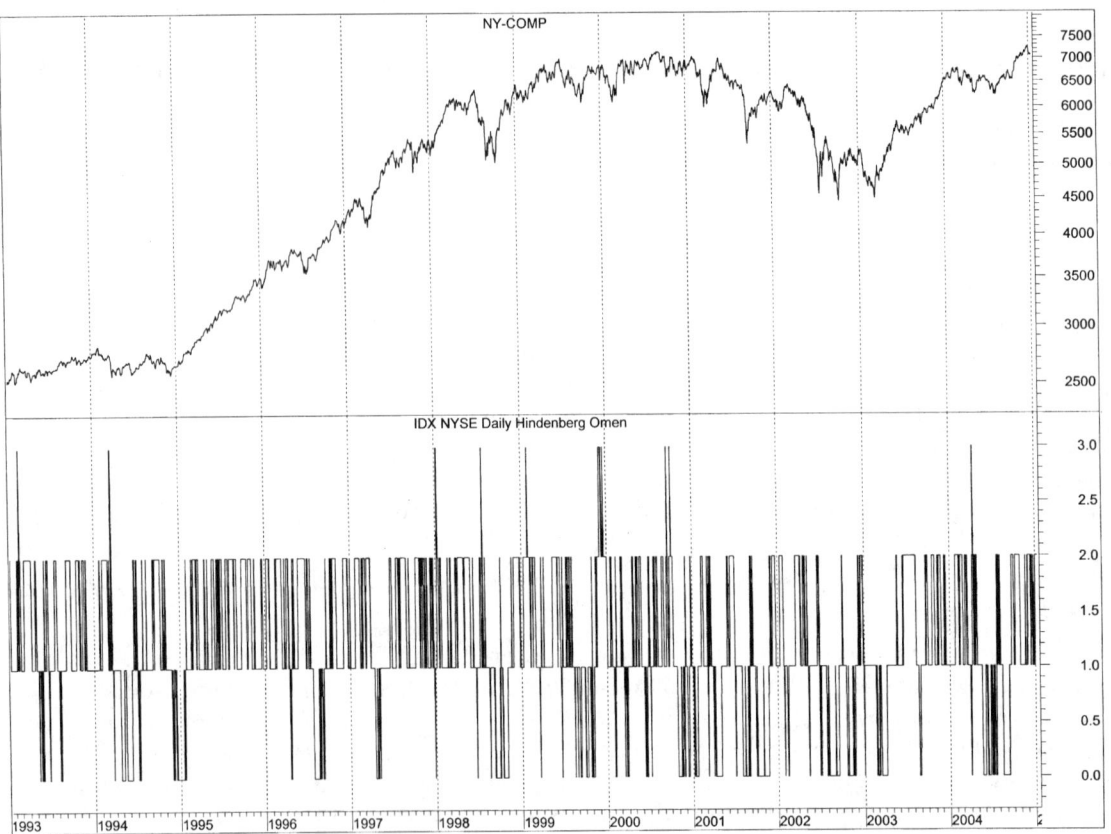

Date Signal Given	NYSE New Highs	NYSE New Lows	NH or NL* as % of A + D	McClellan Oscillator at Start	# of Days Short**	G/L in Old NYSE Points
02/22/93	177	61	3.1	−43	20	−0.80
03/15/94	93	80	3.7	−5	22	+9.68
10/28/94	89	114	3.9	+22	22	+18.55
10/10/96	66	68	2.9	−117	15	−6.56
11/26/97	128	91	3.2	+24	12	+6.21
07/09/98	120	96	3.3	+109	20	+38.64
01/29/99	96	91	3.0	−48	23	+9.69
04/08/99	97	122	3.2	+37	3	−0.97
10/29/99	117	90	2.9	+161	14	+12.57
12/20/99	90	291	2.9	−38	11	−14.22
06/30/00	104	98	3.1	+9	13	−14.32
09/18/00	90	111	3.1	−118	30	+18.77
12/22/00	206	96	3.3	+79	0	+0
10/01/02	92	152	2.8	+5	12	−23.34
04/13/04	114	111	3.3	−174	26	+24.08
					NET	+77.98

* New Highs or New Lows, whichever is smaller.
** Short only when the McClellan Oscillator is negative for 30 days after signal is given.

References

Gammage, Kennedy, 2004, *The Richland Report*, LaJolla, CA.
Miekka, James R., *The Sudbury Bull and Bear Report*, St. Petersburg, FL.

Market Thrust

Author/Creator: Tushar Chande
Data components required: Advances (A), Declines (D), Up Volume (UV), Down Volume (DV)

Description

Tushar Chande offers this as a way to overcome some of the perceived limitations in the Arms Index. The advantages of this indicator are that it subdivided the product of advances and up volume, and the declines and down volume. This helps identify a strong up or down day. It also shows the net balance between bullish and bearish activity using relative volume flows, and it presents consistent information.

Interpretation

This indicator, as shown in Chart 9–21, is basically used to spot large moves in the market. Using the product of advances and up volume will generate significant up moves in this indicator if volume is flowing into the advances and many stocks are advancing. Likewise, the down moves are signaled by the product of declines and down volume.

Chande further refines his concept to create a Thrust Oscillator. This is the Market Thrust concept put into a dimensionless ratio and shown in Chart 9–22. He states that this may be considered a volume-weighted advance decline ratio variation.

Author Comments

In the same article that Tushar Chande outlines his Market Thrust indicator, he states that you can cumulate the daily values (like the advance decline line) to identify underlying trends. Like many of the indicators created before market volume increased, the change to decimalization, and the addition of many interest sensitive stocks to the NY exchange, this summation index does not seem to add much to the picture. Any interpretation must be kept within a short period of data to remove the above-mentioned effects. In a later article Tushar Chande shows many charts to give weight to his Market Thrust Summation indicator over the more common Advance Decline Line. The argument is convincing, as I have always liked a volume component to price-based indictors. That is what I did with the McClellan Oscillator and Summation Index. Chart 9–23 shows the cumulative Market Thrust indicator.

Chart 9-21 Market Thrust.

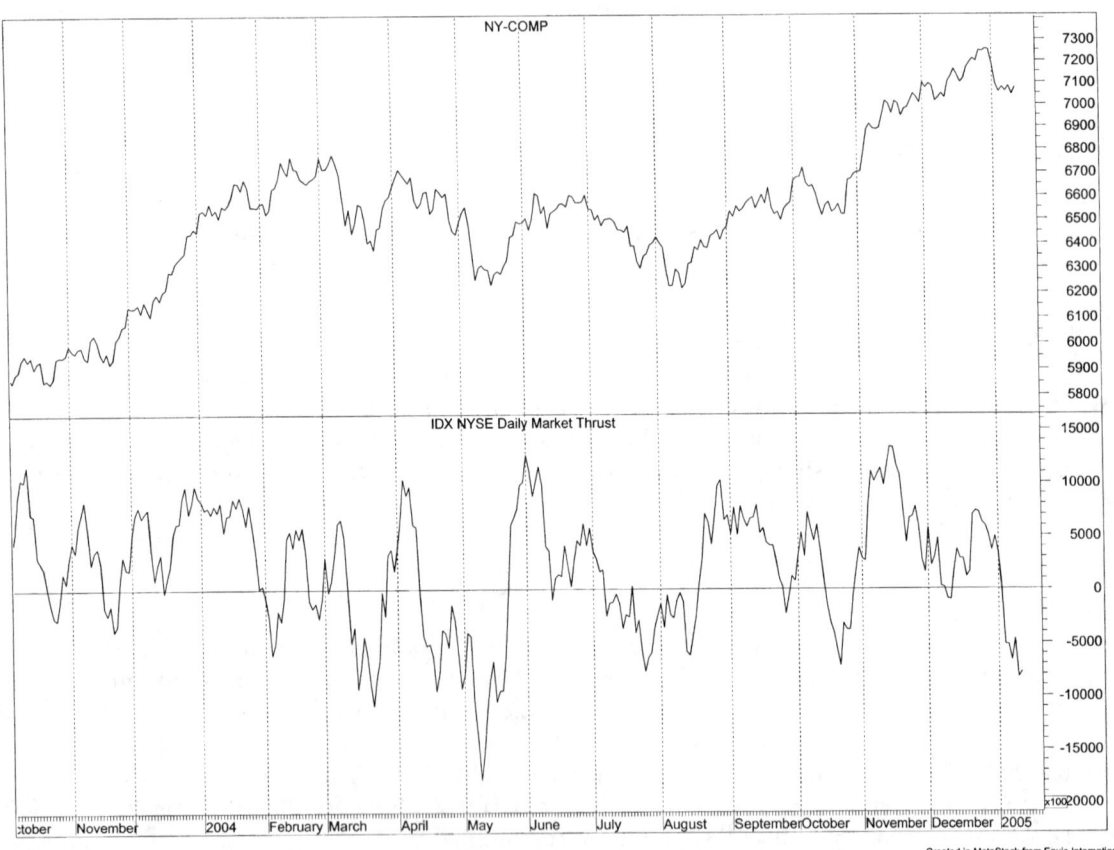

In his book, *The New Technical Trader*, Chande points out that the Arms Index is bounded between 0 and 1 for up days, but unbounded beyond 1 on down days. This, he states, is why smoothing the Arms Index makes it difficult to use. If you think about it, he has a good point. Weak market action can produce an Arms Index reading of 3, 4, and higher, and, in fact, has done so many times. However, the strongest breadth day cannot ever get to 0 on the Arms Index. In other words, the scaling is skewed. This is not so with his Thrust Oscillator, which helps identify strong up and down days equally.

Chande offers a couple of trading strategies in his book with Stanly Kroll. One is to take a 5-day simple moving average of his Thrust Oscillator and overlay a 5-day exponential average on it for trading signals. This is somewhat like Stochastics %K and its 3-day smoothing for %D. A longer-term term strategy would be to plot a 50-day simple moving average of the Thrust Oscillator and use its crossing of that smoothed value for signals.

Stuart Meibuhr suggested in a later article to use Chande's Thrust Oscillator in a similar manner as Richard Arms used his Open Arms indicator. Additionally, Meibuhr said that Chande's Thrust

Composite Indicators

Chart 9-22 Market Thrust Oscillator.

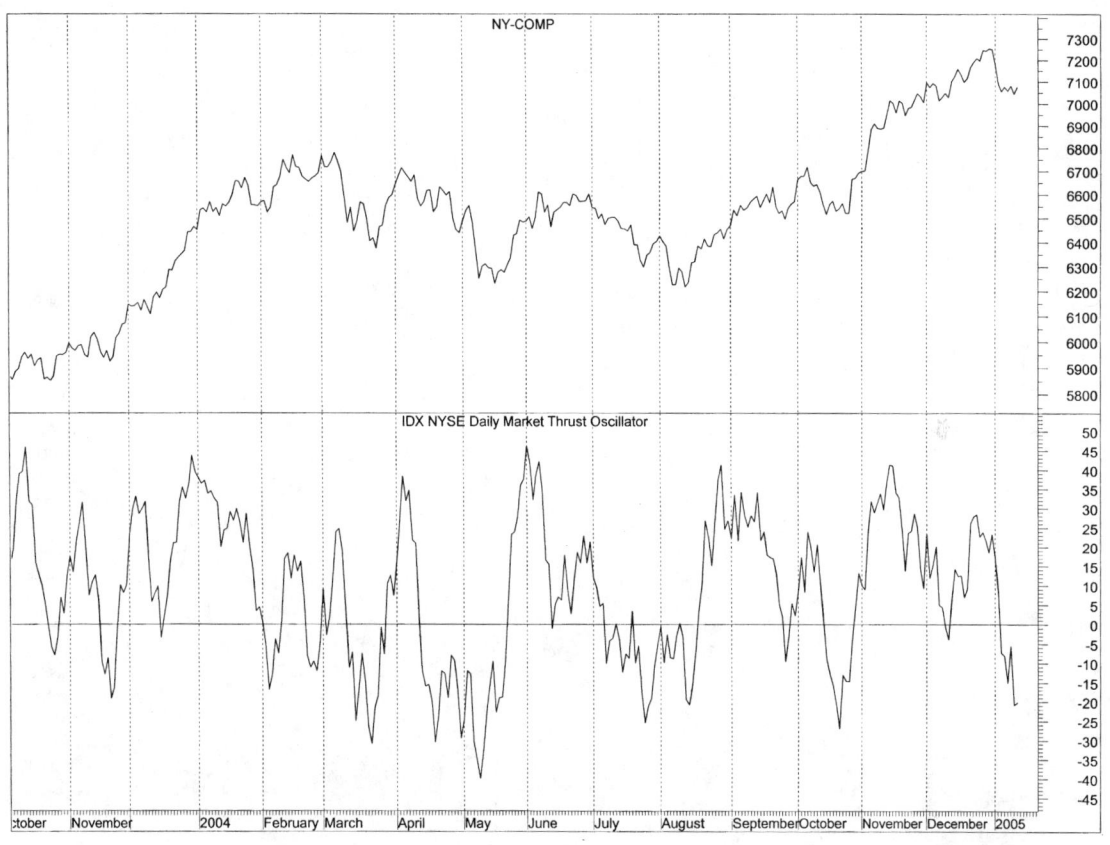

Oscillator, when it went below −0.30, and smoothed by 21 days, was very good at pointing out market bottoms. This was looking at the 21-day and 55-day average of the Thrust Oscillator. Chart 9–24 is a plot that shows the two averages and the difference between them. I took the concept a simple step further by smoothing the difference with a 5-day average. One can easily justify trading using the crossing of the zero line.

$$\text{Formula: } ((A * UV) - (D * DV)) / ((A * UV) + (D * DV))$$

References

Chande, Tushar S. and Kroll, Stanley. *The New Technical Trader.* John Wiley & Sons, 1994.
Chande, Tushar S., "Market Thrust," *Stocks and Commodities*, Volume 10, August 1992, pp. 347–350.
Chande, Tushar S., "The Cumulative Market Thrust Line," *Stocks and Commodities*, Volume 11, December 1993, pp. 506–511.
Meibuhr, Stuart, "Oex and the Thrust Oscillator." *Stocks and Commodities*, March 1993, pp. 127–132.

Chart 9-23 Market Thrust Summation.

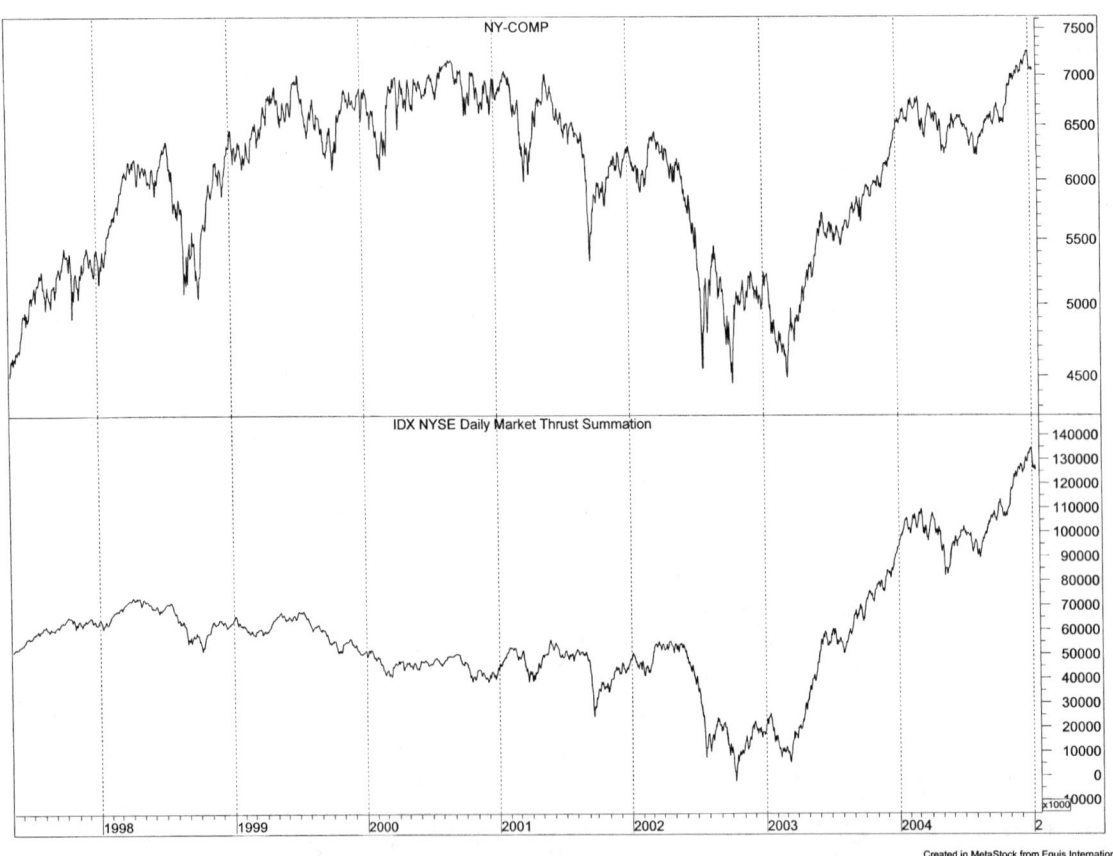

Rusin, Jack, "An issue/volume-weighted long-term Arms index," *Stocks and Commodities*, Volume 9, October 1991, pp. 419–421.

Rusin, Jack, "The Internal Dynamics of Trin," *Stocks and Commodities*, Volume 10, January 1992, pp. 22–25.

McClellan Oscillator with Volume

Author/Creator: Greg Morris

Data components required: Advances (A), Declines (D), Up Volume (UV), Down Volume (DV)

Description

This is the McClellan Oscillator with a volume component calculated into the formula. Instead of using just advances (A), I have used advances times up volume ($A * UV$). Similarly, instead of using

Chart 9-24 Market Thrust Oscillator 21 and 55.

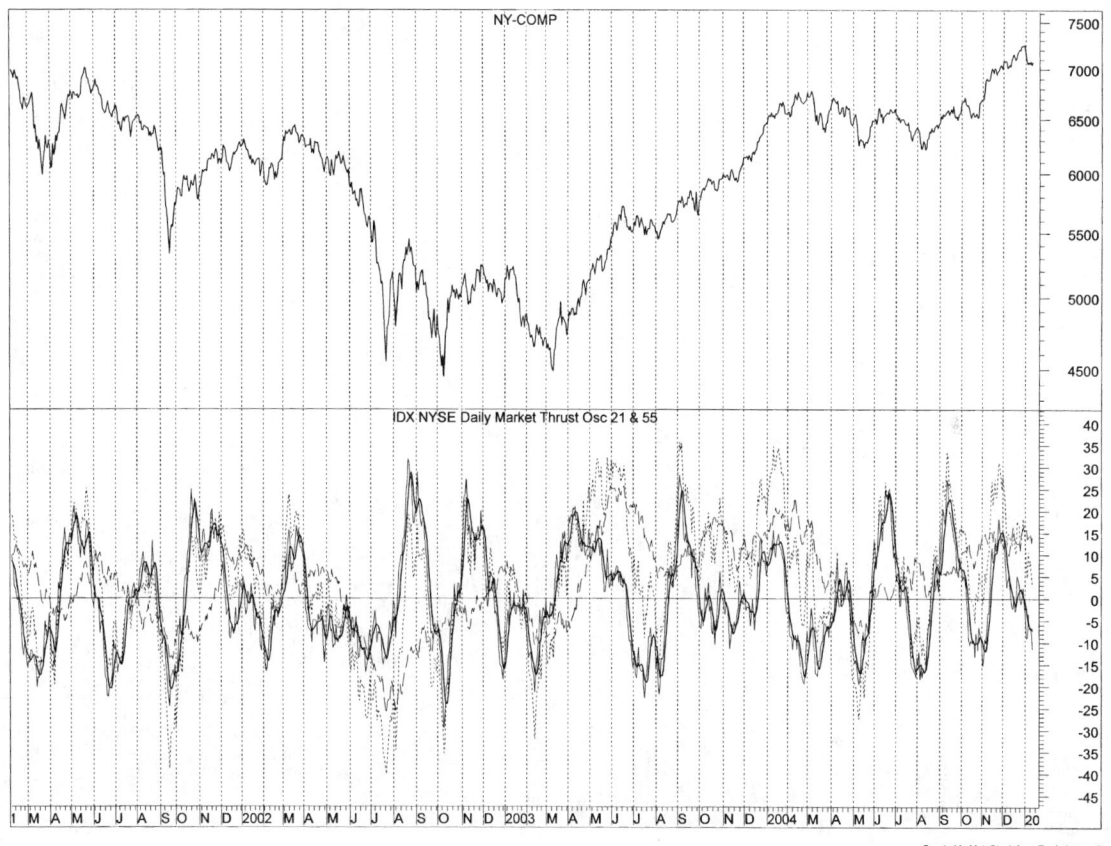

just declines (*D*), I have used (declines times down volume (*D* * *DV*). The formula is identical to the original McClellan Oscillator other than that.

Interpretation

The interpretation is exactly the same as that used for the McClellan Oscillator. This is somewhat of a combination of the McClellan Oscillator and the McClellan Oscillator using volume. This one uses both the advance decline data enhanced with volume and is shown in Chart 9–25.

Author Comments

I have always preferred the influence of volume on most price-based indicators. This seems to generate some great signals for picking market bottoms, similar to the volume only oscillator that the

Chart 9-25 McClellan Oscillator—Morris.

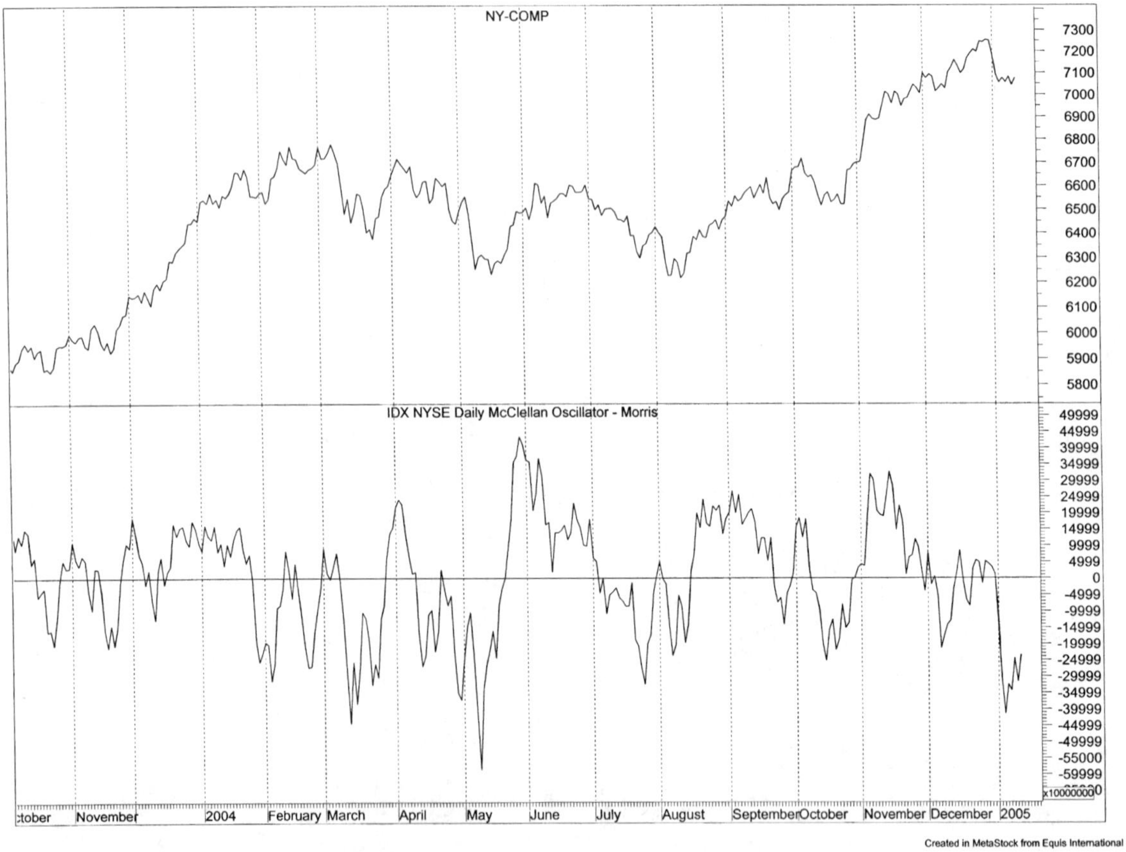

McClellans use. However, this one seems to identify market tops quite well using the extreme oscillator readings. Whenever this indicator peaks and reverses, a top, even if just a trading decline, is occurring. I would imagine that smoothing this oscillator to dampen it and using an exponential smoothing overlay to give signals would work well. Chart 9-26 smoothes the volume-based oscillator by a 10-period exponential average and also by a 3-period exponential average. You can see that the use of the zero line crossing from below to above is good for buy signals and the crossing of the 10- period smooth (bolder line) below the 3-period smooth is good for sell signals.

Formula: Previous Value + ((Today's 19 exp average of ($A*UV - D*DV$)
$\quad$ - (Today's 39 exp average of ($A*UV - D*DV$))

References

McClellan, Sherman and Marian. *Patterns for Profit*. Lakewood, WA : McClellan Financial Publications, Inc., 1989. This book was originally published by Trade Levels in 1970.

Chart 9-26 McClellan Oscillator—Morris with Smoothing.

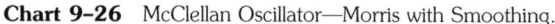

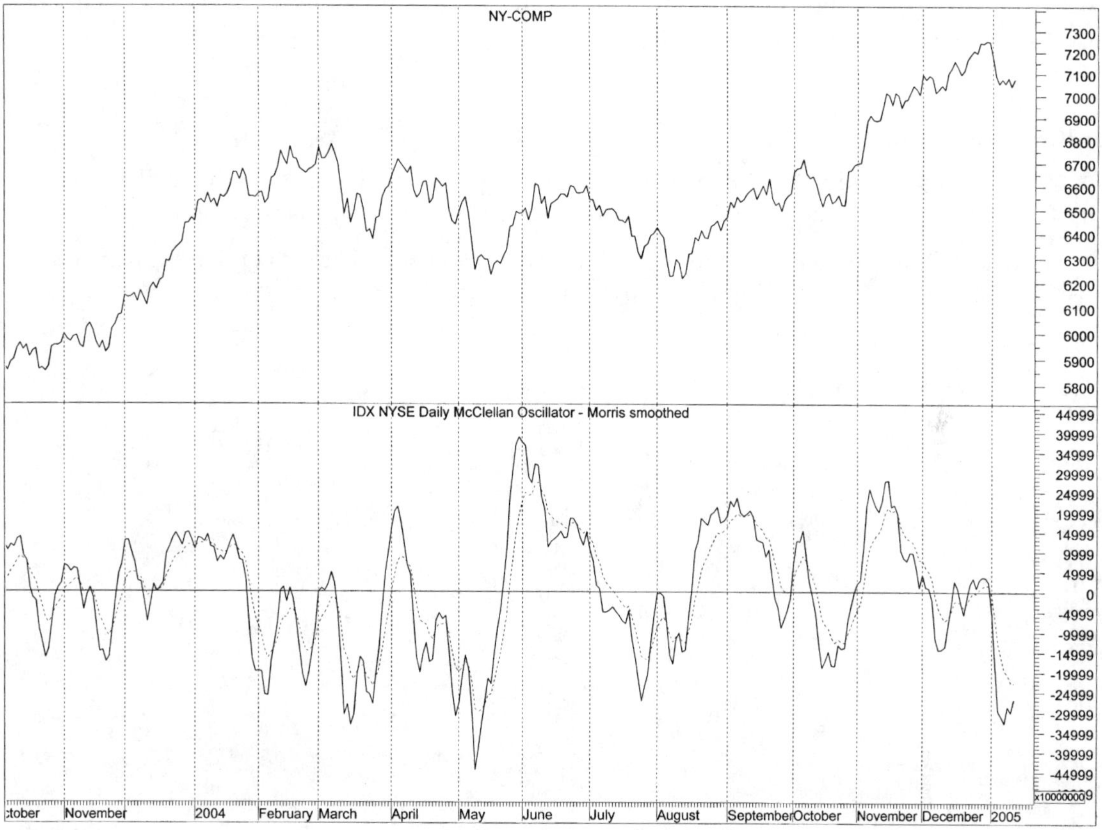

Created in MetaStock from Equis International

McClellan Family Interview, "It's All In the Family: Sherman, Marian, and Tom McClellan." *Stocks and Commodities*, Volume 12, June 1994, pp. 264–273.

McClellan Summation Index with Volume

Author/Creator: Greg Morris
Data components required: Advances (A), Declines (D), Up Volume (UV), Down Volume (DV)

Description

This is the McClellan Summation Index with a volume component added to the calculation. Instead of using just advances (A), I have used advances times up volume ($A * UV$). The formula is identical to the original McClellan Summation Index other than the added volume component.

Interpretation

This summation index should be interpreted just the same as the other two versions, including the original, and is shown in Chart 9–27.

Author Comments

I have always preferred the influence of volume on price-based indicators. Like the original McClellan Summation Index, the direction and the level of this indicator are important.

> Formula: This is the accumulation of the McClellan Oscillator that uses both advances and declines, and up volume and down volume.

Chart 9-27 McClellan Summation—Morris.

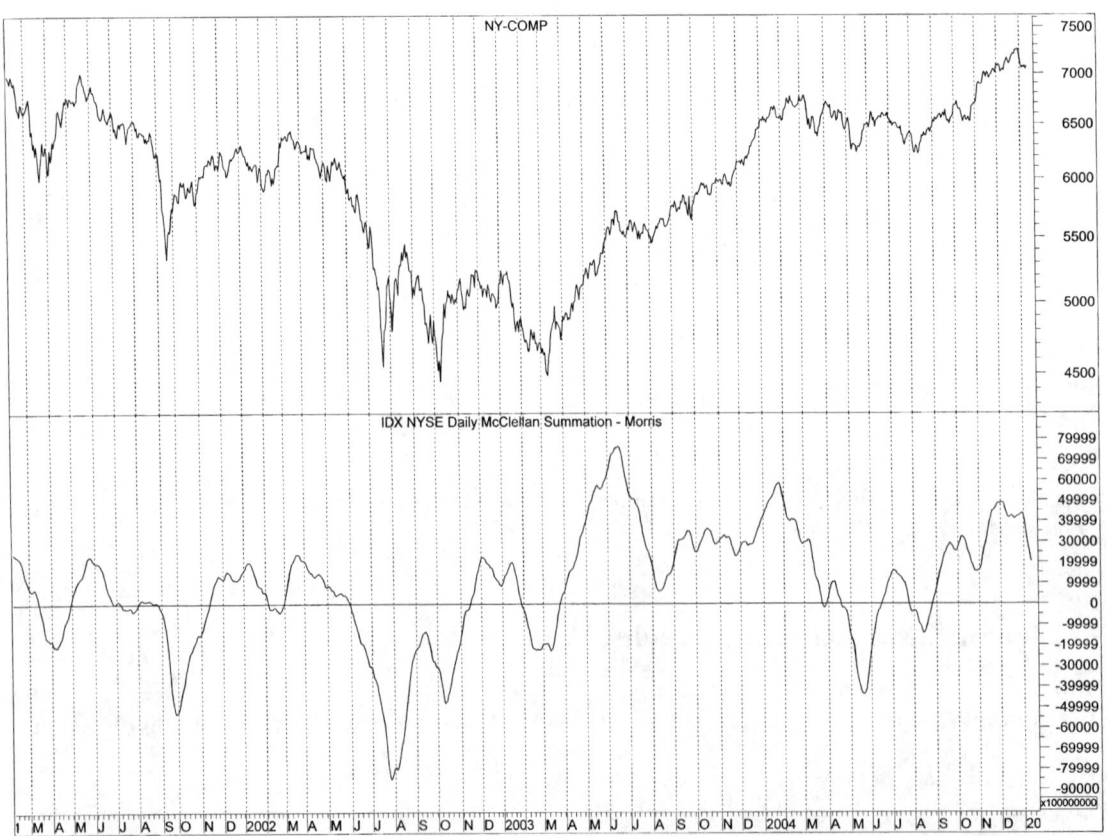

References

McClellan, Sherman and Marian. *Patterns for Profit.* Lakewood, WA : McClellan Financial Publications, Inc., 1989. This book was originally published by Trade Levels in 1970.

McClellan Family Interview, "It's All In the Family: Sherman, Marian, and Tom McClellan." *Stocks and Commodities*, Volume 12, June 1994, pp. 264–273.

Meyers Systems

Author/Creator: Dennis Meyers

Data components required: Advances (A), Declines (D), Up Volume (UV), Down Volume (DV) New Highs (H), New Lows (L)

Description

These are relative strength systems based on new highs, new lows, a market index, and combinations of up volume and down volume, or advances and declines.

Interpretation

Meyers, a Ph.D. in applied mathematics in engineering, wrote four articles in *Stocks & Commodities* magazine describing market systems using various combinations of breadth data. The market index shown was the Dow Jones Industrial Average, however all his testing was done on the Standard & Poors 500 Index.

The Advance-Decline, New-High, New-Low Market System

This one used weekly data and looked at the advance decline line relative to the market along with the relative strength of the new highs and new lows. With these three indicators, he identified thresholds for buying and selling.

A/D Volume, New-High, New-Low System

With this one, Meyers moved to using daily breadth data instead of weekly. This is similar to the first one, but instead of using the advances and declines, he used up volume and down volume. The volume was calculated in a ratio similar to what the McClellan's and the Carl Swenlin use, ($UV - DV$) / ($UV + DV$). Like the first system, he calculated the relative strength of the volume to the market in addition to using the same new high and new low indicators.

A Daily $A - D$ New-High, New Low Market System

Appearing almost a year after publishing his first system, this one uses the same breadth components, but for daily data. Meyers also smoothed some of the raw data in this system.

The Turbo A/D, NH, NL Market System

Meyers came out with this system after discovering a problem he denoted as a lockout condition. This is common in internally normalized equations as strong moves will lock a normalized indicator at its extremes with very little fluctuation.

Author Comments

Everyone who has an interest in designing breadth-based systems needs to read the four articles by Dennis Meyers. He did not uncover anything earth shattering, but his approach to the full understanding of the markets and these components is good. Meyers addresses the downfalls of blind optimization, which would serve as a good primer for anyone undertaking the task of creating a system. The systems did not do well after the market top in 2000, which is not surprising because the data used to test the four trading systems did not contain a significant bear market. My thanks to Dennis for sharing the details on these systems with me.

References

Meyers, Dennis, "The Advance Decline, New High, New Low Market System." *Stocks and Commodities*, Volume 14, February 1996, pp. 69–75.

Meyers, Dennis, "A/D Volume, New High, New Low System." *Stocks and Commodities*, Volume 14, July 1996, pp. 302–310.

Meyers, Dennis, "A Daily A − D New High New Low Market System." *Stocks and Commodities*, Volume 15, January 1997, pp. 11–19.

Meyers, Dennis, "The Turbo A/D, NH, NL Market System." *Stocks and Commodities*, Volume 15, August 1997, pp. 337–346.

Moving Balance Indicator

Creator: Humphrey E. D. Lloyd
Data required: Advances (A), Declines (D), Up Volume (UV), Down Volume (DV)

Description

Dr. Humphrey Lloyd developed the Moving Balance Indicator (MBI) in the mid–1970s. He wanted to find an indicator that would identify extremes in overbought and oversold areas. He came up with an indicator that contained three distinct components. The three components were: The $A - D$ component, The Up Volume component, and the Trader's Index (TRIN) component.

The $A - D$ component: This is the 10-day simple moving average of the advancing issues divided by the 10-day simple moving average of the declining issues. The difference was then multiplied by 10.

The Up Volume component: This is the 10-day simple moving average of Up Volume. This component was used to help identify really strong up moves. As time progressed and market volume increased, he changed this to moderate its effect on the MBI. This change was to make Up Volume a percentage of active volume (Up Volume plus Down Volume), and divide it by 3.

The Traders' Index component: This is the advances divided by the declines, then divided by the up volume divided by the down volume (see formula for better understanding). This is also known as the Arms Index. Because TRIN is an inverse indicator, Dr. Lloyd used a "look up" table to assign values for various levels of TRIN to reverse its value and give it a better component weight equal in magnitude to the other two components.

The Moving Balance Indicator is then completed by adding the three components together and dividing by 1.5. This was done to give it values in the 20 to 100 range so it could be used with other popular indicators such as Welles Wilder's Relative Strength Index (RSI).

Interpretation

Dr. Lloyd laid out several methods of determining buy and sell signals using actual MBI values. Volume on the various exchanges has increased so much since he developed this indicator that those actual numbers are no longer valid. However, the concept he used was good and is as follows:

Buy Signals

1. The MBI has to penetrate a particular level.
2. A valid break of a trendline that consists of at least three peaks.
3. A positive divergence between the MBI and the market.

He further stated that it was rare to find all three signals at once, but if you did, it was probably a very good trade. A good trade was also expected with any two signals.

Sell Signals

This was much more difficult to define. He used a number of different methods but finally resorted to using MBI primarily for entry (buy) signals, and using MBI in combination with other indicators for sell signals. Chart 9–28 shows the Moving Balance Indicator using Dr. Lloyd's signals.

Joseph T. Stewart, in his book, *Dynamic Stock Option Trading*, used MBI, but further smoothed it using a simple 5-day moving average of MBI. You can see in Chart 9–29 that if you also include a longer moving average you can generate some good buy signals. In Chart 9–29 a 17-day moving average was used. Notice that it is not a good system for trending markets, but only good for oscillating markets.

Author Comments

Joseph Stewart noted that the MBI also has a cyclic interpretation to it, so you should get in sync with that cycle. He states there are often 10–20 days in which the MBI will decline. Watch to see if it has it gotten to a level in which it has risen in the past.

Chart 9-28 Moving Balance Indicator Using Lloyd Signals.

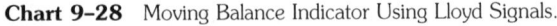

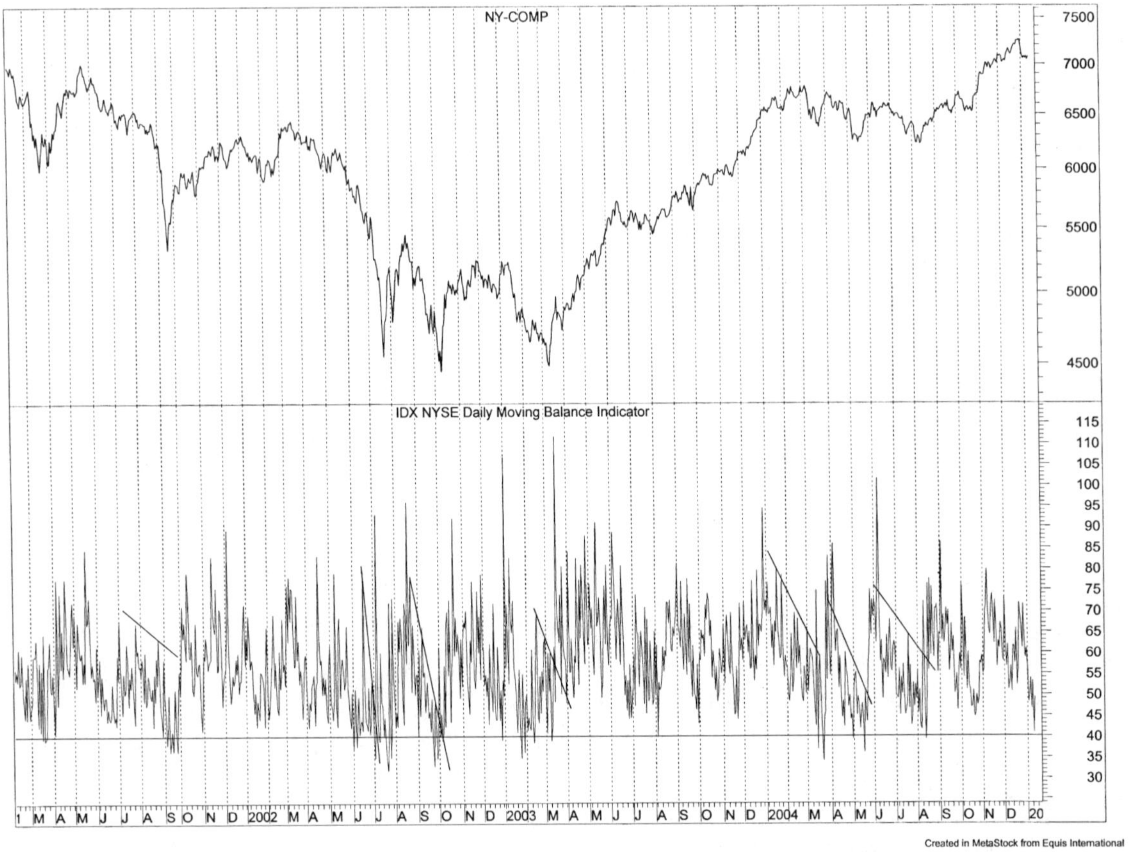

When I first read about Dr. Lloyd's new indicator in the very early 1980s, I programmed it into my Apple II computer using N-Squared Computing's Market Analyzer software. I dealt with the TRIN look up table issue by inverting TRIN and including a multiplier of 10. This seemed to generate similar results as the original MBI. Like Dr. Lloyd, I found that using MBI for entry signals was better. Of course this goes with most indicators because of the nature of market bottoms being quick and decisive and market tops being long, drawn-out distributions that are much more difficult to define. I used to use a value of 57 for determining a buy signal on MBI. This was when MBI crossed from below to above 57. However, in more recent times because of changing market conditions, a buy signal using an MBI value of 40 seems to work well. In Chart 9–30, instead of showing where MBI was below 40, I drew vertical lines at good market bottoms so you could see that MBI was coincident or leading as an indicator of market bottoms.

Joseph Stewart points out a phenomenon during bullish moves that one needs to be aware of. That is the act of the moving balance index to slip into an overbought situation during strong

Composite Indicators

Chart 9-29 Moving Balance Indicator with Stewart Smoothing.

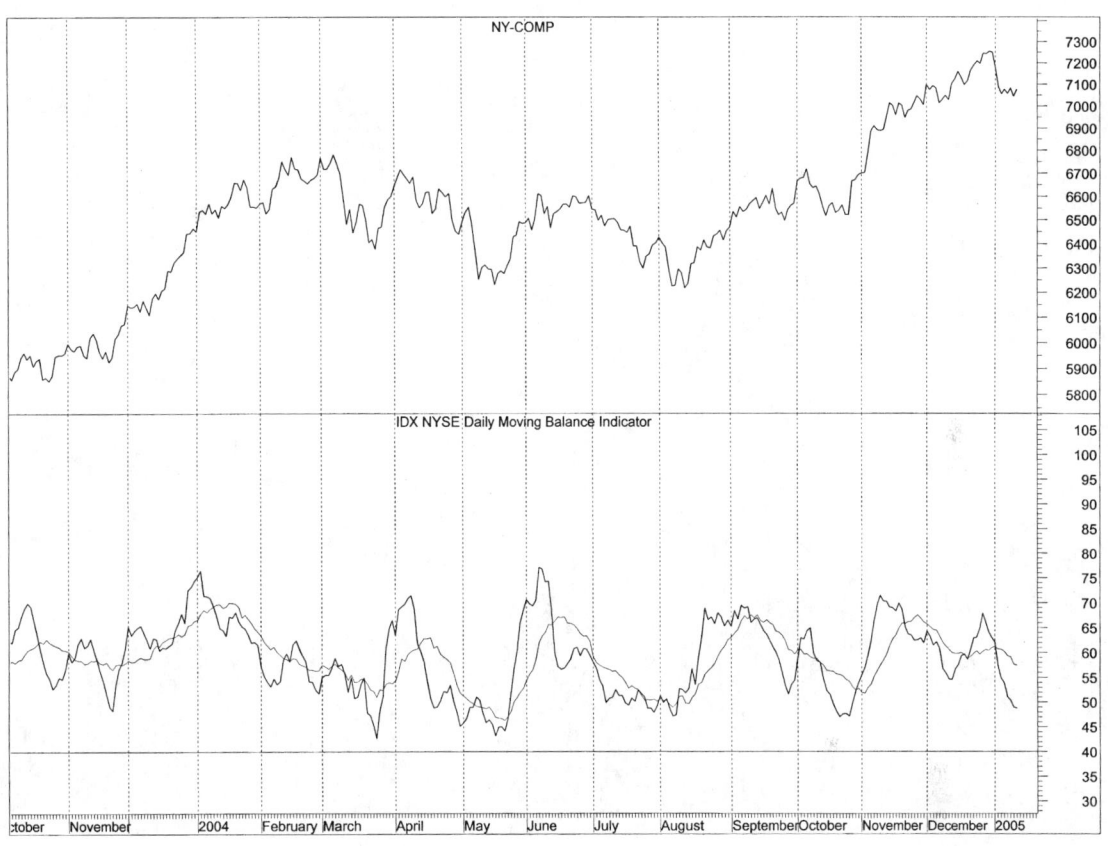

upward moves accompanied by heavy volume. His warning is to not be fooled by the action of the indicator and use other tools to help identify the top. This is sound advice from Stewart, but it applies to any oscillator during the type of upward thrust he is talking about.

$$\text{Formula: } ((((10dayMA\ A) / (10dayMA\ D)) * 10) + ((10dayMA\ (((UV) / (UV + DV))) / 3) + (1/((A/D) / (UV/DV)) * 10)) / 1.5$$

References

Lloyd, Humphrey E. D. *The Moving Balance System, A New Technique for Stock and Option Trading.* Brightwaters, N.Y., Windsor Books, 1976

Lloyd, Humphrey E. D., *The RSL Market Timing System.* Brightwaters, N.Y.: Windsor Books, 1991.

Stewart, Joseph T. *Dynamic Stock Options Trading.* New York : John Wiley and Sons, 1981.

Chart 9-30 Moving Balance Indicator Buy at 40.

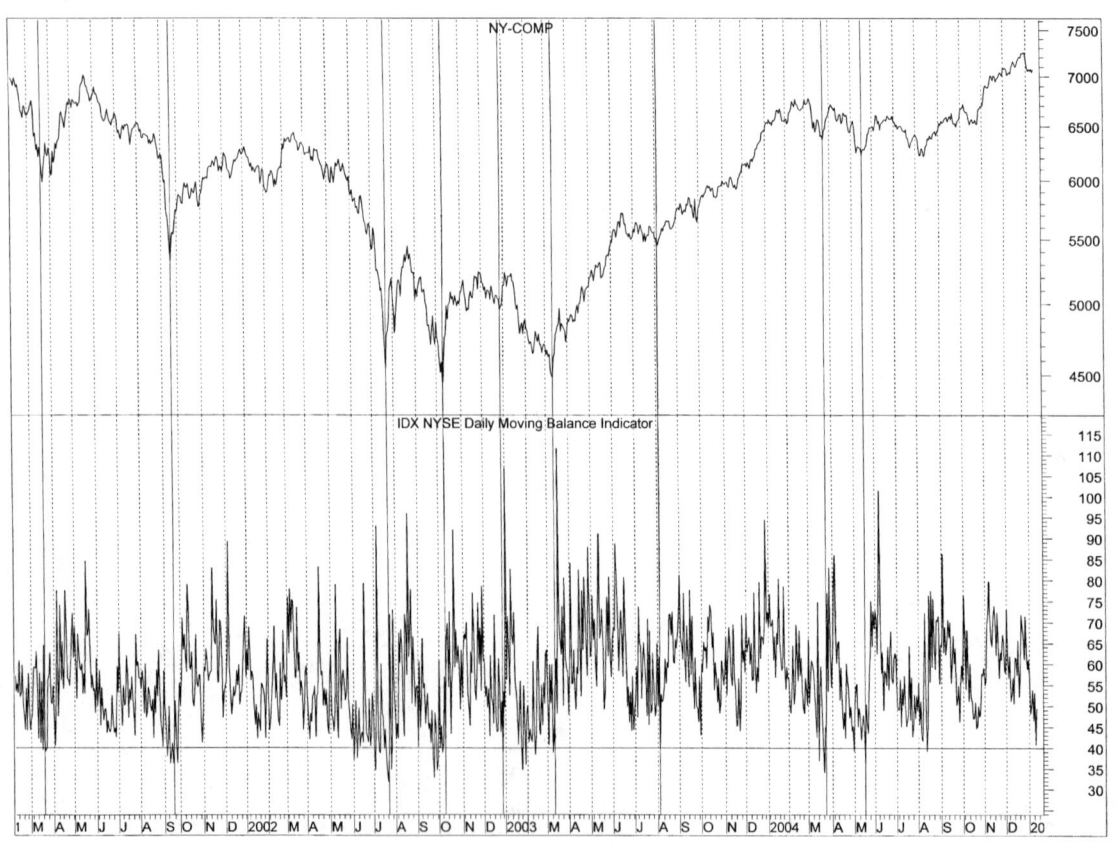

Technical Index

Author/Creator: William Mason

Data components required: Advances (A), Declines (D), Up Volume (UV), Down Volume (DV), New Highs (H), New Lows (L), Total Issues (TI), Volume (V)

Description

The Technical Index is created by taking the net difference of the advances and declines, up and down volume, and new highs and new lows; expressing them as a percentage of their respective base; combining them to get a new value; and accumulating this value similar to the advance decline line. Mason said that the reason for using percentages is that no single parameter will dominate.

Interpretation

Like most accumulated breadth indicators that look at differences, the disparity between them and their base index is what is looked for. The divergences will usually happen near market tops and bottoms, as shown in Chart 9–31.

Author Comments

I really like the concept of composite indicators, and as you might expect, I especially like it when the components are those of breadth. This indicator could be viewed as the all-encompassing breadth line. Like most breadth indicators, look for divergence with the market. One can also use a rate of change of the Technical Index. Chart 9–32 is a 21-day rate of change of William Mason's Technical Index. Above the zero line is generally good for the market.

Chart 9–31 Technical Index.

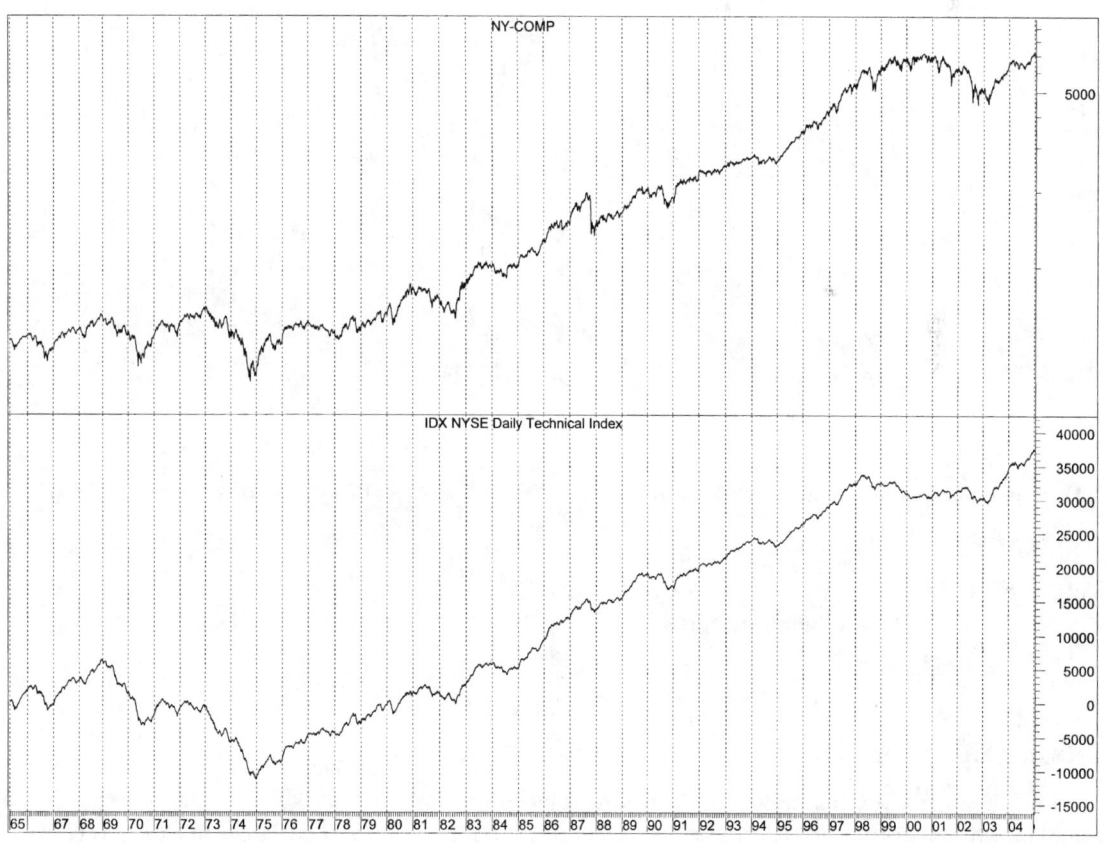

Chart 9-32 Technical Index Rate of Change.

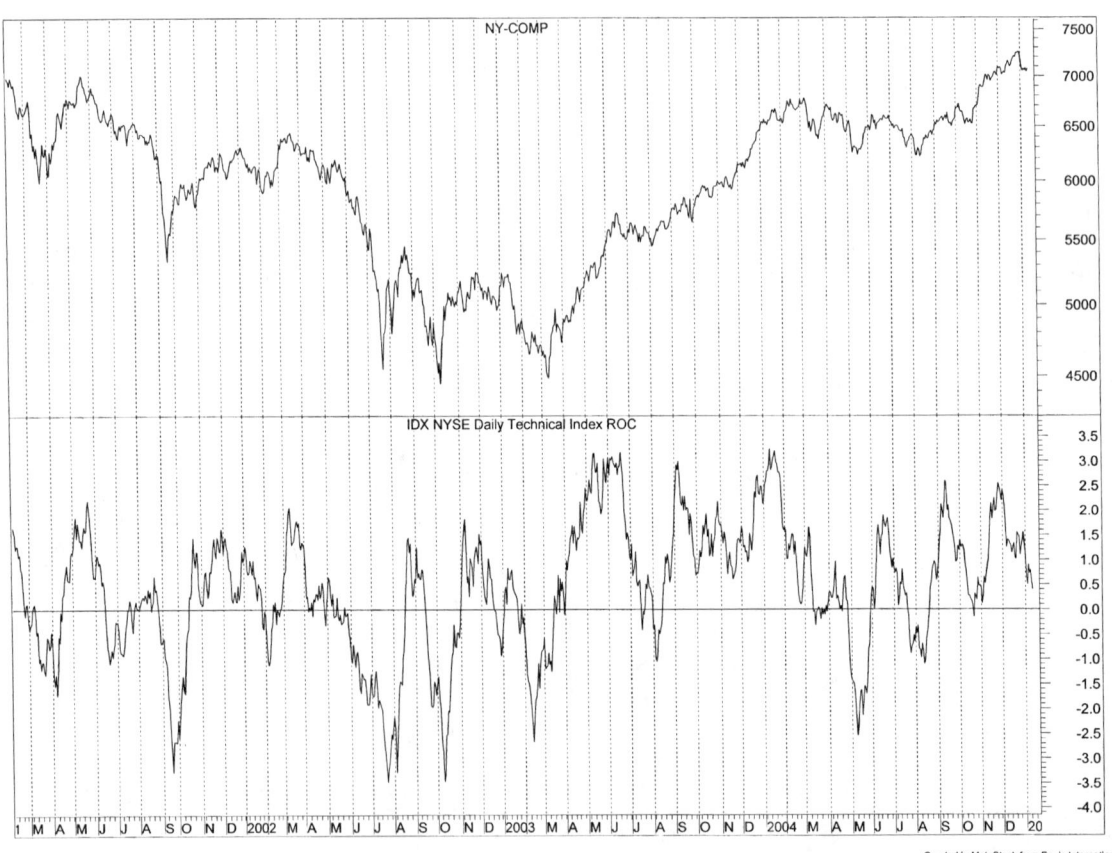

Formula: *Previous Value* + Today's $(((A - D) / TI) + ((UV - DV) / V) + ((H - L) / TI))$

References
Mason, William, "Technical Index Measures Market Breadth." *Stocks and Commodities*, Volume 7, January, 1989, pp. 9–12.

Titanic Syndrome

Author/Creator: Bill Omaha, with modifications by Dennis Myers
Data components required: Advances (A), Declines (D), Up Volume (UV), Down Volume (DV), New Highs (H), New Lows (L)

Description

Bill Omaha first wrote about his idea in *Stocks & Commodities*, November, 1988. He coined the name after looking at a series of market tops in the mid-1960s and stating that, like the Titanic, it was full speed ahead, presumably unprotected against disaster.

Interpretation

When the Dow Jones Industrial Average hits a new high for the year, and in the time frame of 7 days before or after that date, the number of new lows on the New York Stock Exchange exceeds the new highs. This excess of new lows is the iceberg that Omaha refers to.

Bill Omaha also adds that in addition to the new high, one could also use the signal whenever the Dow Jones Industrial Average rallies over 400 points. At the time of his writing, the Dow Industrials were at 2150, so a 400-point rally was about 18.5 percent. Incidentally, the Titanic Syndrome appeared on August 25, 1987; the Dow Industrials hit an all time high at 2746.45, and 6 days later the new lows outnumbered the new highs on September 2, 1987. On October 21, 1987 (less than 2 months later), it was at 1951.76, at drop of almost 29 percent. Chart 9–3 shows the Titanic Syndrome in its original form.

In 1991, Bill Omaha provided an upgraded version of his Titanic Syndrome in the Equis Monitor, a publication by Equis International, the creators of MetaStock. Here he included many of the confirmation indications that he only mentioned 3 years before. This time he offered buy and sell criteria.

Sell Criteria

1. The DJIA makes a new 52-week high.
and
2. Seven days, either before or after that new high, the NYSE new lows are greater than the new highs.
and
3a. After the new high in the DJIA, the declining issues are greater than 1000 for two consecutive days, and one of those days shows an advance/decline ratio less than 0.25.
or
3b. After the new high in the DJIA, 4 out of 7 days have the declines greater than 1000.

Buy Criteria

1. A 10 percent drop in the DJIA from the new high.
and
2. After the 10 percent drop, the advances are greater than 1000 for 2 consecutive days and one of those days has the advance/decline ratio greater than 4.0.
and

Chart 9-33 Titanic Syndrome—1988.

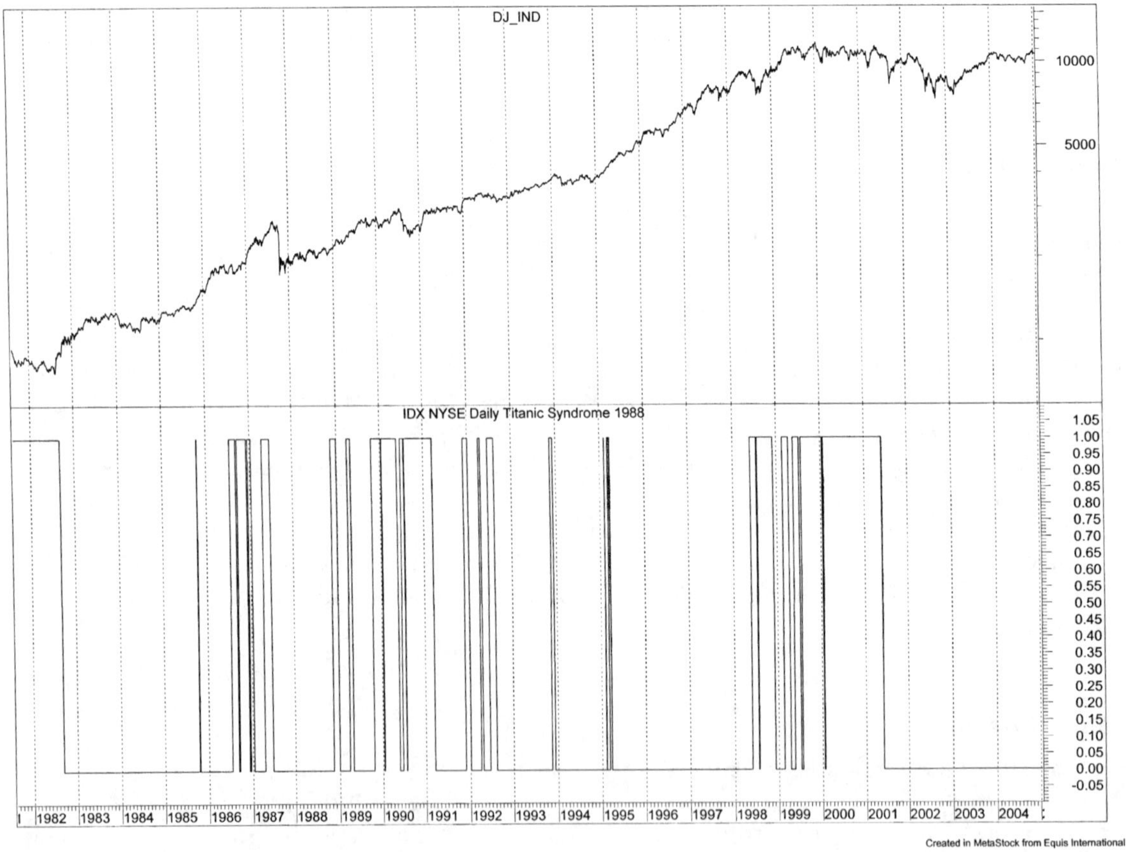

3. After the 10 percent drop, the advance/decline ratio is greater than 9.0 (a) or less than 0.11 (b).
or
4. After the 10 percent drop, 4 out of 7 days have advances greater than 1000.

A sell signal reverses to a buy signal if the yearly new high in the DJIA (the new high that generated the sell signal), is penetrated on the upside by 2 percent Chart 9–34 is a rendition of the Titanic Syndrome with Omaha's last modification.

Dennis Meyers, a frequent contributor to *Stocks & Commodities* magazine, further refined Omaha's Titanic Syndrome in 1995 by added additional components. Meyers removed the buy criteria that after a 10 percent drop in the DJIA, the advance/decline ratio is less than 0.11 (Buy Criteria 3(b)). Meyers also realized that the advance and decline issue using 1000 as a criterion had to be increased. Meyers applied what most have had to do lately, and that is to use a ratio of advances and declines—a dimensionless variable. He applied this logic throughout the Titanic

Chart 9-34 Titanic Syndrome—1991.

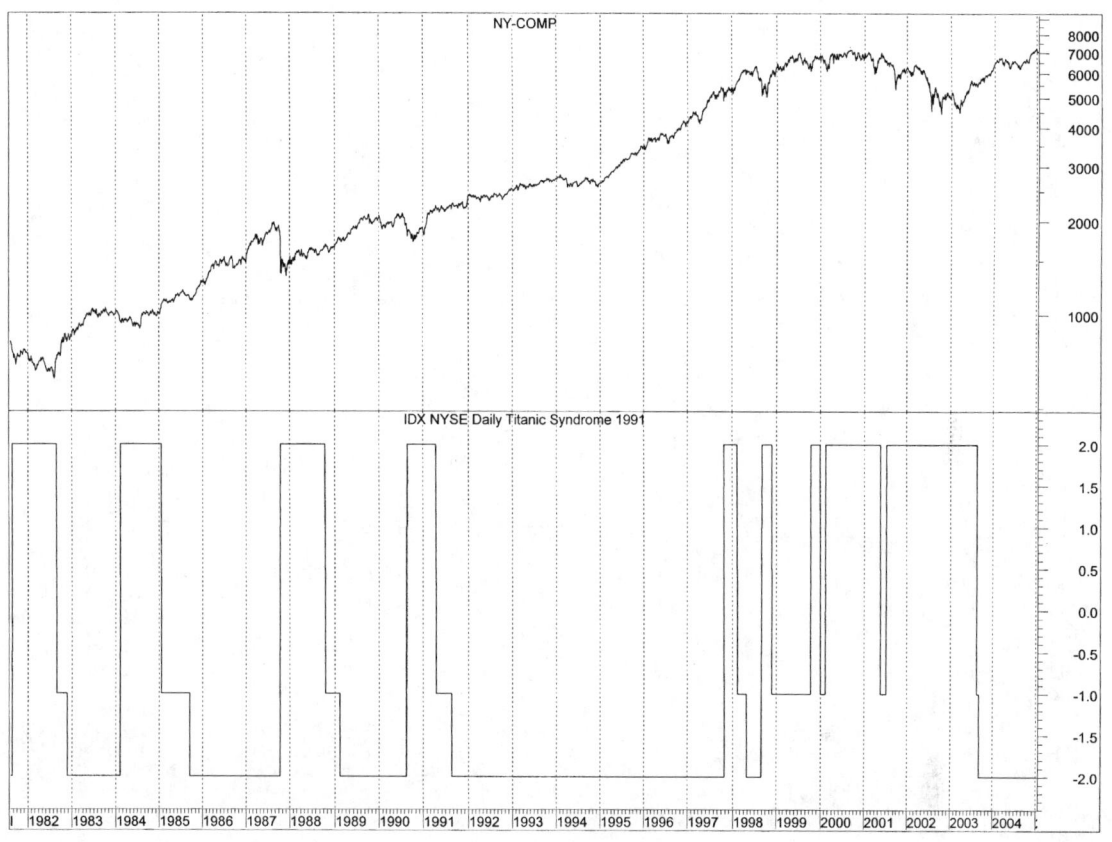

Syndrome. Finally, he added the one breadth component that was always missing, volume. He used an up volume, down volume ratio of 9 to 1, just like Martin Zweig used in his book, *Winning on Wall Street*. Chart 9–35 is a portrayal of Meyer's modifications to the Titanic Syndrome, which he coined the Flying Titanic.

Author Comments

This is good stuff. Someone has an original thought on an indicator and then modifies it publicly, only to be modified further by someone else later on. This is how good indicators are created. I also like indicators that use most of the major components of breadth. This one does. However, creating formulae to represent the full impact of the indicator was next to impossible because it was beyond the formula language I was using. The charts showing the Titanic Syndrome should be viewed as an attempt to reflect the concept.

Chart 9-35 Titanic, 1995—Flying Titanic.

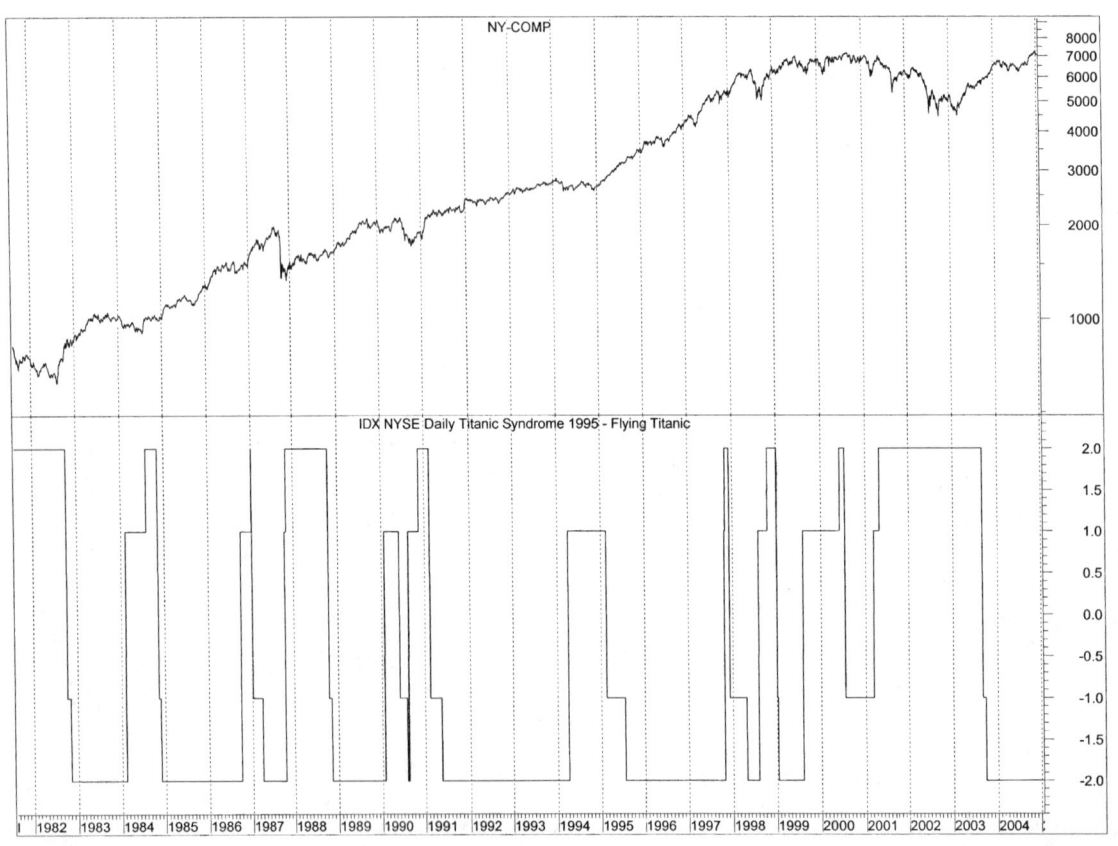

References

Omaha, Bill, "Patterns that Detect Stock Market Reversals," *Stocks and Commodities*, Volume 6, November 1988, pp.416–421.
Omaha, Bill, "How to Avoid Sinking with the Titanic," *Equis Monitor*, June/July 1991.
Meyers, Dennis, "Making the Titanic Fly." *Stocks and Commodities*, Volume 13, May 1995, 189–195.
Zweig, Martin E. *Winning on Wall Street.* New York: Warner Books, 1986.

Trend Exhaustion Index

Author/Creator: Clifford L. Creel
Data components required: Advances (A), New Highs (H).

Description

This is a 10-day exponential average of the New Highs divided by the Advances.

Interpretation

Creel states that during a bull market, many stocks are making new highs and thus a large proportion of advancing stocks each day are also making new highs. This results in a high value for TEI. As the market tops, there is generally a shift to more conservative blue chip stocks. While the top plays out, with occasional rallies, the results will generate advances, but not new highs. This will cause the TEI to decline. The Trend Exhaustion Index is shown in Chart 9–36.

Chart 9-36   Trend Exhaustion Index.

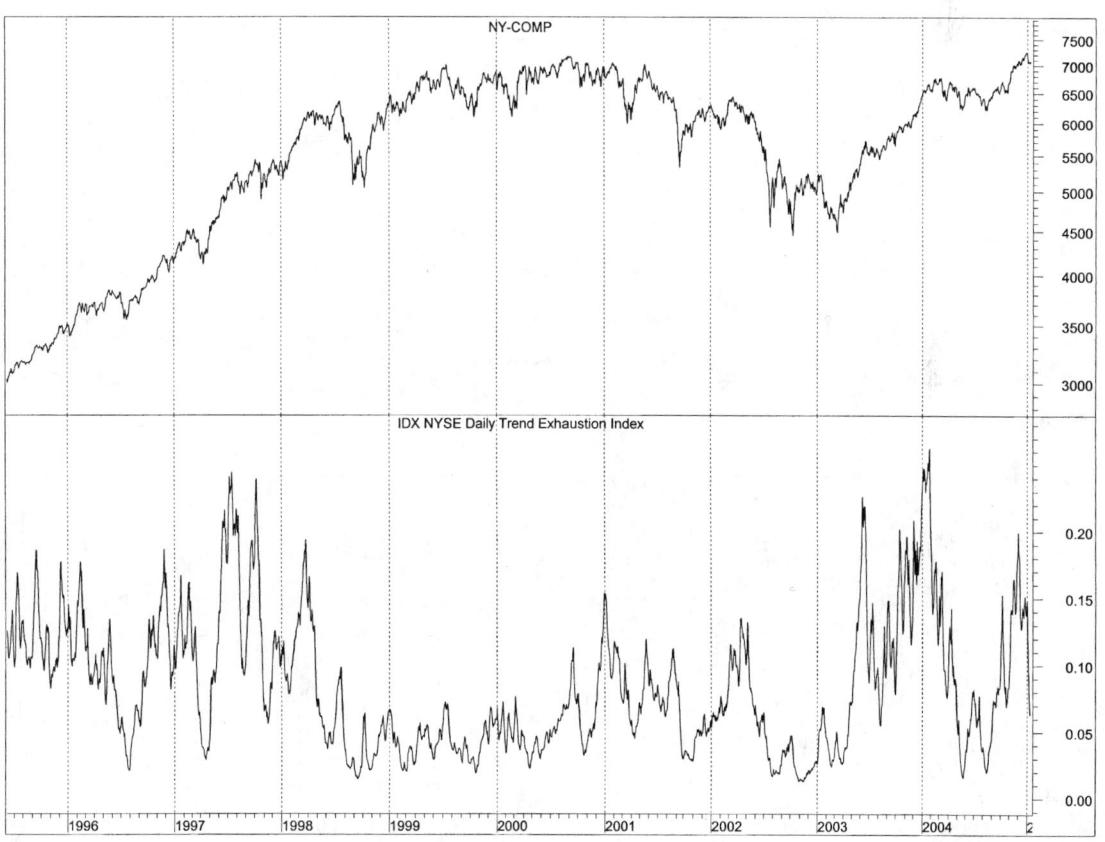

Author Comments

Using new highs and advances is an unusual twist to using breadth, as most breadth indicators stick with like pairs such as advances and declines, new highs and new lows, etc. Chart 9–37 is a plot of new lows and declines using a similar formula as the trend exhaustion index. A good name might be trend explosion index. It seems, visually, that whenever this indicator rises above 0.15, a market bottom has been put into place. If anything, the Trend Exhaustion Index and Trend Explosion Index will assist you in warning of a change in market direction.

$$\text{Formula: } (H / A)$$

References

Creel, Clifford L., "Trend Exhaustion Index." *Stocks and Commodities*, Volume 9, January, 1991, pp. 9–11.

Chart 9-37 Trend Explosion Index.

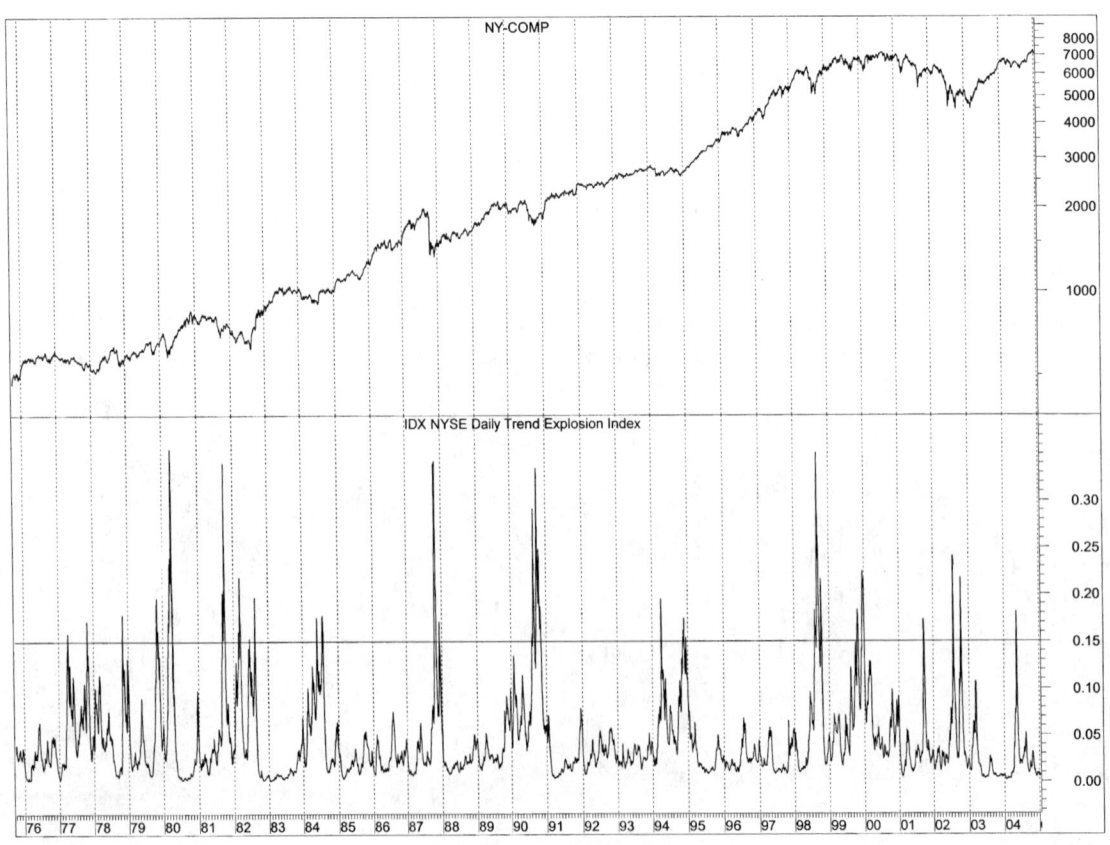

10
The McClellan Indicators

This chapter consists of contributions from Sherman McClellan, Tom McClellan, and James Miekka. It is the author's opinion that the McClellan indicators, and in particular, the McClellan Summation Index, is the single best breadth indicator available. If you had to pick just one, this would be it. This chapter elaborates on its creation, its concept, its modifications, and its usefulness. An important concept in using and understanding the McClellan Summation Index is also in Chapter 12, Conclusions. Also, don't forget the traditional coverage of the McClellan Oscillator and Summation Index in Chapters 4, 8, and 9.

Tom and Sherman McClellan use a lot of different breadth indicators in their analysis, including those discussed here, plus variations based on them. Tom McClellan shares a few of them with us:

One interesting permutation of using the A − D and Volume numbers is to draw comparisons about their strength. This is not easy to do because they are in different units, but when we employ the Summation Index calculations to this data, it makes such comparisons possible.

We use "ratio-adjusted" values for both the daily A − D and UV − DV breadth:

$$\frac{(A-D)}{(A+D)} \times 1000 \qquad \frac{(UV-DV)}{(UV+DV)} \times 1000$$

We then calculate a ratio-adjusted McClellan Oscillator for each, and from those Oscillator values we can calculate ratio-adjusted Summation Indices (RASIs) for each. If the volume numbers are persistently stronger than the A − D numbers, then the Volume RASI will rise faster than the A − D RASI. If we calculate the difference between the Volume RASI and the A − D RASI, we can get a sort of a relative strength line for the volume versus the A − D numbers, as shown in Chart 10–1.

When this indicator is moving upward, it indicates that the Volume breadth numbers are acting stronger than the A − D breadth numbers, and those conditions are usually associated with rising prices. It can also show extreme conditions when it moves outside of the +/−500 area. Notice that during 2000, the NYSE Comp was making higher highs while this indicator was making a series of lower highs, indicating that the volume numbers were no longer showing as much strength as they had been, and foreshadowing the weakness in the general market that was to appear later on.

Chart 10–1 McClellan NYSE Ratio Adjusted Volume Minus Ratio Adjusted Advance Decline Summation Index.

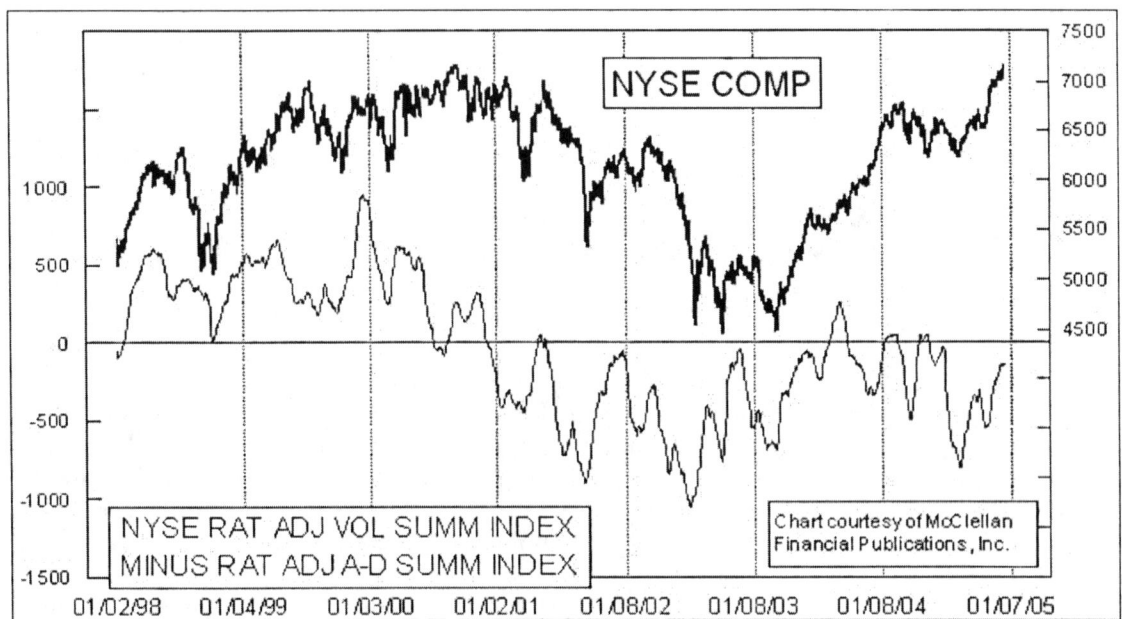

Author Note: The following two paragraphs from Tom McClellan are no longer valid as the NYSE has changed the way they determine common and uncommon issues. I decided to leave this information here to demonstrate the creativity of the McClellans.

We do something similar with another comparison, this time between the NYSE A − D numbers and what we call the "Uncommon" A − D numbers. Each day the NYSE publishes the number of Advances and Declines for what are known as the "Common Only" issues traded on the NYSE. The NYSE filters out issues that have more than three letters in their symbols, which thereby eliminates preferred stocks, rights, and warrants. These types of issues are generally very interest rate sensitive.

When we subtract the Common Only Advances and Declines from the composite NYSE Advances and Declines, we get the breadth data for these issues that have been filtered out. We call this the "Uncommon A − D" data, and it is quite useful for tracking interest rate sensitive issues such as T-Bond prices, as seen in Chart 10–2. We calculate a standard McClellan Oscillator and Summation Index based on this data, as well as ratio-adjusted versions. In Chart 10–2, we show the Uncommon A − D RASI. Very high values above +1000 can indicate likely topping points for T-Bond prices. And when bond prices advance without confirmation from this RASI, it is a sign that there are big problems for T-Bond prices such as the big spike top in late 1998, with the collapse of the big hedge fund Long Term Capital Management.

We employ a similar technique of looking at what has been cast off when it comes to the Nasdaq market. A few years ago, we thought it would be interesting to look at the A − D and UV − DV

The McClellan Indicators

Chart 10-2 T-bonds and McClellan Uncommon Advance Decline Ratio Adjusted Summation Index.

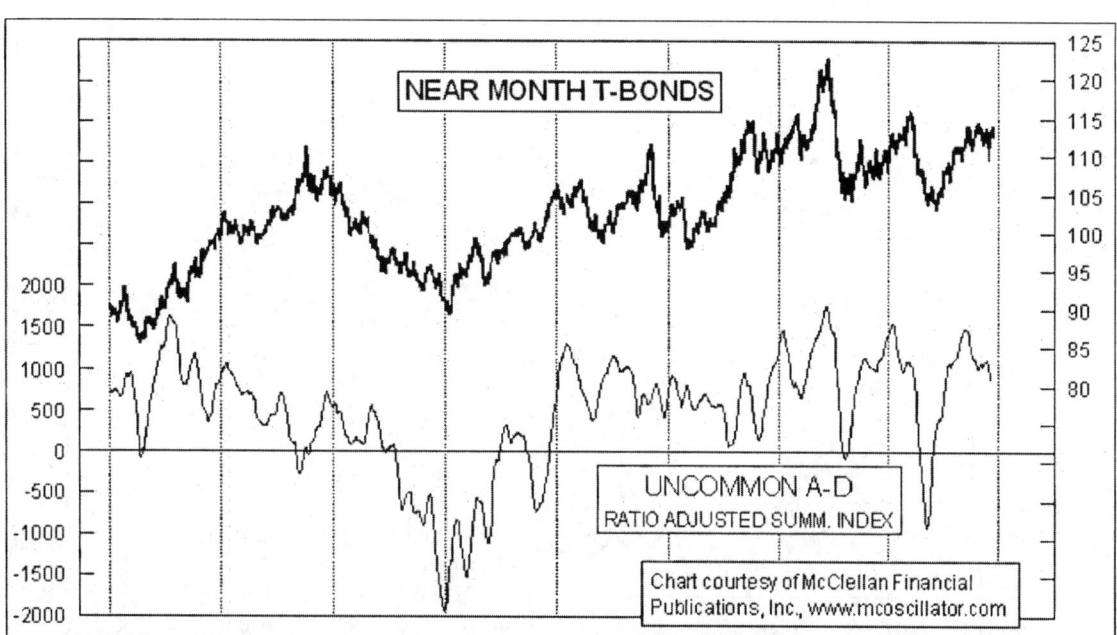

statistics for the stocks that make up the Nasdaq 100 Index (NDX). Because those are not reported in any of the normal financial media or data services, we had to do it ourselves. So we built a big spreadsheet file to track the prices and volume for these 100 stocks (the file is at 56 megabytes and counting). Calculating one's own breadth statistics is not something that we would recommend for the neophyte. One must be adept at data management, and then also stay on top of stock splits and component changes.

What we found through this exercise was that the A − D and Up-Down Volume data for the NDX stocks is very noisy, with a lot of whipping back and forth, which is not something one looks for in a nice, well-behaved technical indicator. The stocks that make up the Nasdaq 100 Index tend to trade as a collective herd. It is not uncommon to see 90 advances versus 10 declines one day, and then the opposite condition the next.

In pondering this revelation, we realized that because the 100 NDX stocks usually account for about half of all the trading volume on the entire Nasdaq, something interesting might be happening in the volume statistics for the stocks that are not in the NDX. These are the "junior varsity" Nasdaq stocks that are not (yet) big enough to make it into NDX, which contains the largest nonfinancial stocks traded on the Nasdaq.

Once we had the Up and Down Volume numbers for the NDX stocks, it was easy to calculate the Up and Down Volume numbers for the rest of the Nasdaq market. All we had to do was subtract the NDX volume statistics from the composite Nasdaq Up and Down Volume numbers. It turns

Chart 10-3 Russell 2000 Index and McClellan Up Down Volume Line.

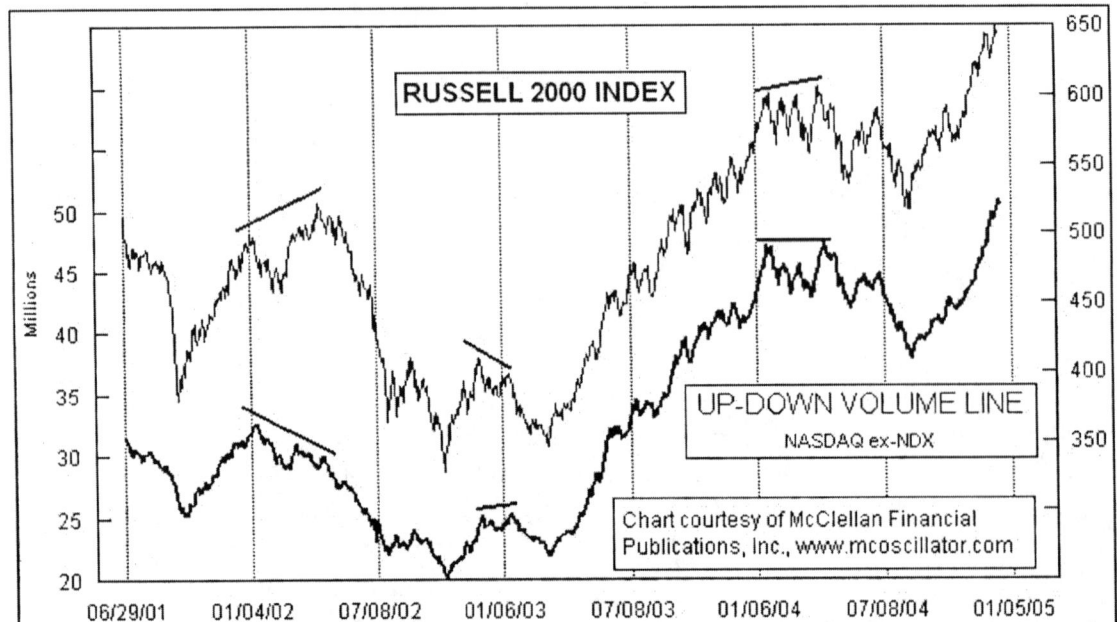

out that these "ex-NDX" volume numbers are a lot less noisy, and they offer us good insights about the health of the small cap market.

Chart 10-3 shows this ex-NDX Nasdaq Volume Line compared to the Russell 2000 Index, which is a small-cap stock benchmark. The two correlate quite nicely with each other, at least most of the time. The insights come from the rare instances when they diverge from one another. In these instances, it is usually this ex-NDX Nasdaq Volume Line that tells the true story about the strength of the market.

In cases when the Russell 2000 Index makes higher highs and this Volume Line fails to confirm, the result is a big decline in the Russell 2000. Prolonged strength in this Volume Line, like we saw in early 2003, tends to foretell continuing strength for the small cap market.

Thoughts on the Continuing Validity of the A − D Line

Some critics have complained that the A − D Line is not useful as an indicator of what the overall stock market is doing because of the "pollution" of the A − D data by certain interest rate issues. This refers to the "Uncommon" issues referenced above, plus certain closed-end funds that are traded like stocks on the NYSE. It should be understood that these complaints have been around since the A − D Line first came into popular use in the early 1960s, but that has not stopped a lot of analysts from finding utility in the A − D stats.

Chart 10-4 After-Tax Profits as Percent of GDP and McClellan NYSE Ratio Adjusted AD Line.

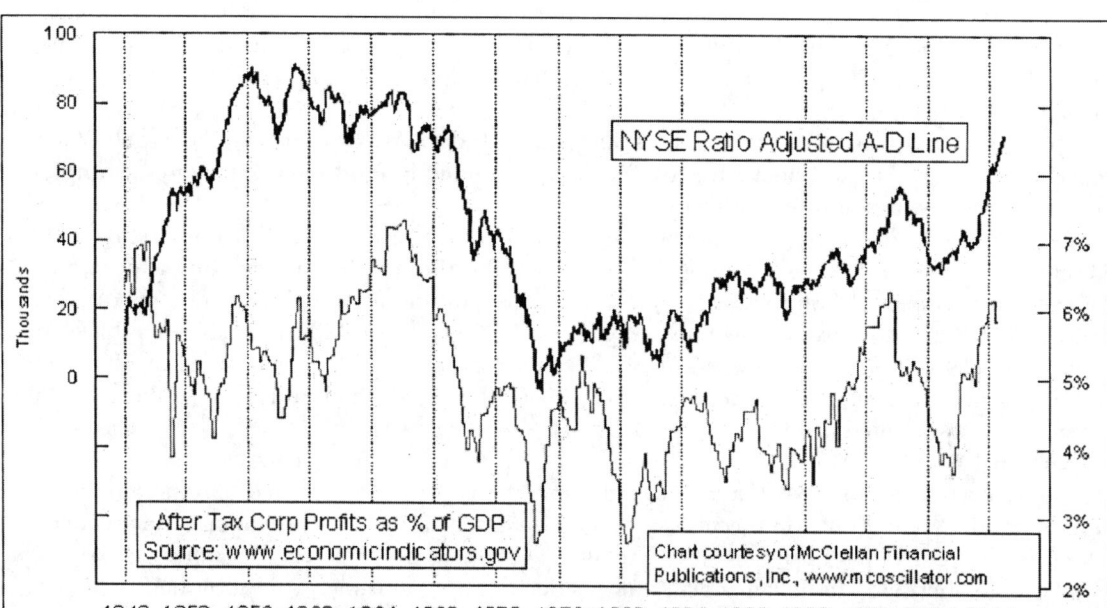

What many technicians, and most fundamentalists, do not understand is that the A − D Line is still the best indication of liquidity out there. Every issue that gets a vote in the daily A − D statistics represents a war between the bulls and the bears, and so reviewing the overall battlefield statistics gives us a useful review of how the war is going. This liquidity concept is often lost on analysts who focus on earnings projections, dividend yields, book value, and other fundamental factors. In truth, there are only two fundamental factors that matter when it comes to the subject of where the overall market is going: (1) How much money is there? And (2) How willing is that money to be invested in stocks? The first of these explains why liquidity matters, and the second explains why sentiment indicators matter, since investors who are already bullish cannot get more bullish.

To see how the A − D Line matters in the real world, take a look at the comparison in Chart 10–4. The ratio-adjusted NYSE A − D Line is on top, and the bottom line shows after-tax corporate profits as a percentage of GDP. What this illustrates is that when liquidity is strong, thereby driving up the A − D Line, it also helps companies achieve relatively greater profitability. This is why it is important for even the fundamentalists to follow what the A − D Line is doing.

The Relationship between an Exponential Oscillator and its Summation Index

by James R. Miekka and Richard G. Miekka

The McClellan Oscillator and Summation Index

The purpose of this article is to show that there is a simple, direct mathematical relationship between the McClellan Oscillator and its Summation Index, and to derive that mathematical relationship. The second part shows the relationship using a simpler algebraic step-by-step format.

The McClellan Oscillator (MCO) and its Summation Index (MCOSI) are standard tools of technical analysis of stocks and stock indexes, which are included in most technical analysis computer programs and listings of tools/indicators.

The MCO is the difference between two exponential moving averages (EMAs) or "trends" of the (daily) difference between the number of advancing and the number of declining issues on one of the stock indexes (NYSE, NASDAQ, etc.), but most commonly the NYSE. The two EMAs are called the fast and slow trends or indexes. Specifically, Sherman and Marian McClellan have chosen the 19-day (10 percent) EMA minus the 39-day (5 percent) EMA as the value of MCO. The MCOSI is the sum of all consecutive values of the MCO, starting (by convention) at a value of +1000 when both exponential moving averages are zero.

Early in 1991 James Miekka determined that the MCOSI could be calculated directly from the fast and slow trends of the MCO. Prior to that time, it was generally assumed that the Summation Index was dependent only on the history of the Oscillator and was not mathematically related to the then-current values of the fast (10 percent) and slow (5 percent) trends. James disclosed his equation to Sherman McClellan shortly after its derivation, and it was soon published in *Stocks & Commodities* as part of an interview between the magazine and Sherman McClellan, and dubbed the "Miekka method" for calculating *MCOSI*. Since then, the formula has been widely used, but its mathematical derivation has never been published. This article will show how the relationship between the *MCO* and the *MCOSI* was derived.

Let's begin with a review of the mathematical expressions for the McClellan Oscillator, its fast and slow trends, and its Summation Index.

The *MCO* is given by the expression:

$$\text{Equation 1: } MCO_n = F_n - S_n$$

Where *F* is the faster, or 10 percent trend (*EMA*), *S* is the slower, or 5 percent trend (*EMA*), and the subscript *n* denotes the *n*th value of MCO and its trends. In turn, *F* and *S* are defined by the equations:

$$\text{Equation 2: } F_n = F_{n-1}(0.9) + \triangle_n (0.1), \text{ and}$$
$$\text{Equation 3: } S_n = S_{n-1}(0.95) + \triangle_n (0.05),$$

Where $\triangle_n$ is the new (current) value of daily advancing minus declining issues on the New York Stock Exchange, and the subscript $n-1$ denotes the preceding (yesterday's) value of *S* or *F*.

Note that $\triangle$ can be positive or negative, so *S*, *F*, and *MCO* can also be positive or negative.

The McClellan Oscillator Summation Index (MCOSI), which is the sum of all oscillator values beginning at some convenient starting point or zero point, can be expressed mathematically as:

$$\text{Equation 4:}$$
$$MCOSI_n = \sum_{i=1}^{n} MCO_i$$

where the subscript *i* refers to the *i*th value of the Oscillator.

The McClellan Indicators

In more generalized terms, let's express the multiplier (0.1) for the faster trend by the letter P, and the multiplier (0.05) for the slower trend as Q, because we may not always want to use 0.1 and 0.05 as the multipliers. Thus:

Equation 2a: $F_n = F_{n-1}(1 - P) + \triangle_n (P)$, and
Equation 3a: $S_n = S_{n-1}(1 - Q) + \triangle_n (Q)$,

The 10 percent trend of the MCO is nominally a 19-day EMA and the 5 percent trend is nominally a 39-day EMA, where the number of days in each trend is given by the formula

Equation 5: $P = 2/(D_P + 1)$, and in the case of the McClellan Oscillator, $P = 2/(19 + 1) = 0.1$
Equation 5a: $Q = 2/(D_Q + 1)$, and in the case of the McClellan Oscillator, $Q = 2/(39 + 1) = 0.05$

Where D_P and D_Q are the nominal durations (days) of the faster and slower trends using the multipliers P and Q. About 86.5 percent of the values of F and S are contributed by their changes in the last D_P and D_Q days, respectively.

Let's now examine a short sequence of days with $\triangle$ chosen in such a way that we can observe the relationships among F, S, MCO, and MCOSI, and in particular the relationship between MCO and MCOSI. Table 10-1 gives the desired sequence, beginning at our chosen starting point.

Although the sequence chosen is short, and the values of $\triangle$ were chosen to illustrate certain factors, the same behavior would be observed for very long sequences of $\triangle$.

From Table 10-1, one can make the following observations.

Table 10-1
Desired Sequence.

A DAY NUMBER	B $\triangle$ A − D	C 10% TREND	D 5% TREND	E MCO	F MCO SI
0		0	0	0	0
1	1000	100	50	50	50
2	1000	190	98	93	143
3	1000	271	143	128	271
4	1000	344	185	158	429
5	−1000	210	126	83	513
6	−1000	89	70	19	531
7	−266	53	53	0	531
8	0	48	50	−3	529
9	−1500	−107	−27	−80	449
10	−1500	−246	−101	−146	303
11	−1500	−372	−171	−201	102
12	−1500	−484	−237	−247	−145
13	1500	−286	−150	−136	−281
14	1500	−107	−68	−40	−321
15	647	−32	−32	0	−321
16	0	−29	−30	2	−319
17	0	−26	−29	3	−316
152	0	0	0	0	−1
153	0	0	0	0	−1
154	0	0	0	0	0

1. If *MCOSI* is positive and *MCO* is 0, then if the next $\triangle$ is 0, *MCO* becomes negative (days 7 and 8).
2. If *MCOSI* is negative and *MCO* is 0, then if the next $\triangle$ is 0, *MCO* becomes positive (days 15 and 16).
3. If one repeatedly enters the value of 0 for $\triangle$, one returns to the starting values for *F*, *S*, *MCO*, and *MCOSI*, which in our case are all equal to zero (days 153 and 154).

Thus, one can see that some direct mathematical relationship must exist between MCO and MCOSI, because MCOSI can never drift off into values unrelated to the then-current F, S, and MCO.

The Neutral Point Concept

In Table 10–1 we observed that if *MCO* = 0, then if the next $\triangle$ = 0, *MCO* rises if *MCOSI* is negative, and falls if *MCOSI* is positive. What value would *MCO* need to have in order that it would not change if $\triangle$ = 0? Let's calculate, in general, how to arrive at such a value for *MCO*, starting from any random *MCO*. To do this we will determine the $\triangle$ required to move the *MCO* to a new value from which, if the following $\triangle$ = 0, then *MCO* will be unchanged. Let us call this the "neutral point" and use the subscript "*NP*" to designate the mathematical functions that relate to the neutral point. The following equation must be satisfied in order to arrive at the neutral point:

Equation 6: $MCO_{NP} = [F(1-P) + \triangle_{NP}P] - [S(1-Q) + \triangle_{NP}Q] = \{[F(1-P) + \triangle_{NP}P](1-P) + \triangle P\} - \{[S(1-Q) + \triangle_{NP}Q](1-Q) + \triangle Q\}$

Where $\triangle$ on the right-hand side of the equation is zero, so the equation simplifies to:

$$MCO_{NP} = [F(1-P) + \triangle_{NP}P] - [S(1-Q) + \triangle_{NP}Q]$$
$$= \{[F(1-P) + \triangle_{NP}P](1-P)\} - \{[S(1-Q) + \triangle_{NP}Q](1-Q)\}$$

Where: *F* and *S* are values of the fast and slow EMA trends at any random point, $\triangle_{NP}$ is the $\triangle$ required to move *MCO* to its neutral point, and MCO_{NP} is the "neutral point" value of the *MCO*.

Solving for $\triangle_{NP}$ in terms of *F*, *S*, *P* and *Q* yields the equation:

$$\text{Equation 7: } \triangle_{NP} = \frac{FP(1-P) - SQ(1-Q)}{(Q^2 - P^2)}$$

Substituting equation 7 into (the right-hand side of) equation 6 yields the following formula for MCO_{NP}:

$$\text{Equation 8: } Osc_{NP} = MCO_{NP} = F(1-P) - S(1-Q) + \frac{(FP^2 - FPQ)(1-P) - (SQ^2 - SPQ)(1-Q)}{(Q^2) - P^2}$$

In the case of the standard *MCO* where *P* = 0.10 and *Q* = 0.05, this equation reduces to:

$$\text{Equation 9: } MCO_{NP} = \frac{9F - 19S}{30}$$

While routinely calculating *MCO*, *MCOSI*, and MCO_{NP}, one of us (James) noted that a), when *MCOSI* was positive, MCO_{NP} was negative, b), when *MCOSI* was negative, MCO_{NP} was positive, and when *MCOSI* was zero (or + 1000 in the case of the standard *MCOSI*), MCO_{NP} was also zero, leading to the suggestion that an inverse mathematical relation existed between *MCOSI* and MCO_{NP}. To

The McClellan Indicators

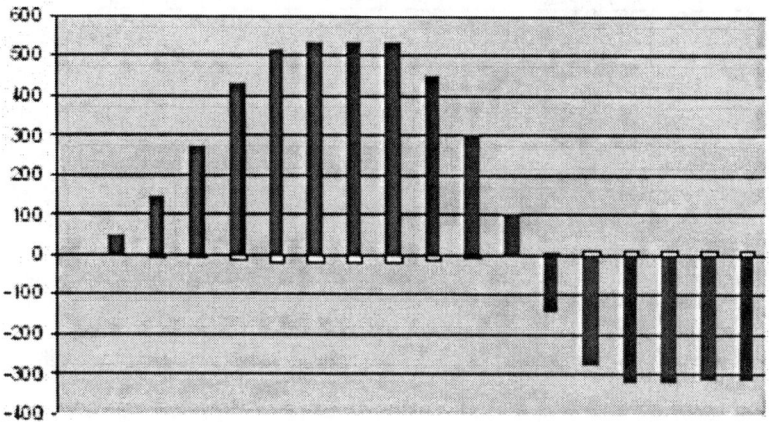

Figure 10-1 McClellan Oscillator with Neutral Point.

illustrate this behavior, if one plots together the first 18 values of $MCOSI$ and MCO_{NP} in Table 10-1, one gets Figure 10-1.

The dark bars in Fig. 10-1 are the $MCOSI$ and the light bars are MCO_{NP}. Note that MCO_{NP} is a mirror image of $MCOSI$ but with a shallower slope. If, however, one multiplies MCO_{NP} by 30, one gets a perfect mirror image of $MCOSI$ (!!) as shown in Figure 10-2.

Finally, if one multiplies MCO_{NP} by -30, one gets exactly $MCOSI$. The formula for the $MCOSI$ using the conventional values of $X_F = 0.10$ and $X_S = 0.05$ thus becomes:

Equation 10: $MCOSI = \dfrac{(-30)(9F - 19S)}{30} = 19S - 9F$

And, if one adjusts for the fact that, by convention, the published $MCOSI$ is normally increased by a constant of 1000:

Equation 10a: $MCOSI = 1000 + 19S - 9F$, or
Equation 10b: $MCOSI = 1000 + MCO + 20S - 10F$

Equations 10a and 10b are the commonly published forms of the "Miekka method" for calculating the McClellan Summation Index.

Acknowledgement: The authors wish to thank Suzanne Schulz of Greely Colorado, Richard A. Fotland of Franklin, MA, and James and Edward Hanson of Maynard, MA for their helpful suggestions in clarifying the text and nomenclature and correcting some wrongly transposed equations.

A Step-by-Step Process

The derivation of the mathematical relationship between MCO and $MCOSI$ was straightforward, but contained rather complex algebraic formulas. Here is another way of calculating the neutral point Oscillator and Summation Index consists of a six-step process as follows:

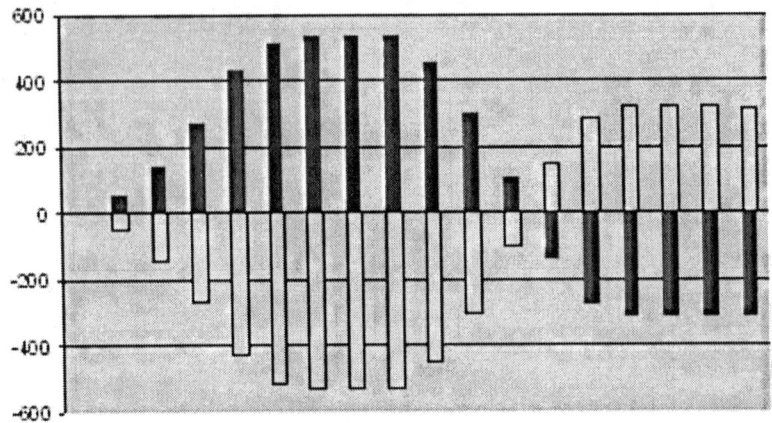

Figure 10-2 McClellan Oscillator with Neutral Point Multiplied by 30.

Step 1: Add the McClellan Oscillator to its 10 percent trend (= MCO + 10 percent)
Step 2: Divide by 3 (= [MCO + 10 percent]/3)
Step 3: Subtract above from MCO (= MCO − [MCO + 10 percent]/3)
Step 4: Multiply by −30 (= −30*{MCO − [MCO + 10 percent]/3})
Step 5: Add 1000 (= 1000 −30*{MCO − [MCO + 10 percent]/3})
Step 6: Add MCO (MCOSI = 1000 + MCO −30*{MCO − [MCO + 10 percent]/3} = 1000 + 19* (5 percent) −9* (10 percent)

The logic of the above is as follows:

Step 1: Calculate the value advances minus declines $(A - D)$ that would keep the Oscillator unchanged (i.e., that would make tomorrow's Oscillator the same as today's Oscillator):

$$(A - D)nc = 2*(10\%) - (5\%) = MCO + (10\%)$$

Where $(A - D)nc$ is the "no change" value of advances minus declines needed to keep the Oscillator unchanged, and (10 percent) and (5 percent) are the 10 percent and 5 percent trends, respectively.

Step 2: If we happen to be at MCOSI = +1000, and if the MCO is at, say, +100, then to keep it unchanged, $A - D$ would have to be +300. Or, if the Oscillator were at +150, then $A - D$ would to be +450 to keep MCO unchanged. In each case, the Oscillator value would be given by the formula:

$$MCO\ nc@neut. = (A - D)nc/3$$

Where MCO nc@neut is the value MCO would have if MCOSI were at its neutral or zero point of +1000.

So, for the moment, let's pretend that the Summation Index is at +1000. If this is true, then MCOnc is given by the formula above.

Step 2: Divide $(A - D)nc$ by 3, or

$$MCO\ nc@neut = (A - D)nc/3 = (MCO + 10\%)/3$$

Step 3: But since *MCOSI* is not really at +1000, we must make an adjustment to find *MCOnc* for our real-world case. This is accomplished by subtracting *MCOnc@neut* from the current value for *MCO*:

Step 3 Subtract *MCOnc@neut* from *MCO*, or

$$MCOnp = MCO - (MCO + 10\%)/3$$

Where *MCOnp* is the value *MCO* that will be unchanged if the next $(A - D)$ is zero.

Note: When routinely calculating the daily values of *MCOnp* and *MCOSI*, James noted that there is an inverse relationship between the two, and that the factor is -30.

Step 4: Multiply *MCOnp* by -30
Step 5: By convention, we add 1000 to the "natural" value of the Summation Index.
Step 5: Add 1000
Step 6: The number obtained in step 5 turns out to be yesterday's *MCOSI*, so we need to add *MCO* to get today's *MCOSI*.
Step 6: add *MCO*

The final formula becomes:

$$\begin{aligned}MCOSI &= 1000 + MCO - 30*[MCO - (MCO + 10\%)/3] \\ &= 1000 + MCO - 30(MCO) + 10(MCO) + 10(10\%) \\ &= 1000 - 19(MCO) + 10(10\%) \\ &= 1000 - 19(10\%) + 19(5\%) + 10\ (10\%) \\ &= 1000 + 19(5\%) - 9(10\%)\end{aligned}$$

The final formula is the same as the formula obtained using alternate algebra earlier in this article. Jim Miekka actually uses the first MCOSI formula in the above series in his own calculations of the Summation Index, which he does in his head.

Of course, the real value of the Miekka formula is that when it is used, the *MCOSI* becomes self-correcting, so any errors in adding up all the values of *MCO* are eliminated. A drift in *MCOSI* will almost always occur in the "add-up" method, even if there are no mistakes in the *MCO* values, unless the values contain a very large number of significant figures.

The second part of the *MCOSI* derivation explains the relation between any oscillator that is the difference between two exponential moving averages and its summation index. The summation index (*SI*) can be calculated from the following formula:

$$SI = C + O_{SC} + S/Q - F/P$$

Where: *SI* is the summation index, *C* is an arbitrary constant, if used, *Osc* is the Oscillator, calculated as the difference between a faster trend (*F*) and a slower trend (*S*), *P* is the multiplying factor for the fast trend, calculated as $2/(N + 1)$, where *N* is the number of units (typically days) on which the fast trend is based. In the case of the McClellan Oscillator, $P = 2/(19 + 1) = 0.1$

Q is the multiplying factor for the slow trend, calculated as $2/(N + 1)$, where *N* is the number of units (typically days) on which the slow trend is based. In the case of the McClellan Oscillator, $Q = 2/(39 + 1) = 0.05$.

McClellan Summation Index Buy Signal

by James R. Miekka

The McClellan Summation Index Buy Signal occurs when the normalized NYSE McClellan Summation Index (*MCOSI*) rises above +1500. The signal remains in effect until the normalized Summation Index drops below +1500. To normalize the *MCOSI*, the 5 percent and 10 percent components of the McClellan Oscillator (*MCO*) are calculated from "normalized" values for advances minus declines, $(A - D)_{norm}$, calculated by the formula: $(A - D)_{norm} = (A - D)*(2000/\text{current total issues traded})$. The reason for normalizing to 2000 total issues is historical. The original work was done when there were, in fact, about 2000 issues traded on the NYSE each day. The purpose of the normalization is to compensate for the increasing number of issues traded on the NYSE over time. For instance, if the total number of issues traded is at 3500 per day, the regular (not normalized) MCOSI will be at about +1875 when the normalized MCOSI is at +1500.

The higher the Summation Index, the greater the tendency for the market to rise. This can be defined mathematically by noting that for every 1000-point increase in the Summation Index, it takes 100 additional advances minus declines to keep the Summation Index at that level (*i.e.*, to keep the McClellan Oscillator at zero). By convention, the Summation Index is classified as neutral at +1000. Thus, at a *MCOSI* of +2000, there must be 100 more advances than declines each day, or 500 per week, to keep *MCOSI* constant. Using the estimate of Michael Burke, of Investors Intelligence, that there are 600 NYSE advances minus declines for each 1 percent increase in the market, this would equate to the market changes versus *MCOSI* values tabulated below in Table 10–2.

If *MCOSI* is high and steady, but the market is falling (or rising at a rate less than the listed values), this means that there is a positive divergence between the $A - D$ breadth and the market, and indicates that higher prices are to come. Conversely, if the market is rising faster than the tabulated values would indicate, this is a sign of negative divergence and the market is likely to turn down, since the divergence acts as a leading indicator.

The Miekka Formula, which gives the mathematical relation between the *MCOSI* and the components of the *MCO*, arose from a study to determine the number of advances minus declines needed to hold the *MCO* constant at different Summation Index levels.

Table 10–2
Market Changes versus MCOSI.

McClellan Summation Index (MCOSI) level	Number of daily Advances minus Declines needed to keep MCO at zero	% Change per week of stays constant (MCO stock market if MCOSI averages zero)
+5000	+400	+3.33
+4000	+300	+2.50
+3000	+200	+1.67
+2000	+100	+0.83
+1000	0	+0.00
+0	−100	−0.83
−1000	−200	−1.67
−2000	−300	−2.50
−3000	−400	−3.33

11
Putting Breadth to Work

What better way to see how all this information on breadth indicators and breadth analysis can actually be put to work and used in a successful practice. The following is an interview with Don Beasley, cofounder of PMFM, Inc. PMFM, Inc. is a money management company that, in 2004, Defined Contribution News named them Advice Provider of the Year in the retirement plan industry. PMFM, Inc. currently has almost $1 billion under management.

Question: When did you first get interested in the markets?
Answer: After I lost (several times) a lot of money with "advice" from brokers who just bought stocks and did not ever sell. I made it a personal crusade to learn how to control my personal destiny as it relates to investing for retirement (since the late 1970s). The first goal is not to lose money. As a former coach, sometimes the first prerequisite in playing to win is to not lose. I also had a math background, and that was beneficial in creating a process that would be productive in the future.

Question: Did you start out using a technical approach?
Answer: Yes! As crude as it may sound, it was important to me to have a predetermined sell criterion for anything that I owned. Spur-of-the moment decisions were/are consistently wrong. The first criterion I ever used was a 50-day average (only rule was to never own anything that was below its average . . . period). Originally it was done in a notebook . . . crude, yes, but I knew when it went below an average. I spent a considerable amount of time in the library reading any material I could find about mutual funds, market information, etc. Among the old publications that were influential were *Growth Fund Guide* and *Systems and Forecasts*.

Question: When did you start managing money?
Answer: Initially, money management was for me and a couple of family members. While winding up my coaching career, some of my peers noticed that I would read the business section before the sports section. During the early 1980s several people said to me; "Just do for me what you do for yourself." Instead of making decisions on a few personal and family accounts, I just handled several more for other people

(no charge). Simply put, I just started a management business and after a couple of years joined with my current business partner, Tim Chapman, to establish our present business that we continue to operate today.

Question: Were you always interested in breadth analysis, or did you get to it by trial and error?

Answer: The two most influential reasons for using breadth were brought about by Sherman/Marian McClellan and Gerald Appel. First, Mr. Appel had a trading system developed in the late 1980s that was heavily influenced by breadth measures (advance decline and high low measures). After studying this system, I immediately viewed all of the losing trades and amended most of his rules to eliminate a significant portion of the losing trades as well as reducing the frequency of trading. I cannot stress enough the importance of his "continuation" signals (long term in nature) and his daily signals (McClellan Oscillator). How he linked these two components was real genius and influenced my thinking from that point forward. Secondly, the opportunity to meet and visit with the McClellans to utilize their methods (pamphlet and correspondence) to develop a personal way to use their McClellan indicators was instrumental. Also, Jim Miekka, was helpful in his dialogue on the uses of the summation index as it applied to our trading methodology (summation direction and level).

Question: Can you describe the overall methodology of your approach to the markets?

Answer: We have clearly defined the first step in the investment process to invest when you have an "EDGE." If you do not know when you have an edge, you are probably just investing for excitement. A somewhat original measure we use is what we call our "Dominant Index" indicator. Basically it is a ratio between two indexes (favorites include: Nasdaq / NYSE, NDX / S&P 500, Russell Growth / Russell Value, etc. Chart 11-1 shows our Dominant Index Indicator using the Nasdaq / NYSE.

When using the Nasdaq / NYSE, if the Nasdaq is the dominant index, we use Nasdaq data for our breadth measures. Each indicator that we use has a probability set that allows us to objectively measure its value and weighting in our model approach. For example, our Nasdaq Advance Decline model (Chart 11-2) historically (1979-2004) can capture almost 300 percent of total return in 51 percent of the time. Our Nasdaq High Low Model (Chart 11-3) is similar, capturing almost 200 percent of the total return in only 54 percent of the time.

Question: How did you come up with the breadth indicators that you use today?

Answer: First, the frequency of trading is our basic delimiter in our model-building process. If you are just building a trading approach that does not consider this important fact, you could be trading so much that the cost impact (trading costs) would be very detrimental to your bottom line . . . not to mention that trading frequency is now a major factor if you use mutual funds. We developed breadth based indicators that traded (issued signals) between three to five round trips per year.

Secondly, we think that keeping two sets of breadth statistics is very important as per the previous discussion about our dominant index measures. If a large-cap index is dominant, we use NYSE data and if the small stocks index is dominant, we use Nasdaq data.

Chart 11-1 Dominant Index.

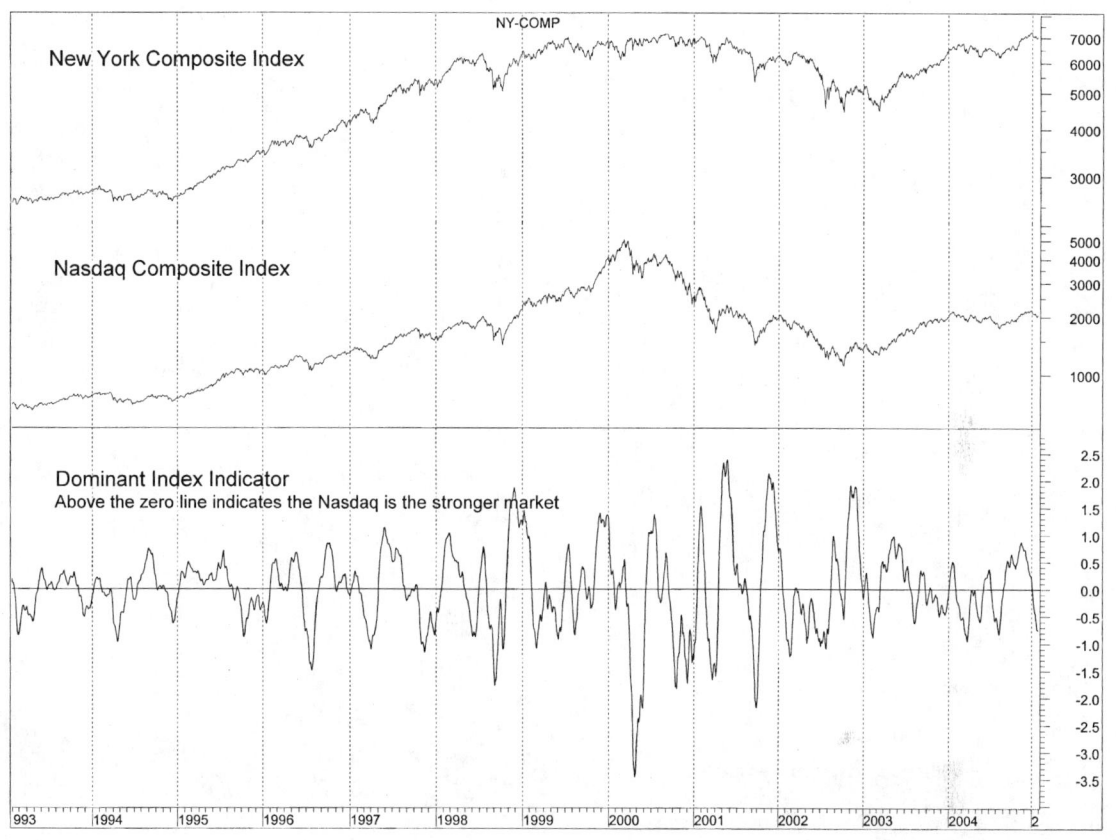

Question: How have these procedures done over the years?
Answer: Our breadth models are major components of our "risk model." We presently have a mixture of breadth and price components in our trading models.
Question: Have you made any changes to them over time?
Answer: We always have ongoing research to improve our models. But the basic philosophy never changes. In fact, we have several mutual funds and management relationships that restrict our number of trades per year, and we can adjust the models to fit these individual constraints.
Question: What changes did you make and why?
Answer: It sounds somewhat like an oxymoron, but we think that you can have both trading discipline and be flexible. The discipline is crucial, as you must follow the current rules for trading. And we never change the rules during an active trade. Only research can amend the current disciplines. Yet we know that things change and we must be

Chart 11-2 Nasdaq Advance Decline Model.

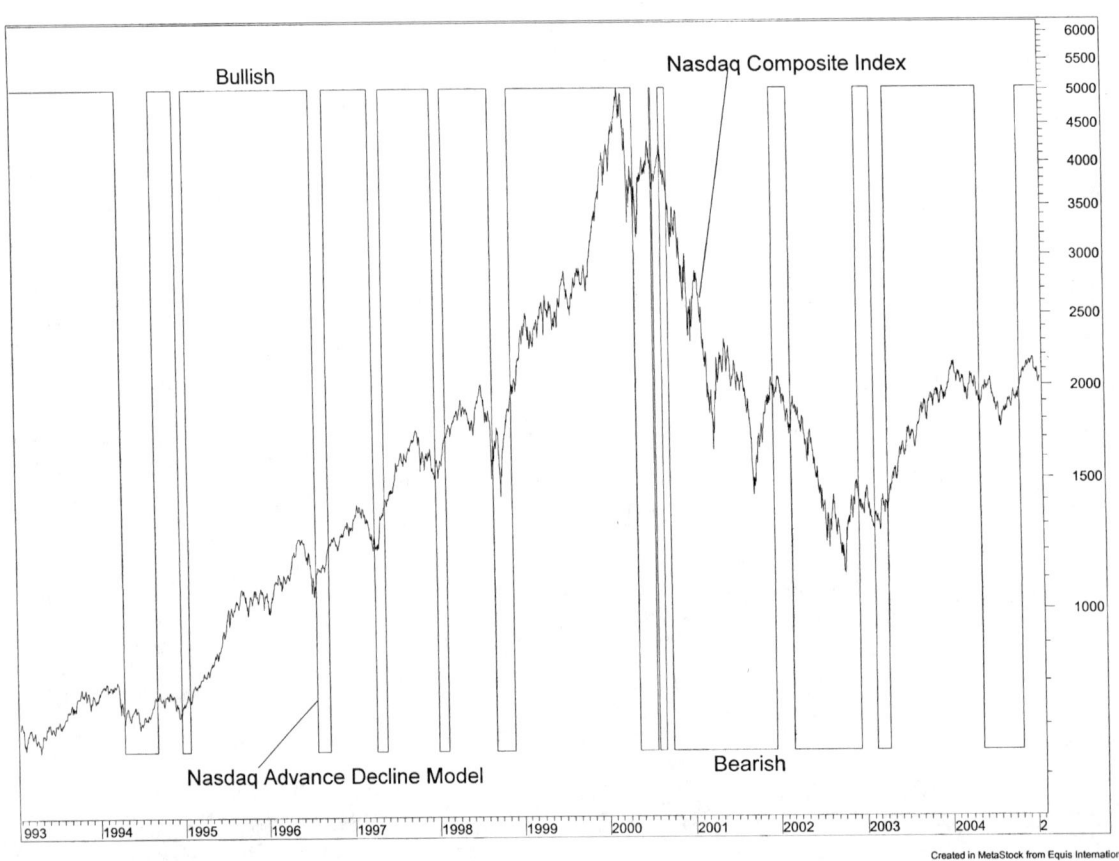

flexible to adjust to these situations. A couple of examples would include: (1) tax law changes, holding periods mandated or backend fees charged, or (2) SEC regulations force a model change. While our core definition of defining an "edge" and creating a model that clearly attempts to take advantage of this process never changes, we are always working on new processes that enhance our risk-adjusted process.

Question: How many funds is PMFM, Inc. the advisor for?
Answer: At this time we have three current mutual funds and a fourth is in registration. All of the funds have risk-adjusted characteristics that amplify our tactical approach. The biggest differentiator is our selection and asset commitment processes.
Question: Is your model used for all the funds or just some?
Answer: Tactical models are used in all of the funds. It is how we attempt to define an "edge."
Question: Why do you think breadth works better than a price-based model?

Putting Breadth to Work

Chart 11-3 Nasdaq High Low Model.

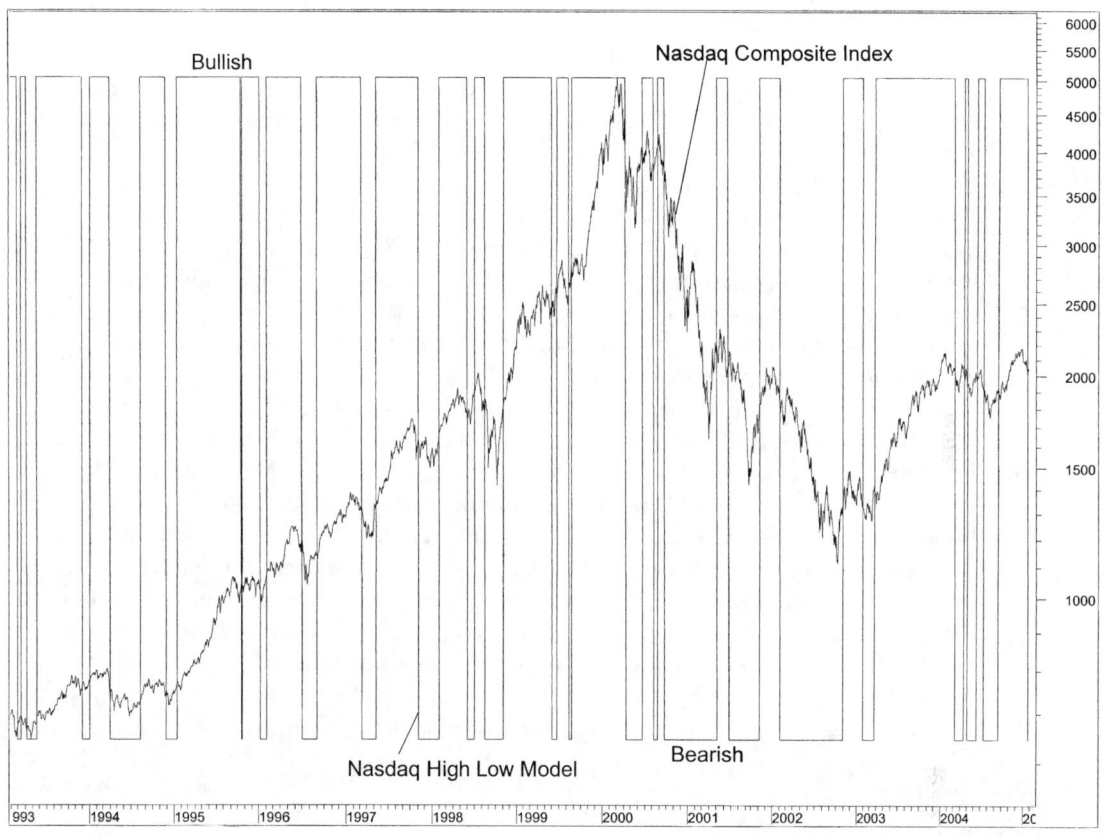

Answer: There is some great historical evidence that clearly indicates that the market averages can be influenced by a few large capitalized stocks while many issues are declining. In fact, a typical characteristic of important tops is that there are significantly more declining issues than advancing issues. We think breadth gives us major input as to the participation level in any market direction. At times, it has leading characteristics as to a change of direction in the markets, such as divergence with price.

Question: What do you think of the NYSE having almost 53 percent of its issues as interest sensitive? Does that mess up your model?

Answer: I'm not so sure that it "messes up" our model, as we strongly feel that the most productive time to be invested in the markets is when the small cap stocks are dominant. This function is very, very important to our selection and asset commitment process. The bottom line is that NYSE issues have significantly changed over the past few years, and it clearly brings into question the historical value of the research we use. Fortunately, there are sources at this time that use equity-only issues to determine their breadth measures.

Question: You said that you look at the NYSE and Nasdaq breadth data. Is there any other breadth data that you use?

Answer: We have access to limited advance-decline and high low data for other indexes and have ongoing research in this area. There is not very much historical data for long-term term research at this time.

Question: Any short bit of advice to investors that you would like to share?

Answer: The single biggest mistakes most people (professional and nonprofessional) make is the need for instant gratification and not being willing to know themselves and construct a personal process in which they can be satisfied. Most have rigid expectations (some yearly percent return function) and flexible decision-making rules attempting to meet this expectation. It is crucial that the exact opposite be true . . . *rigid rules and flexible expectations*. In most cases tactical traders have an obsession trying to change things because it didn't work this time. After all, trading strategies are not perfect; they are simply a set of probabilities that favor you over time.

Question: I believe you said you would share some of the research that PMFM has done in regard to the indicators and models you mentioned earlier. How about it?

Answer: I'd be glad to. Table 11–1 shows the research we have done on the Dominant Market concept. You can clearly see that when the Nasdaq is the dominant market, it is generally a much better time to be invested. The most important number to view here is the Compounded Annual Return while Invested, which is almost twice that of buy and hold, plus you were only at risk in the market 52 percent of the time. That is a very important concept that many forget; if you are in cash half the time, you are assuming half the risk of being fully invested. Also, keep in mind that during the

Table 11–1
Dominant Market Research.
1/2/1979 – 12/31/2004 26 Years

Copyright © 2005 PMFM, Inc.
Statistics from Ultra Financial Systems

Buy	Winning Percentage	Trades per Year	Average Return per Trade	Compounded Annual Return	Compounded Annual Return while Invested	Percent of Time Invested	Ulcer Index
			Nasdaq is the Dominant Market				
Nasdaq	60.00%	3.46	3.54%	14.39%	21.22%	52.68%	14.40%
NYSE	65.56%	3.46	2.03%	9.90%	12.35%	52.68%	10.12%
			NYSE is the Dominant Market				
NYSE	57.30%	3.42	1.18%	7.23%	7.82%	47.32%	6.49%
Nasdaq	59.55%	3.42	0.66%	4.60%	2.29%	47.32%	21.56%
			Buy and Hold				
Nasdaq	N/A	N/A	N/A	11.86%	11.86%	100%	27.75%
NYSE	N/A	N/A	N/A	10.18%	10.18%	100%	10.49%

Table 11-2
Trend Capturing Research.
1/2/1979 – 12/31/2004 26 years

Copyright © 2005 PMFM, Inc.
Statistics from Ultra Financial Systems

Winning Percentage	Trades per Year	Average Return per Trade	Compounded Annual Return	Compounded Annual Return while invested	Percent of Time Invested	Ulcer Index	Maximum Drawdown (entry)
			Nasdaq Advance Decline Model				
49.35%	2.96	4.73%	16.38%	26.00%	50.82%	16.57%	−16.11%
			Nasdaq High Low Model				
48.20%	5.34	2.36%	14.73%	21.47%	54.01%	14.63%	−13.48%
			Nasdaq Buy and Hold				
N/A	N/A	N/A	11.86%	11.86%	100%	27.75%	−77.93%
			NYSE Advance Decline Model				
53.76%	3.58	1.98%	10.09%	12.58%	53.28%	7.78%	−13.63%
			NYSE High Low Model				
49.26%	5.23	1.11%	8.76%	10.14%	53.29%	8.51%	−6.11%
			NYSE Buy and Hold				
N/A	N/A	N/A	10.18%	10.18%	100%	10.49%	−37.85%

period for this study, we had a giant bull market (1982–2000) followed by a giant bear market (2000–2002), especially in the Nasdaq.

Table 11–2 shows our research on two of our Trend Capturing models. Again, it shows that breadth analysis can beat buy and hold by a significant margin. Couple that with the fact that you don't have to be invested in the market full time to get those significantly better results. It also shows that the small-cap Nasdaq version is better than the large-cap New York version, which falls in line with our Dominant Market theory. If you were to buy and hold, you would have had to sit through a drop of almost 78 percent. I don't know how anyone could do that. A decline of 78 percent requires a return of almost 400 percent to get back to even. That could take the rest of your life. And this is just to get even, which is not the name of the game.

Table 11–3 shows our research on the McClellan Summation Index. We use a ratio adjusted version $(A - D)/(A+D)$ and also calculate it using zero as the neutral point, instead of the +1000 in the original version. Our research shows that the McClellan Summation Index is important to watch not only for direction but also its level. One can see from Table 11–3 that if you only invested in the Nasdaq market while the McClellan Summation Index was above zero (>0), you could get a return almost double that of the buy and hold return, plus only be exposed to the market about 45 percent of the time. Now that is pretty darn good.

Question: Don, what is the Ulcer Index?
Answer: The Ulcer Index is a measure of volatility that we use in almost all or our work at PMFM, Inc. It was developed by Peter Martin in 1987. It measures the depth and

Table 11-3
McClellan Summation Index Research.
1/2/1979 – 12/31/2004 26 years
Adjusted for zero level neutral and (A−D)/(A+D) ratio and using Nasdaq data

Copyright © 2005 PMFM, Inc.
Statistics from Ultra Financial Systems

Level	Winning Percentage	Trades per Year	Average Return per Trade	Compounded Annual Return	Compounded Annual Return while Invested	Percent of of Time Invested	Ulcer Index	Maximum Drawdown (entry)
>800	76.92%	0.50	5.89%	8.40%	49.74%	6.75%	1.12%	−2.55%
>700	86.67%	0.58	6.53%	9.26%	50.92%	8.52%	1.18%	−2.71%
>600	70.00%	0.77	5.92%	9.78%	47.91%	10.33%	1.64%	−2.85%
>500	50.00%	0.92	5.65%	10.00%	38.74%	13.32%	2.38%	−4.11%
>400	55.56%	1.04	5.91%	10.88%	36.81%	16.47%	2.91%	−4.11%
>300	55.88%	1.31	5.57%	11.83%	34.08%	21.04%	2.65%	−4.10%
>200	57.89%	1.46	5.09%	11.55%	26.31%	26.78%	5.67%	−8.12%
>100	58.82%	1.96	4.42%	12.51%	24.48%	34.35%	4.33%	−9.59%
>0	54.17%	1.85	5.66%	13.43%	22.38%	44.01%	7.46%	−7.93%
>−100	55.77%	2.00	5.68%	13.64%	20.22%	51.80%	8.93%	−14.47%
>−200	45.61%	2.19	5.38%	13.12%	17.29%	59.77%	12.83%	−18.19%
>−300	56.25%	1.85	8.31%	16.09%	20.71%	66.38%	11.93%	−21.48%
>−400	52.27%	1.69	9.54%	16.02%	19.45%	71.88%	12.76%	−19.95%
>−500	50.00%	1.61	9.55%	14.80%	17.01%	76.40%	18.17%	−22.33%
>−600	55.26%	2.92	4.92%	12.91%	14.04%	80.62%	22.03%	−23.48%
>−700	53.12%	1.23	13.63%	12.83%	13.54%	84.96%	24.37%	−26.55%
>−800	41.38%	1.11	17.98%	13.25%	13.79%	88.22%	23.23%	−26.77%
B & H	N/A	N/A	N/A	11.86%	11.86%	100%	27.75%	−77.93%

duration of drawdowns from earlier highs. Kind of a way to measure the ulcers you can get from buy and hold.

Question: Anything else that you would like to add? I know you don't do all this research by yourself. Not any more, that is.

Answer: Many thanks are in order to our trading and research group: Joe Ezernack, Blake Underwood, Will McGough, Clay Alliston. They have a great command of our processes and are always producing ideas for improvement of existing models and inputs for future products. They are crucial to our tactical approach and are greatly appreciated for their daily actions.

Thanks, Don.

12
Conclusions

By now the need for inclusion of breadth in your analysis should be obvious. Each breadth indicator seems to have its benefits and its shortcomings. The fact that breadth measures the markets in a manner not possible with price is the key element in these conclusions. Breadth measures the movement of the market, its acceleration and deceleration. It is not controlled by General Electric, Microsoft, Intel, Cisco, General Motors, etc., anymore than it is controlled by the smallest capitalized stock on the exchange.

Table 12–1 shows the breadth components needed for calculation of the indicator, whether the indicator is better for picking market bottoms, market tops, or trend analysis, and whether it is better for short-or long-term analysis. Keep in mind that short term is generally some period of time less than 5 to 6 months. Identification of a market bottom can be an event that can last only a few days or launch a giant secular bull market. In Table 12–1, the terms short and long term refer to the frequency of signals as much as anything. A number of the long-term indicators are good for trend following; in Table 12–1 if neither Bottoms nor Tops is checked, it is because the indicator is better at trend analysis.

Some indicators are better at Tops, Bottoms, and both, and at different times, but are only identified by Bottoms and/or Tops below. Great effort was made to determine if one appeared to be better at one or the other. If no difference could be ascertained, they were reported as being good for both Bottoms and Tops. Please keep in mind the nature of market bottoms versus market tops. Bottoms are generally sharp and quick and usually much easier to identify, whereas market tops are usually long periods of distribution where most market indices rotate through their peaks at different times. You will notice that considerably more indicators are noted as being good at Bottoms than at Tops. Add to that the subjective interpretation of the various indicators and Table 12–1 should be viewed as a beginning guide only.

Table Columns

A	Advances	DV	Down Volume
D	Declines	H	New Highs
U	Unchanged	L	New Lows
TI	Total Issues	V	Total Volume
UV	Up Volume	MKT	Market Index

Table 12-1

Primary Indicators.

AD Difference	Breadth Components Used:										Good for use at: Market		Better for: Term	
	A	D	U	TI	UV	DV	H	L	V	Mkt	Bottoms	Tops	Short	Long
Advances − Declines	X	X									X		X	
AD Overbought/Oversold	X	X									X		X	
Plurality Index	X	X									X	X	X	
AD − Fugler	X	X									X	X	X	
AD Line	X	X										X		X
AD Line − 1%	X	X											X	
AD Line − Eakle	X	X									X			X
AD Line − Normailzed	X	X									X	X	X	
AD Line − Bolton	X	X	X											X
AD Line − Adj. Total Issues	X	X		X										X
Big Movers Only	X	X		X										X
AD Line Oscillator	X	X									X	X	X	
Absolute Breadth Index	X	X									X	X	X	
Absolute Breadth − Adj.	X	X		X							X	X		X
AD Power	X	X								X	X			X
Coppock Breadth Indicator	X	X		X									X	
Haurlan Index − Short Term	X	X									X	X	X	
Harulan Index − Med Term	X	X									X	X	X	
Haurlan Index − Long Term	X	X												X
McClellan Oscillator	X	X									X	X	X	
McClellan Summation Index	X	X									X	X		X
Merriman Breadth Model	X	X								X	X	X	X	
Swenlin Breadth Mo. Osc.	X	X									X	X	X	
Swenlin Trdg Osc − Breadth	X	X									X	X	X	
Zahorchak Method	X	X								X				X
AD Ratio	A	D	U	TI	UV	DV	H	L	V	Mkt	Bottoms	Tops	Short	Long
AD Ratio	X	X									X	X	X	
Breadth Thrust	X	X									X			X
Breadth Thrust Continuation	X	X												X
Duarte's Market Thrust	X	X									X		X	
Eliades Sign of the Bear	X	X										X		X
Hughes Breadth Mo. Osc.	X	X	X								X	X	X	

(continued)

Conclusions

	Breadth Components Used:										Good for use at: Market		Better for: Term	
AD Ratio	A	D	U	TI	UV	DV	H	L	V	Mkt	Bottoms	Tops	Short	Long
Panic Thrust	X	X									X		X	
STIX	X	X									X	X	X	
AD Miscellaneous	A	D	U	TI	UV	DV	H	L	V	Mkt	Bottoms	Tops	Short	Long
Advances / Issues Traded	X			X							X		X	
AD Divergence Oscillator	X	X	X							X				X
AD Diffusion Index	X			X							X		X	
Breadth Climax	X	X	X								X	X		X
Declining Issues TRIX		X									X	X	X	
Disparity Index	X	X								X				X
Dynamic Synthesis	X	X	X							X	X	X		X
Unchanged Issues			X								X			X
Velocity Index	X	X	X								X	X	X	
HL	A	D	U	TI	UV	DV	H	L	V	Mkt	Bottoms	Tops	Short	Long
New Highs − New Lows							X	X			X	X	X	
New High New Low Line							X	X			X			X
New Highs & Lows Osc.							X	X			X	X	X	
New Highs New Lows Derv.							X	X			X	X	X	
New Highs / New Lows							X	X			X	X	X	
New Highs & New Lows X							X	X						X
New Highs % Total Issues				X			X					X		X
New Lows % Total Issues				X				X			X			X
High Low Logic Index				X			X	X			X	X	X	
High Low Validation							X	X	X		X	X	X	
Volume	A	D	U	TI	UV	DV	H	L	V	Mkt	Bottoms	Tops	Short	Long
Up Volume					X						X		X	
Down Volume						X					X		X	
Changed Volume					X	X					X	X	X	
Up & Down Volume					X	X					X	X	X	
McClellan Oscillator − Vol.					X	X					X	X	X	
McClellan Summation − Vol.					X	X								X
Merriman Volume Model					X	X					X	X	X	
Swenlin Volume Mo. Osc.					X	X			X		X	X	X	
Swenlin Trading Osc. − Vol.					X	X			X		X	X	X	

(continued)

Table 12-1 (Continued)

Volume	Breadth Components Used:									Good for use at: Market		Better for: Term	
	A	D	U	TI	UV	DV	H	L	V	Mkt	Bottoms	Tops	Short	Long
Up Vol. Down Vol. Line					X	X								X
Cumulative Volume Ratio					X	X					X	X	X	
Up Down On Balance Vol.					X	X			X					X
Volume Percentage Ratio					X	X		X			X		X	
Upside − Downside Volume					X	X					X	X	X	
Upside / Downside Volume					X	X					X	X	X	
Zweig Up Volume Indicator					X	X					X			X

Composite	A	D	U	TI	UV	DV	H	L	V	Mkt	Bottoms	Tops	Short	Long
Arms' Index	X	X			X	X					X	X	X	
Arms' Open Index	X	X			X	X					X	X	X	
Bretz Trin-5	X	X			X	X					X	X	X	
Cash Flow Index	X	X		X	X	X	X	X	X					X
Comp. Tape Index − Short	X	X			X	X	X	X			X	X	X	
Comp. Tape Index − Med.	X	X			X	X	X	X			X	X	X	
Comp. Tape Index − Long	X	X			X	X	X	X						X
Dysart Pos. Neg. Vol.	X	X						X						X
Eliades New TRIN	X	X			X	X					X	X	X	
Haller Theory											X	X		X
Hindenberg Omen	X	X		X			X	X		X		X		X
Market Thrust	X	X			X	X					X		X	
McClellan Osc. − Volume	X	X			X	X					X	X	X	
McClellan Sum. − Volume	X	X			X	X								X
Moving Balance Indicator	X	X			X	X					X		X	
Technical Index	X	X		X	X	X	X	X	X					X
Titanic Syndrome − 1988	X	X		X	X		X	X				X		X
Titanic Syndrome − 1991	X	X		X	X		X	X			X	X		X
Titanic Syndrome − 1995	X	X		X	X		X	X			X	X		X
Trend Exhaustion Index	X						X					X		X

Secondary Indicators	A	D	U	TI	UV	DV	H	L	V	Mkt	Bottoms	Tops	Short	Long
AD Differential − Mamis	X	X									X	X	X	
Hughes Breadth Mo. % Osc	X	X	X								X	X	X	
Advances TRIX	X										X	X	X	
New Highs New Lows % TI				X			X	X			X	X	X	
New Highs Lows − Morris							X	X						X
New High New Low Cohen							X	X			X	X	X	

(continued)

Conclusions

Secondary Indicators	Breadth Components Used:										Good for use at: Market		Better for: Term	
	A	D	U	TI	UV	DV	H	L	V	Mkt	Bottoms	Tops	Short	Long
Wkly New H New L Hayes							X	X				X		X
New Highs Hayes							X	X				X	X	X
New Highs New Lows Burk							X	X			X	X	X	
Low High Logic				X			X	X				X	X	
Up Volume Detrended					X						X	X	X	
Down Volume Detrended						X					X	X	X	
Up Down Volume Oscillator					X	X			X		X	X	X	
Zweig Double 9 Up Volume					X	X					X			X
Zweig Double 9 Down Vol					X	X					X			X
Arms Index 21–55 Oscillator	X	X			X	X					X	X	X	
WTrin10	X	X			X	X					X	X	X	
Market Thrust Oscillator	X	X			x	X					X	X	X	
Market Thrust Summation	X	X			X	X					X	X		X
Technical Index ROC	X	X		X	X	X	X	X	X		X	X	X	
Trend Explosion Index		X						X			X			X

Note: If neither Bottoms nor Tops are checked (X), it means the indicator is better at trend analysis.

Favorite Breadth Indicators

Here is a list of breadth indicators that I believe are good ones to follow. Some are for daily analysis and some are used merely to be kept aware of their indications. There are some really good breadth indicators that have made some very good market calls over the years, they are marked as awareness only below. I try to avoid noisy indicators that require too much interpretation and are very short term in nature.

Breadth Indicator	When Used
Advance Decline Line	long term and usually early
Advance Decline Line Normalized	good breadth overbought oversold
Breadth Thrust	awareness only
Eliades Sign of the Bear	awareness only
New Highs New Lows Line	long-term trend
New Highs New Lows (Chart 7–17)	intermediate trends
McClellan Oscillator	short to intermediate
McClellan Summation with Miekka adj.	longer term and market staying power
Moving Balance Indicator	very good for bottoms (oversold)
Swenlin Breadth Momentum	short-term picture
Trend Exhaustion Index	good for topping alert
Up Volume (smoothed)	good for the beginning of market tops
WTrin10	short-term overbought oversold
Zahorchak Method	good for trend following
Zweig Up Volume Indicators	awareness only

Only one of my choices is a breadth indicator that uses up and/or down volume solely. I have always believed in the value of volume as it moves the market, but quite possibly the breakdown of up and down volume does not yield anything more to the picture. It does appear that up or down volume used with other breadth components can exaggerate or understate some market action, which can certainly enhance those indicators.

McClellan Summation Index for Big Picture of the Market

If there were one indicator that could dominate an investor's overall concept of the market, it would be the McClellan Summation Index. This is not so much for short-term timing, but is excellent to assess the risk of participating in the market. If you look at Don Beasley's research (Chapter 11, Table 11–3) on the performance of the Nasdaq market when the McClellan Summation Index is above zero, it is quite convincing. For the period 1979 through 2004, if you bought the Nasdaq Index whenever the McClellan Summation Index went above zero and then sold it when it dropped below zero, you would have a compounded annual return for the time that you were invested of over 22 percent, while the buy and hold (B & H) return was less than 12 percent. And this is important; you were only at risk in the market less than 45 percent of the time.

Remember, the PMFM study (Chapter 11, Table 11–3) used the Miekka adjusted formula and also used zero for the neutral point instead of the more popular +1000. If you are using the more popular version, then the results would be the same when you bought going above +1000 and sold when dropping below +1000. Chart 12–1 shows the Nasdaq Index with the signals shown for buying as the McClellan Summation Index crosses above zero and selling when it drops below zero. Keep in mind that this is over a 26-year period. You can see that during most of the good up moves, the indicator was bullish.

Breadth Consensus Index

If you were so inclined, one could pick a few dozen breadth indicators, ensuring that they were structurally different to avoid the Multicollinearity trap, (see Chapter 2) then each day keep track as to whether they were giving a bullish, bearish, or neutral signal. This might provide you with a good consensus indicator, hopefully one that would align itself with the market and not one that is psychological, as most consensus indicators tend to be.

I went back and looked at each of the indicators in Table 12–1 and assigned bullish (+), bearish (−), and neutral (0) ratings for all of them as of December 31, 2004. Keep in mind that December 31, 2004, was a significant top in the market. Here are the results:

Conclusions

Chart 12-1 McClellan Summation Study.

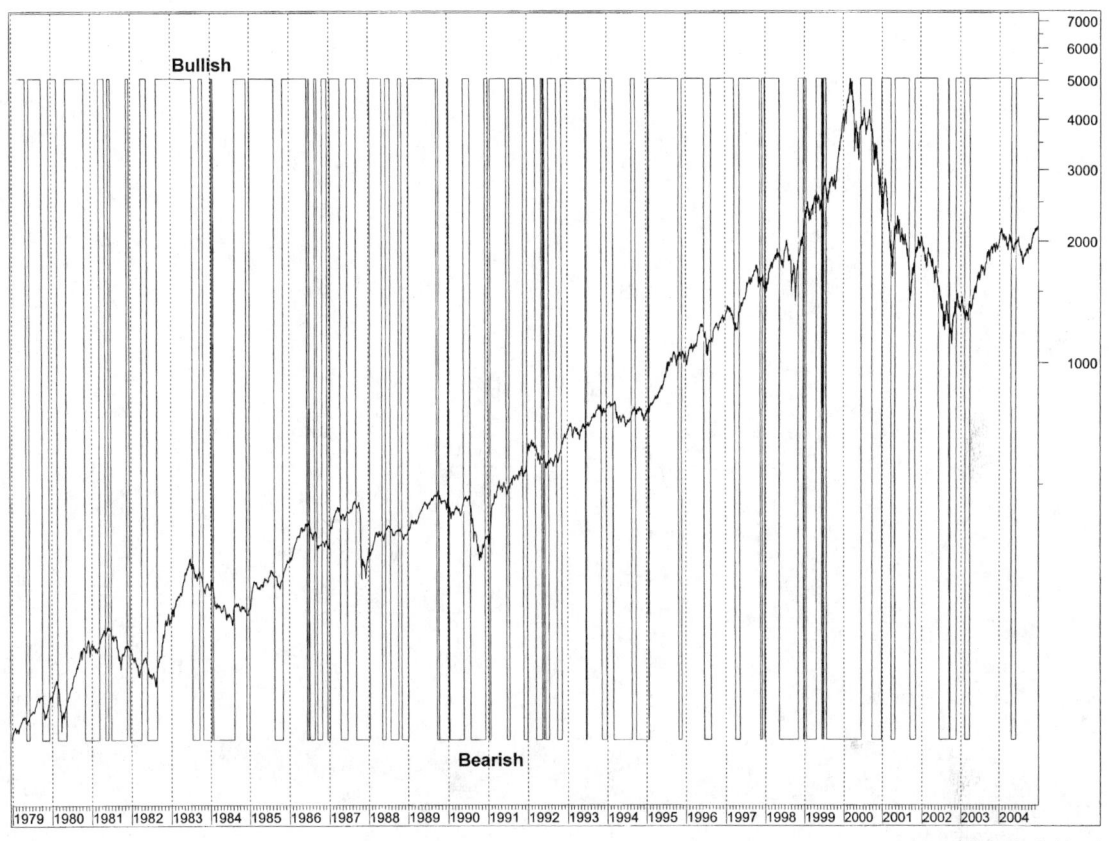

Signal	Primary	Secondary
+	41	12
0	41	7
–	6	2

Generally, an overall bullish reading was registered based on all the breadth indicators. However, 8 of them were decidedly negative and there were almost as many neutral readings as bullish ones.

Appendix A
Indicators and Trading Systems—What's the Difference?

After more than 25 years of developing, reproducing, and building indicators and trading systems, I have realized that many traders and investors do not fully understand the difference between them. Believe it or not, the more sophisticated and experienced traders prefer sound representative indicators, that reflect the trading style that they use and prefer. In my opinion, the folks that are not serious market analysts usually only want a trading system. While this is merely a generalization, and not always true, it has been my experience that it is more often true than not. Well, I have news for those who only want a trading system; they are almost always derived from indicators. Kind of like the chicken and the egg problem. The indicator came first, before the trading system.

Indicators

An indicator is defined by Webster as: "a pointer or directing device, aninstrument for measuring or recording". What then is a technical indicator? Technical indicators are mathematical manipulations of data so that specific values or positions can reflect the market or security being indicated upon. There are other types of market indicators that are commonly used, such as economic time series, interest rates, etc. Most technical indicators deal with price and volume.

One of the first, and possibly still best, indicators is the moving average. In the early days of technical analysis, there was only a moving average. It wasn't as specifically defined as it is today by adjectives such as simple, exponential, weighted, triangular, variable, etc. Using a columnar pad and a pencil, one could easily calculate a simple (arithmetic) moving average, especially a 10-period simple average. This average smoothed price movements and reduced or eliminated any cyclic action whose period was less than that of the average. In other words, it helped eliminate whipsaws and made the prices easier to follow.

The ability to visually display an indicator made computers the ideal mechanism for significant advances in technical analysis. Today, with most technical analysis software packages, you can manipulate data in their formulary and immediately see the results visually. Incidentally, formulary is a word coined by John Sweeney (former Technical Editor, *Stocks and Commodities*), which refers to the system or technique of building or constructing indicators by using predefined mathematical operations and functions.

Indicators come in all types, those that indicate overbought and oversold, those that try to follow a trend, those that indicate reversals of trends, those that indicate excess, and a host of others. You can use an indicator without actually knowing the exact mathematical calculations. Display the indicator with the index or security you want to analyze, using as much data as you can (the more, the better). Attempt to identify times when the indicator reaches a certain threshold or value and the security responds in the same manner. It will be rare to find an indicator that perfectly correlates with the index or security, so learn to accept something less than 100 percent. Experiment with small changes in the parameters that make up the indicator to see if the results improve. Once you have it where you like it, try it on another index or security. Yes, you have just discovered one of the difficulties of overfitting an indicator to specific data.

This is commonly referred to as curve fitting. That is a statistical reference used when performing regression analysis. It works great on the data being used, but it is basically worthless with anything else. That is why so many indicators seem to work on some things and fail miserably on others. Elsewhere in this book is a table of differing time periods. This is so you can develop an indicator using one time period and then test it on a different time period. If it holds up, you have probably created a fairly reliable indicator.

Trading Systems

This could get touchy if I don't offer some preliminary comments. I am going to discuss trading systems in the sense of using signals from indicators for buy, sell, short, and cover. These indicator signals can also provide exit strategies. I will not address money management, multiple futures contracts, averaging up or down, or any of the other more advanced or exotic trading system methods. It is not that I don't use or believe in them; it is just not the purpose of this writing.

Going back to the simple moving average, one can develop a trading system that buys when the advance decline line goes from below to above the moving average. A sell signal occurs when the closing price goes from above to below the moving average. This is a trading system, an overly simplistic one, but still a trading system and is commonly referred to as a crossover system.

Wait a minute! Isn't the moving average an indicator? Yes it is, but when you define how the moving average acts in relation to the advance decline line, you have a trading system. That is, in fact, the essence of all trading systems that are based on an underlying indicator.

Example

This is an elementary example but reflects the concept and point I am trying to make. Chart A-1 shows the New York advance decline line and a 30-day simple moving average.

Indicators and Trading Systems—What's the Difference?

Chart A-1 Advance Decline Line with 30-Day Smooth.

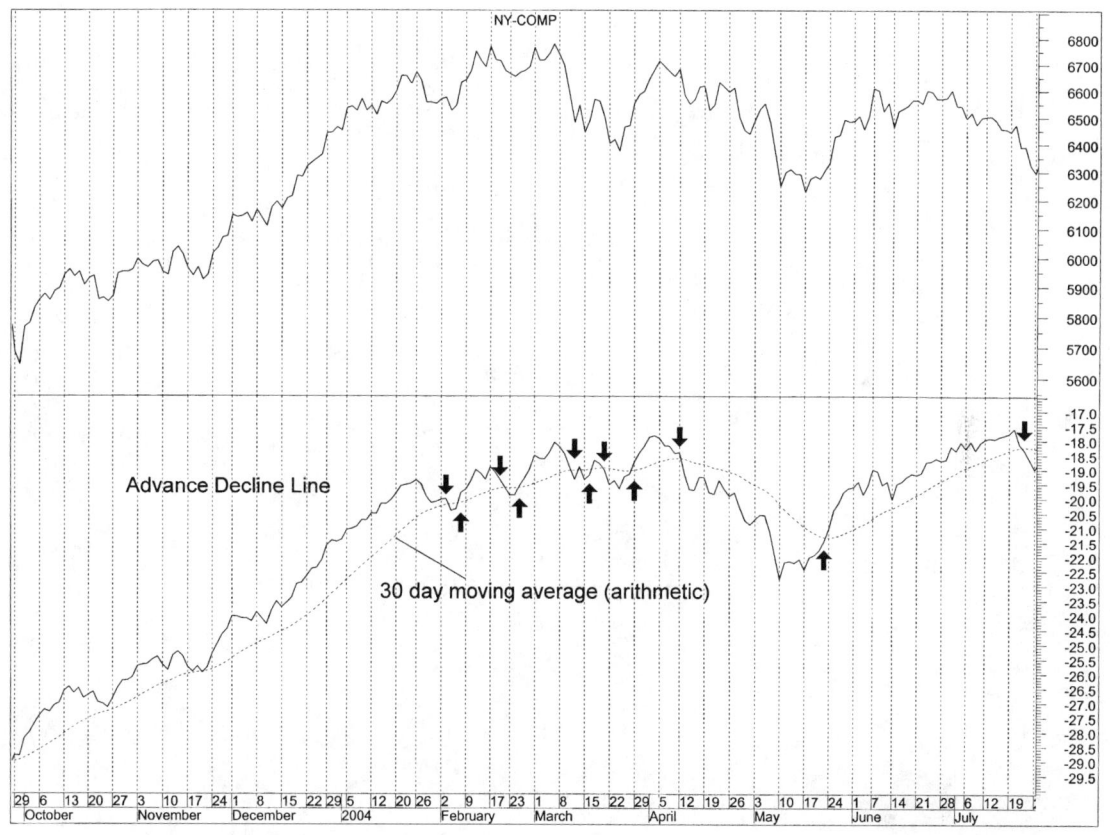

Examining this chart with an eye for detail shows that there were numerous whipsaws using this moving average. The February through March period shows 4–5 buy and sell signals—all in a 50–60 day period. Most traders/investors would selectively choose not to participate in a signal after this many whipsaws. You can see that eventually the signals yielded significant moves and probably resulted in overall profits.

What can be done to this "system" to improve it? The absolute worst thing to do is keep trying different moving average values until you find one that works best. That is curve fitting in its finest form. Pick a moving average based on the time frame that you normally like to trade. Remember that it will eliminate all cycles with a duration less than the average.

You can see that the whipsaws in Chart A-1 only lasted a few days. What if we did not act on a signal for two days before making the trade? In this particular example that would work well; however, in most cases it just would mean getting into a trade later and reducing the opportunity for

Chart A-2 Advance Decline Line Smoothed 7 Days and 30-Day Smooth.

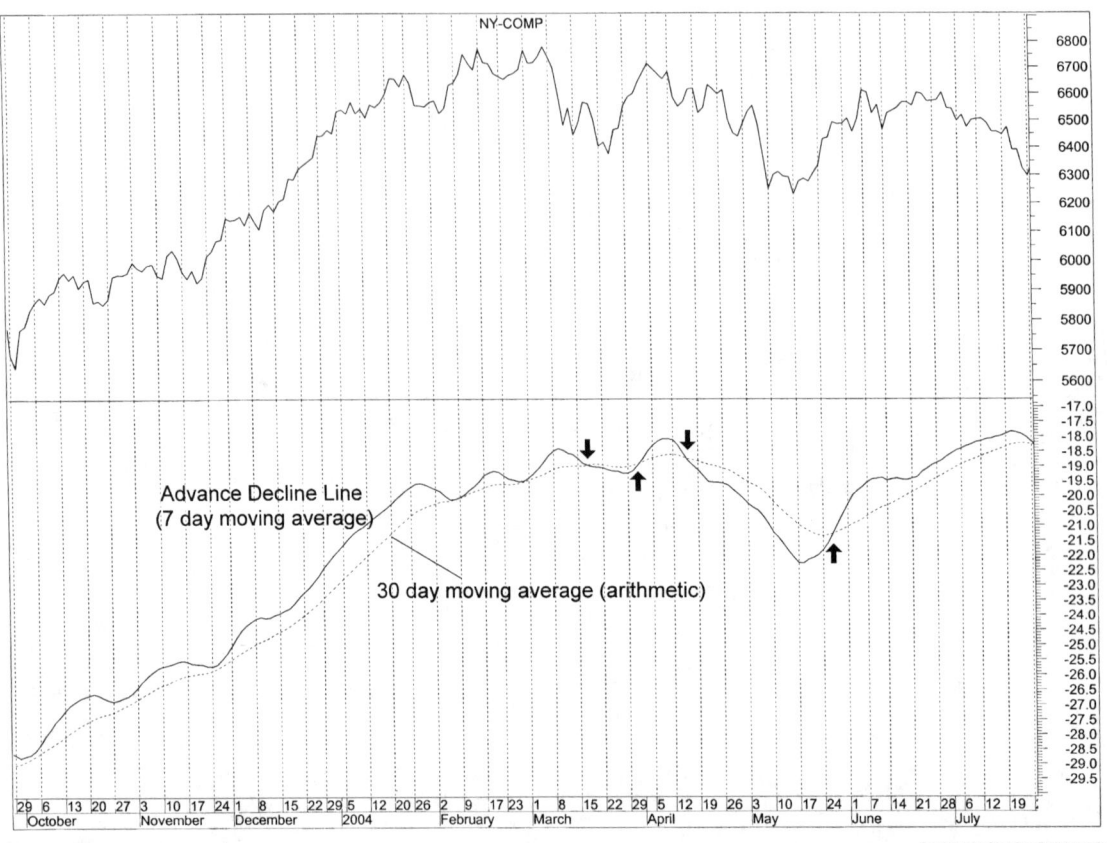

profit. Another way to reduce whipsaws would be to smooth the price data itself. If we smoothed the advance decline data with a 7-period average, what would happen? (See Chart A-2.)

We have successfully eliminated most of the whipsaws. Only one whipsaw still exists in March. Don't confuse a whipsaw with a trade that is not profitable.

Our simple crossover system has progressed into a dual moving average system. By smoothing the advance decline line and then using a larger moving average for signals, we have developed a fairly simple system that has eliminated most of the whipsaws. I want to state again that we have tried to eliminate whipsaws and have not made any attempt to curve-fit the data.

Conclusion

Do not get caught in the trap of optimization without a plan. Optimization can lead one to total failure in a short period of time. It is not the purpose of this article, but one needs to derive a concept from an idea, construct an indicator with variables, then select some data to test it on. Appendix B has a number of different ways to view data. A good procedure would be to optimize over one of the periods in that table, then test it over a few others. If the indicator held up, then you probably have something.

While keeping this somewhat basic and elementary, you can see how the thought process develops and why every indicator can also be turned into a trading system. Most analysis software programs allow you to call (direct reference) an indicator when writing the trading system code. Remember, most trading systems are only indicators with buy and sell points identified.

Appendix B
Time Frames for Analysis

Table B-1 gives a number of different time frames that can be used when performing market analysis. This information is invaluable when analyzing an indicator or a trading system. You must know how something will do in both bullish markets and bearish markets. Many times you will find something that works well in bull markets but is entirely too risky to use all the time because it really falls apart in bearish moves. When developing and testing an indicator, ensure that you use enough different data samples to avoid curve fitting.

Table B–1
Time Frames for Analysis

Secular Stock Markets

Bull		Bear	
Start	End	Start	End
1896	1906	1906	1921
1921	1929	1929	1949
1949	1966	1966	1982
1982	2000	2000	

Bull and Bear Markets

Bull		Bear	
Start	End	Start	End
	1901	1901	1921
1921	1929	1929	1932
1932	1936	1936	1941
1941	1966	1966	1982
1982	2000	2000	2002
2002	2004	2004	

Stock Market Cycles

Bullish		Bearish	
Start	End	Start	End
Apr-42	May-46	May-46	Jun-49
Jun-49	Jan-53	Jan-53	Sep-53
Sep-53	Jul-56	Jul-56	Dec-57
Dec-57	Jul-59	Jul-59	Oct-60
Oct-60	Dec-61	Dec-61	Jun-62
Jun-62	Jan-66	Jan-66	Oct-66
Oct-66	Dec-68	Dec-68	Jun-70
Jun-70	Apr-71	Apr-71	Nov-71

(continued)

Stock Market Cycles

Bullish		Bearish	
Start	End	Start	End
Nov-71	Jan-73	Jan-73	Dec-74
Dec-74	Sep-76	Sep-76	Mar-78
Mar-78	Nov-80	Nov-80	Jul-82
Jul-82	Oct-83	Oct-83	Jul-84
Jul-84	Aug-87	Aug-87	Dec-87
Dec-87	Jun-00	Jun-90	Oct-90
Oct-90	Jun-98	Jun-98	Aug-98
Aug-98	Aug-00	Aug-00	Sep-02
Sep-02	Jan-04	Jan-04	Aug-04
Aug-04			

Political Cycles

Republican		Democrat	
Start	End	Start	End
1929	1932	1932	1952
1952	1960	1960	1968
1968	1976	1976	1980
1980	1992	1992	2000
2000			

Business Cycles

Expansion		Contraction	
Start	End	Start	End
		Aug-29	Mar-33
Mar-33	May-37	May-37	Jun-38
Jun-38	Feb-45	Feb-45	Oct-45
Oct-45	Nov-48	Nov-48	Oct-49
Oct-49	Jul-53	Jul-53	May-54
May-54	Aug-57	Aug-57	Apr-58
Apr-58	Apr-60	Apr-60	Feb-61
Feb-61	Dec-69	Dec-69	Nov-70
Nov-70	Nov-73	Nov-73	Mar-75
Mar-75	Jan-80	Jan-80	Jul-80
Jul-80	Jul-81	Jul-81	Nov-82
Nov-82	Jul-90	Jul-90	Mar-91
Mar-91	Mar-01	Mar-01	Nov-01
Nov-01			

Interest Rate Trends

Bottom (start rising)	Top (start falling)
	6/12/1953
6/25/1954	10/25/1957
6/27/1958	1/15/1960
11/18/1960	9/30/1966
6/23/1967	1/23/1970
4/2/1971	8/13/1971
3/3/1972	9/13/1974
1/14/1977	4/18/1980
7/11/1980	6/12/1981
11/5/1982	9/28/1984
9/26/1986	4/21/1989
10/30/1992	2/3/1995
11/13/1998	11/24/2000
7/18/2003	

Time Frames for Analysis 279

Most of the information in Table B-1 is available on the Internet and in investment books. Here are some URLs (Web site addresses) that will help. Keep in mind that these can change and they must be typed into your browser's address window accurately. Google search offers another good way to find data on the internet.

Business Cycles—http://www.nber.org/cycles.html
Secular Stock Markets—http://www.crestmontresearch.com/pdfs/Stock%20Secular%20Chart.pdf
Bull and Bear Markets—Suggest using a search engine to obtain up-to-date information. Bear markets are generally thought of as when the market drops by 20 percent or more. Some references use 15 percent. Bull markets historically have had increases of 50 percent.
Stock Market Cycles—use a 20 percent zigzag on the market of your choice. If you want more trading action, use a 15 percent zigzag. Keep in mind that zigzag (a name Equis gave to the indicator) and filtered waves (the name Arthur Merrill used when he first introduced the concept) cannot be used to project prices. They only reflect the information on the actual prices, and the last leg is hypothetical. The last cycle on this indicator is only saying that prices have reversed at least as much as the indicator is asking for. Chart B–1 uses 20 percent filtered wave.

Chart B-1 Market Cycles—20 Percent.

Chart B-2 90-Day T-Bills Rate of Change.

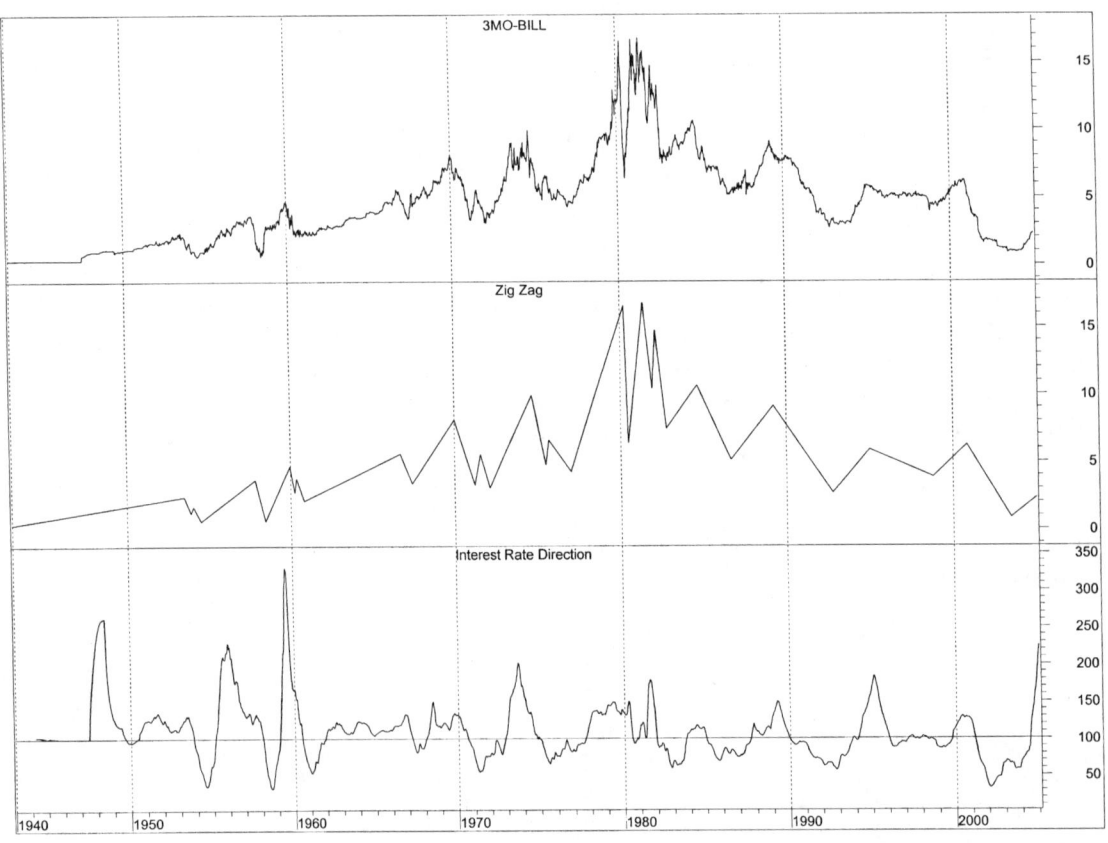

Political Cycles—almost any political Web site or history book.

Interest Rate Trends—use weekly 90-day T-Bill yields and the zigzag (filtered wave) of 30 percent This is a technique of showing changes in direction of only moves greater than a selected percentage; in this case it was 30 percent. That's 30 percent of the underlying index, not 30 percent interest rates. Or you can use a 52-week rate of change smoothed by 13 weeks. Chart B–2 shows both.

References

Dewey, Edward R. *Cycles, the Mysterious Forces that Trigger Events*. The Foundation for the Study of Cycles, Irvine, CA, 1971 This book was written with Og Mandino.

Alexander, Michael. *Stock Cycles*. Lincoln, NE: Writers Club Press, 2000.

Merrill, Arthur. *Filtered Waves*. Chappaqua, NY. The Analysis Press, 1977. This book is privately offered by John McGinley at: Technical Trends, 55 Liberty St., Wilton, CT 06897. $20 delivered or $75 autographed by Art Merrill.

Appendix C
Miscellaneous Information

This appendix contains miscellaneous references and source information that I use and believe reliable. This is sort of a "catch all" for things I believe should be here, plus things I have learned over the years and wish to share.

Selected Smoothing Constants, Trend %, and Related Periods

Below are some common values used to smooth data using exponential averages:

Periods	Constant	Trend %
10	.18	18%
19	.10	10%
39	.05	5%
50	.039	3.9%
100	.0198	1.98%
150	.013	1.3%
200	.01	1%

If you know the number of days (periods) that you want to use, just divide 2 by that number plus 1. For example, if you wanted 39 days, $2 / (39 + 1) = 2 / 40 = .05 = 5\%$.

Breadth Data Sources

Pinnacle Data Corp
1016 Plank Road
Webster, NY 14580
(800) 724-4903
pinnacle@netacc.net
www.pinnacledata.com

Author Note: Pinnacle is the data source used for the analysis and indicators in this book. Mention this book and you will get a 25 percent discount on your first order.

Reuters DataLink
(800) 842–3045
sales@reutersdatalink.com
http://www.reutersdatalink.com

Dial Data
Track Data Corporation
95 Rockwell Place
Brooklyn, NY 11217
(800) 275–5544
dialdata@trackdata.com

Recommended Reading on Breadth

Technical Analysis from A to Z by Steven Achelis
The Encyclopedia of Technical Market Indicators by Robert Colby
Stock Market Logic by Norman Fosback
Winning on Wall Street by Martin Zweig
The Research Driven Investor by Tim Hayes. (this is out of print, but may be available through online stores)

And if you really aren't convinced that technical analysis works, try these two:

The Visual Investor by John Murphy
The Art of Low Risk Investing by Michael Zahorchak. (This great book is out of print. Pay anything for it. It is good.)

Software for Breadth Analysis

SpyGlass 2.5 Add-on for MetaStock

Calculates standard breadth measures such as New 250-day Highs, New 250-day Lows, Advancers, Decliners, etc., plus calculates more unusual breadth numbers such as Number of Stocks above 50-day Moving Average. User can customize many of the periods and run calculations in a batch automatically at night. SpyGlass also calculates External Relative Strength (a percentile performance rank of all stocks versus all other stocks), and Folder Averages (a price-weighted average of all of the securities in a data folder).

www.DeBry.com
support@debry.com
4376 S. 700 E. Suite 204
Salt Lake City, UT 84107

ULTRA Financial Systems

ULTRA contains over 100 fully disclosed market timing systems for stocks, bonds, and gold. A historical database starting in 1942 is included that contains over 100 items of financial data. ULTRA allows for historical testing of systems, combinations of systems, and batch automation.

P.O. Box 3938
Breckenridge CO 80424
970-453-4956

MetaStock by Equis International

MetaStock software comes in an end-of-day (EOD) version and a real time (Professional) version.

90 South 400 West
Suite 620
Salt Lake City, UT 84101
www.equis.com
sales@equis.com
800-508-9180

Internet Charts for Breadth Analysis

Sharefin
c/o Nick Laird
PO Box 224
Freshwater
Cairns, 4870
Queensland Australia
http://www.sharelynx.com/chartstemp/historical.php#US

MasterData

MasterData provides historical composite data on numerous Exchange Traded Funds (ETFs) as well as several market indices. This data, similar to that provided daily by the NYSE, AMEX, and NASDAQ on their broad exchange composites, allows the application of breadth and composite indicators to these more focused markets. For MetaStock users, a plug-in allows full integration of this data into their analyses. Additionally, data is available in MS Excel (.csv) and text (.txt) formats.
www.masterdata.com

Bibliography

Books

Achelis, Steven B. *Technical Analysis from A to Z.* New York: McGraw-Hill, 1995.
Appel, Gerald. *Winning Market Systems.* Greenville: Traders Press, 1973.
Arms, Richard W. Jr. *The Arms Index (TRIN).* Dow Jones-Irwin, 1989.
Bretz, W.G. *Juncture Recognition in the Stock Market.* Vantage Press, 1972.
Chande, Tushar S. and Kroll, Stanley. *The New Technical Trader.* John Wiley & Sons, 1994.
Colby, Robert W. *The Encyclopedia of Technical Market Indicators.* New York : McGraw-Hill, 2003.
Davis, Ned. *Being Right or Making Money.* Ned Davis Research, 1991.
Fosback, Norman G. *Stock Market Logic*, Fort Lauderdale, FL: The Institute for Economic Research, Inc., 1976.
Haller, Gilbert. *The Haller Theory of Stock Market Trends.* West Palm Beach: Gilbert Haller, 1965.
Hayes, Timothy. *The Research Driven Investor.* New York: McGraw-Hill, 2001.
Heiby, Walter. *Stock Market Profits through Dynamic Synthesis.* Chicago : The Institute of Dynamic Synthesis, 1965.
Investor's Intelligence, Inc. *The New Encyclopedia of Stock Market Techniques.* Larchmont, NY, 1985.
Lloyd, Humphrey E. D. *The Moving Balance System, A New Technique for Stock and Option Trading.* Brightwaters, NY,:Windsor Books, 1976.
Lloyd, Humphrey E. D., *The RSL Market Timing System.* Brightwaters, NY: Windsor Books, 1991.
Mamis, Justin. *When to Sell.* New York: Farrar Straus Giroux, 1977.
McClellan, Sherman and Marian. *Patterns for Profit.* Lakewood, WA: McClellan Financial Publications, Inc., 1989.
Merrill, Arthur A. *Behavior of Prices on Wall Street.* Analysis Press, 1984.
Murphy, John J. *Technical Analysis of the Financial Markets.* New York Institute of Finance, 1999.
O'Neil, William J., *How to Make Money in Stocks.* New York: McGraw-Hill, 1988.
Pring, Martin J. *Technical Analysis Explained.* New York: McGraw-Hill, 1985.
Pring, Martin J. *Martin Pring on Market Momentum,* International Institute for Economic Research and Probus Publishing, 1993.
Stewart, Joseph T. *Dynamic Stock Options Trading.* New York : John Wiley and Sons, 1981.
Teweles, Richard J. *The Commodities Futures Game,* New York: McGraw-Hill, 1974.
Weinstein, Stan. *Secrets for Profiting in Bull and Bear Markets.* Dow Jones-Irwin, Homewood, IL, 1988.
Zahorchak, Michael G. *The Art of Low Risk Investing.* New York: Van Nostrand Reinhold Company, 1977.
Zweig, Martin E. *Winning on Wall Street.* New York: Warner Books, 1986.

Software / Online Charting

Online—www.StockCharts.com, www.decisionpoint.com
Desktop—MetaStock, Equis International

Software Manuals

CompuTrac, 1985
MetaStock Professional 9.0 User Manual, Equis International

Web Sites

Carl Swenlin's Decision Point—www.decisionpoint.com
Best charting on the Web—www.stockcharts.com
Peter Eliades Stock Market Cycles—www.stockmarketcycles.com
McClellan Financial Publications—www.mcoscillator.com
Paul Merriman's Fund Advisor—www.fundadvice.com

Periodicals

Stocks and Commodities
Futures

Other Publications/Newsletters/Etc.

Omaha, Bill, 1991. "How to avoid sinking with the Titanic," *Equis Monitor*, Vol. 6, June/July.
McMillan, Larry. *The Option Strategist*
McClellan, Tom. *The McClellan Market Report*
Miekka, James. *The Sudbury Bull and Bear Report*

Index

Note: Boldface numbers indicate illustrations and tables.

1% Advance Decline Line, 49–51, **50, 51**
1% Exponential Moving Average (EMA) of advance declines (Swenlin), 50–51, **51**

A/D Volume New High, New Low System, 229
Absolute Breadth Index, 64, **65**
    adjusted, 65–68, **66–68**
absolute value, 14
accumulated/summed (sigma), 14
Achelis, Steven, 16, 35, 36, 92, 198, 211
Adjusted Absolute Breadth Index, 65–68, **66–68**
Adjusted Total Issues Advance Decline Line, 58, **59**
advance–decline difference indicators, 7, 31–89, **32–35**
    McClellan indicators as, 243, 246–247
    relationships between, 7
Advance Decline Diffusion Index, 113–114, **114**
Advance Decline Divergence Oscillator, 111–113, **113**, 121. *See also* Disparity Index
Advance Decline Index (Eakle), 51–53, **52, 53**
Advance Decline Line, 43–49, **43–48**, 201, 272–274, **273, 274**
    1%, 49–51, **50, 51**
    adjusted total issues, 58, **59**
    Big Movers Only, 59–61, **60, 61**
    Bolton, 55–58, **56, 57**
    divergence and, 46
    downward bias in, 47
    liquidity and, 46–47
    McClellan indicators and, 246–247, **247**
    normalized, 53–55, **54, 55**
    oscillator, 61–63, **62, 63**
Advance Decline Line 1%, 49–51, **50, 51**
Advance Decline Line Oscillator, 61–63, **62, 63**
Advance Decline Miscellaneous Indicators, 109–130
Advance Decline Overbought Oversold, 34–39, **36–39**
Advance Decline Power, 68–70, **69, 70**
advance decline ratio indicators, 91–107
Advance Decline Ratio, 58, **59**, 91–93, **92, 93**
Advance–Decline, New High, New Low Market System, 229
advances, 11–12, 21, **22**
    advance decline difference indicators for, 31–89
    as percentage of total issues, 7–10, **8**, 21, **23**
    bull markets and, 21
    McClellan indicators and, 243, 246–247
    relationships with declines and, 7
Advances/Issues Traded, 109–111, **110, 111**
Advancing Issues TRIX, 118
advantages and disadvantages of breadth, 13

Alphier, James, 39, 119, 199–200
American Stock Exchange, 1
anchoring, 16
Appel Advance Decline Line Oscillator, 62–63, **63**
Appel, Gerald, 33, 62–63, 72, 96, 258
    Breadth Climax and, 115, **116**, 117
    High Low Logic Index and, 157–159, **156–159**, 159
    New Highs/New Lows Ratio and, 141–146, **141–147**
    Up Volume indicator and, 164–166, **164–166**
applications for market breadth indicators, 1
arithmetic averages. *See* simple moving averages
Arms Index, 6, 16, 195–203, **196–202**
    Eliades New TRIN and, 215, **216**
    Market Thrust indicator and, 222
    Moving Balance Indicator and, 231
Arms Open Index, 203–206, **204, 205**
Arms, Richard W., 179, 222
    Arms Index and, 6, 16, 195–203, **196–202**
Art of Low Risk Investing, The, 87
Aspray, Thomas, 197
Astute Investor newsletter, 6
Ayres, Leonard P., 7, 43, 58, 119

bear markets, 6, 7–10, **9, 10**
    Eliades Sign of the Bear and, 100–102, **101**
    time frames for analysis of, 277–280, **277–280**
Beasley, Don, 255–262, 268
Big Movers Only Advance Decline Line, 59–61, **60, 61**
Bollinger bands, Arms Open index and, 204–205, **205**
Bolton Advance Decline Line, 55–58, **56, 57**
Bolton Tremblay, 55–58, **56, 57**
Bolton, Hamilton, 55–58
Bottoms of markets, 263
breadth analysis, 256
    price vs., 12
    relationships among indicators of, 6–7
Breadth Climax, 115, **116**
Breadth Consensus Index, 268–269, **269**
Breadth Thrust Continuation, 96–99, **97, 98**
Breadth Thrust Indicator, 94–96, **95, 96**
Bretz TRIN-5 indicator, 206–207, **208, 209**
Bretz, W.G., 208
broad market indicators, 1
bull markets, 6, 7–10, **9, 10**, 21
    advances and declines in, 21
    new highs and new lows in, 21–22
    time frames for analysis, 277–280, **277–280**
Burk, Mike, 149, 154, 183–184
business cycles, time frames for analysis of, **278**, 279
buy signals, McClellan indicators and, 254, **254**
capitalization-weighted indexes, 12

Carlin, Richard, 113–114
Carroll, Paul, 72
Cash Flow Index, 207–209, **210**
categories of indicators, 20–21
Chande, Tushar, 54, 221
Changed Volume Indicator, 167–169, **169**
charting, 16–17
    Internet sources for, 283
    trendlines in, 5–6
Charting the Market, 77
Cohen, Abraham, 142
Colby, Robert, 67, 94, 102
Commodities Futures Game, The, 3–4
common vs. uncommon issues, McClellan indicators and, 243–244
common-stocks-only breadth indicators, 13
components of breadth, 11–12, 263, **264–267**
composite indicators, 195–242
Composite Tape Index, 209–213, **211, 212, 213**
Coppock Breadth Indicator, 70–72, **71**
Coppock Curve, 71–72
Coppock, Edwin S.C., 70–71
Creel, Clifford L., 240–241
Cross Your Arms indicator, 197, **197**
cumulate, 14
cumulative indicators, 13, 14
Cumulative Volume Ratio, 179–181, **180, 181**
cycles, stock market, **277–278**, 279, **279**

Daily A–D New High, New Low Market System, 229
daily vs. weekly data, 12–13, **13**
data and statistics, and sources of, 256, 260, 281–282, 283
declines, 11–12, 21, **22**
    advance decline difference indicators for, 31–89
    as percentage of total issues, 7–10, **8**, 21, **23**
    bull markets and, 21
    McClellan indicators and, 243, 246–247
    relationships with advances and, 7
    TRIX, 116–118, **117, 118**
Declining Issues TRIX, 116–118, **117, 118**
Desmond, Paul, 13
detrending, 14
Dial Data, 282
differences indicators, 13
Diffusion Index. *See* Advance Decline Diffusion Index
discipline in investing, 257–258
Disparity Index, 119, **120, 121**. *See also* Advance Decline Divergence Oscillator
divergence, 14

Advance Decline Divergence Oscillator and, 111–113, **113**
    Advance Decline Line and, 46
Divergence Oscillator. *See* Advance Decline Divergence Oscillator
Dominant Index Indicator, 256, **257**
Dominant Market concept, 260–261, **260**
double 9 up/down volume, 190–192, **191, 192**
Dow Jones Industrial Average, 16–17
Dow Theory, 7
Dow Theory Letters, 58
Dow, Charles H., 7, 119
down volume, 7, 11–12, 22–23, **26**
    adjusted for total volume, 23, **28**
    as percentage of total issues, 9–10, **10**
    double 9 concept in, 190–192, **191, 192**
    indicators for, 163–193
    McClellan indicators and, 243
    nine-to-one ratio of, to up volume, 190–192, **191, 192**
    semilog scaling in, 23, **27**
Down Volume Indicator, 166–167, **167, 168**
Duarte Market Thrust Indicator (BMTI), 99, **100**
Duarte, Joe, 99
Dynamic Stock Option Trading, 231
Dynamic Synthesis, 120–124, **122, 123, 124**
Dysart Positive Negative Volume, 213–215, **214**
Dysart, Paul, 39, 213

Eakle Advance Decline Index, 51–53, **52, 53**
Eliades New TRIN, 215, **216**
Eliades Sign of the Bear, 100–102, **101**
Eliades, Peter, 100, 203, 215
Encyclopedia of Technical Market Indicators, The, 67
Equalization, Theory of, 39
Equis International, 283
exponential moving averages, 14–15
    Haurlan index and, 72–74, **73–75**
    McClellan oscillator and, 76–77
exponential oscillators and summation index, relationship of, 247–254

favorite breadth indicators, list of, 267–268
Favors, Jerry, 207
Fibonacci series, 4–5
flexibility in investing strategies, 257–258
fluctuations (noise), 17
Flying Titanic, 239, **240**
format of individual breadth indicators, 19–20
Fosback, Norman G., 36, 64, 65, 92
    High Low Logic Index and, 155–159, **156–159**

Index

Fugler Advance–Decline, 42–43, **42**
Fugler, George, 42
fundamental analysis, 2

Gammage, Kennedy, 77, 218
"going nowhere" indicator, 64, **65**, 65
golden ratio, 4–5. *See also* Fibonacci series
Granville, Joseph, 68, 182, 213
group dynamics and market prediction, 3
Growth Fund Guide, 255

Haller Theory, 215–218, **218**
Haller, Gilbert, 215–218
harmonic mean, 6
Haurlan index, 72–74, **73–75**
Haurlan, P.N. (Pete), 72, 77
Hayes, Tim, 133, 152, 154
    Arms Index and, 200–201
    New Highs/New Lows Ratio, 144–146, **141–147**
Heiby, Walter, 120–124, 125
    Dynamic Synthesis indicator and, 120–124, **122, 123, 124**
    Unchanged Issues indicator and, 124–128, **125–128**
herd mentality, 3
high low difference indicators, 131
    New High New Low Line, 134, **135, 136**
    New Highs and New Lows Derivations, 137–140, **140, 141**
    New Highs and New Lows Oscillator, 134–137, **137–139**
    New Highs New Lows, 131–134, **132, 133**
High Low Logic Index, 155–159, **156–159**
high low ratio indicators, 131
    New Highs/New Lows Ratio, 140–146, **141–147**
High Low Validation Index, 143
High Low Validation, 160–161, **161**
Hindenburg Omen, 218–221, **220**
How to Make Money in Stocks, 188
Hughes Breadth Momentum Oscillator, 101–104, **103, 104**
Hughes, James F., 7, 58, 102, 119
Hutson, Jack, 116

indicators, 13–16, 271–272
    categories of, 20–21
    definition of, 4
    trading systems vs., 271–275
industry group analysis, 1
information necessary to breadth analysis, 11–17
    advantages and disadvantages of breadth and, 13
    breadth vs. price in, 12
    components of breadth and, 11–12, 263, **264–267**
    daily vs. weekly data in, 12–13, **13**
    indicators in, 13–16
    normalizing an indicator in, 14
    terminology in, 13–16
interest rate trends, time frames for analysis of, **278**, 280, **280**
interest-sensitive issues, 13, 259–260
Intermediate Term Breadth Momentum Oscillator, 83–86, **85**
Intermediate Term Volume Momentum Oscillator, 175–176, **177**
Internet charts for breadth analysis, 283
investing philosophies, 256–262
Investor's Business Daily, 188

%K stochastic indicator, 15, 138
Kinsman Smoothed Advance–Decline, 38, **39**
Kinsman, Robert, 38
Kuhn, Bill, 199–200

lagging indicators, 5
Lane, George, 15, 53, 138
Lawlor, John C., 179
Leonardo da Vinci, 4
Lindsay, George, 37
liquidity, Advance Decline Line and, 46–47
list of breadth indicators, 24–29
Lloyd, Humphrey E.D., 230–234
logic
    High Low Logic Index, 155–159, **156–159**
    Low High Logic Index, 158–159,1**59**
Long Term Capital Management, 244
Low High Logic Index, 158–159,1**59**

Mamis, Justin, 33
market indices, Advance Decline Line and, 45
market systems, Meyers, 229–230
Market Thrust, 221–224, **222**
Market Thrust Oscillator, 221–222, **223, 225**
Market Thrust Summation, 221–222, **224**
market timing, 2
market-value weighted indexes, 12
Martin, Peter, 261
Mason, William, 207, 208, 234
MasterData, 283
mathematics, 4
McClellan indicators, 243–254
    advance decline and, 243, 246–247

Advance Decline Line and, 246–247, **247**
buy signals in, 254, **254**
common vs. uncommon issues and, 243–244
exponential oscillators and summation index of, relationship with, 247–254
McClellan Oscillator in, 74–78, **76**, 221, 224–227, **226, 227**, 243, 248–253, **249**, 256
McClellan Summation Index, 78–83, **79, 80**, 173, **174**, 227–229, **228**, 221, 261, **262**, 268, **269**
McClellan Summation Index in, buy signal in, 254, **254**
McClellan Volume Oscillator, 171–173, **172**
Miekka McClellan Summation Index, 80–81, **80**
Nasdaq and, 244–246, **246**
neutral point concept and, 250–253, **251, 252**
New York Stock Exchange and, 243–244, **244**
ratio-adjusted summation indices (RASIs) and, 243, **244**
Russell 2000 and, 246, **246**
T-bonds and, 244, **245**
up and down volume ratio in, 243
McClellan Oscillator, 74–78, **76**, 221, 243, 256
summation index (MCOSI) of, 248–253, **249**
with Volume, 224–227, **226, 227**
McClellan Summation Index, 78–83, **79, 80**, 221, 261, **262**, 268, **269**
buy signal in, 254, **254**
with Volume, 173, **174**, 227–229, **228**
McClellan Volume Oscillator, 171–173, **172**
McClellan, Marian, 74, 77, 78, 256
McClellan Volume Oscillator and, 171–173, **172**
McClellan, Sherman, 13, 74, 77, 78, 243, 256
McClellan Volume Oscillator and, 171–173, **172**
McClellan, Tom, 13, 44, 78, 81, 243
McGinley Advance Decline Power, 68–70, **69, 70**
McGinley, John, 13, 40, 52, 68, 203
McGinley Advance Decline Power, 68–70, **69, 70**
New Highs/New Lows Ratio, 142–146, **141–147**
Up Volume indicator and, 164–166, **164–166**
McMillan, Larry, 13, 188
Meibuhr, Stuart, 222–223
Merrill, Arthur, 13
Advance Decline Divergence Oscillator and, 111–113, **113**
Arms Index and, 201
Fugler advance–decline and, 42–43
New Highs/New Lows Ratio, 142–146, **141–147**
plurality index and, 41
Merriman Breadth Model, 83, **84**
Merriman Volume Model, 173–175, **175**

Merriman, Paul, 83, 173, 175
MetaStock, 17, 282, 283
Meyers Systems, 229–230
Meyers, Dennis, 229, 236, 239–240
Miekka McClellan Summation Index, 80–81, **80**
Miekka, James R., 218–219, 243, 247, 254
McClellan Summation Index and, 79–83
Miekka, Richard G., 247
modeling, 256
momentum, 15. *See also* rate of change
Hughes Breadth Momentum Oscillator, 101–104, **103, 104**
Swenlin IT Volume Momentum Oscillator, 175–176, **177**
Momentum Index (Weinstein), 49–51, **50**
money management, 255–256
Morgan, Gene, 77
Morris, Greg, 59, 160, 181, 224
moving averages, 6
exponential, 14–15
simple, 14
trading system using, 272–274
Moving Balance Indicator, 230–234, **232, 233, 234**
multicollinearity, 17

Nasdaq, 1, 256, 260, 268
Advance Decline Line and, 47
McClellan indicators and, 244–246, **246**
Nasdaq 100 (NDX), 12
McClellan indicators and, 245–246, **246**
Nasdaq Advance Decline model, 256, **258**
Nasdaq Composite Index, 12
Nasdaq High Low Model, 256, **259**
Ned Davis Research, 133
neutral point concept, McClellan indicators and, 250–253, **251, 252**
New High New Low Line, 134, **135, 136**
new highs, 6, 7, 9, 11–12, 21–22, **24**
as percentage of total issues, 9–10, **9**, 21–22, **25**, 150–153, **151, 152**
bull markets and, 21–22
indicators for, 131–161
New Highs % Total Issues, 150–153, **151, 152**
New Highs and New Lows Derivations, 137–140, **140, 141**
New Highs and New Lows Indicator, 146–150, **148–150**
New Highs and New Lows Oscillator, 134–137, **137–139**
New Highs New Lows Indicator, 131–134, **132, 133**
New Highs/New Lows Ratio, 140–146, **141–147**
new lows, 7, 9, 11–12, 21–22, **24**

Index

as percentage of total issues, 9–10, **9**, 21–22, **25**, 153–155, **154, 155**
    bull markets and, 21–22
    indicators for, 131–161
New Lows % Total Issues, 153–155, **154, 155**
New Technical Trader, The, 222
New York Stock Exchange Composite Index, 1, 12, 16, 256, 259–260
    Advance Decline Line and, 43–49, **43–48**
    McClellan indicators and, 243–244, **244**
nine–to–one ratio of up to down volume, 190–192, **191, 192**
Normalized Advance Decline Line, 53–55, **54, 55**
normalizing an indicator, 14, 15
Nurock, Robert, 6, 37
    Arms Index and, 203

O'Neil, William, 188
Omaha, Bill, 236–240
On Balance Volume (OBV), Up Down OBV, 182–183, **182–184**
On Balance Volume Indicator, 213
Open Arms Indicator, 222
oscillators, 5, 6, 15
    Advance Decline Divergence, 111–113, **113**
    Advance Decline Line, 61–63, **62, 63**
    Arms Index as, 197–203, **197–202**
    Cross Your Arms indicator, 197, **197**
    exponential type, summation index of, relationship with, 247–254
    Hughes Breadth Momentum, 101–104, **103, 104**
    Intermediate Term Breadth Momentum, 83–86, **85**
    McClellan, 74–78, **76**, 243, 248–253, **249**, 256
    McClellan Volume, 171–173, **172**
    neutral point concept and, 250–253, **251, 252**
    New Highs and New Lows, 134–137, **137–139**
    Swenlin IT Breadth Momentum, 83–86, **85**
    Swenlin IT Volume Momentum, 175–176, **177**
    Swenlin Trading Oscillator on Volume, 176–178, **178**
    Swenlin Trading Oscillator on Breadth, 86, **87**
    Thrust, 221–222, **223, 225**
overbought/oversold, 15, 31–39, **32–35, 36–39**
overlay, 15

Pacioli, Luca, 4
Panic Thrust, 104–105, **105**
Patterns for Profit, 76
percentage indicators, 13, 15
Peterson Up Down Volume Ratio, 189, **189**
Peterson, Dennis, 188

Pinnacle Data Corporation, 281
plurality index, 39–41, **40, 41**
PMFM, Inc., 255, 258, 261, 268, 302
political cycles, time frames for analysis of, **278**, 280
Positive and Negative Issues Traded Indexes, 213
Positive Negative Volume (Dysart), 213–215, **214**
power, advance decline, 68–70, **69, 70**
price vs. breadth, 12, 258–259
price-based models, 258–259, 258
Pring McClellan Summation Index, 82, **82**
Pring, Martin, 57
    McClellan Summation Index and, 82, **82**
Professional Tape Reader newsletter, 33

Raff, Gilbert, 116
rate of change, 16. *See also* momentum, 16
    averaging of, 6
ratio indicators, 13, 91–107
ratio-adjusted summation indices (RASIs), McClellan indicators and, 243, **244**, 243
ratios, 4–5, 16
recommended reading, 282
relationships among breadth indicators, 6–7
Relative Strength Index (RSI), 138, **140**
research, 257, 260
resistance, 16
Reuters DataLink, 282
risk–reward analysis, 2
Rotnem, Ralph, 39
Rukeyser, Louis, 6
Russell 2000
    McClellan indicators and, 246, **246**
Russell Growth, 256
Russell Value, 256
Russell, Richard, 13
    adjusted total issues Advance Decline Line and, 58, **59**

S&P 500 Index, 12, 256
Schultz AT, Advances/Issues Traded, 109–111, **110, 111**
sector analysis, 1
secular stock markets, time frames for analysis of, **277**, 279
Shaw, Alan, 39, 40
    Plurality Index and, 41
Short Term Trading Index (STIX), 105–107, **106, 107**, 196. *See also* Arms Index
simple moving averages, 14
smoothing, 16, 32, 271, 274, **274**
    constants, trend percentages, related periods for, 281, **281**

software for breadth analysis, 282
speculation, 4
SpyGlass software, 282
Stevens, Leigh, 164
Stewart, Joseph, 231–233
STIX. *See* Short Term Trading Index (STIX)
stochastic indicator, 15, 138
stock market cycles, **277–278**, 279, **279**
Stocks and Commodities magazine, 116, 188, 199, 202, 207, 229, 237, 272
summation indexes. *See also* McClellan Summation Index
    McClellan Oscillator (MCOSI), 248–253, **249**
    McClellan, 78–83, **79**
    exponential oscillators and, relationship with, 247–254
support, 16
Sweeney, John, 272
Swenlin IT Breadth Momentum Oscillator, 83–86, **85**
Swenlin IT Volume Momentum Oscillator, 175–176, **177**
Swenlin McClellan Summation Index, 81, **81**
Swenlin Trading Oscillator on Breadth, 86, **87**
Swenlin Trading Oscillator on Volume, 176–178, **178**
Swenlin, Carl, 13, 49–51
    Arms Index (inverted) and, 207, **209**
    IT Breadth Momentum Oscillator and, 83–86, **85**
    McClellan Summation Index and, 79–83
    Swenlin IT Volume Momentum Oscillator and, 175–176, **177**
    Swenlin Trading Oscillator on Breadth and, 86, **87**
    Swenlin Trading Oscillator on Volume and, 176–178, **178**
Systems and Forecasts, 255

T-bonds, McClellan indicators and, 244, **245**
tactical models, 258
technical analysis, 2–4, 255
Technical Analysis from A to Z, 16
Technical Index, 234–236, **235**, **236**
technical indicators, 4–5, 271
Technical Trends, 13, 40
Technician, The (software), 211–212
terminology, 13–16
Teweles, Richard, 3–4
Theory of Equalization, 39
Thrust Oscillator, 221–222, **223**, **225**
time frames for analysis, 277–280, **277–280**
    bull and bear markets, **277**, 279
    business cycles, **278**, 279
    interest rate trends, **278**, 280, **280**

political cycles, **278**, 280
    secular stock markets, **277**, 279
    stock market cycles, **277–278**, 279, **279**
timing. *See* market timing
Titanic Syndrome, 236–240, **238–240**
Tops of markets, 263
total issues, 11–12
total volume, 11–12
trading systems vs. indicators, 271–275
Trend Exhaustion Index, 240–242, **241**
Trend Explosion Index, 242, **242**
trend-capturing research, 260–261, **261**
Trendex Very Long Term Risk Index for Listed Stocks, 71–72
trendlines on charts, 5–6
TRIN. *See* Arms Index
Trin10 indicator, 205, **206**. *See also* Arms Open index
TRIX, 116–118, **117, 118**
Turbo A/D, New High New Low Market System, 230

Ulcer Index, 261–262
ULTRA Financial Systems, 283
unchanged, 11–12
    as percentage of total issues, 7–10, **8**
    Unchanged Issues indicator, 124–128, **125–128**
Unchanged Issues, 124–128, **125–128**
Up and Down Volume Indicator, 169–171, **170**
Up Down OBV, 181–183, **182–184**
up volume, 7, 11–12, 22–23, **26**
    adjusted for total volume, 23, **28**
    as percentage of total issues, 9–10, **10**
    double 9 concept in, 190–192, **191, 192**
    indicators for, 163–193
    McClellan indicators and, 243
    nine-to-one ratio of, to down volume, 190–192, **191, 192**
    semilog scaling in, 23, **27**
Up Volume indicator, 163–166, **164–166**
Up Volume, Down Volume Line, 178–179, **179**
Upside–Downside Volume Ratio, 187–189, **187, 188**
Upside–Downside Volume, 185–187, **186**

Velocity Index, 128–130, **129**
Volume Percentage Ratio, 183–185, **185**

Wall Street Journal, 7
Wall Street Week Index, 6, 37
Wall Street Week, 6, 203
weekly vs. daily data, 12–13, **13**

Weinstein, Stan, 33, 49–51
whipsaws, 42–43, 271, 273
Wilbur, Harvey, 203, 204–205
Wilder, Welles, 138
Winning on Wall Street, 239

Zahorchak Method, 87–89, **88, 89**

Zahorchak, Michael, 87–89
Zinder, Newton, 196
Zweig Up Volume Indicator, 189–193, **190–192**
Zweig, Martin, 92, 94, 95, 210
    Titanic Syndrome and, 239
    Zweig Up Volume Indicator, 189–193, **190–192**
Zweig's Breadth Thrust, 61

About the Author

Since June, 2005, Gregory L. Morris has worked as a portfolio manager for PMFM, Inc. From December, 2003 to June, 2005, Greg served as a Trustee and advisor to the MurphyMorris ETF Fund, which has since been merged into the PMFM family of funds and renamed the Core Advantage Portfolio Trust. He also served as Treasurer and Chief Executive Officer of MurphyMorris Money Management Co. the Advisor to the Fund. He is currently working on a third edition to his bestselling book *Candlestick Charting Explained*. Since October, 2002, Greg (also President of G. Morris Advisors, Inc.) has been working with StockCharts.com, the leading Web-based charting service. He is providing consulting services in marketing, financial development, and business alliances to StockCharts.com. From 1996 to 2002, Greg was CEO of MurphyMorris.Inc., the leading provider of Web-based market analysis tools and commentary, with his partner, John Murphy, a former CNBC analyst. MurphyMorris, Inc. was acquired by StockCharts.com, Inc. in October, 2002. In 1999, Greg and three associates started MurphyMorris Money Management Co. to manage assets for individuals. This focus was later changed to address the firm becoming the Advisor to the MurphyMorris ETF Fund in January, 2004. From 1994 to 1996, he was President of G. Morris Corporation, a Dallas, Texas, headquartered business that provided products and services for investors and traders. His lead product was a series of over 450 indicators and trading systems that supported most Windows-based technical analysis software packages. From 1993 to 1994, Greg was part of MarketArts, Inc., which launched the first Windows-based technical analysis software program, "Windows on Wall Street." In 1992 he published a book on Japanese candlestick analysis called *CandlePower*, now available in soft cover as *Candlestick Charting Explained* (McGraw-Hill). Widely recognized as an expert on candlesticks, candle pattern philosophy, and the developer of candlestick filtering, he has lectured around the world on the subject. In May, 1989, he was awarded "outstanding alumni for 1989" from Pratt County College. From 1982 until 1993, he worked in association with N-Squared Computing, producing over 15 technical analysis and charting software titles, many of which are actively used today. Greg retired in 2004 after 26 years as a Captain with a major airline flying to Europe, Japan, and South America. He graduated from the University of Texas at Austin in 1971, has a B.S. in Aerospace Engineering, has authored numerous investment-related articles, and appeared many times on Financial News Network (FNN). From 1971 to 1977, he was a Navy F-4 fighter pilot aboard the USS Independence. He was selected for, and graduated from, the Navy Fighter Weapons School known as Top Gun. Married with two adult children (both engineers) and two step children, Greg and his wife, Laura, live in the mountains of North Georgia.

Special Offers

Special Offer for Readers of this Book!

Greg Morris' Breadth Indicators Tool Box for MetaStock®

I utilized MetaStock software from Equis International to create almost all of the charts used in this book. The data source I used was Pinnacle Data Corp. I chose these two because I believe they are the best in their fields. As I got further into this project, I realized that putting the complete formulae in the book would cause big problems, from printing errors to copying errors and transfer errors. The frustration from readers trying to reproduce these indicators would have been great.

The good folks at Equis International agreed to assist me in producing a CD that contains all of the breadth indicators found in this book plus many more. The CD will also come with 2–3 years of data from a number of different data services. In developing the indicators for this book, I used a new feature in MetaStock's formula language that allowed me to reference a data set directly from the code. This is what makes these advanced breadth indicators possible, and will make using these indicators on your computer a snap.

If just one breadth indicator in this book is something you want to follow, then my Breadth Indicator Tool Box has all the tools you need to get started immediately. Some of the programming for just one of these indicators would cost more than this entire offer.

Over 165 Indicator Formulae

The Greg Morris' Breadth Indicators Tool Box for MetaStock includes all the indicators in this book, over 3 years of daily and weekly breadth data for the NYSE market and the Nasdaq market. Formulas will work with NYSE, Nasdaq, and/or combined market data (over 500 formulae). All the indicators formulae will be automatically imported into your MetaStock, bringing the power of market breadth analysis to a new level. Market Breadth Indicators will help you feel more confident in your trading decisions, giving you a possible edge in the markets.

The Next Step

Now that you have read this book and have a greater understanding of Market Breadth Indicators, you owe it to yourself to use this information in the actual markets. A special offer is in place for those who have read this book. Visit the website below for prices, details, and special offers.

www.metastock.com/gmi
or call
1-800-772-5797

MetaStock is a registered trademark of Equis International L.L.C, a Reuters Company.

Stocks and Commodities Magazine Special Offer

FREE—Three-month trial subscription to *Technical Analysis of Stocks and Commodities* magazine, *Traders.com Advantage*, and *Working Money*. Three months of the best technical analysis in print and the best trading and investing commentary and interpretation on the Web.

This special three-month trial is available only to readers of *The Complete Guide to Market Breadth Indicators* by Greg Morris!

If you are not satisfied with your three sample issues of *Stocks and Commodities*, your three months of access to *Traders.com Advantage*, or your three months of access to *Working Money*, just return the statement we'll mail you, marked "cancel," and you owe nothing! The three sample issues are yours to keep.

Password for *Traders.com Advantage* and *Working Money* will be provided via the E-mail address that is submitted with the form below.

How to Activate: Visit http://www.Traders.com/Source.html?CHC and complete the form. You must include your E-mail address so we can provide you with the password for your *Traders.com Advantage* and *Working Money* accounts. Or call 1–800–832–4642 and ask for the Three-month trial offer available to readers of *The Complete Guide to Market Breadth Indicators* by Greg Morris.

E-mail circ@traders.com or telephone 1–800–832–4642 if you haven't received your password for *Traders.com Advantage* or *Working Money* within a week or your first copy of *Stocks and Commodities* within six to eight weeks. Please identify yourself as a reader of *The Complete Guide to Market Breadth Indicators* who took advantage of our unique three-month combo trial subscription offer. Tell the customer service representative that the code for the offer is CHC.

Information about the McClellans and James R. Miekka

McClellan Financial Publications, Inc.
P.O. Box 39779
Lakewood, WA 98439–0779
(253) 581–4889
(253) 581–8194 fax
tom@mcoscillator.com
www.mcoscillator.com

The McClellan Market Report

Our twice-monthly newsletter is available by either first class mail or e-mail. The cost is $195.00 per year. Every issue contains our unique analysis of market trends as described by the large set of technical tools we follow, including the McClellan Oscillator and Summation Index. We also provide our proprietary Timing Model dates of forecast future turning points for stocks, bonds, and gold. Our Bottom Line appears on the first page of every issue and sums up our expectations for the market during the weeks that follow.

The Daily Edition

Market followers who need access to more frequent information about market movements enjoy reading our Daily Edition. It is published every day the market trades, and goes out in the evening via fax or e-mail. Each Edition contains a large table of data including McClellan Oscillator calculations for the NYSE and Nasdaq, and even for the 100 stocks in the Nasdaq 100 Index. We also provide calculations of Price Oscillators and important support/resistance levels for the major stock market averages, the XAU, and T-Bonds. Active mutual fund traders appreciate our "Current Opinions" sections. We give our current take, either bullish, bearish, or neutral on stocks, bonds, and gold.

James R. Miekka
6735 14th Street South
St. Petersburg, FL 33705
(727) 866–8682

The Sudbury Bull and Bear Report

A weekly newsletter published by Jim Miekka. Call for a free sample.

PMFM, Inc.

PMFM, Inc.
1551 Jennings Mill Rd.
Suite 2400A
Bogart, GA 30622
800-222-7636